Working
Inside Out

Also by Margo Adair:
Meditations on Everything Under the Sun

Working Inside Out

TOOLS FOR CHANGE

Margo Adair

An Imprint of Sourcebooks, Inc.®
Naperville, Illinois

Published by Sourcebooks, Inc.
P.O. Box 4410, Naperville, Illinois 60567-4410
(630) 961-3900
FAX: (630) 961-2168
www.sourcebooks.com

Library of Congress Cataloging-in-Publication Data

Adair, Margo, 1950–
Working inside out / by Margo Adair.
    p. cm.
Originally published: Berkeley, Calif. : Wingbow Press, 1984.
Includes bibliographical references.
ISBN 1-4022-0032-3 (alk. paper)
1. Meditation. 2. Spiritual life. 3. Success—Religious aspects. I. Title. BL627.A3
2003
158.1'2—dc21

                                                                                    2003006718

Printed and bound in the United States of America
              LB 10 9 8 7 6 5 4 3 2 1

Contents

Using the Audio CD

Five of the meditations from this book can be found on the accompanying audio CD. The meditations are of different lengths, ranging from five to twenty-minutes, to accommodate your schedule.

There are frequent pauses during the meditations to allow time for your own inner work. As everyone has a different rhythm, you may wish to tailor the meditations to suit your preferred pace. Simply pause the recording whenever you would like more time to do your inner work before progressing to the next stage of the meditation.

These meditations are designed to elicit spontaneous responses. You will be doing your inner work at the *same* time as you listen to the instructions. Don't wait for the instructions to finish before beginning to respond. Nor should you wait until the "right" image comes to you—make it up; go with your instantaneous responses. Trust your own experience and give your imagination full permission to play.

To prepare to use these meditations, you will want to turn off your pager, unplug the phone, and otherwise take steps to make sure you will not be disturbed. Find a comfortable place where you can lie or sit with your spine straight. (Sitting up is best for the third meditation.) Before you start the CD, make yourself comfortable. Focus on your breath for a few moments and let it sink into a full and easy rhythm.

You'll find the text of each audio meditation on the following pages:

Relaxing into Well Being: Working with Symbols (20 minutes), Page 29

Make a clear path to your inner dimensions. Unwind and tap into healing energy. Focus deep attention to wherever it is needed.

For an explanation of the techniques used in the meditation, also see page 25, Relaxation: Working with It.

Active Imagination: Aligning Energies with a Positive Vision (15 minutes), page 136.

Work with your imagination to discover and align with the best possible outcomes. Your intuition will guide you to your goals.

For an explanation of the techniques used in the meditation, also see pages 103–111.

Running Energy: Centering for the Day (5 minutes), page 159.

Access universal energies to maintain clarity, focus and personal power while the same time staying open, creative and intuitive.

For an explanation of the techniques used in the meditation, also see pages 141–145.

Receptive Imagination Offers a Gift of Insight (10 minutes), page 246.

Find vision when you have none; gain clarity you are confused.

For an explanation of the techniques used in the meditation, also see pages 81–83 and pages 211–212.

Heart Song (10 minutes), page 289.

In the face of what challenges you, allow what makes your heart sing to soften the edges and to guide you.

For an explanation of the techniques used in the meditation, also see pages 210–211 and page 265.

Tools for Change offers many additional meditations on audio cassette, including most of the meditations in this book. For more information, see page 425.

CD Track List

The beginning of the book addresses how the outside of all of us has affected the inside of each of us, and how we can participate in our own inner world to begin to solve our personal problems.

The end of the book addresses how the inside of each of us affects the outside of all of us, and how working on the outside changes us on the inside—each process necessary for resolving social problems—in other words, how the outside has moved on in all of us, and how to move our reawakened insides out.

Working Inside Out

•1•

Reawakening Innerconsciousness

This book is about consciousness—both its mysteries and its great powers. Applied Meditation synthesizes three approaches to consciousness that rarely cross paths—visualization, intuition, and mindfulness. Working with it will enable you to develop an intimate relationship with your own consciousness. You will be able to come to a deeper understanding and appreciation of what is true in whatever area you focus your attention, as well as learn how to find the specific spots that are most likely to be receptive to transformation. And, just as important, you will come to know how to overcome obstacles and set clear intention so that you may act in alignment with your desire. Working with the principles of Applied Meditation, you can affect transformation whether your concern is deeply personal, in your community, or even the global issues facing us all. Should you decide to take the journey *Working Inside Out* offers, you will come to know that consciousness not only lives inside our psyches, but it also vibrates around us and between us and the inanimate world. Life itself lights up with magic.

Everybody wants change nowadays—that's one thing we all have in common. No one likes the state of the world, and hardly anyone really feels good about the state of their lives either. People may point to different things as being the cause of their malaise, but no one would say everything is okay the way it is. Our lives tend to be so harried that we've lost access to the enormous potential to create change that lies within each of us. Instead, stress-related illnesses have become the number one killers in modern life. This book will enable you to reduce stress, but it will also empower you to change the conditions that cause it.[1] Working with Applied Meditation promises to awaken your creative, intuitive, and healing resources so that you can take charge of your life, envision new directions, and act on them.

People have used reflection, contemplation, and meditation to deepen understanding and increase well-being for millennia. One of the great paradoxes in life is that looking within offers the experience of being intimately connected to *all that is*. The act of meditation brings us into communion with the harmonizing forces intrinsic to life itself.

This book is dedicated to applying these powers for both personal problem-solving and furthering our individual goals, as well as for the purpose of bringing these powers to bear in our process of securing the future for the generations to come. Working inside out, it is my hope that reflection becomes a publicly shared activity.

As the title implies, we begin by addressing the nature of the subjective realm, then progress through our interpersonal relationships, and finally work with the great currents that shape contemporary times. *Working Inside Out* addresses how some of the assumptions and images of mainstream culture have clogged up access to the resilient, creative energies that reside inside each of us. As we release these energies, we can apply them not only to heal our personal lives, but to transform aspects of our culture. Moving our reawakened insides out, we become a much-needed healing influence in the world. *Working Inside Out* continually weaves how the culture's conditioning and images have moved in on all of us and how we might reclaim the great powers of consciousness and shed their light on the world.

When you come to have a better understanding of the nature of consciousness, of the imagination, of intuition, and of creativity itself, and when you come to appreciate the relationship they all have to the world around you, then you won't feel buffeted about by all the turmoil. Instead you can tap the powers within and employ them to deal with challenges you face. When you are not at the will of all that's going on about you, you will be free to participate in life with clarity and vision—a very different feeling from that of being under pressure and constantly on the run just to keep up. You can participate in shaping the future rather than reacting to it when it arrives.

Intuition has been fully neglected in our technological society. But the truth is, it can actually provide the map for each of us to overcome the limitations in our lives, whether that means discarding bad habits, healing health problems, enriching relationships, or even grappling with the massive political issues of our day. You need not hope to get only an occasional glimpse of what your intuition knows. Instead, you can learn to tap its power at will, and you'll discover that it gives you invaluable guidance no matter what your concerns are. This book will teach you how to do just that—how to work with deep awareness and utilize your intuitive and imaginative powers for whatever your particular problems and aspirations.

Creativity, intuition, and healing powers come through innerconsciousness. I use this term to refer to all the intuitive and imaginative capacities of intelligence. Ironically, by looking within, we can tap into the collective knowledge of the human race. It is our innerconsciousness that experiences wholeness, the feeling of being "at one," that is at the heart of all spirituality, the merging of the existential "I" into something greater.

Development of Applied Meditation

In 1972, I was catapulted into the realms of consciousness where my work has been focused ever since. Until then, I had pretty much taken the abilities of my mind for granted, and my attention was focused solely on the external world.

My journey began when a friend told me about his participation in a training that consisted of a series of guided imaginary journeys developed by José Silva, a businessman who was a forerunner of the human potential movement.[2] What particularly caught my interest was my friend's description of the last exercise, called "doing cases." This entailed being given only the name, age, and address of someone you knew nothing about, with the expectation that you would describe this person in full detail. I was intrigued, as I had been brought up in an academic home where reason was paramount. I had always thought that if psychic powers existed at all, only exotic characters born every few hundred years possessed them.

I joined a women's group that was going to try this same set of exercises. We did them without any prior explanation. When it came time for me to do a case, though I felt I couldn't, I went ahead and tried. I relaxed, and a woman gave me the full name and address of a friend of her's named Martha. I proceeded to talk about Martha for forty-five minutes, feeling all the time as though I were simply making up a story. It felt as ordinary as anything that had ever gone on in my mind. When I was finished, I opened my eyes and the woman told me that everything I had said about Martha was true. I had accurately described her character and physical appearance, including a gray print dress that buttoned up the back, and a pair of black "old lady" shoes with brown laces. I'd seen black spots on her stomach and a chalky substance at the base of her spine. It turned out that she had an ulcer and cancer of the spine, and that she did wear that particular dress all the time. My friend said that everything was correct except she couldn't understand my description of the shoes because Martha had always loved to wear the latest style. Two weeks later, I ran into my friend and she told me that the last time she'd seen Martha she was wearing "old lady" shoes—black with brown laces!

I was awed by this experience: my mind had abilities I had never dreamed of! What was so astounding was how *ordinary* it felt while I was describing the case. It was not as if a thunderbolt had come out of the sky illuminating the truth. To this day I view this as the most profound experience of my life. I knew I wasn't one of those weird people born every two hundred years; I considered myself rather ordinary. Everybody else in the group had also been successful at doing these readings.

Having successfully read this case, I was *obliged* to pay attention to what went on in my mind, for all I had done that day was make up a story—I simply used my imagination—yet everything I had said matched the reality of Martha. As a result, I realized that my imagination was real—as real as the ground we stand on. The techniques of Silva Mind Control teach that if you imagine something, you can create it; so I started to direct my imagination toward changes I wanted to make, and that worked too! For the first time I began to pay attention to my mind and to direct my imagination. I discovered that I had powers, that, when applied, changed every aspect of my life. I moved from being acted upon to being an actor; my worldview swung around one hundred-eighty degrees.

I realized that if I could do it, anyone could. This led to my beginning to develop a theory and practice which taps the power of innerconsciousness to facilitate change. In 1975, I started to teach Applied Meditation. Ever since then, I have used a similar exercise in my teaching and have guided hundreds of people through the process of doing cases successfully—all of them, no doubt, ordinary people. I don't understand why it works, but the point is, it does. Somehow our minds have access to information beyond our experience. The implication of this is awesome. You may view this as accessing the collective unconscious or the presence of God, spirit, or the ancestors—however you make sense of the mystery, what is imperative to realize is that we all have access to direct knowing. In some mysterious way, the imagination itself is the medium of psychic awareness. We all have ways of using our intelligence that go virtually untapped. It is as though we are each held by the universe, and that the whole of the universe can be experienced by looking within.

It is when we relax, yet continue to remain alert, that the part of our consciousness which experiences our connectedness and taps into a deep source of knowing surfaces. Creative and intuitive insights arise, as well as healing energy.[3]

It is often more comfortable to avoid the truth. However, it is well known that the condition of the world needs to be changed if we are going to secure our future. Repossessing our innerconsciousness will heal our alienation and help overcome the fragmentation of our society. Our sole reliance on rational processing and our estrangement from other ways of knowing are major contributing factors to contemporary problems. As we reclaim our full selves, we are empowered to live in supportive communities through which we can work creatively to bring about a society which is both equitable and sustainable.

I wrote this book to provide safe structures for exploring the vast realms within you. The training gives you a language to communicate with your deeper self as well as providing methods to employ it for problem-solving and vision-building. The guided meditations create a clear and simple navigational course through your inner dimensions so you can use the resources available within you to improve the quality of your life; this is Applied Meditation. The purpose of this book is to help you to be more effective in making the changes you want, whether that be in your health, your behavior, your relationships, your work, or the larger world. Whatever it is, your innerconsciousness can help you.

The book discusses the subjective—what's going on inside each one of us, our consciousness; as well as the objective—what's going on in the world around us. It clarifies the interplay between them, where the limits and the potential lie, both inside and outside. In gaining a deeper understanding of each, we come to know where to apply our energy to improve our lives.

Repossessing Our Innerconsciousness to Repossess Our Lives

Innerconsciousness—our deepest processes—has been fully mystified; our inner levels are contemptuously dismissed. We are taught to believe that everything is rational and logical, that whatever is "out of control" originates in our "subconscious" and that if psychic powers exist at all, at best they are bizarre, and at worst "evil." We are led to believe that the output of our imagination is, by definition, unreal, that "daydreaming is a waste of time," and that if you can't explain *why* you know something, you don't really know it.

For all intents and purposes, the very ground of our being has been stolen, yet our inner processes are active and have an immense impact on our lives, whether we pay attention to them or not. The very nature of innerconsciousness is that it is suggestible and programmable. It is dominant whenever we are relaxing; it is crucial that we make wise choices about our leisure time.

Spending time in front of the television may be enjoyable, but it has insidious side effects—it provides the images we act out of! Unless we repossess our inner levels, we act more and more like robots. To be autonomous, not automatons, we must reclaim the levels that have been programmed and choose what we want to store there.

The content of your inner awareness regularly seeps into your daily experience; it resides just below your rational surface. However, most of us have never learned to recognize it or know its powers, much less be able to tap it at will. Instead, we have been taught to be suspicious and discount it whenever it peeps its head above the surface. We have a rich language that enables us to use our rational consciousness, but virtually no language for tapping the creative and intuitive powers of innerconsciousness.

Most of us have been raised and educated to ignore our deeper knowledge and to rely only on the "rational." In order to succeed in mainstream culture, we learn to be "objective" and "reasonable." So where do we turn to for "relaxation"? Denying our own creativity, we have become a captive audience for the entertainment industry whose programming clogs the passageway to our deeper experience. We're discouraged from daydreaming—instead we go to the movies or watch television. We get it coming and going. Not only have we lost access to our own creativity, but the very nature of popular entertainment is such that we relax, become passive, and it is done *to* us. Compounding this is the fact that a relaxed state of being is programmable and suggestible; so we uncritically accept the messages conveyed through the media. We find ourselves wanting and buying the latest gadget, the newest "improved" remedies, impractical automobiles and worse, threatening our own bodies with eating disorders and one another with violence. We have been reduced to objects and our culture turned into a consumer society where enjoyment comes from things rather than from each other. All this propaganda has been shoveled into our depths, blocking access to our inner processes, and suffocating both our creativity and our intuition.

It is no coincidence that our inner realms have been denied—they tell us too much. We've been taught not to question the status quo, to distrust our own awareness, and instead to look to authorities for the answers to our problems. Common sense isn't so common anymore. We've come to believe that the authorities certainly know better than we do: when we get sick, we see a doctor; when we have disputes, we see a lawyer; when our families are in turmoil, we see a social worker.

Until we repossess those parts of ourselves, we will be increasingly relegated to leading alienated non-creative lives. Ironically, it is when we look within that we feel connected. It is our deepest selves that experience our heartfelt connections with one another. When we are alienated from each other, it's because we are also alienated from our deepest selves. We often don't know our neighbors, much less how to work together to solve the problems that arise in our daily lives. Suspicious of our inner experience, we find ourselves full of suspicion for one another. We are unable to live together with open hearts, enriching one another's lives; instead, we find ourselves competing for our individual positions in the world.

I believe that reclaiming our inner worlds is best done with others in your life. When we meditate together, we create deep bonds that strengthen the fiber of our relations. Our families, communities, and organizations will reclaim a sense of wholeness when we reflect together. We will also be fully entertained by the richness that comes from sharing the experiences we each gain as we journey through our inner landscapes. I cannot emphasize enough the importance of working with these dimensions with the others in your life. It will greatly enhance your inner experience because the nature of these dimensions makes the experience itself more potent in group settings, and it enables groups to create a field of energy that holds everyone up.

When we resurrect our innerconsciousness, we will have regained our own creative resources for solving our problems, relying on ourselves, our families and our communities, thereby depending less and less on the established, licensed professionals (planned obsolescence). The alienating effect of suspicion will be replaced by the connectedness of trust in our own selves and one another.

Innerconsciousness Is the Ground Out of Which All Behavior Springs

We *always* act out of the messages held in our innerconsciousness; it is crucial to understand this. We move through our daily activities in terms of our past experiences, which are the building blocks of our personal belief systems. Our belief systems are the glasses through which we each view the world and anticipate what is likely to unfold. Our behavior is always loyal with our beliefs. Everyone has had the experience of learning something, but acting to the contrary—thinking one thing yet doing another—and then later hitting oneself over the head saying, "How could I? I know better than that." The cliché, "I just don't have it down yet" is literally true. Your knowledge is intellectual, rational, and does not yet reside in your inner levels where the mass of your memories is stored.

Beliefs are the way we organize our memories into our personal definitions of how the world ticks; they are the assumptions out of which we operate. They stem either from continual repetition of social messages (programming) or from traumatic incidents. For example, you find yourself nervous every time you get in a car because you once had an automobile accident (belief: cars = danger), so you may try to reassure yourself by reasoning to no avail, "It's okay, the brakes have been fixed." This doesn't relieve your tension. Or, for another example, you are a woman who has learned that by being assertive you will avoid many problems, yet you find yourself responding passively (belief: "Nice girls aren't aggressive"). In each case, you are acting out of your stored beliefs. These examples illustrate a dynamic operative in all of us when we find ourselves behaving in ways we know are inappropriate.

You needn't wait months or years before you get the new behavior down. Since you behave out of your inner messages, all you need to do is insert the desired message at an inner level. (Much of Applied Meditation can be likened to the techniques of hypnosis, which work with these same dynamics.) Because innerconsciousness is suggestible if you want to get some new knowledge down, you simply need to put it in at that level. Directing your imagination while in a meditative state will enable you to do so. You will find yourself able to act in accordance with your choices and no longer a victim of thinking one thing and doing another.

Your innerconsciousness is not, by nature, inaccessible or far away. It is always right there just below the surface. Whenever you are relaxing or doing something rhythmic or automatic—not using your rational mind to decide what to do next—innerconsciousness has moved from its usual position beneath the surface to that part of you that is predominantly present. The problem is that because of the prevailing attitudes, it is at these very times that you ignore or discount your awareness. So that your innerconsciousness has become, for all practical purposes, inaccessible and it is only natural for you to be a victim of unwanted behavior. Whether it is the result of a traumatic incident in your past (car accident) or from the programming by the propaganda of our society (women are passive), you will continue to be a victim until you repossess your innerconsciousness.

If you have never taken control and chosen what to keep in your innerconsciousness, then it has simply become the accumulation of everything you've ever experienced. Imagine what it would be like if you never threw out any of your trash. It wouldn't take long to accumulate more plastic packaging than furniture, and you'd find yourself virtually unable to move. *We need to be mindful of what we hold in our subjective landscapes and clear the debris out of our minds.* Let me reassure you, the process for changing what you store in your inner levels of consciousness is simple. It boggles my mind to think of the enormous energy we can release if we rid ourselves of old and constricting beliefs.

There are three ways that you can work with your innerconsciousness. The first is to be mindful of what is taking place in your subjective landscape. Another is to reprogram yourself, enabling you to act the way you want to by *putting* in new information while meditating. This is helpful when you know what you want. I call this the work of the Active Imagination. The third is to gain insights that will help you move forward when you're stuck—*pulling* out new information. This is helpful when you are unhappy with your experience but lack a vision of any positive alternative. I call this the work of the Receptive Imagination.

It is through your innerconsciousness that you have access to universal information, and it is at that level that you receive creative and intuitive insights. It is when you are relaxed that the classic "Aha!" experience occurs. It is also through relaxed awareness that ESP takes place. Once you learn how to enter and use your inner levels of consciousness you will no longer need to hope that an answer to a gnawing problem will dawn on you at some later time. Instead you can enter the meditative state and utilize the mysterious abilities of the Receptive Imagination by simply asking for an answer.

Knowledge becomes available to you when you direct questions inward. Some believe that God resides within and are able to get guidance by looking within through prayer. I think of it is as if a mysterious self-organizing force runs through *all that is*. Physicist David Bohm's theory of implicate order posits that reality is like a hologram.[4] We are all part of the whole and the whole lives in each of us—there is no real separateness in the universe. (A characteristic of holograms is that cutting one in half results not in two different halves but in two smaller wholes.)

Whether you a hold a secular or religious view, it is crucial to understand that clarity does come when one asks while in a receptive state. I believe that the objective and subjective worlds are reflections of one another and *the question itself acts as a flashlight* directing a beam of light on the particular spot in the amorphous collective unconscious where the answer resides. The trick is to have a *clear* question. You will find yourself intuiting an insight that illuminates what is true about your concern and reveals a path toward greater states of well-being.

To fully cultivate the powers that reside in deep awareness, you will come to know your own inner landscape intimately. You will find yourself residing in a quality of quiet awareness which recognizes what is taking place within you and grounds you in the present moment. I call this the Inner Witness, which can be likened with mindfulness of Eastern meditation practices. I do not mean to imply that the Inner Witness is a noun—it is awareness that has no form; it is as though its knowing has neither end nor beginning. This aspect is in a perpetual state of relaxed attention revealing imbalance and what is needed to regain balance.

It is the Witness that recognizes what the beam of light illuminates. When you pay attention to the knowing of the Inner Witness, what is needed— whether to ask a question or to insert a new message—is self-evident. As you embark on your journey you will find yourself working with all of these aspects of consciousness simultaneously. They will always inspire healing, well-being and creativity in your life. You will come to trust your own deepest experience and find that Applied Meditation will always reconnect you with the ground of being itself.

Theory of Consciousness

The abrupt transformation in my life came about in the opposite way from what usually happens. Normally, we're taught something and then learn to apply it— theory precedes practice. For me, it's been the other way around. Over the decades of my working with Applied Meditation, I have always experienced the fact of directed consciousness working, and then later begun to piece together *why* it works. In other words, my rational understanding follows my experience. True, I suspect, for anyone who follows intuition. I have found myself changing and developing techniques, seemingly out of the blue—intuitively. While teaching, changes pop into my mind, and without exception, they are always refinements—always improvements. Each time these changes happen without any planning on my part. There has always been a time lag between my teaching something and being able to explain why it is that it works. In retrospect, I am glad to have discovered that intuition does not work by trial and error.

I would like to emphasize that originally I had no understanding of how consciousness worked, yet my life changed profoundly when I began to direct my own imagination. I want to elaborate my perspective on consciousness and its relation to experience and behavior. You don't need to agree with my explanation in order to explore your inner levels; the power of the experience will speak for itself. I share my ideas with you because they have given me a rational understanding of the phenomena of consciousness, providing a footing that enables me to navigate more easily through my inner dimensions.

I use electroencephalographic (EEG) measures as a language through which to view consciousness. Our brains continuously give off electromagnetic pulsations, which can be measured by an electroencephalograph. EEG levels refer to the different rhythms of these emanations. There seems to be a correlation between what we're subjectively experiencing and the objective brain-wave emanations. The different levels, called beta, alpha, theta, and delta, are each part of a complete spectrum. The divisions are arbitrary—it's like the dividing lines between the colors white, gray, and black: where white stops, gray starts; where gray stops and black starts is arbitrary, yet there is a complete change from one end of the spectrum to the other.

In Western culture, we are most familiar with beta consciousness because it is that level that is rational and therefore recognized as valuable, so it is only this aspect of our consciousness we have been taught how to use. Reading, writing, and arithmetic are all beta functions, as are cause-and-effect thinking, goal orientation, and our experience of clock time. This linear thinking of beta is particular and critical, computing lots of different data all at once, such as talking to a friend while you're cooking, and at the same time thinking of all the errands you need to do. In beta, you're dealing with lots of particulars at the same time in a logical goal-oriented manner. It is a necessary state of consciousness for coping with contemporary urban living, where we have to be dealing with many issues at once. Beta consciousness can also be likened to the activity of the left hemisphere of the brain, which specializes in linear processing.

Beta consciousness both promotes and maintains life in the fast lane. It is overused and at times becomes defeating. Particular thinking, by definition, separates elements of the whole, ordering them in a linear manner. Its natural operating mode is competitive; since it separates elements of the whole and it isolates people from one another. It doesn't make sense to be trapped in competitive mode just because we only know how to function with a beta mentality. We need to be able to relax and connect with others easily, moving out of our isolation and into mutual support. Working with innerconsciousness will do just that.

I think of beta consciousness as if it resides on the surface, and of the inner-consciousness—alpha, theta, and delta—as residing deeper; alpha right below beta, moving down to theta, and below to delta in the depths.[5] These deeper levels of consciousness experience reality holistically. They do not separate things; they make connections. They do not categorize; they synthesize. They are not critical, nor do they order things in a linear manner. Instead they make things whole. They experience reality in images, patterns, sensations, and a quiet knowing that has no form. It is in these states that the imagination lives, and through which intuition comes. It is these deeper states in which awareness becomes spacious and the Inner Witness is present.

To understand the term holistic, imagine that you can't figure out how to solve a mathematical formula; you are absolutely stuck, so you give up and go for a walk (in a relaxing activity such as this, you will be predominantly at the alpha level). As you walk, all of a sudden the solution dawns on you like the proverbial light bulb flashing on—not the specific answer, but an unquestionable sense of the whole pattern. Everything becomes clear; you can go home to your work and your *beta* mind will easily figure out the missing parts of the equation. This is an example of the classic "Aha!" experience referred to earlier.

Rhythmic activities such as running, dishwashing, or repetitive work induce alpha; because you don't need to decide what to do next, linear thinking is unnecessary. While dancing, you've probably had the experience of losing the beat if you begin to think about what your feet should do next. The alpha level is fluid—you find yourself thinking about something and you have no idea what led you there. Most people spend a good part of the day in alpha. When you are relaxed you are on "automatic." When you are in the Alpha state, it is the very time that you ignore the content of your consciousness. This is because we haven't been taught its importance. It is interesting to note that research has now revealed that peak performance in athletes is closely associated with bursts of alpha.[6]

Theta and delta, unlike beta and alpha, are not so familiar. It is these levels of consciousness that are active when your focus is in *one* place. You may have heard the term "one-pointedness of consciousness"—being one with all that is—which refers to the satori experience that is sought after in Eastern religious traditions. It is a complete focus of awareness and occurs at these deep levels.

Whenever your survival is threatened, it is a given that all of your attention is needed to deal with the situation at hand, and anything else is simply not in your awareness. For instance, if you are in an automobile accident, it lasts at most five seconds, yet in memory it feels as if it had lasted half an hour—like a slow-motion movie. All of your energy was focused on surviving, and rather than being spread out on lots of issues, as it is in the beta state, it was all funneled into the exclusive awareness of the threatening situation, having the subjective effect of expanding time. You may have heard of people who thought they were about to die and whose entire life paraded before their eyes—this is complete focus of energy and subjective expansion of time.

At any moment, all the levels of EEG waves are active, but there is a predominant rhythm present. When you are in the beta level of consciousness, the other levels are present as well. However, the slower your predominant brain-wave pattern is, the more synchronized all the levels are. The degree to which brain-wave patterns are synchronized corresponds to the degree to which we feel in sync with what is going on around us.

Thus the spectrum from beta to delta is simply one of the focus and concentration of awareness—at beta it is spread out; at delta it is completely concentrated. At beta it is particular; at delta it is holistic. Let's say you are relaxed and daydreaming. At a time like this, you're aware of your objective circumstances—for example, you know that you are lying on the bed in your room, and that you need to get up at a certain time for an appointment or to take a cake out of your oven—all this is in your awareness while you are still daydreaming. This is the alpha state. On the other hand, if you suddenly realize that you have been dreaming, without being aware of where you are—or that you have already missed your appointment or burnt the cake—you were at the theta level (no longer goal-oriented). This is called the hypnogogic state, wherein the contents of the dream become reality and have a three-dimensional quality—the dream itself is extremely vivid, and your objective circumstances have faded from awareness. This is the difference between alpha and theta. In alpha, your daydreaming consciousness is more spread out, in theta more concentrated. In alpha, you are daydreaming in an offhand manner; in theta your dream is as real as life. In fact, your dream has replaced your objective reality.

The theta level is an extremely receptive state of consciousness because one is *only* aware of what is happening at the moment and has no concept of anything else. Someone at theta level is in a very suggestible state of consciousness because it is noncritical. It does not divide things up, or categorize things; it simply *experiences*. Since theta is exclusively focused on what is occurring in the moment, it is not linear or goal-oriented—whatever may happen next is completely irrelevant. Considering alternatives is not possible while at the theta level.

Some developmental psychologists say that an individual's personality is essentially formed by the age of three. Although I don't think that our personalities are static, I think the basis for this theory is the fact that up until this age, everybody functions predominantly at the theta level. This explains why infants are totally engrossed in whatever is occurring at the moment, and why toddlers cannot grasp the concept of what's happening next. Theta consciousness does not possess the critical capacities of beta or its ability to understand time. So anything that occurs during these years becomes a person's reality, because theta consciousness has no awareness of alternatives. Remember, you act in accordance with your beliefs. For example, if you lived next to a freeway with the constant noise of traffic during the first three years of your life, the chances are you wouldn't be fully comfortable in the quiet of the country—something would be missing—because your belief system defines the world as noisy. This discomfort may be something you're not fully conscious of, but only experience in a vague and ill-defined way.

This example illustrates how we act in terms of our past experience. Our belief systems—our memories—are stored deep in our consciousness at the theta level, so to speak. We remember things holistically: if you smell the scent of a flower you're not going to remember what you learned about that flower in biology class; instead, a *whole* scene in which that scent was present will flood your awareness. Our memories function associatively, not logically. The beliefs from which we act stem either from childhood experiences, life-threatening events, or from an accumulation of repetitive programming.

When children are of elementary school age, they are predominantly at the alpha level (actively getting programmed). It is not until puberty that we have full access to our critical capacities, and begin to function predominantly at the beta level (except when watching TV). So it's our deepest levels of consciousness that house the totality of our past experience and through which our behavior is directed.

Alpha, residing between beta and theta, is composed of the characteristics of each, and it is so powerful because *it can be both active and receptive, simultaneously. It is the threshold between inner and outer consciousness.*

To sum up, when you meditate, you will be predominantly in alpha. In alpha, you can choose what you want to work on (active) and then be effective in doing so (receptive). You can actively reprogram yourself, i.e., give yourself the messages you choose, by changing the beliefs you act out of; your deeper levels, being suggestible, will absorb the new information. Or you can call up information from these receptive states of awareness, discovering new ways to approach your concerns. Through Applied Meditation, you will find yourself relaxing into that calm place that resides inside each of us, recognizing what is needed, and easily working with the active and receptive powers of your imagination.

•2•

Bringing Meditation into Your Life

How can you apply all this? When you want to change your behavior, you simply use the Active Imagination to get the information in at the appropriate level. If the information that you want to put in doesn't have anything contradicting it deeper down—in other words, if there are no counter messages at the theta level—then putting in a new message is a simple, straightforward process, and one application is usually enough for it to sink in. For example, if you need to awaken at 7:15, all you need to do is enter the alpha level and tell yourself, "I will awaken at exactly 7:15 in the morning" (active). If there is nothing contradicting the suggestion at the theta level, such as a childhood message from your mother who always said, "You *never* get up on time," it will simply sink in. Your innerconsciousness will have a new message out of which you will find yourself responding by awakening at exactly 7:15. This works on the first try because you do not have a lot of energy focused on the issue.

Now if you want to change your response in an area that has some charge to it, such as a phobia or an allergy or a deeply implanted message ("I can't get up on time"), you do it the same way. It simply takes longer. You need more energy around the new message than around the old. You need to replace the messages that reside in your theta level, but you need to work in the alpha level because theta is not goal-oriented, and by the time you have gotten there you've forgotten what you were going to do (spacing out). Since there is less energy at alpha, it takes longer to accumulate enough to replace the old message. All of this is the work of the Active Imagination because you have a vision of a more desirable reality and are inserting it through the power of suggestion into your innerconsciousness.

Putting Theory into Practice

To illustrate, if you have had an automobile accident and feel nervous every time you travel in a car, you can change this by replacing your old picture with a new one. You simply enter the alpha state and imagine feeling relaxed riding in a car. This may be rather difficult, given your past experience, so you should think of something that *does* feel relaxing—maybe it's listening to music. Imagine yourself listening to music until you are feeling wonderful, then imagine yourself in a car listening to music on the radio. If you lose your good feelings at that point, go back to listening to music without the car, and keep doing this. Eventually you will be able to imagine yourself maintaining your good feelings while in the car. Then, after more work, you'll be able to imagine being comfortable in the car without music. It's at this point that you'll have a message you can focus on (it is pleasant to ride in a car) and you will find yourself able to do so comfortably. It's a simple process—just a matter of taking the time to replace the old messages and accumulating new energy around fresh ones. The important distinction is that beta works with thoughts and our inner levels work with feelings, sounds, sensations, and images. The difference is not in thinking the car is safe, but in *feeling* that it is.

To repeat: working with these energies falls into three categories. One is to cultivate the Inner Witness, which is the spacious awareness offering a sense of calm knowing that reveals what is true for you at any given moment, making it evident if you need to work with your Active or Receptive Imagination. Working with your Active Imagination is about setting clear intention and replacing old, inhibiting messages that have patterned your everyday behavior with new, liberating ones. This enables you to be in alignment with your vision and act in accordance with it. The third way of working is useful when you're stuck and have no vision, so you ask for an insight to enable you to move on. Remember the example of the mathematical problem: instead of giving up, you simply need to go into the meditative state and ask a clear question at that level of awareness with the expectation of receiving an answer. In doing so, the solution inexplicably becomes apparent, for the information exists. The question itself angles the light of awareness as though it was a spotlight that illuminates the particular spot in the collective unconscious where the answer resides (the clearer the question, the brighter and more steady the light). All your hunches, inspirations, and creative insights come through inner levels of consciousness where extrasensory perception occurs. So when you don't know, you utilize your Receptive Imagination and ask a question, and when you do, you use your Active Imagination and put in the information.

I make it sound simple. What is profound is that it is simple. The ordinary and the astounding hold a peculiar coexistence in these realms. People have used meditation, contemplation, and ritual to enter altered states of consciousness for millennia. It is time that we in Western culture reclaim these ways of being and the intelligence that becomes available when engaging in these activities, by doing so we step onto a healing path. We've allowed these parts of ourselves to atrophy; we need to exercise them. Like everything else in the world, these abilities work only if we use them. If you decide to take this journey into your inner life, you will discover that the effects are profound.

Using the Meditations: Creating a Context

We expect spiritual work to be surrounded with lights, colors, and whispering voices. In short, we expect to sit back and be entertained by the awesome. What is important to understand is that the alpha state is nothing extraordinary, for you are frequently in that level of awareness. It's just under the surface and easy to enter at will. The common view that meditation, hypnosis, and the like are exotic states is simply part of the mystification—our culture teaches us that these things are extraordinary and strange. Well, they're not. Calm, spacious awareness, creative imagination, and intuition all reside within each of us. You don't have to go far to discover answers to the daily problems that arise in your life. All you need to do is pay attention to—and take seriously—a very familiar part of yourself that you've probably never realized could be of use. Instead, you might have felt slightly guilty whenever you were relaxed because you thought you were wasting your time and not accomplishing anything. It's time to refocus and pay attention to that very level you've always ignored—to listen to the voices within.

Our society tells us we must always be productive (the Puritan Ethic)—that it's not okay to be in the clouds, to live in a fantasy world, or to daydream. Now you get to bring the clouds down to earth, moistening the ground of your life for new growth. You can smooth and soften your edgy existence. You get to be productive in your daydreams. You'll be amazed at how wise inner awareness is. If you're skeptical, give it a try anyway because at least you'll have an excuse to relax, and we could all use a little respite from the turmoil of our daily activities. The journeys through your inner dimension are very enjoyable, full of humor and the celebration of life. Ironically, it is when we look inside that we find ourselves experiencing our innate connectedness to life itself.

The last portion of this and each of the rest of the chapters consists of guided meditation scripts; these are to help you tune into your innerconsciousness and work with it. They are best experienced in a group setting because the nature of the energy with which you will be working is such that the potency expands geometrically with the number of people sharing the experience. I suggest that you set a regular time aside and instead of watching television, bring family and friends together, make some popcorn, and discover the movies of your minds—develop your own programming. Those of you who do not yet have a community to share this work can begin by reading the exercises first and then doing them on your own. Some find that they can read them slowly and work with them as they do.*

The meditations in this book utilize metaphor, repetition, rhythm, and rhyme because the inner conscious mind is extremely responsive to this kind of language. Simply reading them slowly will induce a meditative state. They provide guidance for you to voyage through your inner landscape. If you have your own ways, for instance, to relax your body and mind, use them. The important thing is to work within yourself, not how you do it. There are no "shoulds"; there is no right way of doing this. (If anyone tells you there is, the chances are it costs a lot of money to learn their technique.) The correct approach is to be mindful and pay attention to your own inclinations and use only those techniques you find helpful. Always feel free to make any necessary adjustments. I can't overstate that the only "should" is to pay attention to your own inclinations; they are subtle and it is often hard to catch them because we've been taught to distrust and squelch them and instead to follow the instructions of the experts. But *you're the expert of yourself.* I'm only providing guidance for you to meet that expert within you; each time you meet that part of yourself that knows what's right for you, follow it and do not worry about listening to all of the words in the meditation, for they will no longer be necessary.

This book is designed as a training course. The text and meditations in each chapter build on the ones that precede it. To gain optimum benefit, I recommend you set aside a regular time and go through the book at your own pace

---

* If you would like help contacting people in your area who are also interested in creating an Applied Meditation practice circle with others, please contact us at circle@toolsforchange.org.

from start to finish. Practice the meditations at whatever rate is comfortable for you. There is no set amount of practice necessary between one meditation and the next. Feel free to skip any that deal with issues you are not concerned with, or jump ahead if you feel the inclination. You are likely to find some that you'll want to use over and over again. The meditations are meant to create a context, an atmosphere in which to explore—each word needn't be listened to (or read). For that matter, you may prefer to use only portions of some of the meditations. Tune in and out at will.

I do, however, recommend that you start with the meditations at the end of this chapter because they lay the groundwork for easy access to your inner dimensions. They will guide you in establishing a process that you will then continue to use for each of the other meditations or when you want to meditate on your own, for they open a passageway for you to use each time you meditate. The meditation section in the rest of the chapters opens with an induction, which is followed by a list of affirmations relevant to the issues of exploration. After the meditations at the end of the chapter, you will find a "count-out" that provides a method for ending your meditation session. The inductions, affirmations, and count-outs are meant to be used for all of the meditations in that chapter. You may want to use Post-its or flags on the pages to facilitate movement from one section to another when you are reading. Some of the meditations flow easily from one into another, so feel free to combine them. On the other hand, some are particularly long, so you may want to use only some of the passages while leaving out others. Do what works for you.

If you are doing the exercises by yourself, I recommend that you read them aloud, recording each meditation as you come to it for later listening. The CD accompanying this book contains meditations that you can use when you have a particular length of time in which to practice. I have also produced twenty tapes of the meditations; see page 426 for purchasing information. It's easier to go through the meditations without having to think of what you need to do next—a linear process that will only activate your beta consciousness. Using a tape will solve this problem. If you prefer, you can make yourself a crib sheet—a chronological list of one-liners that represent each phase of the meditation—or highlight particular passages, so you don't clutter your mind trying to remember what to do next. Instead, you can keep the sheet right in front of you and open your eyes for each step (this won't disturb your meditation). Some find themselves meditating *while* reading them. If this works for you, it is good to sub-vocalize as you read.

However, I would like to emphasize that working with a group will greatly enhance the power of your work with Applied Meditation. (And groups of any kind also benefit greatly from the practice.) I suggest that someone read and record the meditation when everyone is together. The leader can then catch up with everyone else by listening to it later. Obviously, this is a responsibility that can be rotated. Meditation with others is always more powerful, and sharing what you get in touch with opens up richness of the inner dimensions. This strategy is best, for the reader will be much more inspired leading the meditations when there are people right there experiencing them, making it easier to intuit the best timing and tone for reading.

As all the meditations are written poetically, you'll find yourself naturally reading in a trance-inducing tone. However, it is important to remember to give people time for their inner work. Some sections of the meditations are simply written to create an atmosphere that invites the innerconsciousness; these sections can be read in one continuous flow. On the other hand, there are many sections that ask people to do inner work on their own, for example, inner conversations, re-shaping of memories, etc. When this is the case, it is important to give people time for doing their inner work, and therefore some silence is necessary. For this purpose, I have inserted marks where pauses are called for. Three periods indicate a shorter pause—the time it would take for one or two deep breaths should do it. When one diamond is on a line by itself, it indicates a longer pause—between thirty seconds and a minute is usually about right. On occasion, there are lists of questions or affirmations; you'll want to give a short pause between each of these as well. Be careful not to leave too much time; innerconsciousness is playful and you may lose the attention of the meditators, who will use the opening as an opportunity to space out. One trick to give people time while also keeping their attention is to repeat a sentence or two. This will both reinforce what is happening and provide the needed time to do inner work. When you read a meditation, you should make a point of breathing from your belly in a relaxed manner. Then you'll find yourself easily falling into a natural rhythm. This will enable you to maintain a relaxed state so that you intuit the best rhythm.

You probably have the impression that you need total peace and quiet in order to meditate, so if you're trying to relax and you find yourself aware of your noisy neighbors, the traffic outside, or the ticking clock, you conclude that you're not relaxing properly and can't meditate because of all the distractions. To the contrary, the more you're relaxed the more you'll be aware of your surroundings and your inner state. For example, it's only when you're relaxing that you may realize how tense your neck is—that's okay—normally you're so tense you're unaware of your stiff neck; it's only when you relax that it becomes apparent. Hearing the neighbors outside doesn't mean that you need to listen to them, it just means you have noisy neighbors. Meditating is simply settling down a bit; your body/mind does not need to be totally relaxed. What will facilitate your process the most is allowing yourself to breathe from your belly and keeping your spine straight.

There are a few requirements, however, for your meditation practice. Arrange not to be disturbed and make yourself comfortable. Noisy neighbors don't interrupt you—they're not asking you for anything—but the phone does, so unplug it and put a note on your door. Then be sure that your clothing is comfortable and your breathing is not constricted. Have a blanket handy because when you meditate, just as when you take a nap, your metabolism slows down so you tend to chill easily.

If you're someone who falls asleep easily, I suggest you sit up for the meditations, with your back supported and straight. Some who are prone to fall asleep nevertheless prefer to lie down while meditating, so they hold an arm up (when it drops it awakens them). If you have trouble relaxing, I suggest that you do the meditations lying down. Feel free to change positions in the midst of the meditations—with time you'll come to know your optimum position for relaxation and alertness. I do recommend, whether sitting or lying, that you keep your spine straight, as this makes for easier movement of energy. It is common to fall asleep while meditating for you're learning to maintain that edge between sleeping and waking consciousness. Don't worry, I've been doing this for more than twenty-five years and I still fall asleep occasionally. In fact, when I originally went through the Silva Mind Control processes, I slept through two-thirds of it.

If you can't remember all that happened in a meditation, it may help to read it over again. In doing so, you'll find yourself remembering more easily what you experienced. If there are still large blanks in your memory, you may want to do the meditation again. On the other hand, the inner work has often taken place even though you don't remember what happened; new pathways have been laid in your psyche.

If you find yourself thinking about all kinds of irrelevant things—feeling "spacey"—don't worry, that's the nature of the deeper states of awareness you are working with; it's very fluid—both active and receptive at the same time. Whenever this happens, just bring your attention to your breath and then proceed with what you had been doing. Breath is your anchor in meditation. With practice you'll be better able to maintain your focus where you choose.

Creating Your Own Practice

In addition to going through the meditations in the book, I think it's highly important that you also meditate on your own, without the outside stimulus of a tape or a group setting. This is so you will discover your capabilities for yourself and avoid becoming dependent on anyone or anything else for tapping your own inner resources. Because this book is meant to enable you to repossess your inner self, it is important that you practice daily on your own, entering and exploring the meditative state. When you do this by yourself, it usually feels different—you may not feel as "deep"—this is because it's easier to follow someone else's instructions than to tell yourself what to do, and then do it. This is particularly true if you have been doing these meditations in a group setting, for exploring these energies is always more potent when shared with others. So in your independent practice, if you don't feel as if you're in a meditative state, *pretend* that you are and go through the motions anyway. If you do, you'll discover that it becomes more and more effective each time you practice.

It's important to remember that you never lose your ability to meditate, for Applied Meditation is simply a matter of paying attention to, and working with, a part of yourself that is always present. However, it only works when you use it. You don't lose all your strength if you don't exercise, but when you do, your body stays limber and strong. You can exert yourself with ease, rather than with effort. In the same way, the more you meditate, the more adept you'll be at working with deeper levels of awareness whenever you need to.

Some people meditate daily, some every few days, and some people meditate for less than five minutes at a sitting while others spend half-an-hour. I don't believe there is any magic formula for how often or how long you should meditate, but I do feel *regular* practice is important because then Applied Meditation will become a part of your daily routine. If you don't practice regularly, it is not likely to occur to you to meditate when it would be particularly helpful. With time you'll come to know when and how long is best for you. Everyone has their own particular relationship with their inner dimensions.

It is my suggestion that after meditating you always take time to write down briefly what you've experienced in any combination of words and pictures that feels comfortable. Keeping a journal of your meditations will greatly enhance your ability to remember what occurred in them. This begins the process of moving your inner sense of well-being into the world around you, and bringing the harmonizing energies into daily activities more easily is what Applied Meditation is all about. Recording your experience will initiate and facilitate this process. It will also track your progress, which will help you develop the best possible working relationship with your inner self.

record

As your practice evolves, you may discover that there are more and more issues that you want to work on. You might find it helpful to make a list so you needn't remember all the different things you wanted to do while meditating. You need only open your eyes for a moment and glance at your list (this is particularly helpful for affirmations). Remember alpha consciousness isn't linear. As you learn more techniques, you can integrate them into your daily practice, using as many in each meditation as you find helpful. When you focus on multiple areas then, it is good to do so in the same order each time; innerconsciousness is especially responsive to repetitive patterns.

Relaxation: Working With It

When you are physically relaxed, you are at the alpha level. The first meditation is a basic relaxation exercise in which you will learn a technique that will enable you, with just a little practice, to relax in a matter of moments whenever you wish. The induction that opens the meditation section of each of the other chapters uses this same technique. Soon you'll learn to recognize the particular quality of inner awareness so that you'll be able to tune in at will, whether or not you're physically relaxed. You'll be able to meditate on a rush-hour bus.

At *every* given moment your body is responding to whatever you're imagining. If at one time you were terribly frightened by a dog, every time you imagine one, your body starts pumping adrenaline even when no real dog is actually present. This dog phobia is an example of the intimate body-mind connection that is continuously functioning. If you imagine yourself on a sunny beach, your metabolism will slow down. In the first meditation, you're going to work with this phenomenon. It will guide you through each part of your body, giving you time to relax. Once you're physically relaxed, you'll create something that symbolizes that relaxation for you: you can make up whatever you want, a gesture, a picture, a sound—anything—but be sure it's specific and easy to recall (butter melting on a stack of pancakes). The next time you want to relax, all you'll need to do is bring your physical relaxation symbol into your awareness, and your body will respond accordingly.

By working with symbols, you are creating a language to speak to your inner experience. Next time you won't need to focus on relaxing each part of your body separately; instead, all you'll need to do is focus on your symbol, and your body naturally responds by relaxing.

You're also going to relax your mind. This doesn't mean that it shuts up, only that it calms down and expands. Your thoughts no longer feel cramped or rushed. Instead, mindfulness is present and you can witness all that is taking place. You begin to experience the spacious quality intrinsic to inner awareness. Then you will create a symbol for mental relaxation. Next, you will be guided through a process for emotional relaxation, so that the entire meditation is not experienced through any strong feelings that may have been present. If this is not done, strong feelings act like sunglasses, coloring your whole meditation experience. Just as the mind naturally relaxes into a quality of spaciousness, the heart, when given the chance, naturally relaxes into a state of compassion. Relaxation is as normal to the mind and heart as it is to the body. If you let your breath be full and easy, then you'll find that you remain relaxed throughout your meditation.

After your body, mind, and feelings are relaxed, you will focus on what you are grateful for and what you hold as sacred—whatever that is for you. Then you'll create a symbol for the creative, self-restoring center from which you will do your Applied Meditation work. Your inner self will come to know that after focusing on it, you are ready to begin your interior work. Henceforth, whenever you want to meditate, you simply bring each of your symbols to awareness and you find yourself in your creative self-restoring level of inner awareness in a matter of moments.

Many people feel that they have to wait until their symbols come to them—only if it "comes" will it be correct. This is another one of the subtle ways we discount ourselves—believing what is right must come from an exterior source. In creating symbols, give yourself full permission to *make up* whatever you like. There is no correct symbol; you're working with your own associative process. Therefore, whatever you make up is the right one for you. If a number of symbols come to mind, arbitrarily choose one, or let them coalesce. If you keep changing, your innerconsciousness becomes confused. If we were to use a different word to represent the color green each time we referred to that color, the words would become useless. This does not mean you can never change your symbols. If you discover one you like better, use it, but just be consistent.

Remember that innerconsciousness is suggestible. When I originally went through the Silva training, we were not given the choice of creating our own symbols. Instead we were told that every time we repeated the number "three" three times, our bodies would relax, then repeating the number "two" three times would cause our minds to relax, and finally when we repeated the number "one" three times it would put us in our "alpha level." Twenty-five years later, I still use this process when I begin a meditation. I don't think that there is some deep connection between the numbers three, two, and one to a relaxed state of awareness. I have simply conditioned myself to respond in a particular way. Creating your own symbols is more meaningful, but the fact is you can use anything if you make the suggestion to yourself and follow through by consistently using it. You are creating paths through your psyche, as they become well worn, they easily bring you into your deep dimensions of awareness.

If you have the same symbol for each stage (i.e., relaxing your body, your mind, and feelings), that's fine, just give each part of yourself time to calm down. After your meditation, if you don't remember your symbols, simply make them up in the next meditation (the ones you make up will, in all likelihood, be the same ones you created in the first place).

In this first meditation, there will be a number of suggestions which you can use to deepen your consciousness and explore your inner dimension, for the inner world is as expansive as the outer. The next two meditations are designed for increased breath awareness. When you are tense, anxious, or off-balance, you are not breathing fully. You are cutting off oxygen—energy flow in the body—which only perpetuates further tension and anxiety. It's amazing what simply stopping and breathing will do to alleviate stress and create a clear mental and emotional atmosphere in which to proceed. The fact that we take a deep breath before we embark on a difficult task is no coincidence. You will find breath is your anchor not only in meditation, but also in life.

In the count-out of the meditation, it is suggested that you "feel revitalized." The meditations do revitalize you, but it also takes time to adjust to outer consciousness levels, so if you don't feel chirpy right away, you needn't worry.

Relaxing: Clearing a Path to Your Creative Self-Restoring Center

Focus on your breathing. Breathing with your belly...Let your breath find its own most comfortable rhythm...Breathing as relaxed as the breath of a sleeping baby...Imagine breathing in calming energy as you inhale—however you imagine calming energy...Imagine releasing tensions as you exhale...becoming more and more present in this place—in this moment with each breath...Whenever you focus on your breath you find yourself settling into the present moment...After each exhalation pause a moment before you inhale and watch the calm of your being expand...peacefulness expand, as you watch the next inhalation approach slowly, bringing in more calming energy...your breath comes in and moves out taking more tensions away...washing them away like ocean waves...

I'm going to direct your attention to different areas in your body...If you wish, you can relax these areas, becoming more and more relaxed as we move through this process.

First become aware of your feet, the weight of your feet pressing down on the floor, the space your feet occupy, clothing touching your skin, skin covering each of your feet, bones, muscles, tendons, blood, nerves, everything inside of your feet...aware of each of your toes...Imagine asking your feet to relax...Rather than breathing out through your nose, imagine as though your breath were moving out through the tips of your toes carrying with it any tensions you had in your feet...Feel your feet relaxing more and more with each exhalation of breath...It feels good to give your feet space to relax...

MEDITATIONS

As your feet continue to relax, become aware of your ankles...your shins...your calves...and your knees...aware of the whole of each of your lower legs, aware of the space they each occupy...Feel the clothing touching your skin, skin covering your legs...and all the bones and muscles inside...Imagine asking your lower legs to relax, give them permission to relax...feel them relaxing...let your exhalations of breath wash away any tensions in these areas, leaving each of your legs feeling very, very relaxed...It's good to give your body the time, the space, it needs to relax...

As your lower legs continue relaxing move your awareness up to include both your thighs...Be aware of the space they each occupy...aware of the shape of the space between your thighs...Be aware of the space inside of your thighs...be aware of the shape of each of your thighs...aware of the bones, of the muscles within...Tell them they needn't carry you at the moment and they can have this time to relax...Send your breath down through your thighs to help them relax...Feel them breathing and relaxing more and more with each exhalation of breath...

As your thighs continue relaxing, move your awareness up to your pelvis...Be aware of the space your pelvis occupies, the clothing touching your skin, skin covering your pelvis...aware of the bones, the muscles, the organs inside...Let your pelvis relax...You may wish to imagine breathing out through your genitals, your exhalations carrying away any tensions...Feel your pelvis relaxing...Feel yourself fully supported by the chair or the floor...It feels good to give yourself the gift of this space for relaxation...

As your pelvis continues to relax more and more, become aware of your belly and lower back...aware of the space that this part of your body occupies, the space between one side of you and the other...space between your belly and your back...All the bones, muscles, organs within this space...all of them functioning in harmony with one another...Relax your abdomen and lower back...As your breath moves in and out of your body let the rise and fall of your belly massage this whole area into a deep state of relaxation, feel it relaxing into a calmer and calmer state of being, very relaxed...

As your belly and lower back continue to relax, become aware of the rest of your back and your chest. Be aware of the space that this part of your body occupies...Feel the size and shape of your rib cage...Feel the movement of your ribcage as breath rolls in and out of your lungs...Move your awareness in deeper, become aware of your heartbeat, the pulse of your heart...sustained by continuous life-force energy...feel the rhythm of your pulsing heart...Know that whenever you pay attention to your heartbeat you'll find yourself feeling calmer...Now be aware of the rhythm of your breath...Allow these rhythms to return you to yourself, wash through the whole of your being...Let them dissolve any tensions you have in your chest and upper back...Feel the whole of your chest and back entering deeper and deeper states of relaxation...Breathe out tension...Breathe in calm...

Now become aware of your shoulders, your arms, and your hands...aware of each of your fingers...Notice the space that each of these parts of your body occupies...Notice what the different parts are touching...Imagine your breath washing down through your shoulders, arms, hands, dissolving all tensions in its path and moving out through your fingertips...as they become more relaxed it's as though they become slightly heavier...Feel these parts of your body becoming more and more relaxed with each exhalation of breath...

As they continue to relax, move your awareness up to your neck. Be aware of the space your neck occupies...You may wish to roll your neck around letting it find its own most comfortable position...Give your neck space to relax...Acknowledge it for the hard work of holding your head up all the time...Tell your neck it can relax now...Feel it relaxing, relaxing more and more with each exhalation of breath...It feels good to relax your neck...

Now move your awareness into your throat, you may wish to swallow, becoming very aware of all the muscles in and around your throat...Relax your throat, let it relax more and more with each exhalation of breath...As your throat continues to relax, move your awareness up into your mouth...Let your tongue relax a little...Move your mouth around so you can become very aware of the hinges of your jaws...Breathe through the hinges in your jaws and feel them relax more and more with each exhalation of breath...Let your mouth hang open if it is more relaxed in that position...It feels good to relax...

Now imagine the many layers of muscles in your face, giving your face full range of expression...Relax all your facial muscles...Imagine a soft breeze caressing your face, soothing it...relaxing your cheeks...Let the relaxation soak in to all the muscles in and behind your eyes...breathing in calm, breathing out tension...your eyelids relaxing...your forehead, your temples...relaxing your whole face...letting that relaxation spread out over your scalp...the whole of your face and head relaxed...

Notice how good it feels to be so relaxed and know that every time you relax you'll be able to enter deeper and deeper states of body relaxation with greater and greater ease...Know that this is so...Know that as your breath is full and relaxed your body relaxes too...It feels good to give your body the gift of relaxation...

Now make up a symbol that represents this body relaxation...Any symbol that you choose...it can be a picture, a gesture, a sensation, a sound, whatever you like. If you have a couple of symbols, pick one or let them coalesce into one...This is your body relaxation symbol which you can use whenever you wish to physically relax...Tell yourself that whenever you bring this symbol into awareness the whole of your body will relax as you are now relaxed in a matter of moments...Tell your body this now...Know that it is so. Expect that your body will come to know this symbol and will always relax whenever you bring it to awareness. Know that every time you use this symbol, your whole body will respond to it more and more quickly, tell yourself you'll remember this symbol for the next time you meditate...

You can also give your mind space to calm down, to feel peaceful...Now imagine being in a place that feels very good to you, a place where you can feel quiet and peaceful. It may be in the country, in the city, at home—wherever you like—if you have a number of places that feel calming to you, pick one of them...If no place is completely calm, make up an imaginary place that would feel serene to you if it were to exist. Now choose one place to be...Imagine being in this special place now...Imagine what's below your feet...what's to your left...to your right...Imagine what's in front of you...and behind you...Imagine what's above you...Sense how the air feels on your skin...Imagine the sounds present...the scents present...Let your imagination make this place real, allow yourself to be fully there in your mind...Create this place for yourself to enjoy...Enjoy this place you've created...Let yourself be fully there...

Take a deep breath, breathe in the peaceful atmosphere...drawing in the good feelings of this place, into the whole of yourself...breathing it in...bringing in the serenity...Feel the calming qualities of this place calm you, calm your mind...Breathe in calm...Feel it spread through your being...peaceful...You are as much a part of this place as everything that is here...Feel how in this place the usual chatter of your mind has quieted down some. Its a good feeling to feel yourself mentally relaxing...

Notice how your mind is very relaxed and at the same time very alert...Here, sounds do not distract you, instead they enhance your inner calm and aware-ness...Here, you are both relaxed and alert. Here, thoughts move in and out of your awareness as easily as breath rolls in and out...in and out...no resistance, no attachment...Here, thoughts move through your awareness as easily as puffy white clouds drift through the spacious afternoon sky…Feel the peace in the sky of your mind…Your mind is expansive, clear and calm…Imagine your mind being the spacious afternoon sky…Feel how relaxed and at the same time how alert your mind is…It's a good feeling to be mentally relaxed…as your mind relaxes, your mind opens into its natural state of spaciousness…Imagine the sky of your mind expanding out as far as the horizon…lots of room for whatever thoughts cross the sky of your mind…Every time you mentally relax you'll enter deeper and deeper states of this relaxation with greater and greater ease…Know that this is so…It feels good to give your mind this time, this space to relax…Now make up a symbol that represents this mental relaxation. Anything you choose—a gesture, a sound, a picture, whatever—choose, create a particular symbol…This is your mental relaxation symbol. Now tell your mind that the next time you bring your mental relaxation symbol into awareness it will relax in a matter of moments just as it is relaxed now…Tell your mind this now…Expect that every time you bring this symbol into your awareness your mind will enter calmer and calmer states of mental relaxation more and more quickly…Tell yourself that you'll remember this symbol to use the next time you meditate…Whenever you bring your mental relaxation symbol to awareness, your mind will relax, as it is now…relaxed in a matter of moments—just as it is now…

When you're ready, be aware of the emotional climate present for you now…If any feelings are clamoring for attention, imagine taking care of them in whatever manner occurs to you…You may want to imagine the rain coming through and clearing them away…or you can imagine all the "shoulds" soaking down into the ground…Let all the feelings that judge how the world should be; how you should be; how your life ought to be—all the pushing and pulling energy, all the dense energy, all the edges, frustration, anger, anxiety, judgment— anything that makes your heart tense up and withdraw from life—let it all soak into the ground…Breathe it *all* out…Give yourself permission to let go…Imagine it dropping away and giving your heart breathing space…as your heart relaxes, your heart opens into its natural state of generosity…Now take a moment to comfort yourself…Appreciate your good heart…Tell yourself about it…Offer yourself some loving kindness…Feel your heart open—smile…It feels good to take time to emotionally relax…

Now create a symbol for emotional relaxation…Know that whenever you bring your emotional relaxation symbol to awareness your feelings will quickly relax as you are now relaxed in a matter of moments…Your heart lightens, opens into its natural state of generosity…Tell your emotional self this now…

Take time to bring to awareness what you are grateful for…to make your heart smile…Feel your gratitude…Let all of this have a quiet presence in the light of awareness…Take time to appreciate what you love…Feel your connectedness…Acknowledge the blessings…Feel reverence…Life is sacred…As you exhale, settle into your gratitude…When you relax your body, mind, and emotions and bring your awareness to the sacred, you enter into your creative self-restoring center from which you can do your inner work. This is the place where you commune with the creative and healing energies intrinsic to life itself…Sense your whole being open…

You are now at the alpha level. This is your creative, self-restoring center where you can feel your connectedness to all that is. Here, you can tap healing energy. Here, creativity is released; probabilities are formed, and intuition comes forth. This is where insight is found…Here, you experience spacious awareness…vast and calm…alert and quiet…The Inner Witness emerges. In spacious awareness the ring of truth can always be heard. Truth is revealed wherever you shine the light of awareness. You discover what is needed for well-being. You can focus wherever you choose. Trust spacious awareness…Here you'll find your imagination, creativity and concentration are all greatly enhanced…Notice the quality of this space that you now occupy…

Now create a symbol that represents your creative, self-restoring center—any symbol you like…Know that whenever you bring your symbol for your creative self-restoring center to awareness, the whole of your self will enter this level of innerconsciousness with ease…Tell yourself this now, tell yourself that the next time you bring this symbol to awareness you'll easily and quickly enter this state of being…Know that this is so. Tell yourself that you will remember your symbol for your creative self-restoring center. Expect that every time you bring this symbol to awareness, you'll enter your creative, self-restoring center with greater and greater ease…This is your creative self-restoring center which you are learning to use for a purpose, any purpose you desire. You'll be working from this level of awareness with greater ease every time you practice. Acknowledge that all of this is true…

To return to your creative, self-restoring center, all you need to do is first focus on your breath, then bring your symbol for body relaxation into your awareness and give your body the space to relax, in a few moments bring into your awareness your symbol for mental relaxation and give your mind space to calm down some. Then bring to awareness your symbol for emotional relaxation and your feelings will respond by relaxing. Then bring to awareness your symbol for your creative, self-restoring center and notice that that particular quality of inner awareness is again present…Feeling spacious awareness, feeling your gratitude, feeling the sacred…ready to do the inner work of your choosing.

Know that you are completely safe at this level and every other level of awareness…If ever you find yourself off-center all you need do is return your attention to your breath…Breathe and healing happens…This is *your* creative, self-restoring center —the threshold between inner and outer dimensions…Here you'll discover the rich and beautiful landscapes ready for your journeying…Here you'll experience vivid and meaningful sensations and imagery…creativity, receptivity…new realities unfolding before you, guiding you to new dimensions of being.

Here you commune with the spacious awareness of the Inner Witness. Listen to the quiet of awareness…Experience awareness…Breathe…be *in* awareness…as though you are held by awareness…Feel a quality of awareness that is all-encompassing; as though it sits in wholeness…Know that you are completely safe at this level and every other level of awareness…If ever you find yourself off-center, all you need do is return your attention to your breath…Breathe and healing happens…Your breath is self balancing and resilient. Know that you can choose to move with it in any direction you like. If ever you get distracted or momentarily lose your balance, all you need do is return to your breath. You can return to your usual waking awareness whenever you wish by opening your eyes. Breathe…Arrive here in this meditation. Breathe…Rest your attention on your breath…In meditation your breath is your home. You can always return to your breath…take refuge in your breath…Your breath centers you…Breathe…Your breath clears you…You can breathe in calm and breathe out any energy you wish to release…Your breath renews you…Your breath heals you…Your breath returns you to the embrace of life itself…In meditation your breath is your home…Breathe…Let your attention rest on your breath. Breathe.

◆

Know that you can enhance your inner awareness whenever and however you like. I'm going to suggest several methods you can use to deepen your inner experience. Then I'll give you time to use one of these methods, or you may wish to explore on your own…Throughout your exploration of inner dimensions you will remain alert and aware—Tell yourself this.

It is always good to watch your breath, to watch the rise and fall of your belly, to feel yourself entering an increasingly enhanced dimension of inner awareness with each breath, with each exhalation of breath, letting your breath soothe you into returning you to yourself…letting your breath wash away any distractions. Breath is your home when you meditate. You can always return to your breath. When you do, you call forth the Inner Witness that brings you into the present moment.

You can imagine yourself to be a leaf upon a tree on a warm sunny afternoon. Imagine that a gentle breeze comes along and lifts you up…Imagine floating through the air as long as you like and when you're ready, slowly fluttering down upon the ground, feeling that you're becoming increasingly aware of yourself with each descending layer of your movement toward the ground. Upon landing on the ground, you'll discover yourself at a much more enhanced level of inner awareness—your inner experience will have become much more vivid…And if you like, you can land in a river and softly, easily float through your inner dimensions, feeling yourself gently bobbing up and down as you safely rest upon the surface of the water, and being carried ashore whenever you wish.

Or you can imagine yourself to be in an elevator watching the elevator lights above the door, feeling the sensations as the elevator goes down, down into the depths of your being…And you can choose to leave the elevator at whatever floor you wish, exploring what that particular level has to offer…Or, if you choose, you can have the elevator go up, exploring the heights of your being.

You may wish simply to count on a descending scale from ten to one, telling yourself that at each descending count, your awareness will go deeper and deeper until at the count of one you'll find yourself at just that level you wish to explore, a deeper level than before. And at the count of one, you'll notice that, in fact, this has occurred…

Take time now to choose one of these methods or to explore one of your own creation, and use it to enhance your inner awareness. As you do this you'll discover the expansive, fluid spaces within you. Take time to do this now…Tell yourself you will remain alert and aware throughout your exploration.

◆

Begin to finish what you're doing...Know that every time you enter these dimensions of awareness, that every time you enter your creative, self-restoring center, you're increasingly able to focus where you choose and maintain whatever level of awareness you choose. You'll be able to enter and work from these levels with greater ease every time you practice...Know this to be so. Expect it to be increasingly easy to focus wherever you choose for as long as you like. Every time you practice meditating, your abilities are greatly enhanced...You'll discover that every time you meditate, you open to your true self and you're connected to all that is. The feelings of wholeness that you experience will carry over into your daily activities, enabling you to fully enjoy life, and be clear, centered, and open...whole and connected in heart and spirit...Know that all of this is so. See yourself carrying this sense of well-being you're now experiencing into your daily activities.

◆

Decide now when you will again work in your creative self-restoring center. Decide when during your daily routine would be good times for you to practice meditating for a few minutes...once, twice, maybe three practice sessions a day...Tell yourself you will remember what you have decided...Imagine doing what it is that you decided...

To return to an outer focus of attention all you need to do is to tell yourself, "I am now going to count from one to five and snap my fingers...at the count of five, I'll open my eyes feeling revitalized and remembering all that I've experienced in this meditation."...Then count slowly, giving your consciousness time to adjust levels, just as I am about to do...

Now make yourself ready to come out to the outer focus of attention, knowing you can return to these inner dimensions whenever you wish.

Count Out

Use this Count Out to conclude your meditation.

In a moment I'm going to count from one to five and snap my fingers; at that moment you'll open your eyes, feeling revitalized, remembering all you've experienced and feeling a sense of wholeness that will carry over into your activities...Know you can return to these dimensions whenever you choose.

ONE—becoming more aware of the room around you...

TWO—coming up slowly now...

THREE—at the count of five you'll open your eyes feeling relaxed, revitalized, and refreshed, remembering all you've experienced...

FOUR—coming up now...bringing with you your sense of well-being...

FIVE!—eyes open, feeling refreshed, revitalized, and relaxed, remembering all you have experienced...having brought with you your sense of wholeness—open heart and spirit...

You may now choose to describe or draw your experience.

Ocean Breath: Riding the Rhythm of Breath for Centering

Close your eyes and focus your awareness on your breathing, breathing with your belly...Feel the rise and fall of your breath...Let your breathing find its own most comfortable rhythm. Breathing that is as relaxed as the breathing of a sleeping baby...Let your breath come down into your belly. Let the rhythm of your breath soothe the whole of your body...Bring in what you imagine to be calming energy as you inhale...Release tensions as you exhale...Bring into your awareness your symbol for physical relaxation...Feel relaxation spread through the whole of your body...Give your body permission to relax, for it can relax now. Let the awareness of your physical relaxation symbol soothe your body into relaxation...It's good to give your body space and time to relax...Breathe through any tensions; let them go...Imagine the tensions sinking into the floor...Feel the weight of your body being fully supported by the floor...Know that every time you bring this symbol into awareness, you will enter deeper and deeper states of physical relaxation with greater and greater ease. Tell yourself this now...

When you're ready, bring to awareness your symbol for mental relaxation...Watch the chatter of your mind becoming calm and quiet...where thoughts move in and out of your awareness as easily as you breathe...Let the rhythm of your breath calm your mind, give your mind permission to relax into the spacious awareness...Let your mental relaxation symbol calm your mind...Here sounds do not distract you, instead they enhance your inner focus. Here, it's as though all your thoughts were the puffy clouds drifting through a sunny afternoon sky, the sky of your mind, spacious clear mind...Feel your mind relax into its natural state of spaciousness...Tell yourself that whenever you bring your mental relaxation symbol into your awareness, the whole of your mind will enter deeper and deeper states of mental relaxation with greater ease every time you practice...Expect this to be the case.

When you're ready, bring to awareness your emotional relaxation symbol. With your awareness go over the full range of feelings that are present for you now...If any feelings are clamoring for your attention, take care of them in whatever manner occurs to you...Let yourself emotionally relax...Let all the "shoulds" soak into the ground. Feel your heart relax into its natural state of generosity...Take a moment and offer yourself loving kindness...Appreciate who you are...Tell yourself that whenever you bring your emotional relaxation symbol into your awareness, your emotional self will relax in a matter of moments...Expect this to be the case.

When you're ready, bring to awareness your symbol for your creative, self-restoring center...Feel your gratitude to be alive...Sense your whole being open...You are in healing space, sacred space... receptive... creative...mindful...alert...relaxed...Now feel yourself at a stable level of innerconsciousness...Feel that special quality of awareness that you have at this level...Here you can experience your connectedness to all that is...Your symbol brings you into that level of awareness that you are learning to work with...You can work from this level with greater ease every time you practice. This is your creative self-restoring center, which you are learning to use for a purpose, any purpose you desire...Here your imagination, creativity, and powers of concentration are enhanced. Here you'll discover a rich and beautiful landscape of your receptivity and creativity unfolding before you. You'll experience vivid and meaningful sensations and imagery...new realities...As these realities appear they'll guide you to new dimensions of being...Here you can make use of the wisdom of your inner self, discovering the expansive power of the Inner Witness...The Inner Witness is a part of the universal energy that permeates all life...the energy that dissolves limitations, enabling you to create change easily. Know that all of this is so...

I will now give you time to explore and enhance your inner awareness by any method of your choosing...You can use the falling leaf or elevator, deep breathing or a countdown—whatever you choose...When you next come back to these words, you'll be fully alert and ready to follow carefully all that I have to say throughout the rest of this meditation.

◆

Now imagine that you're at the beach—an ocean beach on a sunny summer day. You're sitting or lying on the sand—remember times when this has occurred...Imagine as though you were on a beach right now...Imagine the warmth of the sun shining down on you warming your forehead, your whole body...Imagine the sound of the ocean...Feel the warmth of the sand below you as the sun has warmed the sand, letting that warmth nurture you, your body soaking it up. You can sense the shape of the indentation that's made in the sand from the contours of your body, your body is fully supported…You can see the glitter of some of the particles of sand…Smell the salty air, feel the breeze that cools you…refreshes you, hearing the breakers and the occasional sound of the gulls…Imagine it…Let yourself be fully present in this place. Let your imagination fully create this place…

Now notice the ocean…how the waves build and break, the ocean waves build, break, roll on the beach, and roll back in again…building, breaking, moving out, moving in…roll out, roll back in…build, break, roll out, roll back in…the rhythm of the ocean, the inexhaustible movement of the ocean…As you experience the rhythm of the ocean, include in your awareness the rhythm of your breath…air rolling in, air rolling out…rolling in, building, breaking, rolling out…The inexhaustible rhythm of your breath sustaining the whole of your being…Breathing life.

Feel your breath as a part of the universal rhythm of the whole of everything…Rolling in, building, breaking, rolling out…Rolling in, building, breaking, rolling out…Simply sit with your breath and let it soothe you, cleanse you…Keep your awareness on your breath and feel yourself returned to your center, to this moment…Simply be present with your breath, letting your breath draw you into yourself, into beingness itself, moving in, building, breaking, moving out—just as the ocean does…Every cell in your body is breathing, just as the granules of sand are being washed by the waves. Feel breath in your whole body…Imagine in fact that your breath *is* the ocean moving through you…And imagine that your breath can move to any area in your body, rolling in, rolling out, washing away all tensions, all toxins, smoothing the surfaces…rolling in, rolling out…Just as the ocean waves smooth all rough edges, so too, your breath can wash them away…

Take time to let your breath move to any areas in your body and washing away all your tensions, smoothing the edges, pulling in calming energy as it rolls in, washing away tensions as it rolls out…Imagine sending your breath to any area of tension…Imagine the air rolling out through the area of tension rather than out through your nose, taking the tensions, toxins, with it; they're slipping out…Let them slip away…Calm rolling in, they're rolling out…rolling in…softening, rolling out…relaxing…Know that with each breath tension continues to diminish…Over time they will dissolve altogether…Feel how each time you breathe the tensions release more and more…And you sink deeper and deeper into the support of the earth…Sometimes tensions and toxins disappear very quickly, sometimes slowly, either way they have begun to disappear…You are more relaxed, returned to yourself…Just as the ocean cleanses everything it touches, every cell in your body is cleaned and renewed. Breath carries life. Breath returns you home to yourself in the present moment. Rest your awareness on your breath and the Inner Witness comes forth.

Feel your breath a part of the universal rhythms that are constantly present always. Let your breath soothe you, clear you, return you to yourself, to beingness itself…Simply be present letting your breath draw you into yourself, into beingness itself…Fully present with your breath, your breath that is constantly present, constantly renewing you, your breath that is the breath of life itself…As the waves are constant, so too is breath…As your breath is continually present, as you are present with your breath, you fully relax into the life that is yours, relax into your connectedness to all that is…Let yourself be soothed by the presence of breath…whole and connected in heart and spirit…

As you're present with your breath, look out into the future and notice if there is anything that keeps you from being relaxed—what causes you to forget your breath…Notice what you need to do to remember your breath, to be present, connected with your being and beingness itself…Imagine doing this…

◆

Know that every time you meditate, you receive beneficial effects on every level, that every time you meditate, you're increasingly able to focus wherever you choose for as long as you desire...Know that every time you practice meditating your abilities are enhanced geometrically...You'll discover that every time you meditate, the good feelings you've experienced will carry over into your daily activities enabling you to enjoy more fully the life that is yours, enabling you to be mindful, creative, and intuitive...Know that all of this is so...Imagine yourself carrying this sense of wholeness, connected in heart and spirit into your daily activities...Expect it to be so.

◆

Know that you are fully capable of acting on these energies...Know that whenever you bring your attention to your breath you will relax, be clear and present...Finish what you're doing and make yourself ready to come out to the outer focus of attention...Know that you'll bring with you all the energies you've contacted...

Know that you can return to these dimensions whenever you choose. Know that every time you rest your attention on your breath you open to the spacious awareness of the Inner Witness.

Count Out

Use this Count Out to conclude your meditation.

In a moment I'm going to count from one to five and snap my fingers...at that moment, you'll open your eyes remembering all that you've experienced and bring with you the energies you have tapped...

ONE—becoming more aware of the room around you...

TWO—coming up slowly now…

THREE—at the count of five you'll open your eyes feeling relaxed, revitalized, and refreshed, remembering all that you've experienced…

FOUR—coming up now, bring with you your sense of well-being…

FIVE!—eyes open, feeling refreshed, revitalized and relaxed, remembering all that you've experienced, feeling a sense of wholeness with open heart and spirit…ready and able to act on the energies to which you've tapped. Breathing.

You may want to jot down your reflections and decide now when you're going to meditate next.

Relaxing into Well-Being: Working with Symbols

Track 1

Make yourself comfortable, close your eyes…Relax…Focus on your breath…Let your breath be full and easy…as relaxed as the breathing of a sleeping baby…As you exhale, feel yourself relax…Feel your body relaxing into the support of whatever you may be sitting or lying on…Appreciate that the earth has always supported you…Let yourself relax into this support…Each breath renews you…Each breath caresses you. Feel your body breathing…Feel the sensations of breath, as breath comes in through your nose or mouth…you can feel it moving in…Sense it moving through your whole body…Every cell of which you're composed breathes…Sense your body breathing…renewed with each breath…and releasing all the energy that's no longer needed with each exhalation…Breathing…It's good to simply be quiet and rest your attention on breath…

Breath relaxes…Breath renews…waves of breath rolling through…Take a moment and scan your body. Notice if there are any particular areas that are calling your attention…Notice the areas of tension…Move your awareness to one of them…Send your breath to this place…Feel it breathing…almost as though your breath were drawn in and released right from this place…As breath releases, it dislodges any tensions and carries them away…Feel yourself loosening up with each exhalation of breath…more relaxed…more relaxed with each breath…Breathe right through the area…As you exhale, sense your breath carrying out the tensions…Just breathe them out. You may want to envision a color or sound moving out with your breath, as this part of your body releases and relaxes…With each breath feel yourself letting go and settling more into the support of the chair or whatever you're sitting or lying on…into the support of the earth itself…each breath more relaxed…Tell your body it can relax…Feel it relaxing more and more…Send your breath wherever it's needed…from the tips of your toes…through your legs…your torso…your arms and hands…Breathe…Let your whole body relax…Breathe…Send your breath wherever it's needed…It feels good to relax…Waves of breath relaxing you…caressing you…renewing you…Breath heals…It feels good to relax…Whenever you focus on your breath and your breath is full and easy, your whole being relaxes…Send your breath wherever you like and your relaxation deepens.

◆

This is your physical relaxation level. Create a symbol that represents this relaxation for you (or if you have one, bring it to awareness now)…

Know that whenever you bring to awareness your symbol for physical relaxation, your whole body relaxes as it's now relaxed in a matter of moments…Tell your body this now…Expect it to be true…Know that every time you bring to awareness your symbol for physical relaxation, your body responds by relaxing as it's now relaxed in a matter of moments…Tell yourself this…Your symbol for physical relaxation tells your body to relax…it gives it that message…Know that every time you practice using your symbol for physical relaxation you'll enter deeper and deeper states of relaxation with greater ease…Expect this to be the case.

◆

Now, to relax your mind, imagine being in a very peaceful, serene, and quiet place…a place that is magical to you…It could be anywhere you like…It could be a place you've been, or a place you create in your imagination…a place that is especially peaceful and serene…Let your imagination transport you into this place now…Imagine, what would be below your feet?…What would be in front of you?…What would be on either side of you?…Feel the quality of this place…the quality of the air…the smells…the sounds…the colors…the textures…It's a wonderful place…It's a sanctuary…your sanctuary… peaceful…serene…special…

Whenever you come here, your mind opens into its natural state of spaciousness, where you are fully relaxed and fully alert at the same time…Here, your breath is like the breeze that clears the air…Your breath clears your mind…and your mind opens into spaciousness…As you breathe in, you draw in the peaceful qualities of this special place…Feel peacefulness moving through you…through your whole being and your mind relaxes…

Create, bring to awareness, a symbol for mental relaxation…This is your mental relaxation level…Know that every time you bring your symbol for mental relaxation to awareness, your mind will relax as it is now relaxed in a matter of moments…Tell yourself this now…and know that every time you bring this symbol to awareness, your mind will relax more deeply…more quickly…Expect this to be the case…Tell your mind this is true…that when you bring your symbol for mental relaxation to awareness, it will relax…as it's now relaxed…in a matter of moments…Relaxing into its natural state of spaciousness…as spacious as the skies…lots of room for whatever crosses the sky of your mind.

Become aware of the emotional climate present in you…Notice feelings that may be causing you to pull back from life a little…feelings that may be tugging at you, and telling you how you should be or how others should be…All the pushing and pulling…any anxiety, frustration…any feelings causing you to shut down a little…Imagine as though you could breathe right through them all…and your breath carries them out…Imagine that they drop down into the ground by the sheer weight of themselves and the soil transforms them, for all that drops into the earth is transformed into nutrients for new life…Give yourself permission to emotionally relax…Breathe out and release all the difficulties…Feel your heart getting lighter…more open.

◆

Appreciate yourself for all the efforts you've made…Appreciate your good heart…Tell yourself about it…Offer yourself loving kindness…Absorb it into your heart…Feel as though your heart smiles. Feel your heart getting lighter…warmer…Feel your heart relax into its natural state of generosity and compassion.

This is your emotional relaxation level. Create, bring to awareness, your symbol for emotional relaxation.

◆

Know that every time you bring this symbol to awareness, your feelings relax…your heart relaxes, as you're now relaxed, in a matter of moments…Each time you practice working with your symbol for emotional relaxation, you relax emotionally more easily and more quickly. Expect this to be the case. Tell your feelings that next time you bring this symbol to awareness, they'll respond by relaxing as they're now relaxed.

◆

Now take time to remember to bring to awareness what you feel grateful about…what you cherish…what you love…Let these aspects of life pass through your awareness now…Life is sacred…Feel yourself relaxing into your gratitude…In this place, you feel your connectedness to *all that is*…to all of life…This is your creative, self-restoring center, where you can tap healing energies. Create, bring to awareness, your symbol for your creative, self-restoring center…Know that whenever you bring this symbol to awareness, you'll quickly enter this state of consciousness. Tell yourself this now…Expect it to be true.

This is your creative, self-restoring center…Here, you experience spacious awareness…calm…vast…quiet…alert…Here, the Inner Witness emerges… Awareness is vast…This is where insight is found…This is where intuition is awakened…This is where creativity is released…This is your creative, self-restoring center. You can work with this state of awareness with greater ease every time you practice…Here, you are increasingly able to focus wherever you choose for as long as you choose…Your imagination…creativity…and concentration are all enhanced…Your intuition is keen…Trust spacious awareness.

◆

Here, you reside in spacious awareness…The Inner Witness is present…revealing what's true…Wherever you focus your awareness, you discover what's true…Here you activate your imagination…Your imagination is fluid and free…Wherever you focus your creativity, you shape probabilities…Your creative imagination shapes reality…Your Receptive Imagination brings intuitive insight…Wherever you focus your imagination, intuition speaks to you…You discover insight…powerful…Your inner world is as vast as the outer…

If ever you find yourself distracted or off balance in any way, all you need do is return to your breath…Focus on your breath…it brings you to your center…Breath is your home in meditation…Trust your experience.

◆

Take time now to enhance and explore your inner awareness by any method of your choosing.

◆

Consciousness opens…Here, you can listen deeply…Here, the Inner Witness grounds you in the present moment…Your intuition brings you insight and deep knowing…Your Active Imagination aligns you with the best possible realities…

Now, do any work that you would like…You may simply want to reside in this calm by focusing on breath…Or you may want to take a few moments to focus on affirmations, creating an alignment with the realities you choose…Or you may want to share presence with a concern, letting your intuition offer you insight…You may want to focus on a particular upcoming event that is important…Imagine it unfolding in the best possible way for everyone…Remember times of peak experiences and bring that energy into the event…Let it glow…Take time to do whatever work you would like now. This is your creative, self-restoring center…Healing happens here…Creativity arises here…Intuition becomes apparent here.

◆

You may want to channel positive healing energy to anyone who may be in need now…or any situation that could use some positive energy…Do this by simply focusing intention and imagining the situation or the person surrounded by positive healing energy…In this dimension we are all connected.

◆

Know that every time you enter these dimensions of awareness, you receive beneficial effects…Healing happens…Intuition becomes more and more keen and available to you…The Inner Witness is fully present…Creativity is fluid…Expect this to be the case…

You can return to these dimensions of awareness any time you choose on your own by simply working with your symbols for physical, mental, emotional relaxation, and your creative, self-restoring center. These symbols will bring you right into this state of awareness…And you can do whatever inner work you would like…You can return to outer levels of awareness any time by counting yourself out, just as I am about to do…

In a moment, I'm going to count from one to five. At the count of five, your eyes will open, and you'll feel revitalized, refreshed, relaxed, remembering all that you've experienced and bringing with you the energies you've tapped…ready and able to act on them in your life…feeling a sense of wholeness that will be with you throughout this day, throughout all of your activities.

Making yourself ready to come out to outer conscious levels now…

ONE—becoming more aware of the room around you…

TWO—coming up slowly now…

THREE—coming up…

FOUR—bringing with you the energies you've tapped, remembering everything you've experienced…

FIVE!—eyes open, revitalized, refreshed, relaxed, bringing with you all the energies you've tapped, ready and able to act on them in your life, remembering all that you've experienced and knowing you can return to these dimensions whenever you choose.

•3•

Creating a Language to Speak
to Your Deeper Self

Whenever you meditate, you are predominantly at the alpha level, which is suggestible, so you may as well take advantage of this receptivity and develop your own programming—thereby, with an act of will, choosing to program your own development. If a TV ad can con you into buying some kitchen gadget, why not choose to do something you really want? Using affirmations is one of the most powerful ways of doing this.

An affirmation is simply a positively stated sentence of how you'd like to be, such as: "The whole of my body is healthy." That may sound simplistic because you know the whole of your body is not fully healthy; all of us have something or other that ails us. However, since your innerconsciousness is noncritical, it believes anything, and it's your innerconsciousness that directs your body. So if you cultivate a belief within that your body is healthy, it will enable your body to be more effective in fighting off potential sickness, and it will give you a little added strength to heal the ailments it already has. Our bodies are continually responding to our inner messages; remember that simply imagining what you're afraid of activates your adrenal glands. If you put in the message that you are healthy your body will respond accordingly, and this is simply done *by pretending* that it is so.

Affirmations for Aligning Intention

Working with affirmations is extremely simple—so simple that our tendency is to slough it off as silly. We tend to do that with a lot of things in our lives, but it's just these simple things that often are the most enriching. We need to stop denying ourselves that which could so easily be ours. Permit yourself to proceed even though you may think it ridiculous. When I began doing affirmations, I invariably thought to myself, "This is foolish." It's okay to think that—remember the beta mind is critical, but each beta thought has very little energy. Thinking it's dumb doesn't stop it from working—the innerconsciousness is noncritical (i.e., suggestible), and each alpha thought has more energy. The only thing that will stop it from working is not using it, so go ahead, perhaps thinking all the while that it is an absurd activity.

A while back, I had an experience that reignited my knowledge of the power of affirmations. I had a major disagreement with one of my closest friends, and for many months we talked about it often, never being able to come to any resolution. It made it close to impossible for us to be able to enjoy our friendship. We finally decided to go to a mediator who tried to help us work through our problems. That too was unsuccessful. All along our intentions had been good—we each sincerely wanted to work it out—but to no avail. Several weeks after that attempt, it came to me in a meditation to use an affirmation. The specific words that came to my mind were, "I reside in the care we have for each other." I used the affirmation regularly, and wrote a postcard to my friend inviting him to join me in its use. About a month later, we saw each other again and somehow, inexplicably, the year-old tension had completely dissolved. The affirmation must have drawn on the intuitive knowledge available at deeper levels, for we found ourselves moving along a new course. The use of that affirmation was the only new element in our relationship—nothing else had changed. If I hadn't known how to use these energies, I might have lost a friendship close to my heart. It is experiences like this that humble me, for the energy that is available to work with is powerful. In working with innerconsciousness, I have come to realize that the solution comes about without my knowing *why* or *how*. It is never linear or reasonable—it simply is. Sometimes it's very subtle; I can't even point to the solution, but I can't point to the problem anymore either—which is solution enough for me.

It's good to make your own affirmations. To do this, think of aspects of your life that you'd like to change and how you'd like them to be instead. For each one create a sentence, stated simply, *positively*, and in the *present* tense, or think of a particular picture or gesture that represents each change as if it has *already* come about. This process will enable you to create a specific affirmation for any particular transformation of your choosing—take a stand for what you want.

Your innerconsciousness is not linear, but instead very childlike, so you don't have to have an analysis of why something is needed or how it will happen—justification is unnecessary. You simply need a statement of the desired end result. Always state it in the present tense because your innerconsciousness takes things quite literally. You don't want to become healthy because that's perpetually in the future; you want to *be* healthy. As far as your innerconsciousness is concerned, you only exist in the moment; time is meaningless to it. So don't say, "I will be healthy because I eat well," but, "I eat well and I am fully healthy."

Because of the noncritical nature of your innerconsciousness, affirmations should always be stated positively; it doesn't understand negatives. Notice what happens when I say, "Don't imagine a lemon." You immediately and unavoidably think of a lemon. If you use the affirmation, "I'm not sick," it will just hear "sick." It's easy to understand this if you think of young children who are much more responsive when you state things in a positive way. Rather than saying "Stop making all that noise," it is much more effective to say, "Be a little quieter." As a matter of fact we should begin to watch the negative suggestions we are constantly giving ourselves (a friend calls them "neffirmations"). For example, "Whenever I talk in groups, I sound stupid." Notice how this statement is positively expressing something you don't want. Similarly, if you want to feel secure speaking in public, saying, "I'm not stupid," is ineffectual, whereas saying, "I'm intelligent and articulate especially when expressing myself in groups," helps enormously.

In addition, you don't want your beta mind to give your inner self a bunch of alternatives stating it one day this way and one day that. Your innerconsciousness, just like a child, will only become confused. You want to impress it with a *clear* message, using the same picture or statement time and time again (like a symbol).

Affirmations work because you are in a suggestible state of awareness when you are meditating. They enable you to realign yourself and awaken your intuition so that you find yourself with impulses to act in ways that are in accordance with the affirmation. When working with them, it is important to feel as much as possible that they are true. You concentrate on the power implied by the statement itself; pretend that it is so. It is not the words themselves (or the pictures) that have power, *it's the feelings they elicit.* You want to plant those feelings in your innerconsciousness as often as you can so new resources will grow for you to act out of. Be sure not to focus on the inaccuracy of the affirmation, for that will only perpetuate the reality you want to change. If the affirmation were fully true, you wouldn't need to use it. It's a given that there's a contradiction, but don't look at the gap between your experience and the affirmation and conclude that it is not working. Instead, move through your daily activities with the assumption that the power of the affirmation is working under the surface. When you say to yourself, "I am healthy," don't focus on your ailing knee, but concentrate on the vitality your body does have. When you are going through your daily activities and your knee starts to hurt, don't decide that the affirmation has been ineffective, but remember it and assume its power is gradually working and that its reality is slowly manifesting.

It is crucial to be ever aware that we always respond in terms of our beliefs. It is our beliefs that shape our expectations, as though they angle the light of awareness. Like a miner's light, whichever way you turn your head is what you see. We need to be mindful and notice what we are trying to prove. This is operative with affirmations and with all other techniques in this book. We always go through our activities in terms of our attitudes. Thus, if you use an affirmation with the attitude (belief) that it probably won't work—it won't. So try to suspend judgment and just experiment with the process. Watch for its results instead of trying to prove to yourself that it's not working. If you do this, the contradiction between your daily reality and the affirmation will slowly dissolve. Since each of us is constantly looking to have our point of view validated, I'd rather work on the side of proof of benefits than detriments. If you can keep your attitudes positive, you won't give up your power.

Some people prefer to speak the affirmations aloud, for hearing the words gives them an added power. Or you may want to make up a jingle. You might also want to use just one word that connotes the kind of quality you want to bring into your life, such as trust, cooperation, love, joy, generosity, etc. I suggest that you write down your affirmations and post them in places that you regularly see, like the door of your refrigerator or your bathroom mirror; simply catching sight of them out of the corner of your eye will enhance the process of bringing their energy into your life.

You can also repeat affirmations while doing rhythmic activities such as exercising or cleaning, as you are in the alpha state and it will be just as effective as it is when you are meditating. You can use a number of affirmations, one right after the other, or you may want to use just one, repeating it over and over again. Either way, stick to the same wording, which doesn't mean that you can't refine them. As you experiment with the use of affirmations, you will discover the format that's most comfortable for you.

It is important to use them *repeatedly* because innerconsciousness is responsive to repetition. That's one reason why rituals are universally practiced—a major part of every religious tradition is the use of ritual. And a major element of ritual is the repetition of certain words—as in chanting—or the regular use of certain gestures. These chants and gestures always have a specific meaning behind them. Their purpose is usually to set clear intention, to invite particular energy to be present, and to be able to access deeper experience. Similarly, repetition of affirmations is a powerful way to create a channel through which deeper knowledge surfaces. In time you will come to a fuller realization of the power that you are speaking of in each affirmation, moving beyond intellectual understanding and creating conditions in the whole of your being in which the affirmation will manifest itself. None of this occurs logically. You will find yourself unconsciously behaving differently, intuitively acting in alignment with the affirmation. In the induction for each meditation section, there are new affirmations that address the particular issues dealt with in that chapter. It's good to use affirmations every time you meditate.

Here is one affirmation that I think is of particular importance, "I always find *positive* approaches." This protects you from your own negative thoughts and those of others. We all find ourselves acting in ways we don't really approve of; if we tap our own wisdom, we'll find ourselves always behaving to the best of our abilities, for on a deep level we do know what's best.

Another powerful affirmation is, "I maintain balance amidst change." This enables you to be relaxed rather than stressed out so you can respond creatively with the whole of yourself in the midst of turmoil.

One which will move us out of loneliness into trusting both ourselves and others is, "I believe in myself; I believe in my family and friends; we believe in our community; there is a free flow of support among us." This will create an atmosphere of shared trust in our powers and mutual support, and will collectively better enable us to resolve whatever needs changing in our lives.

To transform distrust of innerconsciousness, an affirmation such as, "I have complete trust of all levels of awareness," will be helpful.

In today's apocalyptic times, we can create a safe future by believing in it, and thereby working for it. Using the affirmation, "I trust the future," does this.

Bringing in What's Needed: Using the Power of Symbols

A symbol by definition represents more than itself. For instance, anything you feel sentimental about is a symbol. There may be a kind of flower that has particular significance to you because it represents the person who gave it to you and the love you shared, more than simply the look and smell of that variety of flower. Our lives are full of symbols, some are very personal while others are culturally shared like the wedding ring, or the American flag.

A symbol, being more than itself, is a converging point, the focal point of meaning. A symbol does not need logical or sequential thought processes in order for it to evoke its full meaning. Because our innerconsciousness is holistic, non-sequential, and more focused, its predominant language is symbols. By definition, a symbol elicits a particular set of associations and responses when you bring it to awareness. Therefore, if you want to behave in a particular way, you can create a symbol to represent that behavior, bring it into your awareness at the opportune time, and you will find yourself acting in accordance with it. Your behavior and your inner messages have moved into alignment by use of the symbol. You won't need to go off and meditate about the kind of energy you want or the changes you'd like to make; all you need to do is bring into your awareness the previously created personal symbol you have for the energy. This is very important because when you're in the midst of a situation, you don't have the time, space, or inclination to go off and meditate about it. For example, I am a very goal-oriented person—this trait is often useful because it enables me to accomplish a lot, but there are situations where it becomes a detriment. I feel like I want to be there already and I am very impatient. Often it's when I'm working in groups that this problem surfaces. To resolve this tendency, I created a symbol at a deep level of consciousness—a sailboat. Sailboats get to their destination by utilizing the natural forces around them. So whenever I bring this sailboat into my awareness, it causes me to trust the organic process and to adjust myself to the energies around me rather than "pushing the river." As a result, I find myself calming down, feeling more a part of the process, and understanding how the process (symbolized by the wind and the current) is in fact necessary to move forward. If I hadn't already created the symbol of the sailboat in a meditation to use whenever I might need it, my impatience would continue.

A woman in one of my classes had an image of herself as a klutz. She played left field on a softball team and her body kept responding to this self-image, sabotaging her ability to play well. In class, she went through a fantasy of feeling extremely coordinated and created a symbol for it. She moved from being the klutz on her team to being the star. Every time a fly ball was hit, she brought her symbol to mind, and to everyone's amazement she started catching those flies. It worked because when the ball was in the air, she didn't have enough time to give herself a pep talk, but she could remember her symbol instantaneously.

For you to be able to understand the power of symbols, it's important that you remember the *intimate* connection between what is going on in your awareness at any given moment and its effect on the rest of you—your body, your behavior, etc. Again, the example of dog phobia makes it clear that simply imagining a dog will set the adrenaline pumping. You've probably come to experience this connection yourself by using your induction symbols.

You have numerous associations with any particular behavior you want to elicit. In the symbol, they converge creating a focal point out of which the concrete action you want emerges. Whenever the symbol is in your mind, it creates a channel for you to become intuitively aware of what is needed to behave in accordance with the energy. The symbol acts as a flashlight illuminating that information from the depths of knowingness. The trick is first to get in touch with the energy, create the symbol in a deep level, and tell yourself that next time you bring it to mind you'll respond accordingly. You can create an affirmation by telling yourself you'll remember and bring it into your awareness whenever you need it. Never forget that you act out of your inner messages. The symbol is more than just a beta thought. It becomes a source of behavior.

You can have specific symbols for many kinds of energy: for creativity, personal power, trust, cooperation, clear communication, and anything else you may need. For example, if you're about to go through a round of interviews, it's a good idea to have an appropriate symbol to use while being interviewed. It will greatly increase the likelihood of being chosen for the job you want.

In the symbol-making meditation, you can create a symbol representing any particular kind of energy you choose. To help you connect with that energy, the meditation will guide you through experiences of your past when you felt it most strongly. If there are no such times, *pretend* there were, or do whatever occurs to you to help you *feel* the energy. Maybe imagining yourself embodying the qualities of a role model will work best. Remember innerconsciousness is noncritical. The point is to *feel* the quality you want to cultivate; it makes no difference if you do this by bringing to mind memories of yourself or another. After focusing on the energy, make up a symbol that represents it. Whatever symbol you create is the *right* one, for it's what you associate with the energy that makes it effective. Symbols don't necessarily have to be pictures but it is important that they be specific and easy to recall. You may wish to use a physical gesture or a particular tone—whatever your inclination. I also suggest that you create an affirmation that says you'll remember to bring your symbol into your awareness whenever a situation arises in which it will be of help. Here you will want to create a separate affirmation for each symbol.

The first symbol-making meditation,entitled Internalizing a Quality, is for general use; be sure to choose in advance what you want to create a symbol for. I also recommend that you increase your vocabulary of symbols gradually so your deeper self comes to know each one, rather than confusing it with too many to begin with. Like affirmations, it is good to post your symbols in places where you'll see them.

If you do this, you'll find their effectiveness growing more rapidly, for each reminder strengthens the energy, and you'll be better able to act on its power. It's also good to take time to focus for a few moments on the power and quality of the symbol every time you meditate.

Induction

Close your eyes and focus your awareness on your breathing, breathing with your belly. Feel the rise and fall of your breath…Let your breathing find its own most comfortable rhythm…breathing that is as relaxed as the breathing of a sleeping baby…Feel the rise and fall of your breath. Let your breath come all the way down into your belly, feel the rise of your belly, let your breath move all the way out, feel the fall of your belly…Feel the rise and fall of your breath…Let the rhythm of your breath soothe the whole of your body…Bring in what you imagine to be calming energy as you inhale, release tensions as you exhale…Bring into your awareness your symbol for physical relaxation, feel all the associations you have with this symbol, your symbol for physical relaxation spreads out through the whole of your whole body…Give your body permission to relax…relaxing into the support of the earth; it can relax now…Breathe, breath caresses your body…Let the awareness of this symbol soothe your body into relaxation…It's good to give your body space and time to relax. Imagine the tensions sinking into the floor…Know that every time you bring this symbol into awareness you will enter deeper and deeper states of physical relaxation with greater and greater ease…Tell yourself this now…

When you're ready, bring into your awareness your symbol for mental relaxation. Feel your symbol for mental relaxation cause your mind to relax into its natural state of spaciousness…Watch the chatter of your mind calming down…thoughts move in and out of your awareness as easily as you breathe…lots of room for what ever thoughts cross the sky of your mind. Let the rhythm of your breath calm your mind...Let your mental relaxation symbol calm your mind...Here, sounds do not distract you, instead they enhance your inner focus. Here, it's as though all your thoughts were the puffy clouds drifting through a sunny afternoon sky, the sky of your mind...It's good to give your mind space and time to relax...This mental relaxation is a very harmonious state of being. Tell yourself that whenever you bring your mental relaxation symbol into your awareness, the whole of your mind will enter deeper and deeper states of mental relaxation with greater ease every time you practice.

◆

Expect this to be the case...When you're ready, bring in your symbol for emotional relaxation, with your awareness go over the full range of feelings that are present for you now...If you discover any feelings that are clamoring for your attention, take care of them in whatever manner occurs to you...Let yourself emotionally relax. Imagine letting all the "shoulds" soak into the ground, and nurture yourself, give yourself permission to relax emotionally...Feel your heart relaxing into its natural state of generosity.

◆

When you're ready, bring into your awareness your symbol for your creative, self-restoring center...Remember your gratitude...Acknowledge the sanctity of life...Feel yourself at a stable level of innerconsciousness...Feel that special quality of awareness that you have leveling your creative self-restoring center...That special quality of awareness that your symbol evokes; you are learning to recognize and work from your creative self-restoring center with greater ease every time you practice. This is your creative self-restoring center, which you are learning to use for a purpose, any purpose you desire...Here, your imagination expands and creativity opens, your powers of concentration are equally enhanced and permit you to focus wherever you choose...This is your creative, self-restoring center...Here, you have complete control and you may accept, or reject, or put aside for later consideration anything that I say…Here, you'll discover a rich and beautiful landscape of your receptivity and creativity unfold before you, you'll experience vivid and meaningful sensations and imagery…new realities…As these realities appear, they'll guide you to new dimensions of being…Here, you can make use of the wisdom of your inner self, discovering the expansive power of your inner being. Your inner being is a part of the universal energy which permeates all life…This is the energy which dissolves limitations, enabling you to create change, know that all of this is so…

Now take time to explore and enhance your inner awareness by any method of your choosing…You can use the falling leaf or elevator or countdown—whatever you choose. When you next hear my voice you'll be fully alert and ready to follow carefully the whole of this meditation.

◆

Finishing what you're doing…your consciousness is very receptive, very creative, very relaxed and very alert…You will easily follow these words and remember the whole of your meditative experience.

Affirmations

One powerful way of working with this energy is in using affirmations. I'm going to suggest several affirmations. If you wish to affirm them repeat them to yourself after me. And at the same time, as much as you're able, feel as though each affirmation is fully true…Bring into your awareness pictures and sensations that represent each affirmation as you speak the words to yourself. If you don't like the affirmation simply don't repeat it and wait for the next. Remember not to focus on the difference between any affirmation and your life, but look instead for a grain of truth in your personal experience and let your inner consciousness expand it, making room for new energies to flow through. Feel the power of the words. In so doing, you'll discover that as time goes by you'll find yourself living in ways that conform to the affirmations. You will find affirmations materializing in your daily reality. You'll intuitively be acting out of the power of each affirmation…

I believe in myself…I believe in my family and friends…We believe in our community; there is a free flow of love and support between us all…

I trust the whole of myself…

I am enriched by my deepest dimensions…

I have complete trust of all levels of awareness. I am aware and alert when I meditate…

I always find positive approaches…

The whole of my body/mind is healthy. I have all the energy I need to do as I choose…

My negative feelings guide me to changing their sources…

I face my fears; they are challenges; they guide me to new dimensions of learning…

My life is full of joy…

A spring of creativity continually flows through me and out into the world…

All that I know is available to me whenever I need it…

All my needs are always met—there is enough for everyone…

I am in tune and responsive to my intuition—my deeper knowingness…

Every day the powers of the depths of my consciousness become more and more available to me…

My increasing personal power is for making the world a better place to live for everyone…

I maintain balance amidst change…

I trust the future…

Know that in focusing on affirmations, you've evoked patterns of energy that will begin moving through your life, materializing in your daily experience…Know that these energies have already begun to move and their movement will be empowered every time you focus on the affirmations…You'll find yourself intuitively acting in alignment with the affirmations.

Now create one affirmation of your own choosing. Pick one particular area in your life you'd like to improve…imagine how you'd like it to be…feel it as a present reality…Create a statement…simple, positive, and present tense, of how you would like it to be. If you're more inclined, choose a picture or sensation instead; best of all, do both. Take time to do this now.

◆

Bring your awareness back to these words knowing that you'll remember this affirmation for future use, knowing that the energies have begun their movement. Knowing you'll find yourself intuitively acting in alignment with the affirmation the more you use it. Tell yourself this now.

Internalizing a Quality

Imagine soothing energy, whatever that means to you—it may be sounds, feelings, vibrations, a knowingness. Imagine soothing energy, whatever that means to you…calming energy…the softness of velvet, imagine yourself surrounded by this energy, soothing energy and letting it soak into your body, absorb its softness…feel it gently returning you to yourself, nurturing you…soothingness soaking deeper and deeper into you…comforting you, healing you…soothingness gently moving through you, through the whole of your being, deep into yourself. Enabling you simply to be receptive to yourself…receptive to this soothing energy. As though, if you listen, the soothing energy opens up within you very soft and soothing music…you can sense the tones of your being, you can almost hear the quiet hum of beingness itself—the music, the tones of life itself…Let the music soothe you, let the cells of your body sway with it…surrounded by soothing energy, gentle energy, almost as though you're floating in it, soft soothingness…

From this place give yourself permission to be fully receptive, take care of yourself however you need to, so that you can allow yourself to be fully soothed, all your edges smoothed, fully receptive, soft…quiet in yourself, receptive and soothed…

As you are receptive, quietly residing in yourself, bring to awareness a quality you would like to work with, a quality that you'd like to bring more of into your life. Choose a particular quality you would like to cultivate. Love or joy or grace or humor or another quality…whatever quality you like…Choose just one now, and know you can work on others another time.

Now simply meditate on this quality in this receptive state. Repeat the word to yourself several times…Witness its meaning…Repeat the word over and over and over again…Know the meaning of the word…Reach out to it intuitively…Feel the energy inherent in the quality…You can almost feel the quality, sense it…see it. What color is it?…Feel it…Listen to it, how does it sound?…Taste it…Let it touch you…How does it make your body feel?

◆

Let the quality share the space you occupy…call it by repeating its name—over and over and over again…Share your presence with one another, let it be present with you. Let its full power be next to you…Let yourself be fully present with it…Let it be all around you…Experience it surrounding you. However you imagine it.

◆

Create a vessel into which to put the meaning of the quality…Imagine putting the energy, the vibrations, the knowingness, the full meaning into this vessel. Fill up the vessel with the quality…Now imagine drinking out of the vessel, feel yourself absorbing the quality, let it move through you just as soothingness moved through you earlier…Imagine the quality circulating through the whole of your body, breathe it in. How would that feel?…Let your breath, let your blood carry it to all the nooks and crannies of your body…Let your breath, let your blood carry the contents of the vessel through the whole of your being, feel it flowing, sifting, settling throughout the whole of your being, feel it vibrating through you…sense it emanating from your center.

◆

Know that you are endowed with its power; you are empowered with this quality. Imagine for a moment that you have *become* the energy, *become* the quality— being the energy, the knowingness.

◆

Know that as you become more and more familiar with the energy it will sink deeper and deeper into yourself, into the core of your being. Now extend your awareness to include how it is you can act on this energy in your activities, notice how you can incorporate into your life what you sense and feel, what you know…Decide if you're willing to do that…If you are, feel yourself doing it…Become aware of how it is to have the energy present in your actions…to have your actions be receptive to the presence of the energy.

◆

Know that you are fully empowered with this quality, this knowingness and you will become even more so, the more you include it in your awareness. Know that this is so.

Symbol-Making

Now you are going to create a symbol for a quality or ability you would like to cultivate. You are going to use the vast receptive and creative powers available to you. I want you to know that from this place time is very fluid. You can remember and relive experiences vividly as though they were again occurring, bringing their powers to bear…using their powers and projecting them into the future; retaining their powers by containing their powers in a symbol, a symbol that you can use time and time again to call upon the power inherent in the quality…And, in fact, as you use the symbol you create, you'll discover yourself feeling and acting in ways that are fully in accord with the energy of the symbol. Know that this is so. For symbols are the language that speaks to your deepest knowingness—they are the language of your inner self and you can tap the power of knowingness itself and bring forth whatever power you would like, and empower yourself and empower the situation. Know that you can create a symbol to evoke whatever you choose, for symbols are the language of your inner self.

Now get in touch with the quality you would like to work on, the quality you would like to create a symbol for…What does it mean to you?…In a moment, you'll remember a time in your life when this quality was present, or you can create an imaginary time. Feel this time now…create this time now…feel the atmosphere of the scene, notice how your body feels, exaggerate the quality…If there seems to have been no time when this quality was present, pretend that there was. Imagine someone that does embody this quality, and imagine what it is like to be like this person. Pretend that you too embodied the quality.

◆

Now, either remember another scene where the quality was present or become even more deeply aware, even more in tune with the scene you've been experiencing…Sense the quality, sense its vibrations, its tone…Does it have color, or sound?…As you hear the sounds of these words you'll get further in touch with this quality. Discover the personality of the quality…Now, experience a time in the future when the quality is present…How does this time feel? What are you doing? Exaggerate the quality, feel the scene unfold and the quality getting even stronger…Feel the quality's energy in your body. Feel its power.

◆

Now create a symbol that represents this quality…If a couple come to mind, either choose one or let them coalesce into one; if nothing comes to mind, make one up; What you create is right for you.

This is your symbol, feel its power. I want you to know that whenever you bring this symbol to mind, you'll find yourself feeling and acting in total unity with this symbol…Tell yourself that this is so, that whenever you bring this symbol into your awareness, you'll find yourself acting in accordance with it, intuitively knowing whatever you need to, to act in this empowered way. Tell yourself you will remember to use your symbol whenever you need it…Know that every time you use it, it becomes increasingly powerful…Feel your power; you are fully able to act on this quality.

Enjoyment

Know that as you hear these words you will get in touch with times in your life where you have fully enjoyed yourself…The sounds of these words will evoke from the depths of your being the quality of enjoyment…deep enjoyment. Remember a time where you fully enjoyed yourself…Remember this time…the details…feel as though it were occurring all over again…feel the pleasure this time has for you, delight in the pleasure…breathe it in…Feel your body as though you were reliving this time again…Notice what's around you…Feel the expansiveness of the atmosphere you're in…Feel your connection to others, your connection to yourself…Just experience the light-hearted energy… Communion with spirit…Moving into deeper and deeper levels of enjoyment…Letting the energy of enjoyment move through every layer of yourself, feel pleasure...Breathe it...Feel the satisfaction of enjoyment...as though your whole self smiles inside...Remember other times or remember even more vividly this time you've been experiencing...Relive joyfulness, feel the rich satisfaction, having fun, playing...letting the spontaneity carry you, uplift you, trusting these good times of joyousness, times of enjoyment...Celebrate life.

◆

Now bring these feelings of enjoyment into the present, fully opening your life to the pleasure you can have now. Bringing enjoyment into your life now, in the present...Imagine as though when you exhale, the present begins to glitter with this energy...Notice the times, the places in your daily life that can burst with enjoyment, or that can softly fill you with deep, rich satisfaction...Notice the different situations in your life that you like, that are enjoyable, expand these times, exaggerate their goodness...Feel how others also appreciate these times, share your joy.

◆

Now, like shining a beacon of light, let the enjoyment light up the future infused with a celebration of life. Imagine it...Breathe life into this vision...A future teeming with joy...The future welcomes you; let yourself open to it...a future full of joy. Expect it...Joy carries healing, it is healing...Let it heal the whole of your being. As it heals the whole of yourself, the energy moves out and heals what's around you. All the faces of joyful energy...lighthearted...playfulness...laughter...sensuality...sexuality...sharing, sharing enjoyment...Rejoice in life...Letting this enjoyment permeate the whole of yourself and all those around you...Imagine it permeates the whole of life itself.

Now create a symbol that represents all that you've been experiencing, that represents all this enjoyment, this pleasure, this goodness...If a couple come to mind, either choose one or let them coalesce into one...If nothing comes to mind, make one up, and know that what you make up is right for you.

◆

This is your symbol of enjoyment...Know that it contains all the feelings, the energies that you've been experiencing. Imagine its power...And know that whenever you bring this symbol into your awareness, you'll unleash the enjoyment contained in whatever situation you're in...Tell yourself that this is so, that whenever you bring your enjoyment symbol to mind, you'll find yourself opening to joy...and you'll find yourself acting in accord with it, intuitively being receptive to whatever you need to know to enjoy yourself...Tell yourself this now...Tell yourself that you'll remember your symbol whenever you need it. Expect this to be the case...

Creativity

Now imagine yourself in a very comfortable, quiet, warm place in the countryside; there is a stream there. There is a refreshing feeling about the whole place...You can smell the subtle scent of flowers in the air; you can hear the sound of the water, notice the colors and textures of everything around you...Let yourself fully create this place, let yourself really appreciate this place.

◆

Now focus on the stream. I want you to know that this is a very special stream, this is a stream of your imagination...the stream of your consciousness, the source of this stream is nearby—a spring that continually feeds this stream, go to the source of the stream...Find this spring, this spring can be whatever you imagine it to be, a spring of creativity...water, color, sound, vibrations, energy, this is a spring of creativity. So pure you can't quite grasp it, but you can sense its power...Imagine experiencing the very source of creativity itself...beyond yourself, the source of creativity coming from a universal place, the source of this spring is the very depths of collective consciousness of all people, all living things...the source of collective knowledge, collective creativity, primordial, infinite energy, energy that extends vastly through the universe of the past, of the present, of the future...however you imagine it to be...Imagine going into the very source of creativity itself, however you imagine that, however you create that...Witness the vibrant source of creativity...sense it, imagine it, create it. Breathe it...Breath carries it.

◆

Let yourself emerge from this source of creativity and make yourself a comfortable way of floating on the stream of your imagination...As though this stream has an infinite primordial source, it can carry you to the vast reaches of experience, discovering the unknown, revealing new energies. You may want to float down it on an inner tube or by any method you choose...Imagine yourself floating down this stream, this stream of creativity carrying you, floating down...down...down...letting the water you're floating upon cleanse your entire being...Imagine it moves through you, connecting you to pure forms of creativity moving through your being...so pure you can't quite grasp what they are, just sense them...Feel them. Know that creativity moves through you...Breathe it. Experience this creative energy below you, around you, in you, surrounding your entire being...however you imagine it moving down, down, down the stream...a very magic, special stream coming from the depths of beingness itself, this stream constantly flowing, constantly changing, expression of life, the spontaneity of life itself...never twice the same...creativity...Life is creativity...

As you move further and further down this stream, you can begin to experience ways that this creativity can reveal itself in your life. You may see these ways played out as scenarios on the banks of the stream...You may see imagery in the water as you float over it. You may sense things in the air...New ways, richer ways for creativity to express itself in your life, for you to bring this energy that you're floating upon into the world. New ways to express it…richer ways to express it, expressing creativity on many dimensions, clearly asserting this energy…Manifesting this energy in all aspects of your life…Notice all the different areas of your life in the light of this creativity, let it enlighten your life…relationships with different people…responsibilities that you have…new things you may want to do, or old things you may want to do in a new way…Projects you're involved in. Simply bring different areas of your life to mind and in so doing you let this creativity shed light on them, giving rise to new experience.

◆

Notice if there are any activities you can do that will help the creativity flow out into your life…Is there anything you need to be disciplined about?…Your creativity is a gift to the world.

◆

As you float down the stream, and you experience your creativity evolving in new forms, in richer ways, you are now going to discover those ways which get in the way of this energy flowing. What blocks the energy from flowing, from moving, from expressing itself in your experience, from your acting on it, from your experiencing it?

◆

As you experience what blocks the flow of this creativity, you will also experience what you need to do to remove this block, to let the energy flow…You might want to talk to the obstructing energy; it has a gift for you…Ask what it is doing there. It may not answer you verbally, but you'll sense its experience…Experience what's true for it…Listen deeply…patiently…Trust what occurs. Ask what it is protecting you from…Ask it what it wants…Ask what is needed in order to release…to trust and let go…Sense what is so…

You'll discover exactly what needs to be done releasing creative energy in your life. Your creativity gifts the world.

◆

As you continue to move down the stream and the creativity is manifesting all around you, you'll begin to see the effects of this creativity. You can see how this creativity moves into the world, how people receive the energy and are also inspired to create. All making the stream grow and expand, and become richer and richer…Feel the gifts of creativity, of yours, of everyone's, everyone's creativity building on the creativity of others, creativity spreading everywhere…This stream moves through all consciousness, through all lives. Feel the excitement of expressing this energy. Awesome…

Now create a symbol that represents all that you're experiencing that represents creativity…If a couple come to mind, choose one, or let them coalesce into one. If nothing comes to mind, make one up. It can be a sound, a gesture, a picture…This is your symbol for creativity, your creativity. With this symbol you can tap primordial creativity. Feel the creative power in this symbol. As though it has an intelligence of its own, personify it…Take time to imagine talking to your symbol. As you do, you'll sense what's needed…There may be a concern you would like to ask it now; imagine doing so. Trust what occurs.

◆

Whenever you bring this symbol into your awareness, you'll discover creative energies beginning to flow, for you will have tapped universal energy and you'll find yourself able to act on these energies…expressing creativity. Tell yourself that this is so…Know that as the energy is present in you, others are inspired by these powers, too…It's magnetic…This symbol causes all that resonates with it to come forth. *Expect* this to be true…Tell yourself that whenever you need creativity you'll remember to bring your symbol to awareness. When you do, you'll find creativity flowing from the source of beingness itself.

Count Out

Now go over the details of your meditation experience…Acknowledge the healing and creative energy that revealed itself…Review any insights you have gained…any choices you may have made…Imagine further opening to and acting on this energy…Embody it…Breathe it…Project it into the future.

◆

Make yourself ready to come out to outer-conscious levels…Know that you can return to these dimensions of awareness whenever you choose…Know that whenever you enter these levels of consciousness, you receive beneficial effects and become a more centered being. Each time you meditate, you are increasingly able to maintain your focus of attention wherever you choose and remain at whatever level of awareness you choose, for as long as you choose. Every time you work in your creative self-restoring center, your abilities are enhanced…Know that every time you meditate, you tap the harmonizing energies of the universe; they heal you and offer healing to the world. Know that all of this is so.

In a moment I'm going to count from one to five…At the count of five, you'll open your eyes feeling refreshed, relaxed, and revitalized, remembering all that you've experienced…bringing with you the energies you've attuned yourself to…being fully ready and able to act on these energies in your life, and knowing you can return to these dimensions whenever you choose.

ONE—coming up slowly now…

TWO—becoming aware of the room around you…

THREE—at the count of five, you'll open your eyes feeling revitalized, refreshed, and relaxed…bringing with you all the energies you've connected with, having full memory of all that you've experienced…

FOUR—coming up now…

FIVE!—eyes open, feeling refreshed, relaxed, and revitalized, ready and able to act on the energies you've experienced, feeling a sense of wholeness with open heart and spirit...

It is a good idea to write down or draw any affirmation or symbol you created.

·4·

The Nature of the Inner Dimension

There is a paradox in working with your innerconsciousness that is best described by trying to drink water without a glass—it goes right through your fingers. Innerconsciousness is fluid and it feels extremely nebulous. Sensations are gone as fast as they come. However, you know that if you concentrate and focus your attention, you can get a drink of water without a glass. Because the nature of our inner dimension is qualitatively different from the material world around us, we have no framework for understanding what we experience when working with it.

There's a vulnerability—an insecurity—that you feel when working with the innerconsciousness, for there is no objective world to knock up against and get your bearings. Inside you find yourself in a shifting, amorphous reality that has no evident signposts. Trying to apply everyday definitions, you find yourself doubting your ability to navigate the inner realms, but this is not the case. When you understand the dynamics of innerconsciousness, you will find yourself more able to trust and work with inner dimensions.

Conflict Between Inner and Outer Consciousness

This work is about maintaining a state of relaxed attention, the stage between sleeping and waking awareness—the alpha level is equally active and receptive. However, your beta (rational) consciousness does not go away. Instead, as you've probably discovered by now, it continually judges everything you experience. In our society, beta consciousness is what we've been taught to use and value most—it's been given full control. Your beta consciousness is likely to feel threatened by your beginning to work with other parts of yourself. It doesn't like to lose power; so it reacts by injecting judgments: "I'm not relaxed," "I just made that up," "That's dumb," "I'm going to be late."

People usually mistakenly see this as a reflection of not meditating properly and attempt to silence these thoughts by arguing, "I am *too* relaxed." But argument isn't a very relaxing activity. It's a full-time job to try to shut up the beta mind because it has an infinite store of such distractions, and as long as you're trying to deal with them, you're not focusing your attention on your inner work. The beta mind succeeds in diverting you from your task, thus maintaining its power. You can choose not to respond to all that the beta mind says—just let it run on with its critique; let your beta-voice critics take a box seat in the theater of your mind as you go about your inner work. They can watch, and comment, but they are not on stage.

Understand that *awareness and attention are different*. When you find that you get tangled in an inner argument, simply bring your attention back to your breath. Doing so invites the spacious awareness of the Inner Witness, and you will find that there is ample room for your entire process. You can then choose what takes center stage.

However, while your mind attempts to divert you, your innerconsciousness is likely to be rebelling as well. Once your beta-voices take a box seat, you will find that you have to contend with the spotlight of your attention bouncing at random all over the theater (off-the-wall); your innerconsciousness doesn't want to focus. You've probably spent most of your life ignoring innerconsciousness, so be patient with it; it needs time to get used to the idea of working. It's not fair to expect it to shape up instantly. It is carefree and would rather play than be disciplined. Since it has been free to do what it pleases when you're not focusing your attention on it, it now tries to evade you. One of its diversionary tactics is to bring in off-the-wall images. Sometimes it gets even more rambunctious and tries to scare you with grotesque imagery. When you find any of this happening, don't worry about it. Just move your attention to your breath then go back to center stage.

Always use your breath as your anchor. Putting your attention on the sensations of breath develops mindfulness. You will be able to notice when your attention strays so you can bring it back. Strive to be mindful and notice what you're *choosing* to focus your attention on. You're at the controls behind the spotlight of awareness, and you can choose to focus wherever you wish.

Innerconsciousness is not linear. You may space out, or find your attention wandering. That doesn't mean you have to go back to the beginning of the scene; it just means you left center stage in darkness, but you can choose to re-illuminate it, going back to where you left off. Just breathe and refocus.

You can be aware of noises while at the same time attending to your inner work. Remember, just because you have noisy neighbors doesn't mean you have to listen to them. If you become too distracted by sounds or discomfort, turn them around and make them work for you. You are in a suggestible state, so just tell yourself, "All the sounds will cause me to be *even more* focused on my inner processes." Or be more creative. Recently, I was leading a meditation on the Fourth of July and soon after I began, firecrackers started going off in the street just outside. We were meditating on what our different ancestors were doing in 1776. I incorporated the noise by saying that each bang was taking us back another generation. As a result, the meditation was even more effective.

There are two other common ways innerconsciousness succeeds in avoiding disciplined work. It might make your body feel restless or itchy, or your throat congested—again distracting your attention. You can imagine drinking warm syrup and pretend that it is soothing your scratchy throat. To your amazement you will find your cough receding. The other way innerconsciousness evades you is that sometimes you'll find yourself feeling as if you had been asleep, and you'll come out of the meditation with large blank spots (the play goes on, but the stage is dark).

There are several things you can do to avoid this. You can give yourself an affirmation such as, "When meditating, I remain aware and alert to all that occurs." Sitting up while meditating may also be of help. However, if you continue to have blank spots, there are some procedures you can use to fill them in. Logic won't work because innerconsciousness doesn't have a story line with a beginning, middle, and end; it's more like a patchwork quilt. But musing over an image, word, or vibration that you know was a part of the meditation will often make the rest surface. Glancing over the meditation script will also prove helpful. Simply letting an image linger in your mind will sometimes draw up the rest of what occurred, since memory works associatively, not sequentially.

Conversely, when you're meditating and you're fully aware of your experience, feeling as if you'll easily remember it, all too often you return to waking awareness to find that it has slipped away. As a solution, pick one specific detail *while* you are meditating and tell yourself you'll remember it. This is a lot easier than trying to retain the whole scenario. When you come back to outer consciousness, you'll remember that detail by focusing on it, the rest of your inner experience will surface as well. It's similar to recalling a dream—when in a waking state, you encounter an object that was in the dream itself, the whole dream floods into your awareness. The remembered detail or the familiar object acts as bait on a fishing line, drawing up the rest of your deeper experience, for each detail is, in fact, part of a whole.

It is very important to understand there is conflict between your inner and outer consciousness, so you won't interpret it as a reflection of not being able to meditate. In fact, I've discovered that the more effective my work is, the stronger the conflict becomes. Innerconsciousness is frightened by responsibility and outer consciousness fears losing control.

There are two things related to this that are important to watch for. Sometimes a story that seems off-the-wall pops into your mind. Before bringing your attention back to center stage, you should look carefully for what is taking place. You'll often find metaphors offering insights about the very issue you are working on. Sometimes it happens that you have blank spots in your memory, yet the changes you wanted to work on manifest themselves in your life anyway. (The play does go on.) This happens when your innerconsciousness finds it easier to work below the surface because your conscious awareness encumbers it. In time, you will come to recognize when you're experiencing rebellion, or when it is constructive work—trust your intuition.

The Character of Innerconsciousness

In learning to do inner work, there is often much emphasis on visualization, not because picturing things is the only effective way to work with innerconsciousness, but because when one is leading a meditation or just talking about the experience, it's much easier to describe what something *looks* like than what it *feels* like. But consciousness works in different modes—some of us predominantly feel things in our bodies, some hear things, some simply know things, and for others, seeing is predominant. I happen to be a visualizer, so the meditations I write are likely to be slanted toward the visual. Everyone is endowed with an imagination; how the imagination works, however, differs from person to person. Whatever mode is most natural for you is what you need to pay attention to. This is not to say you can't develop the ability to work in other modalities. The point is not to discount the ways that your imagination experiences reality.

Innerconsciousness is holistic; its language is symbolic and metaphoric. It often expresses itself in rhyme, puns, and sensations in the body. One person's symbol for mental relaxation was a train entering a very peaceful countryside (train of thought). In fact, one of the more pleasurable characteristics of striking up a relationship with your inner self is that it has a good sense of humor.

When some people meditate, they experience various physical sensations and responses. For instance, their body may feel as if it has grown bigger or heavier, or maybe they get tingling or heat sensations, while others find that they start to nod, or feel as if they are whirling, or their eyelids flutter, or their bodies twitch. Whatever the sensations, they are no cause for worry. They are simply natural responses to energies being released and moving in unfamiliar ways. If you find yourself uncomfortable, imagine the antidote (e.g., if you have a whirling sensation, stabilize yourself by growing roots through the floor and into the ground).

In the material world things take time to happen. Time and space create limits and maintain linear and logical progressions. The inner world is altogether different; as it's holistic, and sequence is not something within its experience—it operates in simultaneous patterns—time is meaningless. If I say, "yellow balloon" you don't have to go looking for it to imagine it; it's there the instant you hear the words.

We are accustomed to everything taking time, when you do work in a meditation, the chances are you'll feel as if you didn't do it very well because it didn't seem to take any time or follow any logical progression. All too frequently, when you focus on a healing image, for example, the image is very fleeting. It has no duration, so you feel you must recapture it to ensure its effectiveness—but then it seems redundant. Don't worry; that's just part of the process.

Always pay careful attention to *how* your imagination depicts what you are focusing on. This provides insight into the current conditions. The representation itself metaphorically reflects what is true at the moment. In these dimensions, there is nothing the imagination brings that is irrelevant. You can always gain insight by employing your Receptive Imagination. To work with it, the meditations often direct you to imagine talking to and asking questions of your inner experience; be that your imagery or your sensations. You personify what is taking place, as though whatever you are focusing your attention on has intelligence, and you can converse with it. You use the story-making capacities of your imagination. Just make it up as I did when I did the case reading. Give yourself full permission to activate the childlike world of "make believe." *Making up a story provides a context through which the operative energies reveal themselves.* Remember that the imagination is the medium of psychic information. Like improvisation, this creates the context that evokes intuitive and creative insights.

Since processes occur simultaneously on the inner levels you will find that *as you're formulating the question you already know the answer.* This makes you feel as if you made it up or knew the answer all along; since it's the symbol you're asking, you expect the symbol to answer *after* you have asked and therefore discount what is instantaneously apparent. Alas, inner conversations are non-linear. The point is that you find yourself knowing the answer, not how you got it. If you discount it, you are not allowing yourself the use of your inherent personal power. When you feel as if you knew it all along, the chances are you were ignoring your own knowledge.

Your having known it all along doesn't make it trivial or incorrect. The issue is whether you heed it; the point is that you *know* the answer is right. Remember the process is nonlinear and simultaneous. It's not as if you ask the question and then get the answer; both usually occur at the same time. It is like when you move the spotlight (attention), it doesn't take time to illuminate the new area. So when asking a question within, simply be receptive and sensitive to what you're experiencing *while* you are formulating the question. That experience will contain the answer. As you cultivate mindfulness, you will find yourself able to catch your instantaneous insights.

If you don't seem to be experiencing anything, *make something* up. Don't wait for it to come to you, for if it were going to come to you it would *be there already.* I've done psychic case work for many years, and I've guided hundreds of people through the same exercise. Some people feel as if the information just comes—seemingly out of the blue. Other people feel as if they had made up the whole thing. It doesn't matter how it feels, the *content is always the same.* In both situations, the psychic reading is just as accurate—it just takes longer and feels more laborious to make it up. So when you don't sense the answer to your inner question, give yourself full permission to *invent* it. Listen to your fantasies, for they have the answers. It is impossible to exaggerate the importance of this. Dismissing ourselves when we are bringing in intuitive information is the height of giving up our power, and it perpetuates our alienation. When we open to our connectedness, we come to know what is true directly.

Often the answers you come to seem simplistic. They may be obvious or they may be cliché, corny, or trite. We've all been systematically conditioned to discount these qualities (only complicated solutions can be worthwhile). What we need to remember is that ideas are seen as trite or corny *because* they have been universally experienced and expressed. Innerconsciousness gives us cliché answers because it resides in the realm of universality and, when questioned, dips into collective knowledge. When we say something corny, it is somehow suspect—not to be taken seriously—or downright wrong. This is one way we keep ourselves isolated from one another. When we discount an answer only because it is cliché, we divorce ourselves from the lessons others have learned. The answers we come to may not be original, but they are wise; wisdom is never complicated.

When meditating about the difficulty with my friend the affirmation that came to me certainly was corny: "I reside in the care we have for one another." Had I not taken it seriously, it's likely I'd no longer have the friendship. The assumption that answers to problems must be unique or complicated and that simple answers won't do, keeps us powerless. If we listen to our corny, simplistic answers and take action, we'll pull ourselves out of our isolation and be able to resolve our difficulties. If we'd allow ourselves to act on the obvious, we wouldn't have so many problems. Just as power unused may as well not exist, answers and insights not acted upon will be of no value. The purpose of Applied Meditation is to bring the knowing from the universal realm into the particular issues of daily life; this requires acting on our own insights.

Intuitions, Thoughts, and Feelings

One of the most important aspects of this work is developing a sense for your intuitions and learning to keep beta consciousness or your emotions from suffocating them before you're even aware of their existence. Otherwise you won't realize you had an intuition until it's too late. How many times have you come home from a social occasion saying to yourself, "Why did I go? I knew it would be awful." When you've learned to recognize your intuitions, you'll be able to avoid many undesirable situations, but you need to sense them fully before you can respond to them in time. For me it feels like keeping an eye focused toward the back of my mind.

Part of the process of recognizing intuitions is being able to distinguish them from your beta thoughts and your emotions. Intuitions, thoughts, and feelings are all different aspects of ourselves. Beta is intellectual, categorical, complicated, either/or, sequential, and logical. Its messages are easy to recognize for they are never subtle, but always straightforward. Emotions are pushy; they always have a charge to them—attachments, desires, "shoulds." When you find yourself with a message and you want to be clear where it is coming from—whether intellectual, emotional, or intuitive, ask yourself questions like these: Is it critical? Does it set up an either/or category? Is it complicating? Does the voice seem to be coming from my head (intellectual)? Does the answer have a lot of force behind it? Is it pushy? Is it difficult to ignore (emotional)?

Inner messages are never pushy. They're always holistic—not logical or sequential. They are without conflict, subtle but clear, with no "shoulds"—they simply *are*. You can ignore them, but you *can't* argue with them. You can easily take them or as easily leave them. They are background awarenesses that create a sense of the whole. They are often the first impressions that come into our minds, but in this society the first to be discounted, for their knowing does not have reason attached to it. When you don't know why you know something, you assume you don't really know it. With intuitions, you will have an unquestionable sense of knowing that it is so. Ask yourself how or why you know what you know; if you *can't* answer, then it's an intuition.

With time, you'll learn to distinguish between your intuitions and other aspects of yourself, for each one is different. You'll discover the particular individual quality of your intuitions. It is as though they whisper, in the spacious awareness of the Inner Witness you can hear them. Unlike your intellect or your feelings, your intuition will rarely get you into trouble; instead it will almost always keep you out of it. This is not to say your intellect and feelings are unimportant and better ignored, but that when you recognize which you're dealing with, you will learn to respond appropriately.

Meditation develops mindfulness through focusing on breath, which in turn brings one into spacious awareness. As you become more mindful, you'll find yourself easily seeing the origins of different inner messages as well as catching intuitive and creative insight—in spacious awareness, shooting stars are visible. You will find that the Inner Witness becomes more and more present the more you meditate—not only accompanying you on your inner journeys, but in your life.

We have been conditioned to look for drama in our lives, so we expect it in our meditations. But innerconsciousness is subtle, never forceful, and rarely dramatic, so people often conclude that they must not be meditating properly. You usually will not discover the effectiveness of meditation while meditating. Look for its power not in how it feels when you're doing it, but instead, in the changes that begin to occur in your life. If you don't think you're meditating correctly, *pretend* you are, go through the motions anyway. If you do, you'll find the changes begin to manifest themselves.

Unlike other activities (the more you do them, the clearer they get) it seems that the more you meditate, the less distinct the different levels of awareness become. Going deep doesn't feel so deep any longer, and you also find yourself with more profound insights in regular waking awareness. This is because the passages are clear and the movement of awareness from one level to another has become so smooth it all feels like the same level. Another contradiction to working with your innerconsciousness is that the more you meditate, the less you need to.

Induction

Focus on your breathing, breathing with your belly…bring into your awareness your symbol for physical relaxation and allow the whole of your body to relax…Let your body relax…Relaxing more and more with each exhalation of breath…To enhance your relaxation, you might want to relax your eyelids and allow this feeling of relaxation to flow slowly downward throughout the whole of your body, clear down to your toes…

And when you're ready, bring into your awareness your symbol for mental relaxation…feel your mind begin to relax…Feel the chatter of your mind become calm and quiet…Feel your mind become clear and spacious, as spacious as the sky and your thoughts are like puffy clouds, drifting in and out, in and out the sky of your mind…

And then when you're ready, bring in your symbol for emotional relaxation. Go over the full range of your emotions…Pay attention to your feelings, and if there are any feelings that are calling for your attention, take care of those feelings in whatever way occurs to you. Give yourself permission to relax emotionally. Let go of any "shoulds," any feelings pushing or pulling at you. Breathe them out…Take a moment to offer yourself some loving kindness…Feel your heart relax into its natural state of generosity…Feel your heart open…

Bring to awareness your symbol for your creative, self-restoring center…Feel your gratitude to be alive…Sense your whole being open…You are in healing space, sacred space…receptive…creative…mindful…alert…relaxed…You are now centered at a stable level of innerconsciousness where you find faculties and senses opening out far beyond those that you usually use in your waking awareness.

You are now consciously developing intuitive skills you have always had...You are at your creative self-restoring center—the threshold between your inner and outer realities...Here, you discover a rich, beautiful landscape of your receptivity and creativity...Here, you experience very vivid, very meaningful sensations and imagery, new realities...As these realities unfold, they guide you to new dimensions of being, as your being opens, more and more of these energies shall flow through you...Just as using your muscles keeps your body strong and resilient, so too, working in your creative self-restoring center keeps your intuitive and intuitive powers fully accessible and fluid...From here, you can access the pure awareness of the Inner Witness...From here, you realize the calm expansive power of the spacious awareness brought with Inner Witness. Breathe, and rest in the quiet...the Inner Witness emerges out of universal beingness...From here, you can experience yourself as part of the pure universal energy which permeates all life...From here, you gain the wisdom to make this world a more harmonious place to live.

The Inner Witness illuminates the rich, beautiful landscape of your receptivity and creativity...Here you experience very vivid, very meaningful sensations and imagery, new realities...As these realities unfold, they guide you to new dimensions of being, as your being opens, more and more of these energies shall flow through you...Just as using your muscles keeps your body strong and resilient, so too, using your innerconsciousness keeps your intuitive powers fully accessible and fluid...As you work with the Inner Witness you will find yourself with deep understanding of whatever it is you are focusing on...Now listen very carefully, paying attention only to these words and your responses to these words...If other thoughts drift through your mind, just let them drift and gently, easily bring your attention back to these words...Even when you're not paying attention to these words, your innerconscious mind awareness is taking in this information and these instructions, and you'll be able to use these techniques in the future. You are going to fully remember all that you are about to experience. You will absorb new energies, assimilate and understand these energies...You are going to do all of these things with the whole of your being as you explore these new dimensions...

In a moment, I am going to count on a descending scale from ten to one; at each descending count, you'll feel your awareness move deeper and deeper into your inner dimensions...Ten, moving down now...Nine, deeper and deeper...Eight, relaxing into yourself...Seven, returning to yourself...Six, deeper and deeper...Five, moving deeper...Four, very aware and very alert...Three, moving down...Two, into your deeper dimensions...One, deep in yourself...Here your imagination is extremely fluid and you can direct it where you choose...

I'm going to suggest several affirmations...If you wish to affirm them to yourself, repeat them to yourself after me, and at the same time, feel as though each affirmation is fully true. Bring into your awareness pictures and sensations that represent each affirmation, and as you speak the words to yourself, feel the power of the words...In doing so you'll discover that as time goes by you'll find yourself living in ways that conform to the affirmations, and the affirmations materialize in your daily reality. You'll intuitively be acting out of the power of each of the affirmations.

I believe in myself...I believe in my family and friends...We believe in our community; there is a free flow of love and support between us all...I trust myself, I am enriched by my deepest dimensions...

I am aware and alert when I meditate...

I can focus my consciousness wherever I choose, for as long as I choose...

My imagination is fluid and free…

I am in tune and responsive to my intuition…

Every day the powers of the depths of consciousness become more and more
   available to me…

I remember my symbols when I need them and call them to awareness…

A spring of creativity continually flows through me and out into the world…

My increasing personal power is for making this world a more harmonious
   place to live for everyone…

I maintain balance amid change…

I trust the future…

Now take time to focus on any of your own affirmations…Know that in focusing on affirmations, you align yourself with the affirmations on all levels and you'll discover yourself acting in accord with them. You may also want to spend time reviewing and working with your symbols.

Stretching the Imagination

Imagine a piece of fruit. What kind is it? How ripe is it? What color is it?…Imagine holding this piece of fruit in your hand…Sense the texture of the skin, imagine the feel of it in your hand…the size, the weight of it…You may literally want to move your hand around as you imagine these things. It is as though you were literally holding that piece of fruit…Feel its size…its texture…its temperature…Imagine its weight, its consistency…Imagine taking your fingernail and breaking the peel…bring it up to your nose and imagine what it would smell like. Imagine the juice, the temperature, the feel of it…Notice the quality of this fruit, almost as though it had a tone to it, a vibration to it…Compare it to the quality of other fruits, the vibrations that they have, the tone…If each kind of fruit were to have a sound to it, a note to it, a tone to it, what would you hear?…Imagine the sound if you were to squeeze the juice out of the fruit…How would it sound when the juice dripped?…What kind of sound would the fruit make as you crushed it?…Imagine drinking the juice, what would it taste like?…How would it make your mouth feel?…How does it compare to imagining the taste of other juices?

Now imagine creating a mental shelf…You can place anything on this shelf that you would like to refer to at a later time…Now, put the fruit up on the shelf…if you wish to, you can come back to your exploration of it later…Anything you put on this mental shelf at any time you'll be able to remember. You can then come back to it and it will still be there, ready for you to continue your exploration. Tell yourself this now, that whatever you place on your mental shelf will remain there—retained, ready for you when you return to attend to it.

Know that your imagination is facile; you can choose whatever direction you want it to go. To further explore the fluidity of innerconsciousness we're going to experiment with body sensations…Feel your body…aware of the position your body is in…aware of the space you occupy…Now imagine your body to be the consistency of a stone…a smooth stone that's at the bottom of a stream bed…Imagine water rushing over it…rushing over it, making it smoother…Feel your body as though it were a stone on the bottom of a stream bed…How does it feel?…Listen carefully, detect the sound of the stream flowing…Make it up…imagine the sensations, the sounds.

◆

Now let your body become the water that rushes over the stone…fluid, moving, clear, clear running water, taking the shape of whatever is around it…water, crystal clear water that washes all that it passes by…bringing out all the subtle colors of the stones below you…Let your body *be* the water of the stream…feel it, sense it.

◆

Above the stream imagine a breeze…Imagine becoming the breeze…let yourself be the breeze, dancing over the stream, over the land…The breeze, it goes everywhere…Be the breeze, feel yourself get bigger…be the wind, you are the wind. It goes everywhere, blows everywhere. Feel the shape of the landscape, it feels different to the wind than to the stream. Caress the landscape…Listen to the sounds as you pass by…You might even find that you catch scents and carry them in your travels.

◆

Now notice the rays of the sun…penetrating through with the vitality of fire, the penetrating warmth of the sun…Let your body become the rays of the sun. Feel it in your body, be it in your body…fire, warmth, radiant light, brilliant fire, warmth…Let your body *be* it.

◆

Now bring your usual body sensations back into your body…feeling your usual physical self…Now, listen, listen to the crackling of the fire…listen to the blowing of the wind…listen to the gurgling of the stream…listen to the crackling rocks as they roll over one another where the stream moves very rapidly.

◆

Know that your imagination is extremely fluid, that your psychic senses are very keen—the more you work with them, the sharper they become…Your inner awareness perceives the deepest subtleties of reality…Know that all of this is so, and that as you work with your inner senses they become more and more agile…As you work in directing your imagination, you can change the imagery, feelings, sensations, and sounds. In this magical world, all that is conforms to your intention. You are increasingly able to direct your inner awareness as you choose each time you meditate…Know that all of this is so…Now, with your deep awareness you can witness the different aspects of consciousness and discover their character. Your intellect…notice its ability to figure things out, notice its ability to make distinctions…Your emotions…they are always moving, full of color, full of desire…Your intuition…it simply knows, it experiences wholeness, the whole of what is so…Your Inner Witness is the awareness being aware of itself—it *is* the light of awareness…Spacious, present whenever you bring your attention to your breath, your witness arises. Trust that in the quiet of awareness, clarity is always evident.

Bring different issues in your life to awareness and witness what *you know* about these issues…Notice what you think and what you feel with each issue as you bring it to awareness…Witness when different aspects of yourself are active, when you respond to which.

◆

Engage your Active Imagination by envisioning positive outcomes; engage your Receptive Imagination by conversing with any concern—personify it and talk to it.

◆

Now go back to your mental shelf and if there is anything there, you can attend to it or do any other inner work of your choosing.

◆

Know that every time you meditate, you receive beneficial effects on all levels of your being…That every time you meditate, your imagination becomes increasingly agile and your intuitive powers become more and more finely tuned. Know that each time you meditate, you increase your ability to navigate through the inner dimensions; you become increasingly able to maintain whatever level of awareness you choose, for as long as you choose. Your imagination becomes increasingly fluid. You are increasingly able to keep the Inner Witness present in all your meditation work…Know that this is so. Tell yourself that this is so. Expect that every time you meditate, your imagination becomes increasingly fluid, your intuition gets increasingly honed, and the Inner Witness emerges with greater ease each time you practice...

Count Out

Finish what you're doing and make yourself ready to come out to outer-conscious levels.

◆

Know you can return to these dimensions whenever you wish. You may want to project when you will again meditate...In a moment, I'm going to count from one to five; at the count of five, you'll open your eyes remembering all that you've experienced...feeling refreshed, revitalized and relaxed...

ONE—becoming more aware of the room around you...

TWO—coming up slowly now...

THREE—at the count of five, you'll open your eyes feeling relaxed, revitalized, and refreshed, remembering all that you've experienced...

FOUR—coming up now, bringing with you your sense of well-being...

FIVE!—eyes open, feeling refreshed, revitalized, and relaxed, remembering all you have experienced...having brought with you your sense of wholeness—open heart and spirit...

·5·

It's All Energy

When I first successfully read a case of someone of whom I had had no previous knowledge, it was an awe-inspiring experience. I was no longer a separate entity moving through the world. I was somehow intimately connected to everything. I have never been a religious person, I was raised in an academic home, but for me this was a religious experience. It revealed that we are all a part of a cosmic whole. Consciousness all of a sudden lit up with magic! My consciousness was infinitely more than I had ever imagined.

Until then, I'd always taken my own awareness for granted and paid attention only to the external world. It all turned around. All of a sudden, my imagination was as real as the ground I stood on. If I could get to know someone by simply directing my imagination, there was much more to the intricacies of the universe than I'd ever been taught by rational explanations. Though impossible to adequately put into words, the experience taught me that somehow each of us is held by the web of life—as though there is an invisible energy that connects *all that is*. And consciousness itself is mysteriously entwined with this energy.

The scientific era has taught us to make clear separations between the subjective and objective, the body and mind, the personal and political, spirit and matter, heaven and earth, God and everything else. Western rationalism has taken the life, the soul, out of everything. Before the onslaught of dualism, most inhabitants of the world experienced it as charged with spirit—everything possessed consciousness and was part of a living whole. The scientific revolution ushered in a new viewpoint: the world is made up of separate inanimate parts that together make a vast machine of matter and motion obeying mathematical laws. Science has succeeded in separating us from the whole, and getting us to view the objective as inert—in other words dead. Not only have we lost our place *in* the world, the world itself has died and has therefore become exploitable—this is the beginning of alienation. As Fritjof Capra describes:

> To Descartes the material universe was a machine and nothing but a machine. There was no purpose, life, or spirituality in matter. Nature worked according to mechanical laws, and everything in the material world could be explained in terms of the arrangement and movement of its parts. This mechanical picture of nature became the dominant paradigm of science in the period following Descartes. It guided all scientific observation and the formulation of all theories of natural phenomena.
>
> The drastic change in the image of nature from organism to machine had a strong effect on people's attitudes toward the natural environment. The organic world view of the Middle Ages had implied a value system conducive to ecological behavior. In the words of Carolyn Merchant: "The image of the earth as a living organism and nurturing mother served as a cultural constraint restricting the actions of human beings. One does not readily slay a mother, dig into her entrails for gold, or mutilate her body...As long as the earth was considered to be alive and sensitive; it could be considered a breach of human ethical behavior to carry out destructive acts against it."[1]

All That Exists Is Alive

Western culture views women as closer to nature, and both are suspect. Women are "naturally" emotional and intuitive; men are more rational. (Read "white" men for in racist consciousness, the darker one's skin color, the closer to nature one is assumed to be.) The primacy of human over nature, male over female, white over color have been images that have allowed the exploitation of nature (and of women and people of color). The scientific method studies nature and teaches us not to trust our own natures. To know is, by definition, not to feel—not to be involved—for feelings cloud the issue and make it immeasurable. Scientific methodology has primarily dealt with that which is quantifiable or measurable. The degree to which the human element enters into the experiment is the same degree to which it is invalidated. Science holds a monopoly on knowledge. Therefore, by definition, *knowledge resides outside of us.* If knowledge is exclusively attained externally, that effectively cuts us off from the vast knowing to which consciousness has *direct access.* Not trusting our own nature we find ourselves dependent on the authorities, who are again usually white men[2]. Only experiments reveal the "facts," not direct experience. How often do we discount ourselves for not being "objective?" Our experience is suspect until it is scientifically substantiated.

Western rationalism teaches us to believe only that which has been proven—never trust the obvious. In consequence we are taught to be suspicious of our own experience. After five hundred years of Western Rationalism, most of us in the modern world have fully internalized this. When people do psychic readings in my Applied Meditation training it is the most accurate pieces of information that they discount. Remember, they are given only the name, age, and location of the person they are to read. They have no basis upon which to judge what is accurate and what isn't. For instance, on one occasion, I was giving to one of the participants in my training a case of a man who was paraplegic. The reader kept saying he wasn't getting anything. I told him to make it up. Eventually he said that he saw a man sitting in a wheelchair, whom he didn't think could walk. When he was done, he opened his eyes, and I informed him the individual he had read was paralyzed from the waist down as a result of a fall from a roof. His jaw dropped. He said that immediately upon hearing the name of the person he was to tune in on, a fleeting image of a person falling in midair had popped into mind. He had dismissed it out of hand and told me he wasn't getting anything. The first impressions are always the clearest and the most frequently dismissed.

There are profound implications if the moments when we are most tuned to the truth of the matter are the same ones when we discount what we are aware of. *There is nothing more fundamental to giving up one's personal power than not to trust one's own awareness.*

I don't mean to imply that we dismiss what science has discovered over the centuries, but that we should be very clear that it is not the sole purveyor of truth. Nothing is static, over the last couple of decades there have been holistic trends that are bringing science back into the cosmic whole. As Fritjof Capra relays:

Physics has gone through several conceptual revolutions that clearly reveal the limitations of the mechanistic world view and lead to an organic, ecological view of the world which shows great similarities to the views of mystics of all ages and traditions. The universe is no longer seen as a machine…but appears as a harmonious indivisible whole; a network of dynamic relationships that include the human observer and his or her consciousness in an essential way.[3]

It is not only innerconsciousness that functions in simultaneous patterns, but the very building blocks of the material world also seem to do so. Gary Zukav in his book *The Dancing Wu Li Masters*, describes:

The distinction between organic and inorganic is a conceptual prejudice. It becomes even harder to maintain as we advance into quantum mechanics. Something is organic, according to our definition, if it can respond to processed information. The astounding discovery awaiting newcomers to physics is that the evidence gathered in the development of quantum mechanics indicates that subatomic "particles" constantly appear to be making decisions! More than that, the decisions they seem to make are based on decisions made elsewhere. Subatomic particles seem to know instantaneously what decisions are made elsewhere, and elsewhere can be as far away as another galaxy![4]

Not only does material (i.e. atomic particles) appear to be conscious, but in addition, our consciousness seems to be connected to theirs—*objectivity itself is discovered to be impossible*. Capra explains:

The crucial feature of quantum theory is that the observer is not only necessary to observe the properties of an atomic phenomenon, but is necessary even to bring about these properties. My conscious decision about how to observe, say, an electron will determine the electron's properties to some extent. If I ask it a particle question, it will give me a particle answer; if I ask it a wave question, it will give me a wave answer. The electron does not have objective properties independent of my mind. In atomic physics the sharp Cartesian division between mind and matter, between the observer and the observed, can no longer be maintained. We can never speak about nature without, at the same time, speaking about ourselves.[5]

Our dualistic objective worldview has trained us to ignore aspects of reality that have seeped into the scientific laboratory where there are experiments with results that fully defy the classic materialist explanation. We are now told that the very building blocks of matter—the atoms—have no separate objective reality. It can no longer be an issue of cause and effect when separate subatomic particles respond to one another instantaneously.[6] Quantum physicists refer to these connections as "Nonlocal." They are are unmediated, unmitigated, and immediate. This means that there is no medium carrying a message; that distance does not diminish the effect and effects are simultaneous.

Larry Dossey, a medical doctor who has investigated the power of consciousness and prayer for many years, has coined the term "nonlocal mind." He describes many double-blind studies that have been conducted to assess if prayer or mental intentionality from a distance makes a difference in healing. In a wide variety of investigations, ranging from healing wounds, to impacts on plant growth; from improving heart conditions to AIDS, numerous studies have now shown beyond a doubt that prayer and intention can have a positive impact on health.

He further reports that even *non*-human consciousness affects the material world; as experiments conducted in France with baby chicks demonstrate. As you may know, baby chicks imprint on their mother and follow her around wherever she goes. They can also imprint on anything that moves near them soon after they hatch. Baby chicks were imprinted on a robot that was programmed to move randomly in an enclosed space. They were then separated from the robot by a glass wall and observed to see how the robot and the chicks responded to that circumstance. When the chicks were present and able to see it through the glass, the robot spent two and a half times longer in the area closer to the chicks than when the chicks were not there. When chicks that had not been imprinted were placed behind the glass instead, both they and the robot exhibited random behavior. Eighty groups of fifteen chicks each were tested; in each case, these results were duplicated.[7]

Psychokinesis is the term used for the direct influence of mind on matter. Research with Gellor, Mikhailova, and Kulagina,[8] has proven that objects can be moved simply with the power of mental concentration. Princeton Engineering Anomalies Research (PEAR) studied psychokinesis for over twenty years using random events generators (REG's). PEAR has established through literally millions of tests that the REG responds to mental intentions of operators and it does not matter how close the person applying intent is to the generator.[9] What is fascinating is that people who have a close bond like spouses or whole groups have even more of an effect than an individual does. Is it any surprise that the winning lottery number in New York State on September 11, 2002 was 9-1-1? (Over five thousand New Yorkers won.) [10]

There have been numerous experiments investigating Extra Sensory Perception in which the subjects were asked in advance whether it existed. Those who said they believed in ESP, scored better than chance, those who were not sure scored at chance. Most interesting of all, is that those who said there was no such thing as ESP scored *below* chance! [11]

One of the most active areas of research in the past twenty-five years has been what has come to be called "remote viewing," acquiring information about a person, place, or event which is distant in time or space; when the viewer has no prior knowledge of the subject under investigation. There is extensive documentation of individual remote viewers finding lost people or things and also of their making accurate maps of locations they had never seen.[12] The CIA pursued both research and intelligence activities using remote viewing for over two decades. The most famous program, Stargate, yielded spectacular results ranging from locating aircraft that had crashed to finding kidnapped hostages.[13]

All of these occurrences necessitate rearranging the classic secular view of the nature of the universe.[14] It is only because of our narrow frame of reference that we define such occurrences as paranormal. The impacts are both on what one perceives and what happens in the external world. We are all part of a whole and consciousness itself is a participant in what occurs—not simply reflective and responsive—a participant in the creation of the phenomenon.

Inner and Outer Realms Dance Together

The Silva Method teaches the power of positive thinking—if you want something all you need to do is imagine it, and it will manifest, be it a parking place, an apartment, a partner, or a job. After I discovered the powers of my imagination—its ability to receive information—I was inspired to experiment and see what other powers it might have. All of a sudden "coincidences" became commonplace. All kinds of things started manifesting themselves in my life after I had projected them with my imagination. I didn't understand how or why it was working, but my experience showed me that it did, indeed, work. It was as if the world, up until that point, was out of sync—everything was random—and when I began taking responsibility for what my imagination was projecting, everything moved into synchrony. Random events ceased to occur and coincidence was suddenly pregnant with significance. I like Carl Jung's term "synchronicity," a causal, meaningful coincidence. His illustration:

> A young woman I was treating had, at a critical moment, a dream in which she was given a golden scarab. While she was telling me this dream, I sat with my back to the closed window. Suddenly, I heard a noise behind me, like a gentle tapping. I turned round and saw a flying insect knocking against the windowpane from outside. I opened the window and caught the creature in the air as it flew in. It was the nearest analogy to a golden scarab that one finds in our latitudes, which, contrary to its usual habits, had evidently felt an urge to get into a dark room at this particular moment.[15]

Objectively, consciousness permeates the material world, affecting which of the myriad possibilities transpire. Subjectively, the material world permeates our consciousness in two ways. *The vocabulary of the imagination is composed of past memories.* This limits the possibilities one can imagine—what's *conceivable*. Anticipation prefigures the future; that is, what you anticipate paves the path for your actions, and what you meet on the path. Secondly, intuition is perpetually present. It shapes *how* we imagine what we imagine. Matter affects mind; mind affects matter. The whole lives both subjectively and objectively. We are all part of a great and mysterious co-arising. Author Joanna Macy explains this Buddhist concept, "Things do not produce each other or make each other happen, as in linear causality; they help each other happen by providing occasion or locus or context, and in so doing, they in turn are affected. There is mutuality here, a reciprocal dynamic."[16] We can consciously participate in this process.

Most indigenous cultures view people inside the whole—working with the connections. Rationalism patronizingly views their rituals as "primitive." As a child, I went to many Pueblo rain dances in New Mexico where, by the end of the day, rain usually came down upon us all—often the first rain for many weeks.

Our imagination affects what happens to us, whether we choose to participate in the process or not. Consciousness is always interacting with the environment. I think of it as magnetic energy drawing in particular probabilities while repelling others. The law of this phenomenon is the attraction of opposites within the unity of opposites—energies that resonate with each other attract one another. Kammerer tells us, "We thus arrive at the image of a world mosaic or cosmic kaleidoscope, which, in spite of constant shufflings and rearrangements also takes care of bringing like and like together."[17] When I refer to thoughts and attitudes, I mean a *material* force affecting the environment.

This can easily be seen if you look into your past; you'll notice how events happen in clustered sequences. Seemingly unrelated positive events congregate together, and so too the opposite, difficult incidents happening together. You could call them streaks of good or bad luck. Well, it's true except that luck is by definition something operating by chance—randomly, disconnected from ourselves. The energy you're putting out is an ingredient in causing these "random" circumstances to occur. Notice that some people you know are optimists and have lives full of good fortune, while others are melancholic and their lives are full of misfortune.

I no longer believe that there is such a thing as "chance." Instead there is an elegant coherence in *all that is*. Things occur out of the coalescence of energies. We always hear, "What goes around, comes around," "As within, so without," "As you sow, so shall you reap." The day you're in a bad mood is the day your car gets sideswiped while parked, and the plumbing gets clogged, and likewise, the day you're feeling good you get offered a promotion and a dear friend whom you haven't seen in years unexpectedly arrives in town. I'm not saying your moods created these events, but that it is part of the whole—it is likely that part of you was aware of these probabilities, and therefore you were in a good mood. What you expect is not only determined by your past experience, but is also shaped by the fact that consciousness is perpetually attuned to—and entwined with—what is taking place objectively. In an elegant dance, the subjective and objective continually mirror one another.

Synchronous events frequently occur as puns. A friend of mine recently expressed how tired he felt using the term "deflated"; he got two flat tires that week. Any residual skepticism I had evaporated when I was reading a book called *The Seth Material*, which was the first of a series of books to come out by Jane Roberts. This book was the first material I had come across that enabled me to understand rationally why I could imagine something, and then it would occur. While reading it, I said to several friends, "This book has been turning my idea of reality upside down!" After reading the first book I was anxious to get the second, *Seth Speaks*. Many people apparently were going through the same process as I was, for I went to numerous bookstores only to discover they'd all just sold out. Returning home, I called a number of others, and finally found a store that had one copy left. I asked that they hold it for me. When I picked it up, I discovered that this copy's binding had been put on upside down!

A woman in one of my classes said that when she was younger her life was full of what she'd always thought were coincidences, but they all stopped when she took the advice, "Don't expect anything, you won't be disappointed." For the first time, she understood why they had disappeared. Now she was delighted to cultivate positive expectations again. Yet we let ourselves worry, having no idea that our fretting is adding to the likelihood that the very things we fear most will occur. It's time we turn it around.

Religious traditions hold that prayers work. If you have faith, your prayers will be answered. I think this means that you don't always get what you want, but you *do* get what you expect. Wherever your attention is focusing, wherever your imagination goes, what you anticipate, all of this is a feeding power of probabilities. Personally, I don't believe there is a Higher Being who decides what will and won't occur; but that it's a matter of the grand coalescence of energies. It is as though affinity is the way of the universe, there is a marvelous coherence in *all that is*. Consciousness en masse creates a sea of probabilities in a great cosmic co-arising. It seems to me that the largest concentrations of energy dictate what probabilities materialize. If we know that this is so, then we can participate by taking responsibility for energies we put out, thereby decreasing the likelihood of negative events occurring and increasing the likelihood of positive events occurring. Participating in the world of probabilities is sacred work and a gift the universe offers.

Cultivating Faith

They say getting what we expect is a self-fulfilling prophecy. True, but it's time we stopped being victims and realize that we can be prophets. Great amounts of energy lie in deeper levels of awareness—where more focused and concentrated consciousness resides. When we direct our imagination while meditating, it has that much more potency than in our usual waking consciousness. We can choose where to focus it, thereby increasing manyfold our influence on what happens in the world around us.

Your primary focus should be on what you're wanting or expecting. You should not deny negative circumstances that you may find yourself in, at the same time you should expect change to occur in spite of them. When any dissatisfaction comes to mind, always have your last image be one of movement toward the positive reality. Do not try to prove your projections are working by watching to see if the problem has begun to dissolve. This puts focus on the problem and perpetuates it. Assume energy is working under the surface whether you experience it yet or not. Set clear intention, focus on the projection, then let it go.

A couple of years after I had begun working with Applied Meditation, I had an experience that brought this home. As it often does for many of us, my problem boiled down to economics. At the time, I was making a living doing odd jobs. I spent many of my waking hours worried about how I was going to get the rent together; I spent many of my meditative minutes imagining money coming in. The fact that I didn't know how I was going to pay the rent was entirely more real and had a lot more energy connected to it than all my imaginings of money did. Whenever I finished meditating I still had to face the reality of my bills.

Then one day it dawned on me: I was focusing more on the problem—the bills—than on the solution—money coming. Having more money simply wasn't believable in the face of all those bills. I had to make it believable, so I changed my tactics. I decided that I needed three things: to get out of debt, to have a functional car and, to be able to focus on developing Applied Meditation. I then projected for this to occur within six months. This way what I was currently experiencing didn't contradict the possibility of change. I was building faith in the solution emerging.

I created three images symbolizing this: I imagined taking my friend out to dinner in celebration of paying her all that I owed; I also imagined myself happily driving my fixed car, and lastly I saw myself saying "no" to a job prospect because it interfered with my focus on Applied Meditation. Given my lifestyle, it was fully plausible that in six months all of this could be true. I didn't know how it would come about, I just assumed it would. This released me from the trap of seeing my current situation as a reflection of my failed projection. I did not need to compare my projection with my current situation. In the ensuing months, while meditating I would momentarily picture each of these images. It wasn't hard; after a while I did it less often as other concerns became more prominent. After about four months, I had stopped focusing on it altogether.

Exactly six months later—not a week early, not a week late—it all manifested. I was in the process of rebuilding my car's engine. I had visualized finding a newer Volkswagen bus with a blown-up engine for sale for two hundred dollars into which I could install my rebuilt engine. Time had run out and my mechanic was going to put it back into my old car. The day before this was to happen, I found just what I was looking for—a Volkswagen bus with a blown-up engine for sale for two hundred dollars! If that wasn't magical enough, the engine in the newer bus turned out to be perfectly functional. Coincidentally, the oil light malfunctioned and lit up at the same time that the bus ran out of gas. The previous owner assumed that the engine had blown up. I happily put that bus's engine into my old car and the new motor into the newer bus. At this point I had two running automobiles. Now, another coincidence: the friend to whom I owed money happened to be in the market for a car. I gave her my old car, which was worth more than the original debt; so she gave an additional three hundred dollars to the previous owner of the bus. In the end, everybody was happy. All that I had asked for had come to pass: I had a functional car, I was out of debt, and that was the first week that I began teaching Applied Meditation.

As is usually the case when projecting what you want, events occur in surprising ways. I didn't spend hours in meditation. Whenever my frustrations came up, I would bring to mind the three images of having already resolved the issue, assuming that underneath, the energy was at work. Each of the scenes I had chosen to symbolize my goals were meaningful, plausible, and easy to clearly imagine. It is important to understand that the projections of the Active Imagination are part, but not all, of the process. You also have to act on the energy. It doesn't just come to you; you've got to meet it halfway. If I hadn't been actively looking for a bus, I would never have been told about the one I found.

It seems to me that energizing realities with the Active Imagination does two things: it creates or empowers the probability—and it also sensitizes you to knowing intuitively what directions to turn to bring it about. A word of advice—don't get caught in the details of your imaginings. You work with them in order to generate the energy. It is the intentions and expectations that are operative. The details are just a way for you to wrap your imagination around a new possibility. The universe is much more creative than we are. I couldn't have put together such an unfolding of circumstances in my wildest dreams!

Remember this is a two-way street, the imagination is not only the stuff probabilities are made of, but is also the *medium* through which you receive information psychically. When you use the Active Imagination, you not only breathe life into probabilities, you also familiarize yourself with those that already exist—psychically attuning yourself to them. Not only is the environment responding to you, you are responding to it. You and your environment are moving into sync. For example, if you're projecting a parking place, you'll intuitively make the correct turns in discovering it. Your imagination is also a *receiver* of information. You didn't create the parking place; you became attuned to it. It is as though setting clear intention becomes magnetic headlights. You both attract and are attracted to that which has affinity with your projection.

Finding a Positive Orientation

We get what we expect; the trick is to expect what we want. Wishful thinking and expectations have opposite results. The difference is that a wish rests on the assumption that it is beyond possibility—the cow looking over the fence at the greener pastures, whereas expectation assumes it *will* occur—no fences. The Catch-22 is that the very issues with which you would like to have a more positive experience are the same ones in which your experience shows you otherwise. It is tricky; you don't want to go into denial, yet you have no positive reference point with which to work. Without a vision to move towards, your unsatisfactory past experience is all that your innerconsciousness knows regarding that particular issue. It is the source of behavior by default, and your intuition has nothing to align with in order to orient you toward a more desirable experience.

Always witness when you feel unhappy with your situation or get reactive. When you notice that you are, take steps to move out of reaction and ask yourself what you *do want*. On any important issue, if you have no plausible and positive vision, then you need to find new possibilities which open your imagination. There are a number of strategies you can use to find positive points of reference and get unstuck. One is to ask yourself what would be the opposite state of affairs. For instance, if you are trying to overcome shyness, then think of what the opposite would be. Obviously it is feeling relaxed and communicative with strangers. Then *pretend* this is your experience, and make adjustments to the projection until you find one that is desirable and plausible. It is likely to stretch your imagination, and this is good, but you want it to be plausible. At this point you have a new vision to affirm and energize.

Another way to find a positive reference point is to think of something you *do* excel at and imagine bringing that sense of confidence into the area you are working on transforming. Let's say you are a talented sculptor. Imagine yourself feeling inspired and satisfied by your work; confident that you did what you set out to do. Take this quality of confidence and imagine embodying it when you are meeting new people. This will take some practice, but you will find that you can. As your subjective experience changes, so too will your objective experience. Imagining a role model is also helpful. Witness the qualities that this person portrays, and then pretend that you yourself are filled with these same qualities.

There are a variety of ways you can apply a positive reference point. A student of mine once got into a tiff with her boss. As a consequence, her job was on the line; she was very distraught. She found herself staring at a picture of a holy man with flowers in his hair. This picture always made her happy. She began to imagine the holy man superimposed over her boss' face and her boss became holy. She meditated on this for a week. The next time she saw her boss, she felt love towards her and acted accordingly. With her hostility gone, their relationship was comfortable and she kept her job.

Your beta consciousness will think all of these exercises foolish. However, innerconsciousness is suggestible and it, not beta, is the source of behavior. What you are after are positive points of reference. That way, you won't continue to feel fenced into a reality you would prefer to leave behind.

In addition to these strategies, I recommend that you do some research to find positive reference points to work with. Let's say you want a relaxed relationship with your children. Ask your friends to tell you about an outstanding moment when they felt especially close with their child or a time they got through a difficult situation together. It is also fine to hear a story about an exemplary parent that they know. When you are inquiring, be careful that you don't commiserate with each other about things that aren't working; this only reinforces your sense of lacking. And you don't want philosophy either, you want descriptions of what works. You want to hear shining examples. Be inquiring, find out the details of what happened. How did it feel? What made it so positive for them? It is these details that open the imagination and give a feel for how reality could be. This process expands the repertoire of your imagination and you'll find yourself inspired with possibility. Your Active Imagination will then have rich resources from which to cook up new experience. Envision a desirable scenario with your children, then step into the vision and feel what life is like from that position.

Nothing new comes about without having imagined it first. (If none of the above methods have provided a plausible vision, then you will need to use your Receptive Imagination to discover a way through the situation (see Chapter Eight). When you work with your Active Imagination, you want to be simple and specific in your projection. This will enable you to experience the sensations and feelings associated with what you want.

Well-being doesn't happen in a void, it happens in a context. It's a result of specific conditions. To feel good, you need to imagine *what* would bring this about. Perhaps living in a new space will make you happy; imagine what it feels like to *already* be living there. Use the story-making capacities of your imagination. Conjure up the vision and step into it—see it, feel it, even smell it. Be in it as though it is your experience. Breathe life into the vision. Imagine what it would be like if you were looking back on it as though it had happened already, as if it were a memory. How has your life transformed? Create all of this in full living detail.

All of this works energetically; it's not logical. When you work with the Active Imagination, you don't need to worry about how, why, where, or when something's going to occur. All you need to do is *feel* as if it has *already* occurred. Endeavor to take it for granted, just as you do with your memories. If you do, you'll both project the quality of energy that attracts what you want, and you'll intuitively move in the right direction. It is as though you have created both an internal magnet and a compass.

Always be specific, simple, and positive in your projections. The clearer you are about your goal—how it feels to have attained it—the more powerful your projection is. If you have confusions and conflicts associated with the goal, the power of the projection is diminished proportionately. Likewise, the more you expect your goal to manifest itself, the more likely it will. It works proportionately to your faith in it. It is therefore good to begin with small issues because they are easier to be clear about. If you start in an area you consider trivial, you won't be as likely to have feelings that cloud the issue. But do keep in mind that you still want something that is possible (it's okay if it is unlikely, but it needs to be possible). The clearer you are, the more it will work, the more it works, the more you believe it's going to work the next time. *Faith comes from experience.* You need to cultivate your faith by successful projections, and as you do, you can take on bigger and bigger problems—otherwise you're likely to throw the baby out with the bath water. Start with parking places and bus connections, then slowly work up to the issues that really do make a difference in your life. *It is the faith in its working that makes it work.*

The Inner Witness Sheds Light on Your Projections

The irony is that, although the imagination is seen as unreal, we're supposed to be able to imagine anything. You can *think* anything you want, but to clearly imagine it is another matter. To illustrate, imagine grasping the doorknob on your front door, imagine turning it, and then pull the door open. You probably never bothered to imagine this but the point is, if you did, it would be no trouble. Now try imagining what it is like to be free of an allergy you had your whole life. Clearly imagining yourself liberated from a lifelong issue is not so simple.

There are both external and internal limitations that keep you from being able to imagine whatever you want. On the one hand, your imagination is psychically attuned to what is possible—the environment may not contain the possibility of your desire yet. On the other, your past experiences, your memories, are the raw materials your imagination uses to cook up new meals. If there's no flour in the pantry, it will place severe limitations on the bread you bake. Someone who has lived in poverty all her life is unlikely to imagine what it would *feel* like to be economically secure. She knows only what it's like to wish for it, which is quite a different matter.*

Working with your Active Imagination in the presence of the Inner Witness will enable you to inspect your projections closely. Doing so illuminates what is

---

* In this chapter I am dealing with the dynamics of individual energy projection and do not mean to imply that the solution to our economic malaise resides in the way we each project our imaginings—this is a political issue and will be dealt with in the last chapters.

needed. Being mindful will enable you to notice just what you can and what you currently cannot imagine. You will discover the specific ways your projections may fall short of what you desire. At this point, you can employ your Receptive Imagination to discover what will bridge the gap. This is where deep transformation occurs.

Be mindful that striving to be positive does not mean denying any of the challenges life offers. When you engage the Inner Witness, you'll notice the quality of energy present in your subjective landscape. That is, noticing when you are open, or if you are constricting and withdrawing from life's offerings; noticing when you can imagine something, and when you can't.

As you come to understand the potent energy of consciousness and the reciprocal nature of the inner and outer worlds, it becomes important not only to take responsibility for your own thoughts, but to be mindful how you describe yourself to others. Notice if you ever portray yourself as a helpless victim just for the dramatic effect. Do you want that thought form—the idea that you're a victim—floating around, potentially compounding your problems? I am not saying that you shouldn't share your problems, but that when you do, you should also share what you are doing to solve them, so that the image people carry gives you an added boost.

Since the innerconsciousness is quite literal, it is of extreme importance that you inspect your projections to be sure that you are ready for them to occur. Make your projections detailed enough that you can experience the whole of their implications. Step into it. Use your childlike make believe faculties and discover what the projection would actually *be* like. The Inner Witness will notice if these projections will really increase well-being, discovering if there are aspects that need to be adjusted.

In the presence of the Inner Witness, it is important that you extend your awareness to include others. How do they take to the projection? This will give you invaluable information, revealing if adjustments are needed not only for you, but for others too.

The Ethics of Applied Meditation

This is sacred work and not to be played with lightly. Power, of whatever kind, always needs to be approached ethically. Great powers lie in these dimensions. When you make a projection that involves others, do so with the intention that it will only come to pass if it is desirable for all concerned, and further, that it benefits the planet itself. Listen deeply. Doing so will serve to bring us into deep intimacy with those we share our lives with. When we all do this, we create community that holds us all as sacred.

Maintain humility, you don't necessarily know what is best. Projections are always loyal to the intention in which they were created. Intention establishes the groove through which the energy moves. Be mindful; notice your motivation. I suggest that you think of your projections as offerings to the universe, not demands—suggestions not requirements. Never put forward anything with an investment in the outcome, feeling your way is the only way.

With the Inner Witness present, you will be able to make projections with an open attitude. In *openness, projections move us toward wholeness.* With mindfulness present, attachment recedes and generosity emerges.

The work of the Active Imagination is to set clear intention, make specific projections, focus on them regularly and let them go. *If you are too invested in a particular outcome, you will not be able to avail yourself of intuitive information, which only sets you up for trouble.* Avoid feeling that your way is the only way; you do not want to approach a situation with the motive of controlling it. You want to take the attitude that the best will manifest.

You do not want your ego to be the part of you that employs these powers. Its view is too narrow, it will only cause problems for both you and others. This work is about coming to live in reverence with one another and the earth—not about getting what you want. In a culture of generosity, we won't turn to the greedy aspect of ourselves. Working with these energies with a loving heart secures not only our personal futures, but all the world's.

Conscientious Consciousness

We get what we expect, not necessarily what we want. For example, as women we've been taught to experience ourselves as vulnerable and weak, expecting to be overpowered and needing protection. I know that this is the last feeling I should have when I walk in the streets. I don't blame myself for feeling vulnerable—there are good reasons for my feelings, but I know that vulnerability is just the energy that will draw an assailant (remember the unity of opposites: energies that resonate with each other attract one another). Therefore, whenever I feel vulnerable, I notice the feeling, and do whatever I need to do to feel powerful—whether that be exploring and transforming my worries, carrying a weapon, learning self-defense, or being with friends—but I never allow myself to go into the street alone if I'm feeling insecure.

When you care, it's only natural to have some worries. Worries are a double jeopardy—you're already troubled and now you realize that the concerns themselves are adding to the likelihood that what you fear most will actually happen. Most people want to know whether their worries come from their own emotional limitations or from their intuitive/psychic awareness. The boundaries between objective and subjective dissolve when working with Applied Meditation. That's not the issue, the worry does not live either inside or outside. The very fact that you are imagining it means it is a probability. Denial further compounds the situation.

With innerconsciousness, worries can be transformed into messengers who carry the specific information you need to heed. They become a gift if you let your imagination give shape to your anxieties and play them out. With the Inner Witness, you can look closely at the scene you're afraid might come to pass. Get to know it in detail: the atmosphere, the place, the weather, the people involved, and what everyone's doing. The Inner Witness does not get caught up in worries, so it can reveal the nuances of your imaginings. You will want to use your Receptive Imagination to gain further insights and your Active Imagination to change the scenes into more positive scenarios. This will both shift the operative energy and point to strategies you can act on in your life. Here it is crucial to witness what seems plausible, as well as noticing if the images keep reverting back to your initial worry. Keep working with your Active and Receptive Imagination until you come up with a scene that feels good to you. This process will reveal exactly what you can do or what needs to be avoided so that your worry cannot manifest.

If your imaginary scene keeps reverting back to the worrisome one, take it as a warning, and be cautious about the situation. On the objective level, you want to ensure that the particular ingredients of your worries never have a chance to assemble themselves. Ironically, working with the Inner Witness and the imagination takes you *into* reality, not away from it. With mindfulness and intuition, you have choice. Do not dwell on your worries, but take them as messages and attend to them. If you have changed it, but still have a little residual negativity hanging around, you'll want to transform it.

Mental Housecleaning

The most powerful method I have discovered for transforming negativity is what I call Mental Housecleaning. Years back, I was teaching a class with a friend and we were not getting along—making it difficult to do a good job. I couldn't figure out rationally what to do. Every time we were together after a class, I'd find myself angry at him, or myself, or both for one thing or another. So I tried a problem-solving technique I'd learned from the Silva Training called "The Glass of Water Technique". After using it the next time I meditated, a fountain appeared in my awareness. It was not one of those off-the-wall images that so frequently move through one's mind while meditating; I knew exactly what it meant. I proceeded to place an image of my friend in the fountain to be cleansed by the water springing up through the base. As I imagined all this, I wasn't struck by anything specific, it was not one of those "Aha!" experiences—there was no great emotional feeling when I did it. As usual, it felt like a story I'd made up. Once again, I learned that the results of meditation manifest in daily life—not during the meditation. Subsequently, every time I interacted with my friend, I felt okay about it; no longer did I plague myself with our difficulties. Needless to say, we were better able to collaborate with one another. Using the Mental Housecleaning device cleared a space in my consciousness and made new perspectives possible. It was a symbolic gesture to give my deeper levels the message to transform my stuck position and provide space for new experience.

The innerconsciousness takes things quite literally; so in order to create a Mental Housecleaning device, imagine something that transforms energy and doesn't simply store it—for example, a fire, a compost pit, a fly-eating plant, or simply dropping into the ground to be transformed in the soil. You want to be sure that what goes in, comes out transformed. Always use the same imaginary process so your innerconsciousness will come to recognize your intent. This technique is one about which the beta mind is likely to spew out multiple discounts. Use it anyway—the discounts of beta are ineffectual. It is the alpha level that is suggestible and responsive to symbolic messages. Working with innerconsciousness, it is your *intentions* that always create the effect. They set the path upon which consciousness travels.

Mental Housecleaning is useful in working out problems in all kinds of relationships. You may have found that even when you've discussed your problems together and made agreements to change, you still find yourself being irritated at the drop of a hat. This is because your innerconsciousness is still in the habit of being irritated. You can also use Mental Housecleaning for any habituated thought patterns.

A friend of mine puts his problems into the image of a waterfall. After it has bounced around on the rocks in the stream below, he pulls something different out. I simply put an issue into the fountain, then with an act of will, I move my attention to other concerns, expecting transformation to occur. It is important that you re-focus your attention either on a positive outcome or something different altogether—if you don't, you'll find yourself habitually acting out of the familiar, recreating your problem. Mental Housecleaning clears your mind of bad habits, but it does not necessarily solve the problem itself; rather, it provides space for a resolution to emerge, a resolution that otherwise you probably would not notice. Always have the last thought be positive; this acts as the directive to which your consciousness responds. Intention and expectation set the path upon which your consciousness travels regarding that issue.

If ever you are still plagued with a problem that you have Mental Housecleaned, the chances are your innerconsciousness knows that this is not exclusively a negative habit on your part, but has something positive to offer you—some lesson is still to be learned. Some closer attention is called for. In this case, you can employ your Receptive Imagination to discover the insights you need in order to move on. Once you've acted on the insights, your Mental Housecleaning will succeed.

We Cocreate Reality with Others

Your imagination is a material force affecting the environment, but we mustn't forget that we're social beings living with others who, needless to say, also have imaginations. Your individual imagination does not create reality, it simply interacts with it. By focusing it, you increase the likelihood of things occurring; you do not create the events. If there are more people imagining otherwise, the event will not come to pass. I'm not saying that our imagination isn't effective; I'm just reminding you that it's only a part of a sea of probabilities. When you participate with it, you increase those probabilities that will materialize as a result of the concentration of energies.

The world of probabilities is not private, but shared. Channeling energy by focusing on positive outcomes for those in challenging situations, and by using

Energy Circles to work with others, will offer added support where it's needed, and enable us all to reclaim the experience of being embedded in a larger reality in which we are all interdependent participants in the co-arising realities we share (see Chapter Six).

Mass Media Mesmerizes Us into Mindlessness

If we are to take seriously the many ways consciousness influences reality then we cannot ignore the impact of the media on our subjective landscapes. I've already said that we move through the world in terms of our inner messages. When we watch TV, we are in the alpha level. Much to the gratification of the advertisers, it is a highly programmable state of awareness. For too many of us, television has become a companion who is always there, doesn't argue, and is full of entertainment—the problem is, we are not in the habit of arguing with it either. Remember we don't distinguish between the real and the unreal—we simply act in accordance with the images present in our consciousness. Whether we're actually confronted by a mad dog or simply imagine that we are, as far as our adrenal glands are concerned, it's the same. There's no difference when we watch TV; we are constantly awash in a sea of images and no matter how much we may use rational discrimination, our bodies and psyches respond to them. Notice the bodily sensations you get when watching a horror movie. Once I understood the power of the imagination, I stopped exposing myself to such atrocities, for they are genuine pollution of the mind.

Eric Peper, an expert in biofeedback tells us that:

> The horror of television is that the information goes in, but we don't react to it. It goes right into our memory pool and perhaps we react to it later but we don't know what we're reacting to. When you watch television you are training yourself not to react and so later on, you're doing things without knowing why you're doing them or where they came from.[18]

For many of us, television has replaced life. The image in the box has become more vivid and "real" than our everyday existence. It claims the center of our attention. Witness what communication experts have to offer on the subject:

The people who control television become the choreographers of *our* internal awareness....By (television's) expropriation of inner experience, advertising makes the human into a spectator of his or her own life. It is alienation to the tenth power.[19]

By its very nature, TV impoverishes the sensory environment. Recent studies show that TV viewing induces severe sensory deprivation.[20]

When listening to the radio, or reading, we provide our own images. The insidious aspect of television is that it provides the images. They go directly into innerconsciousness. We become passive receptacles for the images it bestows on us. How often have you heard someone say, "Just like on TV!" as an expression of how real something was? Now we don't live life, we watch it; then the most exciting moments in our actual lives get compared to what we saw on TV.

Television is now being recognized as an addiction in our society—two out of five adults and seven out of ten teenagers acknowledge that they have a problem.[21] How bad is the problem, really? 99 percent of American households have a television set.[22] The average person in the U.S. spends over four hours a day in front of the television though it's likely to be turned on for seven hours a day. This adds up to an estimated nine to eleven years devoted to television viewing in an average life span.[23]

American children also spend an average of four hours a day watching which adds up to twenty-eight hours a week, 2,400 hours a year and nearly 18,000 hours by the time they graduate from high school. This is 5000 hours more then what is spent in a classroom."[24] Now young people can't even escape the influence of television as it invades the classrooms with Channel One:

...a marketing program that gives video equipment to desperate schools in exchange for the right to broadcast a "news" program studded with commercials to all students every morning....Channel One boasts, "Our relationship with 8.1 million teenagers lasts for six years."...According to Mike Searles, President of Kids R Us, "If you get this child at an early age, you can own this child for years to come. Companies are saying, 'Hey I want to own the kid younger and younger.'"[25]

---

* See Susan R. Johnson, M.D., *Strangers in Our Homes: TV and Our Children's Minds*. (Zaytuna Institute, 1999) and Keith Bruzzel, *The Human Brain and the Influences of Television Viewing* (Wyllaned Institute, 1997).

Young people see an average of 100 TV commercials a day…Most kids can list more brands of beer than American presidents.[26]

The spread of television unified a whole people within a system of conceptions and living patterns. Because of it, our whole culture and the physical shape of the environment, no more or less than our minds and feelings, have been computerized, linearized, suburbanized, freewayized, and packaged for sale.[27]

For the first time in human history, most of the stories about people, life, and values are told not by parents, schools, churches, or others in the community who have something to tell, but by a group of distant conglomerates that have something to sell.[28]

We've become mindless consumers, but there's an even scarier aspect:

If commercials are the appetizer and dessert of each TV time slot, violence is its main course, the meat and potatoes that make the sponsor's message stick to your ribs. "To the advertiser, violence equals excitement equals ratings."[29]

An hour of prime-time television includes about five violent acts. An hour of children's Saturday morning programming includes twenty to twenty-six violent acts. The average American child will witness 12,000 violent acts on television each year, amounting to about 200,000 violent acts by the time he turns eighteen years old…In a University of Illinois study, people who had watched the most violent TV between birth and age eight committed the most serious crimes by age thirty.[30]

An appalling number of juvenile crimes—torture, kidnapping, rapes, and murders—have been traced to events portrayed on televisions.…A boy's television habits at age eight are more likely to be a predictor of his aggressiveness at age eighteen or nineteen than his family's socio-economic status, his relationship with his parents, his IQ, or any other single factor in his environment.[31]

Boys are conditioned to be violent towards others, while girls turn the violence inwards: along with all the images of the ideal put forth in TV programming and commercials comes the inevitable inability to measure up and ensuing low self-esteem and self-destructive behaviors. For girls in particular, the ideal borders on emaciation; anorexia and bulimia are now epidemic. Eighty percent of 4th grade girls are on diets and one in five women in the U.S. has an eating disorder. [32]

If we don't want to be homogenized the best thing to do is turn *off* the set or talk back to it for your own self-protection so your deeper levels of consciousness don't absorb it all noncritically in the name of reality. The people responsible for the programs won't hear your arguments, but your deeper awareness will. So talk back! And take back your consciousness! Every time you compare yourself to a movie star bring in the affirmation, "I believe in myself." There is nothing more frustrating than trying to live up to something that isn't real. You can protect yourself from the destructive messages by imagining yourself surrounded by an invisible mirror that bounces back the ones you don't want to absorb.

If our creativity isn't buried under the sludge we'll have better ways of spending our time than in front of the tube. Remember our creativity comes from deeper levels. We have to give it space to surface. And we don't want to energize all the junk we watch by carrying it around in our real imaginations.

Get out the popcorn, invite your friends over and do an Energy Circle together. You'll be entertained with images that fuel *desirable* futures.

Induction

Breathing with your belly, give your body permission to relax...Breathing out tension...Bring to awareness your symbol for physical relaxation. Feel your body relax.

◆

When you are ready, bring to awareness your symbol for mental relaxation. Feel your mind relaxing...Notice how your thoughts become soft and gentle...and you can begin to detect space between your thoughts...Awareness is expansive, lots of room for whatever crosses the sky of your mind.

◆

Bring to your awareness your symbol for emotional relaxation...breathe out any emotional tension...Offer yourself some appreciation...Feel your heart open...Feel yourself emotionally relax...Breathe, it is good to give yourself some space , some time to relax.

◆

Now bring to awareness your symbol for your creative self-restoring center. Take a moment and remember what it is that you feel grateful about...Breathe, let yourself rest in an appreciation of the gift of life...Here your consciousness is fluid and free.

◆

You will remain alert throughout this meditation—tell yourself this now...

I am going to suggest several affirmations. If you wish to affirm them, repeat them to yourself after me knowing that in doing so you create patterns of energy both within and around you, causing your life to align itself with the power of the words. Expect the affirmations to manifest themselves within and around you.

I believe in myself, I believe in my experience...

I trust my nature, I trust nature...

I am a fully intelligent, creative, joyful being...

I live up to my fullest potential...

I expect the best...

I listen to my intuition. It guides me in the right direction...

I only respond to positive suggestions...

My fears are transformed into teachers, empowering me to move forward
    with courage and insight...

I always successfully protect myself...

My life is in harmony with the life around me...

My life is whole, my life is embraced by the whole of life...

All my needs are always met, there is enough for everyone...

What I offer is needed; what I need is offered...

I contribute my best to the world...

I maintain balance amidst change...

I trust the future...

Now take time to focus on any of your own affirmations, knowing that as you focus on affirmations you create patterns of energy to which your life will conform. And you may also want to focus on any quality symbols you have been working with.

◆

Finishing what you're doing...alert and ready to follow what I have to say to you.

In a moment I'm going to count on a descending scale from ten to one. At each descending count you can descend deeper and deeper into yourself—into your center of knowingness—into the center out of which your personality emanates. Breathe and your exhalations carry you down. Ten, moving down deeper now, feeling the qualities of who you are…Nine, relaxing into yourself, breathing, returning to yourself…Eight, acknowledging the essence of your being, the particular way you are an expression of life…breathing…Seven, feel the deepest tones of your being, like musical chords…Six, moving down deeper and deeper into your center…Five, your center of knowingness…Four, your center of receptivity, creativity, spacious awareness…Three, deeper and deeper into yourself, who it is that you are…Two, moving into your center out of which your energy emanates, drawing to you particular events, resonant events…One, this is your magnetic center of deep knowing, potent energy resides here. Here you can adjust energy, align energy, create probabilities. This is your center of receptivity, of creativity. Here you can feel yourself as a part of *all that is*…

This is a very powerful place to do your interior work. From this place you have access to all knowingness. Awareness is spacious, the Inner Witness present. Here you can experience all that is known. Here you can look at any aspect of life and know its true nature…know your own true nature. Here wisdom resides. You can look at any fears, any anxieties, any particular feelings, anything, and you can discover what to do. Here, all your knowingness resides. Breathe, and knowing is present…

Here your inquiring mind can acquire whatever knowledge you need in your life now…All knowing is available—all you need to do is focus your attention where you choose and witness what takes place in the light of awareness. Honor knowing…In this deep place of inner awareness you can discover realities, you can shape realities…Here you reside outside the usual boundaries of space and time. Here you discover and create reality…It is in this dimension that magic is born…

Rehearsing the Future

Feel the quiet space you now occupy, fully relaxed—yet there is much potency—like the atmosphere right before the morning sun rises, the dawn of a new day…very peaceful, yet pregnant with potential…very quiet, yet charged with possibilities…Feel this quiet, receptive space you now occupy…Know that this very space is full of creative energy. Here you can create possibilities. Here you can create probabilities. In this space the future takes shape. This space is very powerful…

Know that you have different vortexes of energy inside of yourself where there is a concentration of energy. Move your attention to the particular vortex of energy in the middle of your forehead, your third eye. Imagine you could rest your awareness in your third eye; feel the quality of energy that's present in this area. From here you can best discover and shape probabilities. It is from here the future dawns. Imagine that you are sitting in a theater, where you have control of the spotlight. Imagine as though this were a magic theater, where the future rehearses, and this spotlight is very powerful, for you can direct it to illuminate the future—all the possible futures…The future is the stage this spotlight illuminates. You can set the stage however you choose.

Imagine what your third eye illuminates…Look down the beam of light. Wherever you turn this light it can illuminate possibilities…Then you can create probabilities of how you'd like things to unfold…for yourself, your family, your community, the world. You can focus this beam of light personally, collectively, and planetarily. You can focus it here, you can focus it there, seeing possibilities that exist, and you can create positive probabilities…

First observe possibilities as they already exist and let your third eye illuminate the immediate future…Imagine…Notice the probabilities. Let the next week unfold before you, and watch it occur…watch what you do…watch what happens…Let the scenes arise in your awareness…sense the atmosphere around each…as though you're watching previews…Witness how each day unfolds…Be aware of the atmosphere surrounding the unfolding of scenes.

◆

Now go back to the beginning of the week, and this time let the spotlight illuminate day by day exactly how you would like it to be…Familiarize yourself with the best of possibilities…Feeling good about yourself, energize what you would like to have occur, how you'd like to feel…Endeavor to expect the best to occur…

Feel yourself being fully deserving of all this…Know that in experiencing it occurring in this way, you have energized it…You move into coherence with the best of probabilities—for consciousness is magnetic energy. You are drawn toward circumstances that resonate with the good qualities you imagine and so, too, circumstances are drawn into your goodness.

◆

Now let the light illuminate how, if it unfolds in this manner, it will affect others…Notice all the ripplings…Notice how this unfolding affects others…Make the shifts needed…If you discover any detrimental effects on others, make whatever adjustments are necessary, so that all that occurs is good for everyone.

◆

Now, once again, go back to the beginning and this time enter the scene. Travel down the beam of light and enter into the image of yourself that you've been watching. Feel all the events unfolding around you…Notice what you're wearing…how your body feels…any sounds, smells, vibrations that are present as the week unfolds around you…Feel yourself going through the events…Feel the excitement of these events developing in this desirable manner…As you experience all of this, if you come across anything that would benefit from having an adjustment made, reshape the scene. Here reality is malleable…Feel your connection with all those that you share these events with...Feel it all happening, experience it happening around you. Feel as though it were happening right now...from the beginning of the week to the end.

◆

Now extend the light of awareness further in time...Project yourself into a time when this week that you have been imagining has become memory. It has *already* happened...Notice the difference the occurrences made...How they lead to this particular place in the future. Witness how it is here...How you'll be doing...How others are...Notice the quality of energy.

◆

Bring yourself back to the present moment. Bring with you the energies you have discovered in the future times...Breathe...As you exhale, you infuse current time with this energy...You breathe life into it...Know that this energy has been set into motion...Sense how you have aligned yourself to it. A subtle shift has taken place...You intuitively know how to bring these events into being...Allow yourself to believe in yourself...to believe in your experience...to believe in the world...to believe in the future. Acknowledge that the very fact that you can imagine these experiences makes them real, your imagination is real, imagination is the stuff probabilities are made of...

Now notice what you are inclined to do to bring these energies into being...How can you seed them?...How will you cultivate them?...Notice what you personally need to do to bring these events into reality...or maybe there's something you need to give up...Choose if you want to commit yourself to this energy...Imagine what you are willing to do...Make agreements with yourself about what you're willing to do to make room for this energy to manifest...Imagine how and when you'll do it...Know that in doing so you bring this energy out into the world...knowing what you have to offer the future...knowing what the future has to offer you.

Tell yourself that if ever you find yourself frustrated with the way it has been, you'll move your attention to a sense of change that has already begun to take place...believing in the future...

Be the change you want to make. The future lives in you now. Breathe it into the present moment. Expect the best.

Mental Housecleaning

Know that your consciousness is your consciousness, your dominion...Your consciousness is loyal to your choices...You choose the qualities of energy that reside here. The whole of your innerconsciousness is your realm, your sphere, and fully responsive to your influence. Your innerconsciousness is responsive to your suggestion.

Now create a ritual of transformation in your consciousness. Create a Mental Housecleaning ritual—use the transmuting powers of nature. Create something like fire, a compost pit, whatever you like—be sure it transforms energy...recycling the old making space for the new.

◆

This is your Mental Housecleaning device. Know that you can use your Mental Housecleaning device to convert, to transform any negativity, making space for new creative perspectives to reveal themselves. Tell your deeper consciousness this now, tell your deeper consciousness that whenever you symbolically put anything through your Mental Housecleaning device, your consciousness will then transform the constricting energy, making space for new energy to emerge...Know that this is so, trust it...

You can use your device whenever you are stuck in negative patterns; simply symbolize the habituated pattern and put the symbol into your Mental

Housecleaning device...When you do this keep your intentions clear and positive. After using your device always move your consciousness in a positive direction or focus on an entirely different concern trusting that deeper within you a conversion is taking place...Your imagination is real and when you imagine a transformation you speak to the deepest levels of knowingness within you which respond; the energy shifts and a metamorphosis occurs. You've transformed the old and created space for the birth of new liberating experiences to manifest themselves. Know that this is so.

Whenever you do Mental Housecleaning, always be specific...Recreate the concern in your awareness, be aware of the atmosphere in which it lives, symbolize it, and put the symbol through your device, then move your consciousness into a new direction expecting the transformation to take place deeper within you. You can take time to work with your Mental Housecleaning device now...Choose one specific area of habitual negativity that you wish to free yourself of.

◆

Know that you have released yourself from patterns of the past...transformation is taking place within you. New experience is available to you now. Expect it...

Tell yourself that you will remember to use your Mental Housecleaning device whenever you need to clear the debris in your mind and it will enable you to be fully present, clear, and creative in the situation...Your consciousness is your dominion, and you can choose the qualities that reside within you.

Self-Protection

Think of times when you've felt very safe, what safety means to you, protection, security, safety...Feel yourself safe, secure, protected...Let these qualities move through your awareness. Like snapshot pictures, remember times of safety, protection, security. The times in the past where you've felt these qualities present. Let them be present now.

◆

Breathe in the sense of safety...Exhale and feel yourself settle into security...Feel what it is like to be safe, how it feels in your body...Bring the energies of safety and protection into the present, into the room right now...As you breathe in, imagine your body filling up with this sensation of security, of safety...Fill yourself up with this sensation. Breathe safety...Imagine it...As you exhale, breathe the energy out and create a bubble of protection surrounding you. You might imagine it like a warm cozy fire-lit room, or white light, the feeling of being held in a loved one's arms, soft music—whatever security is to you...In fact, you may want to literally imagine yourself in a bubble of protection. You may want to imagine yourself in a bubble of light, energy, music, however you wish to imagine yourself surrounded by, and immersed in, protection.

◆

Create a symbol for this experience. It may be the bubble itself or it may be something different...Know that whenever you bring this symbol into your awareness, you'll bring this energy of protection into your sphere, into your space. In so doing you'll protect yourself from any influences that might threaten you. You will find yourself intuitively knowing what you need to do to protect yourself...Whenever you use your symbol of protection, you fully claim your space...you embody your full power...you engage your dominion and protect your autonomy. Feel how powerful this is...You cause others to respect your integrity...Whenever you use this symbol, you create boundaries allowing only positive influences to penetrate...Know that this is so, that this symbol energetically creates a quality of dignity around you, to which everything responds, bouncing off the negative and absorbing only the positive...Sense how this is the case...With your symbol of protection you become immune to all detrimental influences. Suggest to your inner self that whenever you bring this symbol to mind you will receive the information you need, knowing just what is necessary to remain safe and secure…

Wherever you are, you can protect yourself from other people's energy, from germs, from attack, from advertising…whatever it may be, by simply bringing this symbol into awareness you surround yourself with this energy of protection and safety and you *are* safe…Know that this is so, tell yourself this. Whenever you need protection, you just bring your symbol to awareness and your space will be honored…You'll inspire respect. Witness how your symbol inspires your courage and you always successfully stand your ground. Take it for granted that you always stand your ground…fierce…Your symbol not only protects you from the outside, but also evokes deep power inside, power that rises to the occasion…Imagine it…Breathe power…Feel it…Expect that your symbol always secures the scene.

◆

You can also use this symbol to protect anyone who may be threatened, anything that may be threatened. You can use this symbol to surround anything with protective energy…Imagine using this symbol now, moving through your activities to notice how it feels…When you use it, you intuitively know what to do to protect yourself or others…Tell yourself that next time you bring this symbol to mind, the whole of your being will respond, doing what's needed to protect yourself and everything around you…Know that everyone will respond to this energy.

Tell yourself you'll remember your symbol and use it whenever you need it.

Stretching Your Confidence into a New Area

Experience the warmth you feel for the beauty of life, the wonder of the world, spectacular landscapes…delicate flowers…a child fumbling as she learns to make her own way through the world...Feel your compassion, feel the compassion you have for all of life, your love of life itself.

◆

Draw this quality you are now experiencing into yourself...Breathe in compassion...compassion, for who it is that you are. Breathe it into the whole of your being...Breathe in tenderness for your own nature...Immerse yourself in compassion, let yourself be affectionate towards who you are.

◆

Remember yourself in the past, all the years that have gone into making you who you are...Unique experiences, a combination of experiences that only you have had...Believe in the lessons of your experience...Recognize your intelligence...Appreciate who it is that you are, love yourself. Acknowledge the true nature of who you are...Tell yourself what you appreciate about who you are. Honor yourself, appreciate yourself.

◆

Witness how you receive this acknowledgement, sense if there are any places that this love bounces off, where it doesn't go in...or any place that needs the love to go in even deeper...With breath, send loving right into those areas that haven't accepted this acknowledgement. As you breathe into them, feel them open to caring energy...Breathe, feel them softening...becoming receptive...Let them be nurtured with loving compassionate energy...Massage yourself with loving energy.

◆

Now bring into your awareness your sense of competency, your sense of intelligence...Become aware of your sense of security with your abilities. To do this, you may want to remember an area in your life in which you are fully competent, an area you have fully mastered. It may be something you think of as insignificant and simple—no matter, choose an area in your life where you believe in your experience; don't worry if the area seems trivial or unimportant—what is important is that you are fully proficient...Acknowledge your proficiency...Feel your know-how...Breathe in your competence...Exaggerate it.

◆

Create a symbol for self-confidence...Now choose an area in your life that you would like to enhance, be it creativity, a skill, whatever you choose...Choose one particular ability that you would like to develop...

Know that within you, you have the ability to tap universal collective consciousness. Know that within it resides the knowledge, information, and powers that will enable you to acquire exactly what you need to develop yourself. You have the ability to tap knowledge directly; you can go past ordinary ways of learning by tapping directly into the source of all knowingness. Pretend that you can...

Your symbol for self-confidence enables you to be fully receptive to the insights and qualities that will help you bring about this new way of being. Your symbol acts as a magnet drawing to you exactly what you need from deep within and from around you...Imagine shining your symbol into the arena you have chosen to embrace...as though your symbol were to infuse the scene with power, however you imagine this...Imagine your symbol flooding the area with the powerful energy of competence...Imagine it glowing, pulsating, charged with power...Breathe it, let it sing inside you...Feel the energy.

◆

Now shine this energy into the future. Imagine your future self immersed in all this energy...Witness transformation...Powerful...Step into the vision and feel your future self fully able in this new way...Dynamic...Be your future self...Feel your confidence symbol make your steps steady in this new area of your life...How does it feel?...Notice how your confidence gives you courage to manifest your desires, to believe in yourself...slowly, your steps are no longer tenuous but instead steady and strong. Feel it; open to it. Breathe this way of being.

◆

Talk to your future self and your symbol for self-confidence to discover what it is you can do in your life to bring all of this about…Sense if there is anything you need to give up in your life or in your self-image to make room for this new way of being…What can you do to cultivate this way of being?…

◆

Are you willing to do these things? Make the commitment you are willing to…Know that if you can imagine it, you can create it…You'll find yourself knowing intuitively just what to do, just where to go, just what to ask, just what to say…Your body, your mind, your feelings, and your spirit are now all aligned with this energy. Know that this is so…Give yourself permission to believe in yourself, to believe that in fact all this *can* come about, *will* come about. You deserve it…Let any residual skepticism soak down into the ground to be transformed by the soil, or put through your Mental Housecleaning device, making room for this new energy to come through.

◆

Know that as you are confident in some areas, you can become confident in all areas that you choose to focus on; confidence can spread throughout the whole of your experience, throughout the whole of your life, believing in your experience in all areas of your life…Know that your potential grows every day…Believe in yourself. You have transformed a wish into a belief.

Fear As Challenge

Now imagine a spot that's a very powerful spot for you, a place of power…It could be one that you create in your imagination, one that you've been to before, a place of power…a place that's charged with potent energy for you.

Create your place of power…Let yourself be in this spot, feel the power of this place…Breathe in the energy of this place…Remember times in your life when you felt relaxed, creative, and powerful…Exaggerate the greatness of these times…Fill this place with the qualities of those times…Sense power, strength, vital forces in this place…Breathe power…in and out.

Imagine yourself standing in this place and drawing up all the power it has to offer you, through the arches of your feet, the palms of your hands, or anywhere it's inclined to come in. Breathe it in…infusing the whole of yourself with the power, letting the energy move through you…throughout your whole self…feeling extremely powerful and balanced and with a vital force…empowering the whole of your being, every cell, every thought, every feeling—the whole of your experience charged with strength…Feel how centered you are with this energy moving through you…Feel that quality of being fully powerful and balanced all at once.

◆

Now bring to awareness your symbols for protection and confidence. Or if you have none, bring into the scene the quality of safety and feel your confidence…You are courageous; it is from these wellsprings of energy that your courage emerges. Experience courage, experience your courage. Breathe it in from your symbols, draw it up from the earth. Courage, it lives in you.

◆

Now choose one particular fear or anxiety you would like to work on…Bring into your awareness something that you find very intimidating, scary, fearful. As you bring it to awareness, know that you can breathe out any tension that might arise. You can always breathe out tension, as you do, the Inner Witness reveals what is true for you…Here in the light of spacious awareness, there is room to witness. Breathe out the charge and witness what is so…Recreate the times you've felt this particular fear…don't bring the fear too close, just bring it close enough so that you can keep your energy moving smoothly…continuing to feel courageous and protected…Witness this fear…take the fear and look at it…Separate yourself from it and witness…Breathe out whatever anxieties you carry…Let them drain away. Give the fear form and color and personify it…Give it a personality…The fear is no longer within you at all; it is personi-fied before you…Imagine it. Talk to it…Get to know it…It has a character all of its own…Find out where it is coming from…Notice its quirks…Endeavor to make friends with it…See what it has to offer you…Bring your symbols into the conversation and hold council.

◆

Be receptive, listen to what you need to know from your place of power, from your symbols, from this character before you…Witness how it has transformed into a challenge…Experience transformation. Ask the character for a gift. Know that in fact fear is your greatest teacher. When you are open to it, it magically transforms into a highly sensitive friend who offers crucial information…What gifts does it have for you now?…Let it give you power, let it teach you…as if it were a door through which you can discover new ways of being.

◆

The energy that used to aim into you and cause constriction is now transformed into positive light…Imagine that your newfound friend has a beam of light with which it can illuminate possible futures and you can see what it illuminates and explore potentialities…Witness the opportunities for learning…Witness where caution may be useful…Witness what awakens the old familiar fear…Notice what the fear is protecting you from.

◆

With your newfound friend and your symbols find the places receptive to a shift in energy. Shape positive potentialities. From this power stop you are the creator…You might find these places inside you…or around you…or both…that welcome opening to a different way…Illuminate a new empowered future…

This light can be used to attune yourself very finely to potential situations. It can give you the knowledge that you need to move through those situations in a very courageous and protected way…It can give you the information you need to rearrange probabilities, making the potential scenes positive.

◆

If you wish, you can decide to walk down the path created by the beam of light and embrace the challenges, make them your own, let that beam of light empower you to move forward…With the light, the unknown is illuminated, and all becomes known and you become wiser…See where you can go with it. Step into your liberated self.

◆

Appreciate the fear that has become your friend, your challenge, bringing you the gift of learning.

◆

Imagine that as you move forward down your path fears always transform into friends gifting you with new perspectives…making life interesting. Imagine that whenever you come across fear you talk to it and receive the gift of the challenge that it has hidden inside it…learning from it, becoming a wiser, fuller human being.

◆

Know that you can always do this, protected, powerful, courageous, and learning…Tell yourself you will remember to transform the negative into a positive light…Fear transforms into challenge which transforms into the wisdom lessons learned…Acknowledge that this is so.

Count Out

Just as the sun gives birth to a new day, your imagination gives birth to a new future…Your imagination is real, in it, probabilities are born. Appreciate your imagination for all that it gives you. It gifts you with intuition as well as visions of new ways of being. You can sense what is so and work with it, creating positive transformation.

Go over all that you have come to in this meditation, insights, choices…Know that the very fact that you imagine it makes it real, the energy now exists…Trust it…Expect the best.

◆

Finish what you're doing and make yourself ready to come out to outer conscious levels by knowing that you'll bring with you all the energies you've contacted; ready and able to act on them in your life.

In a moment, I'm going to count from one to five, at the count of five, you'll open your eyes remembering all that you've experienced…feeling refreshed, revitalized, and relaxed…

ONE—becoming more aware of the room around you…

TWO—coming up slowly now…

THREE—at the count of five, you'll open your eyes feeling relaxed, revitalized, and refreshed remembering all that you've experienced…

FOUR—coming up now, bringing with you your sense of well-being…

FIVE!—eyes open, feeling refreshed, revitalized, and relaxed, remembering all that you've experienced, sense of wholeness—open heart and spirit.

Track 2

Active Imagination:
Aligning Energies with a Positive Vision

Focus on your breathing...Let your breath be full and easy...each breath rolling through your body like waves...breathing...Bring to awareness your symbol for physical relaxation...Give your body permission to relax...Feel your body relax more and more with each exhalation of breath...Breathe through any areas of tension and feel your body relaxing into the support of the earth...relaxing more and more as you move through this meditation.

When you're ready, bring to awareness your symbol for mental relaxation...Let your breath be like the breeze that clears the air...Let your breath clear your mind...and your mind relaxes into its natural state of spaciousness...as spacious as the skies...relaxed...open...clear...alert throughout this meditation...

As your mind continues relaxing, become aware of the feelings present in you now...Give your feelings permission to relax...Bring to awareness your symbol for emotional relaxation...Let go of all the feelings that push at you or pull at you...any anxieties or distractions or frustrations...any feelings that somehow cause you to constrict yourself...Give yourself permission to let them all go...down into the ground, transformed in the earth...breathe them out...

And take a moment to appreciate yourself...to offer yourself loving kindness...To appreciate your goodness...Feel your heart lighten...as though it smiles...Sense your heart relaxing into its natural state of generosity and compassion.

◆

When you're ready, bring to awareness your symbol for your creative, self-restoring center...Remember the goodness of life...Remember what you hold sacred...what you feel grateful about...what you cherish...Feel yourself relaxing into the sanctity of life itself…Here, awareness is spacious…You're held by awareness…The Inner Witness is present…The receptive imagination brings forth intuitive knowing…The creative imagination awakens your inner visionary…Here, you can align yourself with energies…discover energies…create probabilities…Here, you shape energy…This is your creative, self-restoring center, where you feel yourself a part of *all that is*…Take a few moments and appreciate this space…Know that each time you exhale you move deeper into this quiet space…potent place…alert…aware…open…Feel the space you now occupy…fully relaxed…yet there is much potency…like the atmosphere right before the morning sun rises…the dawn of a new day…Very peaceful, yet pregnant with potential…Very quiet, yet charged with possibility…It is in this space that probabilities are created…This space is where the future takes shape…This space is very powerful…Here, you can discover what's possible…you can shape what's probable…This is where the future dawns…

Imagine that you're sitting in a magic theater. You have control behind the spotlight, and you can choose whatever you'd like to illuminate…The light illuminates possibilities in the future, and you can shape what takes place by simply changing the act on the stage…however you'd like to change it…This is a powerfully magic space…Take a moment to choose what you'd like to focus on…It may be this day…it may be the coming week…it may be an important event…You can focus the light in the immediate…you can focus the light in the distant future…Here, time stretches…You can focus it on issues that are personal…You can focus it on issues regarding your family, or your community, or even the world…Choose what you'd like to focus on now.

◆

Focus the beam on the particular area that you would like to explore…Create a scene…Imagine how it might unfold…Watch it on stage…Witness what's so at the moment…What's likely to unfold?…What are the currents of energy?…Let your imagination give detail to the scene…Imagine it in full detail…the different people involved…What's taking place?…How are you doing?…The mood…let yourself imagine it…Like watching previews…What unfolds?…What's the quality of energy present?…Create it…imagine it…listen deeply…sense it…feel it…Watch carefully as your imagination brings you the possibilities…Witness…

Now go back to the beginning of the scene and shape it so it unfolds in the *best* possible way…Imagine that it draws out the best in you…and it draws out the best in everyone…Let your imagination paint the most wonderful scene…It's *so* good, it glows…Feel it…let it sing…Imagine it sparkling…Imagine it unfolding in a way that is really wonderful for everyone…joyous.

◆

Imagine it in detail…feel it…Now sense what ripples out as it unfolds in this way…Witness how it affects others…See what unfolds…Notice how others experience it…Make any adjustments so that all that occurs is good for everyone, and for the earth itself.

◆

Now, enter into the scene…as though you could travel down the light and enter into the scene…be in it…Feel it unfolding around you…Feel your body inside the situation…the smells…the sounds…the atmosphere…Feel yourself in it…pretend you're there now…These events are unfolding around you…Feel the excitement awakening inside you…Feel your heart sing in this situation.

◆

Now, move into the future and look back into this time you've just been exploring…Feel as though it has *already* occurred…it's become a memory…Notice how life is *after* it has all unfolded…As you explore, if you come across anything that needs an adjustment, make the adjustments, so that all that unfolds is good for everyone it touches…If you come across any resistance, listen in…discover the story…Your intuition will offer the insight needed…Work with the vision till it settles comfortably for everyone, and everyone looks forward to it.

◆

Now you can bring these energies into your present…into your life now…Know that you're in alignment with these energies…Know that in working with these energies in this way, you've brought yourself into alignment with the possibilities…You've energized these probabilities…You intuitively will know just what is needed to make space for them to manifest…Expect this to be the case…Believe in the future…Acknowledge the very fact that you can imagine these energies *makes them real*…Imagination is the stuff probabilities are made of…Like energies attract like energies…You are drawn into these experiences…and all that is resonant with these experiences in the world is drawn toward you…Know that this is so…Notice if you are inclined to do anything to bring these energies into the world…to plant them in your life…If there's anything you want to express to another…Notice what you might do to cultivate them…Or, if there's anything you need to release to make space for them…Choose what you'll commit yourself to…Imagine doing it…Know that in doing so, you bring this energy into the world…you embody it…you open to it…

Expect the best…Offer your best…Trust the future…Just as the sun gives birth to a new day, imagination gives birth to the future…With each exhalation of breath, know that these energies move out into the world…With each inhalation of breath, you draw resonant circumstances into your experience…Trust it…Affinity is the way of the universe…

Take time to go over any insights you've gained…any choices you've made…Channel positive energy wherever it may be needed…Appreciate the gifts life offers…

Make yourself ready to come out to outer conscious levels…Finish what you're doing…Know that the energies exist, all you need do is act on them…Know that you are now in alignment with these visions, and you will intuitively act in accord with them.

In a moment, I'm going to count from one to five. At the count of five, you'll open your eyes, remembering all that you've experienced, feeling refreshed, revitalized, relaxed, and bringing with you the energies you've tapped, in full alignment with the best of your visions.

ONE—coming up slowly now…

TWO—becoming more aware of the room around you…

THREE—at the count of five, you'll open your eyes, revitalized, refreshed, and relaxed, remembering all that you've experienced, and knowing you can return to these dimensions whenever you like…

FOUR—coming up now…

FIVE!—eyes open, revitalized, refreshed, and relaxed, open heart and spirit, ready and able to act on the energies you've tapped, trusting the future.

◆6◆

Tapping Universal Energies

Meditation is one of the most effective ways to become aware of your intuition; it is the aspect of yourself that won't get you in trouble. How do you put it in charge so you can act in the best way possible amid your activities? When we can access it in the midst of daily life as well as when we are in meditation, we profoundly increase our ability to live well. Intuition resides in the realm of universality. The imagination is real; though it sounds simple, all you need to do is imagine universal energies continually moving through you. The technique of running energy does just that.

For most of us, our natural inclination is to spend our energies primarily focused on our personal lives, our trials and tribulations. We tend to forget our connection to the earth, to the sky, to each other, to the life that's constantly percolating around us. When we forget our connection, we wind up feeling drained and isolated. When we remember it, we become energized, inspired, and feel supported by and a part of all that's around us.

Running energy as an individual practice is powerful. Running energy in a group for the purpose of healing and weaving visions together is the most potent way to work with Applied Meditation.

Running Energy: Shifting Out of Ego Attachment
Running energy moves one out of personal isolation into connection. When you run energy, you experience yourself as being part of, and held by, universal energy. The process itself is simple: you just imagine the energies of the earth and sky to be constantly moving through you, just as the air continually

moves through you. Don't let its simplicity fool you; it can literally change your life.

A couple of years after I had begun working with the power of consciousness, I took a class at The Psychic Berkeley Institute where I learned this technique.[1] Until then, whenever I taught a full-day workshop, I would be so exhausted at the end of the day that I would not have the energy to cook dinner for myself. I'd just collapse into bed. The next time I had to teach an all-day workshop, it occurred to me that there was all this energy around; I needn't depend only on my own. Right before I started my class I ran energy and continued to run it throughout the day. When the workshop was over, I made dinner and went out dancing for the next four hours. The difference it made was astonishing; never again have I gotten drained from teaching because now I always run energy.

When I'm running energy I don't actually *feel* anything; it's just a picture I make up in my mind—I'm a visualizer. As with Mental Housecleaning, the results are profound and are felt in the midst of activities, not in the meditation itself. When I first applied the technique, I didn't understand why it worked: I still expended as much physical energy as I ever had. In retrospect, I can see why in the past my teaching so exhausted me. My ego had been too involved, and I had let it take a front row seat. Much of my energy was engaged with how people were hearing me, and what people thought. The fact is, I have no control over how people hear me or of what they're going to think of what I say—nor should I. All I can do is present the material in as clear a way as possible, respecting people's choices as to how they will respond. It's only natural for me to want both approval and agreement, but it confuses my clarity and drains my energy, and it certainly doesn't help people hear me any better.

Before I started running energy in my classes, if I had information that I thought would help someone with a problem, I'd restate it many different ways in order to convince them to follow my suggestions. Now when I run energy, it doesn't occur to me to try to convince anybody of anything. Instead, I find myself communicating with greater clarity and with a sense of security, knowing that's enough. My expression is precise for the very reason that I'm not caught up in the opinions of others. Running energy causes me to respect people's processes automatically because my ego is no longer separating us. If someone doesn't take my advice, that's okay, it's their choice, not mine. Clear communication occurs because my personal feelings are not clogging up the process; it isn't as though they go away, they're just no longer in the driver's seat. Running energy moves you from an individual ego-separated perspective into a spirit-connected perspective. Your feelings move into the background and your intuition comes forward.

Running energy is the single most effective technique for overcoming stress, since much stress grows out of isolation, that feeling of having to fend for yourself. It is particularly helpful in difficult situations, like being around relatives who are hard to get along with. If you run energy in the midst of such a situation you'll surprise yourself, you might actually enjoy being with them. Or you may find yourself in a conflict with your supervisor; you know that if you express all that you're feeling, negative consequences are likely to fall on you. On the other hand, you know you need to assert yourself. If you run energy, you'll find yourself intuitively knowing exactly what to do and say.

Just as running energy reduces your need for approval, it also enables you to steer clear of negative energy. You won't find yourself internalizing other people's problems. This is important especially when working with others, whether you are providing leadership, teaching, or healing. It is also useful for avoiding absorbing other people's energy. Many women suffer from this because we have been socialized to respond to other people's needs before our own. As a result, we often have fuzzy boundaries. Running energy puts everything in perspective so that one can respond to both one's own needs and those of others.

Running energy can be used as a barometer to reflect your state of being. If you find it easier to imagine the earth energy, the chances are that most of the practical affairs in your life are taken care of: your kitchen is clean, but you may frequently be bored. On the other hand, if you find it is easier to imagine the sky energy, you probably have a sink full of dirty dishes but lots of good ideas, few of which are put into action—you are scattered. Everyone needs a balance of both. If you find it hard to imagine the earth energy, then that's what you need to work on; as you do, you'll be less absentminded. If you have a lot of ideas and don't know where to start, ground yourself and you'll find you are able to focus. If you're in the midst of a project and you get stuck, bring through the energy of the sky. It will help you move on. In my experience, people who are depressed can't imagine a future that is desirable. It is understandable that they remain low, for they have nothing to look forward to. They also find it difficult to focus on the sky energy, but deliberately making an effort to do so in time brings about a change of heart. Some people have an easy time imagining both earth and sky energy, but have trouble mixing them together; invariably these people's lives feel compartmentalized. Concentrating on mixing the energies will bring about a sense of integration.

Running energy is also valuable for living in alignment with your sense of greater purpose and meaning. It enables you to stay true to your intention, making it easy to sift through and know just what you should be paying attention to, and what you shouldn't. One client who had struggled for years with bulimia would run energy whenever she felt the compulsion to purge, and thereby maintained self control. It is important to note that running energy can also be helpful in healing many bodily problems such as headaches, carpal tunnel syndrome, or even more severe conditions like epilepsy.

It's good to begin by sitting with your back straight, either in a chair or on a pillow on the floor. It's important to sit comfortably while keeping your spine as straight as possible. Running energy does not need an induction before working with it. It stands on its own.

You can, however, run energy as a substitute for going into your meditative state with your relaxation symbols. This is an especially good way to enter meditation if you tend to fall asleep while meditating. It will enable you to enter a deep state of consciousness while at the same time remaining alert. You can also use it in conjunction with your symbols, in which case, connect with the earth while relaxing your body, and connect with the sky while relaxing your mind.

The essential thing about this practice is that energy is constantly moving *through* you; you've created channels so that nothing gets stuck. When you use it in your daily life, before you start any activities take a few moments, close your eyes, and begin the energy moving. Then set the intention by telling yourself that it will continue to move through you as you go about your activities. Throughout the day, occasionally pause for a moment to focus your attention on the energies moving through you. With time, you will find that you'll automatically run energy whenever you need to.

Running energy is helpful to make meetings more effective. For example, if your group is stuck on an issue and you can't seem to bring it to resolution, stop the discussion for a few moments and have everybody draw in sky energy. Afterwards, you'll find yourselves knowing how to move forward. Similarly, if the group seems to be working all over the agenda, unable to take one thing at a time, stop and draw up earth energy and ground yourselves.

Energy Circles: Concentrating Consciousness

Meditating in a group is exponentially more potent than when you're alone. When a whole group is meditating on the same thing at the same time it becomes even more powerful. It is as though everyone's deeper experience merges, dissolving isolation and heightening people's creative and intuitive capacities. Just as our individual consciousness creates probabilities when more people focus on creating probabilities, they become much stronger. I have named this process "Energy Circles."

I developed Energy Circles as a form for collective meditation over twenty-five years ago. It is so effective that it has not changed in all these years. Energy Circles are a potent antidote to the isolation endemic in our society. Circles are an extremely effective way to unify people before everyone goes about a common task. They inspire a community spirit and invite both creativity and intuition to inform the work. The Circle causes everyone's energy to move into a deep resonance with one another which facilitates easy access to innerconsciousness.

People have been praying together for millennia. Energy Circles are similar to prayer circles. They allow people who hold different religious beliefs—or none at all—to tap the power of spirit together. The power of this form is that it offers an easy way for diverse people to come together, whether the purpose is to align energies, gain insight, channel healing, or weave vision. (For readers who would like to investigate, we can be glad that science has begun to shift. There are now many interesting studies on the impact of prayer, especially how it facilitates healing.)[2]

The form is as simple as running energy. People sit in a circle holding hands and a leader guides them into imagining earth and sky energy moving through themselves and then around the circle. Once all of this is happening, the leader brings the group's attention to the specific concerns people would like to focus on, or people take turns directing everyone's attention. It is inspiring and helpful when people share with each other what they imagined afterwards.

You can use Circles in all kinds of settings. They can be large or small—two people or hundreds; they can take as little as three or four minutes or as long as a half an hour. An Energy Circle allows us to align ourselves with our goals, energize events, and investigate situations. This investigation leads to helpful insights that illuminate strategies for addressing concerns. It is particularly powerful because, in my experience, it is virtually impossible for individuals to hide their intentions from psychic perception. So if ever you're in a quandary about what or whom to trust in a situation, an Energy Circle will provide helpful information.

Energy Circles can be used to start a meeting or any kind of group activity, especially planning. It takes only a few minutes, yet will shorten your meeting overall because it establishes an energetic coherence enabling people to work together more effectively. I was in a group that was to do an all-day workshop and, rather than having the usual drawn-out discussion in planning an event like this, we did a Circle. Every few moments one of us would throw out a question like, "How many people are there?" "What's the mood in the room?" "What are the different roles each of us is playing?" After the Circle, we each shared what we had imagined—our visions wove together. Clear patterns emerged and we planned the day in about half an hour rather than the usual two or three hours. It also got all of us into alignment of shared purpose, setting the stage for shared leadership that lifted everyone up. Needless to say, the workshop was a great success.

If you are under a tight time schedule, taking a moment to begin with a Circle assures ending exactly when necessary. There are many times when I have done this and the meeting ends precisely when we said it would—not a minute under or over. Circles set in place a magical field in which to operate.

They are also great for opening a conference to set collective intention and move into coherence from the start. Large gatherings generate great energy. Yet often they are accompanied with a deflated feeling at the end when people are getting ready to return to their separate lives. Closing with a Circle channels the power generated by the conference, and bridges the gap between it and people's individual lives. It makes it possible for all that was shared and the power created by the conference to be carried back easily into participants' lives. (If you are in a setting where people would be reticent to Run Energy or hold hands, it is still possible to lead a reflection exercise which will augment the purpose of the gathering.)

Energy Circles As Life-Support Systems

Energy Circles can qualitatively change one's life when used on a regular basis. They have been the central component in my weekly Applied Meditation support groups for over twenty-five years. Working consistently with one another for a length of time, we've come to develop an entirely new kind of relationship. We're intuitively attuned to each other, an attunement that grows with time—an experience of knowing people in a wholly different way. We witness one another's transformation from the inside out, instead of the other way around. Doing Circle work supports maintaining well-being no matter how challenging one's life becomes. They are also beneficial because using them clarifies what is most important to you and what is a positive approach for the issues you really care about. Circles become an invaluable resource for finding positive points of reference, which in turn creates an upbeat approach to life. They also make one set intention that helps you stay on track in the midst of daily activity.

Circles have become the major source of support in my life. In fact, if it weren't for them this book would never have been written. The effects of energizing and the insights gained are extremely helpful. For instance, my cat Madeline once developed a limp that I hoped would go away by itself. After a couple of days, it was still bothering her so I made an appointment with her vet following the next day's Circle. When I returned home, she was prancing around as if nothing had ever happened. Stories like this begin to pile up when you do work with Circles. In addition to the mysterious ways that healing and intuition show up in Circle, having the opportunity to view the creativity and humor intrinsic to innerconsciousness is inspiring in and of itself. It lightens the heart. The sacred does not always have to be somber.

Just as important to me is the uncanny sensation I get in the Circle itself, as if I'm being fully supported by the energy—suspended in it. For the duration of the Circle it feels as though I'm relieved of carrying my own weight. Sometimes it feels as if the whole room fills up with energy. Once, right in the middle of a Circle, an unopened bottle of wine sitting on the table next to us popped its cork. To me, it feels as if this energy in which I'm suspended extends out beyond the space and time of the Circle and becomes an underlying support as I go through the activities of the week. Life gains buoyancy.

If you already meditate in a group context, start with a Circle. Otherwise, get some friends together to try it. I recommend coming together regularly because it takes time to get the hang of it, and to discover how powerful Energy Circles can be.* Working in Circles will become a potent resource for healing and

---

* If you would like help connecting with others in your area for doing Energy Circle work, please contact us at circlework@toolsforchange.org.

insight, as well as boosting your confidence in the intuitive power of the imagination. Remember, the more you expect it to work, the more it does.

How Circles Work

When doing a Circle, sit comfortably and close enough to hold hands. Have lots of pillows around to prop up your arms and hands so you can be comfortable for the duration. (For really long exploratory Circles, some elect to lie on the floor with their heads to the center.) When you do a Circle, one person should lead. This person gets everyone imagining the earth and sky energies moving through them then moving around the Circle. The leader gives cues to each individual to take their turn asking the group to focus on specific concerns. These concerns can be personal, for loved ones, and about the larger world. Individuals can ask for as many as half a dozen issues at a time.

Each request needs to be to the point, positive, and in the present tense, or targeted to a specific time. Expressing the "whys" and "hows" is cumbersome, distracting, and evokes beta rather than deeper awareness. Before the Circle, it's good for each participant to briefly describe the general scenario of the concerns for which they will ask for energy. If you want an apartment, don't say "energy to find an apartment because I don't have enough room to do my artwork." Tell people beforehand the reasons why, and then in the Circle simply say, "I would like energy to easily acquire a spacious, affordable apartment by September first."

We frequently need help in figuring out how to state a request in brief and positive terms. Most of the time, we are more aware of what we don't want than what we do. This is another way the group can be helpful because others can help you frame a request. You may think that saying "Energy to overcome my stage-fright when I give my speech this Tuesday" is a positive frame. Someone in the group is likely to catch it, and ask you "What would that be like?" As you think about it, you might say, "Well, I'd be relaxed and eloquent." So you would ask "I would like energy to be relaxed and eloquent when I speak on housing at the City Council meeting this Tuesday."

Group members offer a fresh perspective and can help figure out how to state an issue positively, providing a vision to move toward rather being stuck in reaction. When it is difficult to find a positive vision, think of the opposite state of affairs and then make adjustments to that until you find a desirable outcome that you can ask for. If you do not arrive at any positive vision, simply ask for energy to learn from the situation and to be at peace with it. Replace words like "effortlessly" with "easily," or instead of saying "heal my headache," say "healing energy to my head that it be clear and comfortable."

You want to target the energy by full names, events, times, and locations. If you're applying for a job, name the employer, the company, the address, and the job title. If a friend is to have surgery, give her full name, and location, the part of the body (not the disease), the time of surgery, the hospital, and the surgeon's name. For example, "I would like healing energy channeled to Jennifer Burton of Santa Monica Avenue in Berkeley, particularly to her abdominal area for her surgery with Dr. Tom Blake at Highland Hospital at three o'clock this Friday; that the surgery goes smoothly, is successful and Jennifer Burton has a speedy and full recovery." (Avoid saying: "with no complications.") If you don't have all the information, simply give what you do have. It may seem cumbersome to give all the details, but it's my experience that it's a lot easier to focus when the specifics are mentioned in the Circle. When the request is a long one, repeat the name of the person at the end.

When you are working with influencing probabilities that involve other people, questions arise as to whether it is ethical to use psychic energies to influence others. Here, as with the work of the Active Imagination's projections, view it as sacred. Nothing is to be sent energy with an investment that it is the *only* way it should come to pass. Approach all requests with humility and openness. Hold the intention that only those requests that are beneficial to all manifest.

You have to be careful when energy requests involve someone else. For instance, if you are asking for energy to deepen a friendship, you need to respect the autonomy of the other person, so end it with "in a way that is mutually beneficial." It is important to put forward any request concerning others in the spirit of respecting everyone's free will, and intend that only what is agreeable to everyone manifest.

Although it is ethical when you value the free will of your equals, asking only for mutually beneficial results, I do feel that it is appropriate to energize things with the spirit of a "should" when you're working with a situation in which the other person is in a more powerful position specific to your problem. It is okay to energize that your landlord remember your leaky faucet, or that your surgeon be clear and coordinated. For example, one evening we did an Energy Circle for the purpose of channeling energy to a judge to give lenient sentences to anti-nuclear protestors for civil disobedience. Five hundred people had been arrested, and when the judge began levying sentences everyone was startled at how stiff they were. The day after our Circle, his sentencing greatly relaxed. On the other hand, energizing your friend to call you or lend you money with a "should" behind it is inappropriate.

You can ask for energy for many issues. Because of the simultaneity of inner-consciousness, it doesn't take long to focus on each request (maybe ten seconds or the duration of three full breaths). In my support groups, there are usually about five of us and each of us addresses about six to eight different concerns. It takes an average of twenty minutes for the whole Circle to be completed. People usually write down each of their requests, and when it is their turn, they open their eyes and read them. This is so you don't have to think about how to say it when you are in the meditative state. It also gives you a journal in which you can write feedback and refer back to it later. This will prove to be another resource for developing your appreciation for inner powers.

You can ask for the same thing week after week. One would expect this to be boring, but to the contrary, it is a very interesting way of tracking the progress of an issue. If you have multiple requests, put them in a sequence from the general to the specific. For example, if you're asking to be calm and clear and you are also asking to state your case as well as possible in court, ask in that order. In one Circle, occasionally people would come up blank not knowing what they wanted to ask for. If this ever happens to you, look over some of the affirmations in each of the chapters and see what speaks to you. This will help you find both the issues and provide ways to frame concerns in a positive manner. You can ask for energy on anything. Think of a challenge you would like support in, or a new habit you would like to reinforce, or a goal you are aiming for. Channel energy to your neighborhood or peace in the world—the sky is the limit!

Psychic energy knows no boundaries, so we must create them. It is important to focus on *one* issue at a time, re-centering between issues, and one person at a time; otherwise the energy from the last person or issue gets carried over to the next. Re-centering is simple, it just means letting go of what you were imagining and focusing on the energy moving around the circle or on your breath. If you're channeling healing energy to someone, she doesn't need the residues of the energy for the job you just focused on. Re-centering only takes a moment, but you need to remember to do it. If you have more than one request to be energized, it's necessary to ask for one thing—be silent for a few moments to give people time to imagine it. Take a few breaths or imagine the energy moving around the Circle twice, and then suggest that people re-center, and proceed with your next request.

When moving from one person to the next in the Circle, there should be a few moments between each person's speaking so that people can clear and ready themselves to focus on the next person. It is good for the leader to reinforce the process by saying something like "grounded and open, earth and sky energies moving around and around…" Then the leader invites the next person to take a turn. This helps both maintain the momentum and gives people a moment to re-center themselves before moving their attention to the next person.

When you are making your requests, consciously imagine yourself receptive to the energy. In our culture, many of us feel we must fend for ourselves and that we don't deserve support. This belief effectively bars us from receiving the support we need. Channeling energy, as with all work with innerconsciousness, follows intention.

Channeling energy simply means focusing one's consciousness. Consciousness itself is energy. But it is important to think of it as *channeling* energy—universal energy. *Do not think of it as sending your energy; you need your energy, and others don't.* A while ago, a counselor who worked primarily with people's emotions joined one of my groups. The first few Circles exhausted her. When it was pointed out that she was to channel energy—as opposed to "personally being there" for each person—she found Circles energizing rather than draining.

During the Circle, as with individual meditation, your beta consciousness is likely to discount what is occurring—it may seem hokey—that's okay, just go through the motions anyway. The only thing happening in an Energy Circle is that everyone is focusing their attention simultaneously. After you've experienced the power of Circles, the messages of your beta mind will subside.

Everyone has her own individual way of channeling and focusing energy. Some people experience a knowing which has no form, others experience bodily sensations, some hear song or tones, many visualize colors, or symbols, or miniature dramas. In whatever way you imagine a positive outcome for each request, this is what's right for you. Trust whatever occurs and play with it—if you get an image or a sensation, *embellish* upon it. If none comes to mind, create one and work with that. Your first impression is like the outlines in a coloring book—when you color it in, it comes to life. Trust your process, remember that making it up versus having it come to you are equivalent processes when working with innerconsciousness.

If you ever imagine a scene or have sensations that do not feel good to you, that is, when things don't seem to be moving in a positive direction, it is important to try to shift it as best you can so that you reorient the probabilities. Don't come down on yourself if you can't come up with a positive outcome—it's not your fault. You are intuiting that the conditions in the given situation are simply not ready and able to change. This doesn't mean the situation will remain negative—you also may have a limited idea of what is positive. Whenever you imagine constricted energy in a Circle, simply do what you can to create movement. When you are working on shifting the energies you have tuned in on, you might find that you do not have enough time to complete the process before the next request. If this happens, at the end of the Circle go back and complete your work, then remember to re-center yourself before you open your eyes so that you do not carry that energy with you after the Circle. If you change the negative imagery—moving to a positive outcome—after the Circle share how you worked with the images and sensations. What you did with them will often be significant—symbolically representing a positive approach the individual can take. Refrain from judging whether something is accurate in these dimensions; you don't know. And it is important to note that the subjective world is not the same as our objective experience. Meaning is usually found by the person who asked, not the one who channeled.

After the Circle, it is good to share what each of you imagined. This sharing is always delightful. People love to hear issues about which they care deeply imagined in a positive light. If you work with Energy Circles in this way it won't take long before you experience the psychic nature of the imagination. Afterwards, you will feel as if all that had happened was just in your own head, with no connection to the outside world. It is only by taking the risk and expressing what happened that you get validation for your intuition. When sharing afterwards, it helps to take turns giving feedback to one person at a time. The person who receives feedback first starts by listing the different things she asked for. This often jogs memory. Frequently, more information comes to people in the process of describing what happened in the Circle;

that's okay too. If your imagination "feels" rather than "sees," make yourself describe what you felt even though it might be hard to put into words. This will be helpful to the recipient, for insights often come in the process of articulating how something felt.

In the sharing after the Circle, you'll discover in what ways your experience is significant to the receiver of the energy. For example, Janet was asking for energy to feel good while working. Clara had imagined her smelling roses in the midst of her work. When asked what color the roses were, Clara said they were orange. Janet then told the group that the owner had just brought orange roses and placed them on all the tables in the restaurant where she worked. This was very validating for Clara, enabling her to trust her intuition that much more, and it was helpful to Janet as an idea she could use to maintain her well-being while working. When Clara had seen the roses, she didn't feel there was anything particularly significant about them; one never discovers the significance of one's imagining in the midst of the Circle—that only comes later through the feedback process. It may take a while before you become aware of what is going on in the Circle and are able to articulate it. Give yourself time to become comfortable with the process. Also keep in mind that the language of innerconsciousness is symbolic and chock full of metaphor.

I must add that the point of Energy Circle work is not to prove your intuitive powers but to align energy, fuel probabilities, and gain insight. They are not a game; they are sacred. When you work with them, you'll be able to reclaim the great powers that are our birthright—they are not extraordinary, they offer nothing less than reconnecting with the fullness of our humanity.

I think Circles are the best way to experience the power of the imagination. The more you experience it working, the more you'll believe it will work again, and subsequently, the more your powers are enhanced. Most of us can more readily come up with lots of issues in life to complain about and not as many visions of what we are cultivating. Without vision, we are perpetually stuck in the mire of what we complain about. The great power of Energy Circles is that they provide a way for creating vision and further ways to weave our visions together. Given how isolated many of us feel, they are a powerful way to reclaim our interconnections. For it is in meditation that we feel ourselves embedded in the greater reality of *all that is*. When we come together in these states of awareness, we heal ourselves and our communities.

Energy Circle

*The person designated to begin the Circle can suggest an approxima-
tion of the following.*

Focusing on your breathing, breathing with your belly, breathing in calming energy, gathering any tensions and distractions,
breathing them out and down your grounding cord...sinking your
grounding cord down into the center of the earth, all the way
down through all the layers of the earth...letting your grounding
cord carry any tensions, any distractions into the ground to be
transformed by the earth...

Imagine that we are all a circle of trees—roots intermingling in
the ground, drawing up earth energies, up our grounding cords, up
our roots, into our bodies...feeling the earth energy in our bodies...feeling our connection to the earth, feeling attuned to the
substance of which we're made...feeling attuned to our
bodies...feeling the support of the earth below us, the nurturing
energy of the earth, focused and relaxed...Draw on the great wisdom of the earth which has witnessed all of history...Earth energy
offers sustenance and courage...Feel Earth energy move through,
magnetic connection between ourselves and the earth...held by
the earth...Breathing with the earth...

As we continue to breathe with the earth, let us move our
attention to the sky to the air around us, as trees reach to the sky,
feel the air around us, be aware of the vast sky above us, the patterns of weather, the radiant sun...the luminous moon...the planets...the millions of stars...the whole sky...Open to the vastness of
the skies. Imagine that these energies drop down through the tops

of our heads. Bring through the energy of the sky into our bodies, mixing it with the energy of the earth, let it move in and out continually, just as air moves in and out continually. However you imagine this to occur, feel yourself as open on the inside as the skies above…Feel possibility, sky energy brings with it the spirit of the future, creativity, fresh perspectives…open to it. As it moves through you, it cleanses and clears you…As the energy continues to move through us in this manner, imagine it moves around the circle, as though it were moving in your left hand and out your right hand…around and around, potent energy, magnetic energy…building momentum as it moves around and around, getting stronger and stronger…Feel the pulse of the energy…the life of the universal energies moving around the circle, the energies of the earth and sky moving through us…wisdom of the past, possibilities of the future all here now…energy moving around and around…

This energy supports each of us…it brings insights…It is the stuff probabilities are made of…energy moving around and around…energy that will continue to move around as we focus it on different issues to gain insight and align ourselves with the best of possibilities…energizing the probabilities that benefit all beings…powerful energies moving around and around, gaining momentum…

Now the leader can suggest to the first person that she state what she would like energized. Then the first person asks one request at a time, saying "thank you, now re-center" after a moment of silence, before going on to the next. After that person's requests have been energized, the next person can imagine the energy moving around the Circle a couple of times and then say the following.

Re-center yourselves…clear your awareness…feel the energy of the earth and sky moving through you…moving around the circle…in one and out the other…around and around…powerful energy.

Then she can ask for whatever she wants energy focused on; then the next person does the same thing. Proceeding all the way around the circle in the same manner, going through the clearing process each time (i.e., when the next person to ask for energy is finished sending energy to the person before her, she leads the group in clearing their minds and feeling the energy continuing to move around the circle). When the last person's (the leader's) requests have been energized, the first person who requested energy can lead the following ending process.

Re-centering yourselves…feeling the energy moving around the circle…go back over in your awareness what you sensed each time you channeled energy for each of us…Finish anything you did not have time to finish earlier, having your last sensation be a positive one…Take as much time as you need…

Know that the energy we've generated will continue to move as we move on…Open your eyes when you're feeling ready and inclined.

Opening a Meeting or Group Planning

Either have someone read or ad lib an approximation to this. To begin, use the first three paragraphs of the Energy Circle meditation and then continue with the following, starting after the pause marks. If the group is uncomfortable holding hands or running energy, sit in silence with eyes closed and substitute the next paragraph for the Energy Circle part. Elaborate or shorten to suit your group's sensibilities. Also see meditations designed for group use in Chapter Eleven.

For group planning, replace the second paragraph about the agenda with the suggestion that everyone imagine the future event(s) as though they were unfolding right now in their mind's eye. Set the context by naming some specific plans or times in the future. Then suggest that each person around the circle ask a pertinent question, one at a time, with three breaths of silent time in between (e.g. What is the atmosphere?

What are each of us doing? What roles do the different people play? How does every-thing unfold? How many people are there? What are they doing? What is happen-ing to us a year from now?). When finished, read the rest of the meditation. After the Circle, share how each of you imagined the event. You may want to do this by speak-ing one at a time without interruption, and then discussing it later after everyone has had a chance to share. This will insure not losing any insights. (Obviously this med-itation can also be easily adapted for opening a conference.)

Let our silence give us the space we need to adjust ourselves to the tasks at hand. Feel the energy we create together in this room...letting ourselves settle into being together, affirming our common concerns...Feeling our collective power...feeling what connects us. However you imagine it, align yourself with our shared intention...Feel yourself supported by and supporting the group...as though we breathe together...We create a field of energy that lifts each and all of us up.

◆

Now focus on what draws us together today, our common purpose...what brings us together...what goals we share...Notice what will strengthen our work together...Breathe energy into our bonds...powerful...Be aware if there is any-thing coming up that needs addressing, that is keeping our energies from unify-ing. Decide when and how to work on this issue...Imagine us moving through our work creatively and efficiently.

Go over the agenda in your mind. *[Name items on the agenda slowly.]* See us working through issues with ease and creativity, making clear decisions, har-nessing and organizing our energies for our shared tasks. Sense how all this is happening...Imagine that we tap into our collective genius and release great team spirit.

◆

Imagine us all working together in an atmosphere of warmth and mutual respect.

◆

Sense the timing being smooth and easy...Sense everyone energized, feeling good about our shared work, a renewed, reenergized commitment to our shared purpose, feel the spirit of our group...See ourselves succeeding in our overall goals. Notice what needs to happen for this to occur...

Review your feelings/thoughts, any choices you've made, and open your eyes when you feel inclined, knowing that this energy will continue to be present, enabling us to fully cooperate and work together creatively.

Conference Closing

Use portions of Energy Circle Meditation that are appropriate and proceed with the following.

Remember your choice to come here...Remember your arrival, everyone from different places coming together to share, to learn, to grow...Go over in your mind's eye the events that have transpired, what has happened between us...the collective power we've created.

◆

You may want to name some of the specific activities now.

Remember the connections you made...the leaps of understanding you experienced...what inspired you...what still needs work...Remember the sparks in you, between you, among us.

◆

Now imagine these sparks becoming little seeds which we can each plant in our own communities...Imagine that all we've shared here, all that's grown out of our collective experience takes root in each of our communities…And it grows even bigger than it is now. Envision it.

◆

Notice what you personally want to do to carry on…Choose what you will commit yourself to in cultivating all that we've begun together…Notice how you can make space for this new growth to take place…Notice what support you have for this, both here and at home.

◆

Imagine the ripple effect of all our work…Feel how the energy we share transcends space and time. Feel our collective power…It creates a pool of support we can dip into whenever we need to replenish our spirits. Feel our collective commitment—it transcends space and time; it always feeds our spirits…and we have the power to create change.

◆

Know this energy continues to be present. You can open your eyes when you are so inclined.

Running Energy: Centering for the Day (5 minutes)

Track 3

Make yourself comfortable sitting with your back straight…Focus on your breath…Move your attention to the area around the base of your spine…Feel the energy there…Sense a core of magnetic energy there…Imagine as though, as you exhale, you were to drop a cord of energy from this center down through the floor…all the way down…down into the earth…Imagine that this cord of energy sinks down through the soil…through the clay…through the underground waters…deeper and deeper through all the layers of the earth…each exhalation carrying it down further and further…way down until it settles…in the center...like an anchor...

Imagine there's a magnetic connection between your center and the molten center of the earth...Imagine as though gravity were to absorb any tensions or distractions...anything you want to release and transform you can breathe it out and gravity draws it down and it is transformed in the earth, making nutrients for new life...Breathe out anything you want to release...

This energy cord can also bring earth energies up into your body...just like the trees draw nutrients directly into themselves...Imagine pulling up earth energy like you had roots...draw earth energy up into your body...however you experience this...Feel earth energy...feel it coming up into you and moving through your whole body...grounding you in this present moment...present in your body...focused...relaxed...relaxing into the support of the earth...Feel it...This is your grounding cord. Whenever you ground yourself in this way, you can release anything to be transformed, and you can draw up earth energy...the earth that has witnessed all of history...When you draw up earth energy you always find yourself fully present...wise...focused...relaxed...supported with all the endurance, patience and courage that you need in the activities before you. When you are grounded you are centered...

Now bring to your awareness the great spacious skies...the stars...the planets...the radiance of the sun...the magnetism of the moon...the great skies...The patterns of weather...the winds...the rains...the snows...the clouds...the breezes...all the patterns of weather...Imagine sky energy funneling down into the top of your head...pouring into your body...moving through your whole body...mingling with the energy of the earth and moving back out again...either out through the top of your head, or out your hands or your feet, or out the grounding cord...Let the sky energy come in and out continually just as breath moves in and out...Imagine it...however you experience it...sense it...feel it...Feel yourself as spacious inside as the skies above...sky and earth mixing together inside as they do all around you…Whenever you bring sky energies through you in this way, you open to the vast possibilities that life offers…Clear…creative…open…insightful…

Tell yourself that both the earth and the sky energy will continue to move through you as it's now moving through you throughout this day. Imagine moving through the day grounded, focused and clear. Expect this…

Take time now to do any inner work…Open your eyes when you're ready and inclined…Take as much time as you like…When you open your eyes, know that you'll continue to be centered in this way throughout the day, more than equal to the challenges before you.

·7·

We're All Healers

With the mystification of innerconsciousness came the mystification of the healing process. The separation of body and mind became complete. By repossessing our inner selves, we repossess our healing powers. Scientific thinking has made all that is mysterious become invisible. The regenerative healing process is one of life's greatest mysteries. To understand it rationally is like trying to understand colors with your ears. But just as your eyes know color, your deeper self knows healing. Traditional healers throughout the ages have entered trance states to understand and heal ailments. It is in our interest to stop regarding such behavior as "primitive." Indigenous healers have long taught that life is healthy when in equilibrium, and disease is a result of imbalance in the material, emotional, and spiritual realms. They treat the whole person, family, or community by restoring balance to the situation.

Health results from living in harmony with yourself and your environment. To be healthy is to be in sync with life: all the rhythms harmonizing, breath with bodily functions, bodily functions with life activities, and life activities in rhythm with the cycles of the earth. But it is not exactly easy to be in sync living in our modern technological world. We are lucky if we can just keep up. We can no longer take for granted that the air is clean, or that our water is drinkable, or that food will give our body sustenance. It is as though our society itself is carcinogenic. The most pervasive health problems in the U.S. are related to stress and to what we take into our bodies.

Studies have shown that between 60 and 90 percent of the population's visits to the doctor are stress-related.[1] Our body's natural self-protective system, the immune system, is suppressed by the presence of chronic stress[2] and environmental toxins, compounding our susceptibility to illness. Rather than addressing the causes of stress and disease, in order to prevent illness or regain balance, three billion prescriptions are dispensed each year.[3] It is as if the medical system has forgotten the wisdom of the healers.

Instead of cleaning up the environment or supporting us to live healthy lives, high-tech medicine proposes to replace worn-out body parts, genetically screen out the "weakest" of us,[4] or even to reengineer us to adapt to unsafe environmental conditions![5]

Health is a sociopolitical issue, not a private one. What is called for is a slowing down so that reflection is an intrinsic part of our culture, cleaning up our environment, and creating an accessible health-care system focused on healing. But as we work toward that goal, we need to maintain our health as best we can. Understanding the entwined relationship of body and mind is crucial to our healing; innerconsciousness has a major impact on the state of our bodies, regardless of our participation with the process. Your conscious participation in the processes perpetually transpiring between your body and mind may have more impact on your health and well-being than any other single change you choose to make in your life. To mystify the innerconsciousness is to destroy the mysterious. When we dip into our psyches, we are no longer victims. We become participants; we become healers, for innerconsciousness is where both healing wisdom and energy reside.

From Machines to Living Beings

In the same way that the advent of rationalism took life out of the objective world, justifying its exploitation; so too the body has became divorced from the mind to become a machine that only the mechanic doctor understands.[6] You, who inhabit the body, are seen as and treated as though you have nothing to do with the causes of disease, and further, nothing to do with the healing process either. What is more, environmental influences are rarely considered in the analysis at all. Most of us are led to believe that only the all-powerful doctor is able to save the day. The patient is assumed to have no ability to make a judgment about what's in the body's best interest. I don't mean to paint a picture that blames individual doctors. My intention is to examine the way that overdependence on allopathic medicine can be a roadblock to healing. In the past two decades, there has been well-documented medical research on the influence that spirit and matter, or mind and body, have on one another and the power of innerconsciousness for healing. Unfortunately, the medical mainstream continues to operate as though this is not the case.

In our culture, physicians enjoy more moral authority than any other professional group. If we are to reclaim our own healing abilities, it is essential to wrest our belief away from the medical model and reclaim the natural healing powers that are our birthright. Given both the enormous costs of medical care and its limited orientation, it is not clear that the present "health-care" system isn't creating more problems than it is solving:

> The pain, dysfunction, disability, and anguish resulting from technical medical intervention now rival the morbidity due to traffic and industrial accidents and even war-related activities, and make the impact of medicine one of the most rapidly spreading epidemics of our time.[7]
>
> There are 2,000 deaths/year from unnecessary surgery; 7,000 deaths/year from medication errors in hospitals; 20,000 deaths/year from other errors in hospitals; 80,000 deaths/year from infections in hospitals; 106,000 deaths/year from non-error, adverse effects of medications—these total up to 225,000 deaths per year in the U.S. from iatrogenic causes which ranks these deaths as the No. 3 killer.[8]

In fact, there is evidence that in many ways, technical medical interventions have little or no positive effect on populations:

> Life expectancy is no greater in regions that have more intensive medical care, the researchers find, and Medicare surveys find that their quality of care is no better…Another recent study, on the distribution of newborn intensive-care specialists and the death rate among infants, reached a similar conclusion. A tripling of the numbers of these specialists did not result in any improvement in infant mortality.[9]

The medical model defines health as the absence of disease, which gives you about as much understanding of it as defining exercise as the absence of rest. With the concentration on disease, health itself recedes over the horizon. It's as if the medical establishment, in the face of continual burning, studied all the most efficient means of performing skin grafts, rather than simply turning off the heat.

The complexity of the body/mind has been reduced to a series of mechanical parts often treated as being unrelated. If the body/mind goes wrong, the medical establishment introduces a new ingredient or replaces some part.

> Following the Cartesian approach (the idea that the body is a machine that can be understood completely in terms of the arrangement and functioning of its parts), medical science has limited itself to the attempt of understanding the biological mechanisms involved in an injury to various parts of the body. These mechanisms are studied from the point of view of cellular and molecular biology, leaving out all influences of non-biological circumstances on biological processes.[10]

Television and especially advertising reinforces this image of the human organism—that of a machine which is prone to failure unless supervised by the medical system and treated with high technology interventions. The notion of the body's inherent healing power and tendency to stay healthy is not communicated, and trust in one's own healing power is not promoted.

Researchers even claim that now that they have successfully sequenced the entire human genetic code, they can predict and cure all diseases.[11] From this point of view, there is no focus on human beings living in balance with their environment while listening intuitively to their bodies. Neither is there any emphasis on our individual participation with the healing process itself.

The concept of "spontaneous remission" does not invite an inquiry into the power of healing but instead makes it sound as though healing just happened by chance. Any transformation that has taken place in the ailing person's heart, soul, and/or life remains invisible. This not only disempowers the individual, it disempowers us all, for it reinforces the attitude that there can be no cure except through medical intervention. Medical models promote beliefs that encourage suspicion of the body and of nature—the intrinsic healing powers of life itself are systematically ignored. Our most sacred process of giving birth has been pathologized, as these days, labor is often looked upon as if it were a disease. And lastly, our deaths—it is as though medicine's ultimate goal is to eliminate this natural outcome of the life cycle. The greatest expenditures of the "health-care" system are in the last weeks of life.

Disease is viewed as an enemy to be conquered, and medical scientists pursue the Utopian ideal of eliminating, eventually, all diseases through the application of biomedical research.[12] We've been taught to regard illness as a problem that only doctors have the expertise to understand and solve. Our complaint is often diagnosed with a four-syllable word that we can't even pronounce, but we are given a play-by-play account of the progression of destruction the illness is likely to take through our bodies. We get all the appropriate messages to keep us ill; *knowing precisely what to expect, our bodies respond with disease.*

One cannot be healthy without being life-affirming; one cannot be life-affirming and at the same time deny death. Life and death are united opposites; we cannot have one without the other.

In fact it is our *belief* that is key to our health. For example it is common knowledge that the placebo effect is due to the patient's belief in the efficacy of treatment.

> In 75 percent of all cases the usefulness of the prescribed medication is not the active principles but in the faith that the patients have in the technology. In other ages people *believed* in miracles; today they *believe* in science, and so the medical ritual takes on the appropriate guise.[13]
>
> Approximately 80 percent of the response to [anti-depressant] medication was duplicated in placebo control groups…Improvement at the highest doses of medication was not different from improvement at the lowest doses. The proportion of the drug response duplicated by placebo was significantly greater than the medication.[14]

But how many diseases are caused or made worse from negative images given by medical practitioners? Recent studies have shown that illness can be brought on by a loyal response to the doctor's suggestions and predictions regarding one's health:

> Another study looked at the following train of events. They examined 4,000 people who were feeling well and confirmed that 30 percent were clearly ill without being aware of it, and that 60 percent had latent diseases to which they were well

adjusted. Only 10 percent were in clinically good health. The authors' conclusion: when these people who were feeling fine were informed of their clinical profile, that was all it took to transform 90 percent of them into patients and bring on in most of them the appearance or worsening of symptoms that they had ignored up to then.[15]

We have all heard stories of doctors who tell patients that they have only two months to live. The effect of such an announcement on the patient can set in motion a self-fulfilling prophecy which may justify the doctor's prognosis but which convinces the patient that she will become increasingly ill. Andrew Weil, in *Spontaneous Healing*, talks about a patient whose doctor diagnosed her with MS and immediately ordered a wheelchair so that she could practice sitting in it![16]

We can begin our return to health by becoming aware of the beliefs that we hold. If we pull ourselves out from under the spell of the all-knowing doctor, we can begin to believe in ourselves. Trusting the resilience of life and reclaiming our healing process offers the greatest health insurance yet.

Making Miracles Commonplace

One of the most significant changes in my life since I've come to learn how to work with the power of consciousness has been my own health. I used to feel that whenever I got sick it was something that had happened *to* me. I had to follow the doctor's instructions, go to bed, take medication, and wait until my illness left. I used to be sick an average of ten days a year. Now, I virtually never get sick for more than a day at a time. If I get the flu, I participate in it, passing it through my body very rapidly. I've learned that I'm not a victim of whatever illnesses cross my path. Instead, I can listen to my body, participate with my healing processes, or avoid responding to potential threats altogether.

Meditation slows us down, reduces stress, and creates an acutely receptive state of awareness through which we can sense the subtle messages of our bodies. The Inner Witness reveals when we are in balance and when we are not. All that is needed is to stop, breathe, and pay attention; then we can respond to messages our bodies give us. When you can imagine what you want, that is, feel what it would actually be like; you can then project this with the Active Imagination. When you cannot do this, an insight is called for, so you then engage the Receptive Imagination, ask questions, and then respond to the information you get. Your body can respond to the messages you give it, and you can respond to the messages your body gives you.

When I was younger, I had a runny nose throughout each winter. That was a given state of affairs for me. During the winter after I learned the techniques of Silva Mind Control, when my sinuses started to act up I meditated, imagining my mucous membranes drying. I pictured that it was like cotton evaporating. I did this for only four or five times. My sinuses cleared up, and I haven't had this problem ever since. Until I learned to work with my imagination, I continually gave my body the message: "This runny nose will be here all winter," it had never occurred to me to imagine the problem clearing up.

Effecting change with the power of consciousness works in direct proportion to how strongly you believe that it will work. As I described in Chapter Five, the more you believe, the less confusing your inner messages will be; clear messages are directives for your body to respond to. The catch is that your belief comes from your experience of success. So I recommend you begin by doing modest experiments, ones that have little emotional charge in which it is easy to give yourself clear messages. I focused on avoiding mosquito bites, imagining an impenetrable wall around me that the mosquitoes could not get through. That didn't work—the mosquitoes didn't seem to see the wall. I tried another approach. I imagined talking to my skin, telling it that when the mosquitoes came, that it and the rest of my body would be happier if we let them come and go without responding. This tack was successful, from then on whenever a mosquito bit me, a welt would appear for perhaps twenty minutes and then go away, and the bites never itched. It is experiences like this that build confidence in the power of innerconsciousness.

The more you experience success, the stronger your faith in the power of your body/mind becomes—remember, the agent of change is belief. Eventually, with the accumulation of experience you'll find yourself spontaneously giving clear messages—without premeditation—always expecting what you want. Instead of being a victim to whatever dangers may cross your path, you will be able to maintain your power.

Expecting what you want does not mean that you get to transform into having the body all of us have been conditioned to strive for. Each of our bodies has differing abilities, yet the cultural messages are to be strong or beautiful, thin, not too short and not to tall. Health doesn't mean conforming to the norm, but to be in alignment with the resilient life force energies moving through our bodies. To reclaim healing powers, we each need to affirm who we are and work *with* our bodies. Striving to be something one is not only takes one further away from the attunement needed to maintain good health. With the Inner Witness present, you will be able to tell if you have succumbed to the conditioning that diminishes the integrity of your body. If you do, you can use Mental Housecleaning to shift into a healthier perspective. Coming from an appreciation of our bodies is necessary if we are to work with the great healing powers that reside within.

Three years after I began meditating, I had a profound experience that revealed the degree to which I had come to know the power of the body/mind and how much I had *regained* mine. I was moving a refrigerator on a dolly, pulling it backwards down a driveway into the street. The driveway, rather than the gradual decline I had expected, moved from sidewalk level to street level very quickly. All of a sudden, the refrigerator was pushing me—I wasn't pulling it—and then I tripped on a four-by-four. As I fell, I instantaneously called on healing powers. One would expect that the leverage created by the bars of the dolly and the corner of the four-by-four would have snapped the bones of my legs under the impact of the refrigerator. If I had responded with fear, expecting to hurt myself, my body would have responded by receiving the full impact and my legs would have been crushed. Instead, when I landed on the pavement I felt an incredible mushroom of energy holding up the refrigerator. Afterwards, my legs didn't hurt and that energy continued to buzz through me for the rest of the move we were making that day—as if I'd had a few cappuccinos.

A friend of mine had a similar experience on his motorcycle. He made a left turn in downtown traffic, not seeing a car coming toward him—nor did the driver see him. When my friend realized what was happening, he stopped the bike and put his foot down on the pavement while screaming at the driver. The driver hit his brakes and his front tire stopped on top of my friend's left foot. The moment my friend saw the car approach his foot he flashed a feeling/sense through his mind: "My foot is safe and sound and will stay healthy and strong." When the driver realized what had happened, he backed up and the tire rolled off my friend's foot. He shook it gingerly, discovered that his foot was not even sore, and then proceeded to drive on. At home later, he took off his shoe and sock and found that his foot was not even bruised.

What is vital to understand about each of these examples is that the last and prevailing message the body received was positive. Trusting the power of the body/mind to maintain itself leaves no space for the idea of being victimized. In a study of one hundred and fifty-two cancer patients "the most significant finding was that a positive attitude toward treatment was a better predictor of response to treatment than was the severity of the disease." The Simontons, who conducted this study, pioneered working with cancer by visualization; their patients have a survival rate twice the national norm.[17]

Whether positive or negative, our bodies are always responding to whatever images we hold in our imagination at any given moment; It is crucial to appreciate how much our bodies and minds are tied together. Notice what messages your mind is giving your body. Prevailing wisdom says: "If you have a problem, Have a drink. Got a stuffy nose? Take Seldane. Got indigestion? Take Alka Seltzer. Can't sleep? Take Sominex. Can't cope? Take Zoloft." These messages promote total distrust in the body's own ability to heal itself. We're led to believe that the innate wisdom of the body/mind simply doesn't exist.

"A drug ad denies your ability to cope. The result is that you become further separated from yourself. Your natural abilities die from lack of practice and faith in their efficacy."[18]

The multibillion-dollar diet industry coupled with the prevalence of eating disorders reflects the contempt we have for our own bodies. Instead of believing in our bodies many of us hate them because they are not the right size or shape. Most of us could use a little Mental Housecleaning.

The powers of body/mind are not exotic; it isn't as if only a few exceptional individuals are endowed with them. They sleep inside each of us and can be reawakened. Just as muscles atrophy with lack of use and exercise brings them back to life, we just need to *use* this power that each of us has. So-called miracles can become commonplace when we take the time to be *with* our body/mind and to work with the energies that reside there.

We can celebrate the fact that over the last two decades there has been a burgeoning of body/mind medicine which affirms the intimate relationship between body and mind and offers holistic approaches to health care. Mainstream medicine, however, has a long way to go before the wisdom it offers informs more than the margins of the practice. But now there are resources available to the general public that simply didn't exist twenty years ago.[19]

Hearing the Voices of Your Body

Spending time with our bodies while in meditation establishes conscious communication between body and mind. For this reason, I recommend regularly focusing on the resilience intrinsic to life that is your body's birthright. Also, scan your body with your imagination. Witness if any area is calling your attention. This need not take long but you'll find yourself able to respond to your body's needs *before* you get ill.

When you're meditating on a health problem, strive to give your body a clear message of what you want. Imagine what it would be like to be healthy in that particular area—problem-free. To find positive points of reference, think of areas in your body that are in good health, or remember times when you felt full of vitality, or a time when healing happened easily. Endeavor to transfer this positive sense into the area of distress. If you can't envision yourself healthy, then working with the Receptive Imagination will be of great benefit. Imagine going inside and visiting with the area of your body that is having difficulty. Assume that you really can do this, and further, that it makes a difference. If this is hard to do, just pretend; give yourself a placebo. Talk to your body. Comfort it; talk with it and with the ailment. *Witnessing what happens when you strive to experience the area as healthy will offer you deep insight into what is taking place.* You just have to pay close attention. When the vision of well-being you are trying to hold keeps reverting back to the status quo, then your body is not ready to heal—there is likely to be a message to attend to. In the presence of the Inner Witness you can both discover insights that help you heal, and just as importantly, you can also find peace with what is occurring in your body—make peace with yourself.

Sickness is a result of imbalance. It's a message that something needs to change to enable you to regain balance. Tune in and respond; you'll find that your life is changing for the better. With any illness or pain, your body is talking to you—you need to listen. If you keep taking aspirin for headaches, not stopping to discover why you have headaches, your body doesn't stop signaling you. Its reactions will get louder and louder until you can no longer ignore them. Down the road, you may find yourself with a condition that is much more difficult to heal.

Doctors spend their time looking for the symptoms of a disease, rarely acknowledging that illness itself is a symptom. Treating the symptom may bring comfort in the short run, but it is ultimately ineffective in resolving the problem. Our automatic reaction whenever we get sick is that something is wrong with our bodies rather than with our lives. This discounts the wisdom of our bodies, for they give us our early warning system and know just what is healthful. If being sick is thought of as being wrong, we diminish ourselves and abdicate our power. To repossess our healing powers we must repossess our illnesses.

> Might not the illness be the inevitable response of a healthy individual to a situation that is not? Aren't the digestive troubles, headaches, rheumatism, insomnia, and depressions that switchboard operators, key punch operators, assembly line workers, and electronics solderers suffer from, more than anything the 'healthy' protests of an organism that cannot adjust to the violence done to it daily, at an eight hour stretch?[20]

Ill health is an invitation for introspection. If you listen deeply you will find what is out of sync in your life. As suggested above, this can be done easily while meditating, by simply going inside your body and talking with the ailing part. Put your Receptive Imagination to work. Be inquisitive and imagine what this part of you body would say—let yourself make it up—your fantasies will tell you what is happening. You'll discover simple things, some easier to respond to than others, like needing more rest, or establishing a better eating pattern, or making a change in a relationship. The answers are often simple and may feel like something you already knew. There is a felt sense that the answer is right. The issue is what you are willing to *do* with the insight. Are you willing to act on it? If not, some negotiation is called for. Make an agreement with your body as to what you'll do about it. Some of the messages are harder to respond to— they may be about your working environment, which is usually out of your control. If this is the case, at least you've discovered the specific cause of the problem and can take protective measures against it. Maybe you're plagued with headaches and discover they're from the fumes at work. Use your imagination to find out what can be done to compensate. *Notice your inclinations* (other than telling off your boss). Maybe your head will tell you that a regular run in the countryside will be of help, or that you should get your lungs to be on guard so they can push the toxins back out before they make it into your bloodstream. Ultimately what's called for is clean air, so organize to get proper ventilation at work. But this takes time. If you listen to your inner messages, you'll know how to compensate for the problem in the meantime.

You've got to be careful not to blame yourself for getting sick and not to ignore the conditions of your life that need change. Placing all the blame on conditions outside of yourself entirely leaves you in a powerless, victim position. The way out is to get rid of the detrimental influences and at the same time discover how it is that you *collude* with them. Your internal response to an event is as important as the event itself. The clothing of two people catches on fire. One person panics, runs, and fans the flames, severely burning herself. The other remains calm and consciously chooses to roll on the ground, thus smothering the fire and ending up with only minor burns. The environment is increasingly full of substances that are hazardous to our health. Everyone exposed to carcinogenic substances does not develop cancer. No matter what is going on, despite how we may feel, we are not victims, but participants. Since we are participants, we can be creative in how we participate.

Sometimes you're getting more out of having your problem than you would from being healthy. Many times the problem itself provides a solution for something else. Ask your body what made you come down with the malady. What is the ailment protecting you from? What are you getting out of it? Your immediate reaction to this question is likely to be defensive, but blame is not the issue here. Even the worst of things have their positive side. If you allow yourself to look under the surface, you can know what is true for you. Maybe your illness offers the chance to get a much-needed rest, or alleviation from overwhelming responsibility, mourning a loss, or a way out of a seemingly irresolvable situation. When you find out what the advantages are for you, you can take steps to get your needs met in other ways. Then you'll be able to focus your energy effectively on healing yourself and your environment.

Remember to tune in to the condition of your body regularly. This needn't take long; it can be momentary in the midst of your meditative work. Notice how your body feels, where the energy seems to be—if there's too much or too little anywhere, or if the energy is getting stuck someplace. Then try to imagine balancing out. Focus on any areas that you're working toward healing, tune in, and sense how the process is going—give it a little added support. If you are working with Energy Circles, I especially recommend regularly focusing on any challenges to your health. Doing so will provide an extra energetic boost and offer insight from the other participants who will easily be able to tune in since they have no emotional charge on the issue.[21]

In meditating on healing yourself, it is good to have a framework to work with, it is helpful to find a health-care provider with whom you can collaborate. Form a partnership, assert yourself, and make the provider work *with* you, not on you. Rather than asking her what's going to happen with the illness, find out what needs to happen for your body to return to a healthy condition—what will it feel like, what will it look like? Find out exactly what transpires physiologically in the healing process as opposed to the course of disease. Give yourself positive points of reference by reading up on the subject or talking to people who have successfully healed themselves of a similar condition. Find an anatomy chart—you need to give your imagination food for thought.

Some years back, I got a toothache. I went to the dentist and was told that I had an abscess and would need to have a root canal performed, which was going to cost five hundred dollars—money I didn't have. I asked him to explain the physiology of what was occurring in my mouth—precisely what a root canal was. He was very cooperative and took the time to explain in detail what was going on. Then I told him that I wanted to try healing myself with meditation. He wasn't very optimistic, but I appreciated his giving me a chance. He drained the abscess and put in a temporary filling, saying he would give me two weeks, and if I had no further problems he would make the filling permanent, which would avoid the root canal work. I went home with a clear picture of what to imagine while I meditated. I was motivated—I didn't want to borrow five hundred dollars. So I meditated three or four times a day for the next two weeks—each time I visualized the details of my tooth healing. When I returned to the dentist the problem had disappeared and he put in a permanent filling, which has sufficed for twenty-five years. Each of us gained more respect for the body/mind's regenerative healing powers.

On another occasion, I was exposed to infectious hepatitis. I've never liked having shots and once again I wanted to prove to myself the power of my body/mind. I asked the nurse what gamma globulin shots actually do. She told me that gamma globulin is simply something that the body already produces to ward off disease. If I had little trust in my ability to protect myself, I would have gotten the shot. Instead, I wanted to exercise the powers I knew I had. I imagined my body producing gamma globulin overtime—armies were being created. I imagined little armies of gamma globulin marching through my blood and standing in formation around my liver creating an impenetrable fortress. It worked—I didn't come down with the hepatitis that I had definitely been exposed to. I once again confirmed my power to maintain my health, and thus my power was further increased. Here I am not recommending that you ignore medical opinion but only that you bring yourself and the power of consciousness into the healing process and further that you find out what healing might look like rather than be preoccupied with disease.

Your Body Is the Home of Yourself: Home Maintenance

All ailments are messages we need to hear to keep a harmonious balance in our lives. Ailments are not something wrong, but are signposts pointing to what is right. When we follow their directions, we live in health; when we ignore them, we get lost and wander around aimlessly in a hazardous environment on a collision course, getting sicker and sicker. It is our ailments that know how to live in health. Health problems are always a reflection of the innate wisdom of life itself.

In beginning your practice with meditation, use your consciousness for healing, and cultivate your patience, particularly if you have quite a number of conditions bothering you. It took time for your problems to develop, it will also take time for your body to develop and maintain healthy habits. Your body has become accustomed to the problem, and it will need time to become accustomed to the solution. It bears repeating here, honor what is true for your body, don't impose what you think it ought to be from a superficial level. For myself, I was born with a bone condition, which brings with it some disabilities. It has never occurred to me to "heal" myself of this condition. It is simply part of who I am. Each of our bodies has its own limitations. This work is not about turning us all into "superwoman" or "superman," but reclaiming our wholeness and being attuned to healing energies.

I relate to my *whole* self as conscious—not just my brain, but to every cell in my body—as possessing intelligence, as indeed it does. You don't need to explain to your cells how to replenish themselves. Consciousness moves along habitual grooves. Sometimes healing is simply a matter of re-educating your cells, letting them know the situation has changed. When your body goes through some trauma, it responds in the same way as your consciousness does. You find yourself acting as though the threat is still present because the scene remains in your theta level even though the situation has changed. Similarly, your cells store trauma and behave as if their lives are under constant assault when that is no longer the case.

This work is not a quick fix. You have to do your part in bringing about change, so keep the agreements that you've made with your body. If you don't, your body will feel duped, and will stop cooperating with you. It is the same as when a friend makes promises that she doesn't keep; eventually you get fed up and write her off. Often people discover that it's hard to keep the agreements they have made. This is because when you go inside you become aware of *all* the solutions; inside lives all-knowingness. You find out all that needs to happen to return to health, making lots of agreements. A week later, you find you haven't been keeping them. It's as if you tried to eat a banquet in one mouthful—inside there are no limitations of space and time, but in the outside world you have to contend with lots of them. If you find yourself not having kept all the agreements, next time you meditate, talk it over with the ailing part of your body and come up with a more realistic and manageable course of action so you can take it one bite at a time. Patience is likely to help.

If you have any constant problem—chronic pain, for example—tell yourself that the pain is dissolving ever so slowly, that it's *imperceptibly* getting better, and over time it'll be gone altogether. This way, you haven't let your experience of the problem become a reflection of your inability to heal it; instead, you've allowed yourself to experience the problem while *knowing* that it's continually getting better.

Another method of working on a recurring health issue is to work on it at a time when it is not immediately affecting you. Do the necessary inner work ahead of time so when the need arises you're ready for it—the same principle as working with symbols. The first day of my menstrual period I used to feel really awful. Once, I was scheduled to do a workshop on the day it was due to occur. I could not afford to be under the weather since I was working with a new group of people. So I began talking to my uterus three weeks in advance. I was feeling fine at the time so it was *believable* that I would feel fine later. And, in fact, I did.

This approach is particularly useful because when you're feeling bad, you're not inclined to meditate at all, much less convince yourself that you could feel otherwise. Remember the agent of change is belief, so you want to be in a place to project what is *believable*. Somehow you figure out how to offer yourself a placebo. Trick yourself into believing, and you change your situation.

Since your body is always responding to whatever is in your awareness at every given moment, be mindful of what you are thinking as you move through your activities. Mind/body medicine reminds us of the importance of taking responsibility for our inner dialogue because it is a continual stream of directives, which become actualized in our brains and bodies.

> Remember that the "nocebo" is equally powerful. Unfortunately, remembered wellness has a flip side. It can have negative side effects, called the nocebo (as opposed to placebo.) Our agitated minds may inappropriately trigger the fight-or-flight response in the body. Similarly, automatic negative thoughts, bad moods, and compulsive worrying eventually take up physical residence in our bodies. People who dwell on worst-case scenarios, who exaggerate risks, or who project doubt and undue worry keep the nocebo effect busy in their physiologies. They signal their brains to send help when no physical sickness is present; persuading the body to get sick when there is no biological reason sickness should occur.[22]

Notice if you're spending more time and energy thinking of the problem, being irritated and victimized by it, than you are focusing on its moving into a state of health. Your body simply is going to respond to the strongest messages you give it, and whatever you spend the most time on will have the most energy. It's hard to focus more on the solution when you're experiencing the problem, but the important thing is the prevailing last message whenever the area of concern comes to mind. If you think of the problem, always have your last image be your recovery—your sense of change, and that will be the direction in which your body goes, cutting new grooves for consciousness to move in.

Don't focus on the problem to see if it has begun to heal yet. I learned this lesson well when trying to rid myself of headaches. In Silva Mind Control, you learn that to get rid of a headache you just go into meditation and tell yourself that at the count of five your headache will be gone. So, whenever I got a headache I would do just that. Then when I returned to the outer focus of attention, it was only natural to check to see if I was successful. I had just had a headache; I knew full well what it felt like, and there it was as soon as I looked for it. It took me a while to discover what I was doing wrong. Now, whenever I get a headache I meditate and tell myself that over the next half-hour my headache would gradually dissolve. Afterwards, it is okay that my headache is still there because I know it is going to take a while to go away. In a half-hour, I am occupied with other concerns. There is no line to be drawn between success and failure, yet my headache disappears in the same amount of time it takes to digest an aspirin.

Since your body is tied to your mind, it's important to bring your beliefs into conscious awareness. They pave the road that your thoughts move over, leading them in very specific directions. Even though they are subtle, you can become fully aware of them by taking the time to bring them to light. Being mindful of what you say to yourself as you move through your activities reveals them. What you are discovering is *not* reality, but your attitude *about* reality—and that you can change. Once you become aware of a negative attitude, you can transform it into its opposite with an affirmation.

To help you uncover the defeating beliefs about your body that you need to change, ask yourself some of the following questions: Is my ability to be healthy different from that of others? Am I victimized by anything? Do I think of bodies as degrading and impure? Do I think of food as fattening or nourishing? What am I susceptible to? Am I stuck with any burdens? Do I like my body? Am I fully vulnerable to all germs I am exposed to? Think of three negative feelings about your body, then think of their opposites and notice how you can cultivate those. What do they feel like? Whatever insights you come up with will become food for your meditation work. You will find that as you take action to change these attitudes, you'll greatly increase your health and be more attuned to what is actually taking place in your body.

As in all inner work, building positive points of reference is crucial. It is of equal importance is to remember the resilience intrinsic to life. Regularly focus on the innate wisdom of your body. Build your confidence. Give yourself a placebo daily. Remember how your body has healed in the past; acknowledge the ways it does function well.

If you are struggling with a life-threatening disease, it may seem impossible to have an image of yourself as healthy. You may wish for it passionately, but expecting it is another matter. It is only possible to heal when you can sense what it would be like. It also may be the case that healing isn't about extending one's life, but about coming to peaceful terms with one's self and one's life, which in turn is a preparation for death. I don't mean to imply that being given a medical prognosis of imminent death means you are fated. Many people whom doctors "put in their graves" years ago are still alive and well. But in our youth-worshipping, death-denying culture, there is a way that we deny ourselves the ability to come to terms with the natural processes of our bodies—we will all die sometime.

If you can't imagine being well in the area of your body that is afflicted, then you can use the resources of your innerconsciousness to come to terms more easily with what is happening to you, discovering what you need in order to live in more comfort, and/or coming to a sense of completion with your life and letting go. Working with innerconsciousness offers a way to intimately know what *is* happening inside and what you need. It is truly profound when facing death. Innerconsciousness not only offers healing, it offers access to wisdom and knowing in the spiritual dimensions beyond the body.

Induction

Make yourself comfortable. Focus on your breathing…Bring to awareness your symbol for physical relaxation. Breathe through any tensions you may be feeling…Breath releases them…Let them drop into the ground…Relax into the support of the earth…Draw up nurturing earth energy into your body…Breathe. Breath carries life.

◆

When you're ready, bring to awareness your symbol for mental relaxation…Breathe. Let your breath be the breeze that clears the sky of your mind…Bring through the energy of the sky. Experience your mind opening into spacious awareness.

◆

Bring to awareness your symbol for emotional relaxation…Breathe out any feelings that are tugging at you…Acknowledge your goodness…Offer yourself some loving kindness…Feel your heart relaxing.

◆

When you are ready, bring to awareness your symbol for your creative, self-restoring center. Take a moment to acknowledge your gratitude…Acknowledge the sanctity of life.

◆

Now take time to enhance your level of awareness on your own by whatever method you choose. You can simply rest your awareness on your breath…Or you may choose to go to a relaxing place, or listen deeply to the pulse of your own heart, or any other methods that you are inclined to work with to deepen your awareness…Tell yourself you'll be fully relaxed and alert throughout this meditation.

MEDITATIONS

Beginning to finish what you're doing…You are now consciously developing the intuitive skills you have always had. You are at your creative self-restoring center—the threshold between your inner and outer being. Here the Inner Witness emerges and you discover a rich, beautiful landscape of receptivity and creativity. As you open, more and more of these energies flow through you. Just as using your muscles keeps your body strong and resilient, so too, working in your creative self-restoring center keeps your intuitive powers fully accessible and fluid and enables you to tap the wellspring of healing energies…Breathe and the Inner Witness emerges. Here you experience the calm expansive power of spacious awareness. You feel yourself as a part of the pure universal energy which permeates all life…From here you discover the powers to heal yourself and others. Here you become a healer.

I'm going to suggest several affirmations; if you wish to affirm them, repeat them to yourself, feeling as though they are fully true; knowing that in focusing on affirmations, you'll create patterns of energy that will move out into your life, materializing in your daily experience both within and around you.

Life is resilient; I believe in life…
I love my body; my body is resilient…
The whole of my body/mind is healthy…
My life is whole, my life is a part of the whole of life…
Energy flows easily and clearly throughout the whole of my being…
I am in harmony with the natural rhythms of life within and around me…
I honor my sexuality and celebrate the joy of life…
I give myself the time I need to remain centered…
I honor my body with care…
I eat only those foods that nourish my body…
I rest all I need to replenish my body…

I exercise all I need to maintain my health and vitality…

My body is a self-healing, self-clearing organism…

My body/mind is whole and fully attuned. My mind responds to the messages my body offers; my body responds to the messages my mind offers…

I maintain balance amidst change…

I trust the future…

Now take time to focus on any of your own affirmations or symbols. Know that in focusing on affirmations, you set intentions in place and you'll find that your experience conforms to the affirmations. Expect this to be the case.

◆

Know that in focusing on affirmations, you have created patterns of energy that will move out into your life and materialize within and around you…

In a moment, I am going to count on a descending scale from ten to one. At each descending count you'll be able to relax into yourself, into your body, even more than you now are. As you relax, you become increasingly sensitive to the state of your being, to the state of your body. At the count of one, you will be fully attuned to the healing powers of life itself, aware of the healer that resides deep within you.

Ten, moving deeper now…Nine, returning to yourself…Breathing…Eight, relaxing into who it is that you are…Seven, relaxing into your body…Six, your body relaxing into the universal life energies that carry it…Five, deeper and deeper…Four, moving down into the center of your life…Three, relaxing…Two, very aware…*One*, feel the expansive energies of life itself. Breathing…here is where healing energy flows…Here you experience the intimate connection of body and mind. You are fully attuned to what is so in your body.

Tell yourself you will remain alert throughout the whole of this meditation, and you will remember all that you experience.

Vitality of Life

Now extend your awareness to include whatever you imagine to be the very source of your vitality, the spring from which your life forces come…Breathe, feel life moving through you…Breath carries life. However you imagine the source of vitality, the source of the life force energy…You may wish to imagine the radiance of the sun, imagining that you have a golden sun within you, emanating this life force energy…brilliant energy that your life rides upon…Or maybe a spring of water that sparkles with the light of the sun dancing on the surface as it flows…Radiant, resilient energy that is life, your life. Sense the spring of energy, the source of vitality…However you experience it…It's the continuous flow of being, your being…breath, heart, life moves through, life carries you…animating who it is that you are.

Witness it…Feel it. Sense it, as though your energy were coming up from an underground spring…continually coming up…continually moving, like a river that is never twice the same…the continuous spontaneous flow of being…the spirit of life itself…sometimes quiet, sometimes loud…Breathe it…It breathes you…Witness that you are carried by the radiance moving through your body and out into the life that is yours. Feel the continuous and inexhaustible resilient life force energy…However you sense it…vibrant energy.

Feel the life force energy moving through the whole of your being, every cell of your body infused with the pulse of life…sometimes it is soft, sometimes it is surging…resilient life energy always carries you…Breathing you. Spontaneous, inexhaustible energy…vibrant, radiant energy moving through you. Feel the rhythms of this energy, sometimes slow, sometimes fast…Your life rides on it…Feel it teeming in every cell of your body, through every pore, every organ…energy…Feel this energy's connection with all of life energy that permeates everything…The glow of life.

Identify with the constantly new life being born within you. The cells of which you are composed animated by life, vibrant with life…cells continually being created, continually growing, as old ones die…the continuous transformation of energy…constantly transforming energies, bringing energies in…and releasing, discarding what's no longer needed. Life is fully resilient. It rejuvenates itself. Acknowledge this…Feel the self-perpetuating, self-healing regenerative powers that your body has…It continually renews itself…Witness the innate intelligence that your body possesses, its ability to heal and regenerate itself…Witness the intrinsic intelligence of every cell of which you are composed…

Acknowledge the intelligence of life itself. Let yourself trust life. Let yourself reside in the sanctity of life. Now create a symbol for all that you're experiencing. Create a symbol for vitality, for your health, for the vitality of life itself…Know that whenever you bring this symbol to awareness it will move you into harmony with the life forces within you…it will revitalize you, energize you…Know that whenever you bring this symbol to mind it creates a channel to receive the information you need to regain your health and vitality…Expect this to be the case. Tell yourself this now…Feel the energy of this symbol…Imagine that the energy of this symbol pours into the whole of your body…Experience the life forces vibrating inside you, throbbing in every cell of which you are composed…Acknowledge life. Trust life. Acknowledge your gratitude for the gift of life…Acknowledge the gift that your body is.

Developing Rapport with Your Body

You are going to journey through your body…Your imagination will transport you through your body's inner landscape. You will be able to experience directly the vitality in all the parts of your body. In the next meditation, you will have time to go over any areas you may be having difficulty with so that you can understand the difficulties and energize the healing process. As you move through the different areas within you, you may wish to imagine yourself very tiny, riding a pinpoint of light...light that illuminates the internal workings of your body...Know that it is fine—in fact it is good—to simply make up what you imagine it to be like inside yourself...You needn't imagine it literally, you may instead wish to symbolize the internal parts of your body. However your imagination depicts what is happening inside is what is true for you...

Bring to mind your symbol for health and vitality and keep it in the background of your awareness as you explore the inner workings of your body; in doing so your symbol will enable you to fully experience the innate intelligence of each area within you.

Feel your bones...Explore what they look like...Imagine what they'd feel like if you were to touch them with your fingertips...Become aware of the strength, the durability of your bones, of the whole of your skeleton giving your body a frame to stand on...Sense the strength of your bones...Experience your bones...know that within them they create your blood, your life blood. Imagine blood being manufactured...

Imagine the layers of muscles connecting your bones...Be aware of their strength, their flexibility, their texture, their color, their tone...Feel how it is that your muscles give you movement...Explore the whole of your musculature...its strength and durability. Notice how it shapes your body...

Become aware of your heart, the rhythm of your pulse...the sound of your heartbeat...Witness your heart pumping blood, keeping it flowing throughout your whole body...rivers moving through the landscape of your body...Imagine all the blood branching out throughout the whole of your body...Imagine moving through a vein and exploring the whole of your circulation, feeling the blood moving easily and rhythmically throughout the whole of your body keeping the whole of your body fully nourished…bringing to each of the areas in your body what they need and carrying away the wastes…Your blood carries on the regenerative processes of life itself, keeping your body in a harmonious balance.

Feel the rhythm of your breath, like waves rising and falling. Feel your breath renewing, cleansing and sustaining your body…feel your breath moving through the whole of your body, carried by your blood…Witness each cell of which you are composed breathing and releasing what is no longer needed…Breath carries life. Every single cell of which you are composed breathes.

◆

Now become aware of your digestive system…You may wish to imagine riding on a piece of food…Go through the whole of your digestive system…Notice its feel, its color, its sound. Experience your digestive system transforming food into energy…keeping every cell of your body well-nourished…

Become aware of your reproductive system, its harmonious balance…how it looks, how it feels, where it is in the cycle of life…Appreciate your sexuality as a celebration of life itself…

Become aware of your brain, sense it, feel it…Become aware of your spine…aware of the whole of your nervous system branching out to the full reaches of your body…Feel how alert and responsive your body is…Imagine the networking of impulses throughout the whole of your nervous system keeping your body in clear communication, all your body parts in communication…Feel how acutely aware your body is…Acknowledge the intelligence residing within you…

All of your senses are sharply attuned, intimately connected to your nervous system…Explore your five senses, see them, feel them, fully sense them…Explore each of your senses, your sight, your eyes, your hearing, your ears, your touch, your skin, your taste, your mouth, your smell, your nose. Now take time to explore them.

◆

Imagine your lymphatic system, your immune system maintains the integrity of your body...keeping your body safe and secure...always on the lookout for and clearing away anything that doesn't belong...maintaining the peace and well-being in the landscape of your body so all parts can do their job well...Now become aware of each of your glands producing the appropriate fluids for all of your body to function in cooperation...maintaining equilibrium...Notice how each of your glands plays a role in keeping your body in a state of balance.

◆

Now further explore on your own areas you've been through or areas you have not yet gone into. Remember your symbol for health and vitality and explore with it. Take time to do this now.

◆

Take time to finish what you're doing and bring your attention back...Take a moment to fully appreciate the nature of your body...Feel its integrity...Believe in your body, make friends with it...Feel how all the areas in your body cooperate with one another. Your body is always able to replenish itself, providing you with a good home for yourself...Love your body for the home it gives you. Breathe in loving, healing energy. Imagine offering it loving, healing energy...As though as you breathe you bring loving, healing energy into your body...Love your body. Acknowledge your gratitude for the gift of life...

Self-Healing

From this place be aware of the resilience intrinsic to life itself, for life is healing, self-clearing, regenerative...To heal yourself, know each symptom is the clue offering insight into just what is needed...Each problem contains within itself the seeds of its own healing. Any ailment you might have is a signpost pointing you towards just what is healthful. Trust your body's ability to heal itself…When you cut your skin, it rebuilds itself of its own accord, your body knows how to regenerate itself…Acknowledge the self-healing capabilities intrinsic to your body. Remember times when your body has healed itself…The cells with which you are made are fully influenced by your attitudes. Trust the nature of your body…in so doing, you treat it kindly. Your trust gives your cells added support for their healing work. Give yourself permission to believe in your body.

◆

Now become aware, fully aware, of the whole of your body, the position it's in…the condition it's in…the pulse of life percolating through your body…the pulse of life percolating in every cell of which you are composed…Know that you are becoming as aware of your internal physical environment as you are of your external physical environment…With your keen inner sense, become aware of any areas in your body that you would like to heal…To promote and maintain good health you can communicate with any area of your body…You can hear its messages and discover what is needed to increase well-being…Your body will hear new messages you offer…Your body is loyal and responsive to whatever messages you give. Appreciate that this is true…

Choose one particular area you would like to work on…If you have a number of different areas, choose one, and know that you can work on the others another time.

Imagine this part of your body, imagine what it looks like, what it feels like. You needn't imagine it literally—imagine it however you like…Feel the area…Sense its condition. Be aware of the atmosphere in which it lives…Be aware of the quality of energy present in this part of your body…If it were to have a mood, what would it be?…What sounds and smells are present?…What colors and textures are present?…Sense what is so here. Let your imagination create a sense of how this area is doing…Trust what occurs to you. Let it all come through your imagination.

Imagine this part of your body having a consciousness of its own, an intelligence of its own, as indeed it does. Imagine that this part of your body sends out a messenger who represents it...Imagine the representative...Welcome the representative. Give yourself full permission to pretend that indeed you can talk to this area. Let the child within you make up this conversation. Talk to the messenger; listen to what it has to say about what's true for this part of your body...Ask it how it feels...Imagine what it would tell you. Use your imagination, make up a story...What is the story?...Be sensitive to how it communicates, it might not be verbal, it could come in the form of direct knowing...You might find yourself knowing at the same time that you are asking...Pay keen attention to what occurs. Be receptive to whatever you sense...Trust what happens. Ask the messenger what is going on...Be receptive to the area's experience. Trust your experience.

◆

Ask if there is anything it is defending you against...anything in your life it is protecting you from...or what it wants protection from...understanding happens.

◆

Come to ways that work to take care of needs...Ask it if there are particular exercises, foods, rest, or whatever it may wish to help it...Ask what it wants, sense what it has to say. Trust your sense.

◆

Decide if you're willing to give it what it wants...Decide if there is anything you want from it and ask for it...You can tell it how you feel, what you want...You may need to re-educate the cells—tell them what is happening now or reassure them about the future...You and your body may need to let go of some old habits and make ways for energies to move along different routes.

◆

Sense if the area is willing to give you what you want...What agreements might you make so that you can cooperatively take care of one another?...Compromise when need be...Ask it what you can now expect of it...Tell it what you're willing to do...Be patient with one another...Endeavor to make life easier for one another...Bring kindness into the scene. Breathe some kindness into the area...Put any difficult feelings through your Mental Housecleaning device.

◆

Bring your symbol of health and vitality into the scene. Imagine asking the symbol if it has any light to shed on the healing of this area...Come to agreements with the area, and when you come to agreement, imagine acting on it. Witness what that feels like...Notice how the mood in this part of your body changes, feel the area healing. Breathe in healing. Breathe in vitality...As you inhale, gather vital healing energy...As you exhale send it to the area, shine it onto the messenger...Feeling healing happen.

◆

Witness if there is any part of you that somehow is a little hesitant; not so sure this change is such a good thing. Talk with this part too. Imagine what it is you need to do to take care of that part of yourself...Decide how you are going to act on this...and imagine doing so.

◆

Now imagine your vitality symbol hovering above your body. Let it pour its healing energy into the area...Feel vital, healing energy coming into the area, healing the area...Breathe healing into the area...Imagine it breathing in healing...This healing process will always be what's last in your mind whenever you're aware of this area in your body. Tell yourself this...Know that whenever you bring this symbol to mind, it will help your body in its healing process...Know that this is so.

◆

Know that every day you're getting better...Expect the best...Your body/mind is united...Trust your ability to heal yourself to be in harmony with the whole of yourself and all that's around you...Now, if you have one, bring to awareness your symbol for self-protection, experience what it feels like to be fully protected...If you don't have a symbol, evoke the quality of protection—whatever that is to you...Now surround yourself with this energy, let it form a protective bubble around you...Your symbol for protection creates a bubble of safety, security, and strength. Immerse yourself in the energy...Know that whenever you wrap yourself with this energy, you protect yourself from danger. Know that this is so...that this symbol keeps you safe by shielding you from any threats to your health. This energy keeps your body's immune system strong and sound...protecting you from any influences that may threaten your health, protecting you from germs, bites, whatever may come your way...Expect that you can protect yourself with this energy...You may imagine asking the energy if there's anything you need to do to protect yourself from any influences that may hinder your health...Sense what you can do to keep yourself safe and healthy.

◆

Decide if you are willing to do this, and if you are, imagine yourself doing so...If you're not, see what alternatives there are and experience yourself acting on those...Know that you do have the ability to maintain your health and to protect yourself from any threats. Imagine that this is so...Acknowledge your gratitude for the gift of life...

Healing Attitudes

In this state, you are very clear, much clearer than usual. Here you can witness the patterns of your own consciousness. Here you witness what you tell yourself is so. Here your beliefs become sharp and clear. Not only are the patterns of your consciousness revealed to you here, but you can re-pattern your attitudes so consciousness moves only in positive directions. You can transform negative ideas and pave new roads for your consciousness to move down—moving in a healthful direction...

Be aware of the position your body is in at this moment. Feel your breath rolling in and out of your body...Feel the movements that accompany breath...In the quiet of breath, just breathing, take a few moments to simply be *with* your body...breathing and aware of your body...As you breathe, and tune into your body, witness what comes up for you...

◆

Notice what crosses your mind as you breathe and focus on your body. Breathe...What comes to awareness as you quietly be *with* your body? Notice, are you glad to be with your body?...Do you have aversion?...Witness...In the quiet as you rest your attention on your body, note what comes up for you...Breathe.

◆

Witness your responses as you hear the following questions...Witness when you respond in a way that causes you to withdraw from your body. Witness when you feel good. First simply notice, at the end of the meditation you will have time to transform attitudes and cultivate new ones that empower you to have a loving relationship with the whole of your body, with the whole of yourself...

Witness what is usually true for you. As you move through your day, when do thoughts and feelings about your body come up?...When you are dressing?...When you are eating?...When you are moving about?...When you are with others?...When you are resting?...When you are exercising?...Witness what is true for you.

◆

Do you ever talk to your body?…What do you say?…Are you friendly?…What feelings are there?…What do you tell yourself?…Are the thoughts affirming?…Are they wanting your body to be different than it is?…What are you telling your body?…

◆

How strong, flexible, are you?…How is your stamina?…Witness your sexuality…Witness your body's ability to protect itself…What are your body's strengths?…What does wellness feel like?…Explore your inclinations to health…to challenges to your body…to sickness. What limitations do you have to contend with?…What are you always vulnerable to?…What do you assume to be so?…How do you care for your body?…What do you assume the future holds for your body?…What beliefs do you hold about your body?…What do you anticipate?…Explore all this.

◆

Now transform any attitudes that are limiting with your Mental Housecleaning device, or ground them with your grounding cord, know the earth transforms them. Symbolize the attitudes and all their accompanying thoughts and feelings…Imagine doing a ceremony and let them go…Tell yourself you are changing your approach…and let the old demeaning assumptions go.

◆

Bring to awareness your symbol for vitality. Remember the resilient qualities of life itself. Life regenerates itself—heals itself. Life is vitality…Feel the sanctity of life…of your life…of your body…Offer your body loving kindness…Have gratitude for your body, be generous toward your body…

◆

Now invite the specific beliefs and affirmations that assume health and well-being are as natural to your body as breathing…Be specific…Go back to the particular attitudes you just released and make beliefs that empower you and your body...Cultivate beliefs that are life affirming. Work with one at a time. Create affirmations that affirm the integrity of your body. You deserve it.

◆

Breathe in these different perspectives...Get a feel for them...Imagine going about your day holding these beliefs to be true...Believe in your ability to change. Believe in your body. Believe in your wellness...Imagine exaggerating your belief. Stretch your faith, make it even greater...Feel how your life will be after these changes have fully taken root.

◆

Notice what you can do in your life now, to acknowledge this life-affirming perspective you are cultivating. Think of a symbolic act that is in alignment with your new beliefs. Imagine doing it...Tell your body what you are going to do.

◆

Feel resilience...Life always brings change...Expect the best...Trust yourself, trust your body, trust life itself. Acknowledge your gratitude for the gift of life...

Creating a Healthful Routine: Food, Rest, and Exercise

You are now going to explore the routine of your life—the life of your body. You now occupy an extremely receptive and knowing state of awareness. Acknowledge the fact that within you lies the knowledge of what you need to care for your body, to care for yourself, to honor your life, to honor your body...

Food is sacred. Food nourishes your body. Some food your body will resonate with, some food your feelings may resonate with. Some foods may hum, some may scream. Be aware of what part of you is desiring different foods. Simply bring a food into awareness and witness whether it's your body that desires what this particular food has to offer, or another aspect of yourself that desires this food...Explore what parts of you desire the different foods in your life. Bring these to awareness one at a time. Imagine it in detail and witness what occurs. Be in your body and notice what happens.

◆

When you are finished exploring the different foods, if there are foods that you are wanting with other parts of yourself other than your body, talk to those parts of yourself and see how you can meet their needs in new ways, so you only eat those foods that your body wants...Choose what you want to eat for healthful life, meeting the needs of all of yourself, your body, and your feelings. Notice if there are foods that your body wants which you have not been giving to it...Imagine offering your body all the foods it needs for optimal health. What food does your body want for its strength, balance, and vitality?...Breathe...Be in your body...Open to your experience.

◆

Choose how you want to relate to food as you move through your daily routine...If you have in any way been compulsive about food, breathe through it...Forgive yourself. Remember you are sacred as you are, and food is sacred...Mental Houseclean the pushy energy.

◆

Focus on meals, on that part of eating that is connected with others...Imagine that everything is a part of a healthy process of living, of sharing, of nourishing yourself, nourishing others...Choose how you want to relate to food in a fully healthful way, healthful for all the parts of yourself, your body...your feelings...your mind...your spirit...your family and community...Feel, see yourself acting on your knowingness, caring for the whole of your being...nourishing your life with food...Acknowledge the earth for sustaining your life, providing your body with food.

◆

Now take time to be aware of what your body needs in rest and relaxation on the one hand, and activity and exercise on the other…Talk to your body about it, notice how it feels…Does it get the rest it needs?…Does it get the stimulation it needs?…Be in your body; how does it experience the rhythm of your life?…Take joy in your body in motion…Imagine how exercising fits in the routine of your life…Exercise feeds your resilience…Rest is comforting, replenishing. Appreciate this…Sense what resonates well with your body…Create a routine in your life that is balanced with vital activity and replenishing rest. Imagine the optimal rhythm. Life thrives in rhythm. Offer your body what it needs to maintain optimal health.

◆

Decide what you are willing to do…Make agreements with yourself. Imagine acting on your choices…caring for your body, the home of yourself…Acknowledge what you need, honoring the life that is yours, honoring life itself…Acknowledge your gratitude for the gift of life…

Sexuality: The Dance of Life

Imagine going to a place that's sacred; create this place for yourself now. Imagine a temple…a temple that's enchanted with music in the air. This place is a healing magical space. This is the place where you can reclaim and celebrate the fullness of your being.

◆

Not only is this place sacred, but it's extremely sensual. Life is vibrant here, energy is revealed in its pure, naked forms…here you can affirm all life-giving sensuous energies. This place is a powerful place, a sensuous place. Create this place now, let it be enchanted...Know that when you are in the place new insights and new energies reveal themselves...These are particularly important in healing, integrating, and growing with your sexuality...From here you can make peace with your sexuality and celebrate it at the same time...a very safe, splendorous, and sacred place. Bring your Mental Housecleaning device to mind so whenever constricting feelings or thoughts come up you can transform them by putting them in your device or simply letting them soak into the ground.

In this place you are keenly aware of the connection your body has to the life cycles of the earth and heavens, the cyclic nature of life itself...the coming into being and the passing away—birth and death. Sexuality is the richest experience of life itself. Feel your attunement to the rhythmic nature of life...The spirit of the movement of life, the cyclic nature of life itself, your sexual, sensual self...Affirm your love of life...sexuality is a celebration of life itself...Feel the spark of joy within you...

Make yourself fully comfortable in your temple...Move your awareness inside of yourself to what you imagine to be the center of your sexuality...Let yourself experience the motion of the vitality of life itself...Your sexuality that springs from the source of life, the regeneration of life...Affirm your physicality. Affirm your sexuality. Affirm the life force which surges up through you...Let your sexuality spring from the core of your being...To bring forth your sexual experience remember good times you have had...sexuality—sensuality—has brought you pleasure...attuned you to the gifts of life itself.

◆

If anything comes to awareness that makes you withdraw from affirming your sexual energy, you can release it, you can transform it. Symbolize whatever comes up and put it through your Mental Housecleaning device...Breathe space into the scene and release the old energies. As you breathe healing happens...You might want to talk to it first and see if there is any learning to be gleaned...Breathe out any old pains...Give yourself permission to experience sexuality in new ways. You can also give any negative messages back to whoever told them to you in the first place...Claim your sexuality...It is yours.

◆

Experience it as a gift for yourself, which you and only you may choose to share with another—a gift from life force energies themselves. Sexuality, your sexuality is sacred. Take time to be with it now. Take time to heal any old wounds...claim sexuality as a celebration of life, your life...Take joy in your own sexuality...

Feel the splendor of life itself...as though your sexuality were the music of your body...Know that as you heal your sexuality, as you clear your sexual center, you are fully connected to the earth...to the spirit, to the dance of life your body naturally moves to...that the earth and spirit are one and the same. Imagine that you merge with the cosmic whole with loving orgasmic energy...In merging with the whole of sensual, sexual orgasmic energy you empower yourself, power from within rises up...Life is sexual. Open to your sexuality...receptive and powerful. Life energies are received—sexual, sensual, intimate energy is received and all meets within you and you are one with the pulsating dance of life. Feel it. You are blessed with life.

◆

Now imagine that as you heal, you'll be more and more able to be fully present and attuned to your sexuality and the sexuality of those around you. Honoring it as a sacred part of our lives...Honoring your choices and those of others...Feel how you do this...Enabling you to be a fully spontaneous, sexual being, connecting where it feels good, where you're attuned to another, where loving energy flows, sparks, moves...letting that connection express itself...

You may choose to experience your sexuality within yourself, letting it reveal all the levels of yourself and your self-love...Loving ourselves, loving each other, our bodies dance with soul…Intimacy vibrates within and around us. We are sexual beings, we celebrate the joy of life within ourselves and with others—sexual alone, with another connecting where it feels good and dancing love of life together…

Know that in reclaiming your sexuality, you are very clear; you *know* what you need…Affirm who you are, affirm your ability to express your sexuality, while fully sensitive to others and respecting another…Knowing that life is sexual. Affirm your choices. Acknowledge what commitment is for you…If you are committed to one in particular, affirm your choice, your bond…honoring the bonds that sexuality creates…Know that in affirming sexuality you affirm life itself…Take time to imagine expressing your sexual energy in ways that are a celebration, an integration into the wholeness of life itself—the orgasm of life…Sexuality is so powerful, so potent, that it is only in sexuality that life itself can be created…Honor sexuality—both yours and others'.

◆

Create whatever you need to protect the integrity of your sexuality; if you wish, do an imaginary ritual to protect its sacredness…Take time to protect yourself from all those ideas in the world around you that degrade and hurt your sexuality. If you have a symbol for protection, bring it to awareness. Surround yourself with sacred energy that inspires respect. Energy which inspires honoring of boundaries…honoring of the integrity of your being. Feel it…Breathe it…

◆

Honoring your sexuality, you let it flow, flowing from the depth of your being out into a joyous celebration of life. Sometimes you keep the energy, sometimes you share the energy…sometimes you express it in other ways…You choose when and when not to act on your sexual energy…Explore your feelings of love…your feelings of celebration, of intimacy, the bonds your sexual sharing creates…your spirit, your soul, alive in your body…Take time to explore and choose the ways you can be in the world that affirm sexuality.

◆

Create a symbol for all that you're experiencing. Know that you can bring this symbol into your awareness whenever you wish to affirm your sexuality…You may wish to ask your symbol what you need to do in your life to affirm and honor your sexuality…If you have concerns about another, talk it over.

◆

Take time to acknowledge yourself as a sexual being. Imagine thanking anyone you've been sharing this energy with…Know that in affirming sexuality, you affirm life itself—for life is sexual…Life is sacred…Acknowledge your gratitude for the gift of sexuality; for the gift of life. Life is sexual.

Wise Self: Meeting Overwhelming Challenge and/or Life-Threatening Illness

Imagine a sacred place for you to be; it may be a temple, a place in the country, a place you've been, or a place in your imagination…Let your imagination transport you to a place, a special sacred place, a very peaceful place, so peaceful you can almost hear the quiet of it…So quiet, the quality heals your spirit…Imagine what is all around you. Imagine the details…the colors, the textures…the sounds of life…be aware of the qualities of energy here…Breathe in these qualities, let them soothe you…You can come here to commune with your spirit. In this place, peacefulness keeps deepening. Sense this…In this place, you can rest your spirit and just be…Be peaceful. Here you also gain the wisdom you need…Breathe the peace that is here…It is quieting to the heart to be here…Let your spirit be replenished by this place…Breathe the peace that is here.

◆

In a moment, I am going to snap my fingers, and at that moment you're going to meet an aspect of your knowingness, an aspect of yourself, which may be manifested in many ways. This aspect of yourself is very, very wise…all-knowing. She might reside in the deepest core of your being. She may quietly make her home in your heart or speak through your soul…She may have no form; she may simply have a presence…This aspect of yourself may come to you in the form of light, an imaginary being, an animal, a spirit or maybe another you. However she shows herself, she is part of you, yet she is more than you…[*snap*] Imagine this aspect, very, very wise, very gentle, and yet very powerful…strong, full of compassion. Meet this part of yourself now, very wise…all-knowing. Sense her. She is fully present, always present—feel her presence now…Let yourself feel comforted in her presence…Ask this aspect of yourself how it is that the rest of you can gain the courage you need to either keep up the fight, or to let go, to move on, to trust the future…Imagine what this aspect would tell you, sense your knowingness…You may receive answers in energy form, they may not be verbal; you may simply find yourself knowing, feeling, having the courage that you need to keep up the fight or to let go, to move on, to trust the future.

◆

As you breathe, imagine breathing in this knowingness…Imagine breathing in this courage…Breathing in this strength so that it spreads through every aspect of your being…every cell of your body…every thought in your mind…every feeling in your heart…your whole being vibrating with courage, with patience, with knowing…Feel your whole self become as wise as your wisest, deepest self…Breathing wisdom…Breathing loving kindness…Breathing.

◆

Notice things that you need to do in your life to be able to come to completion in any areas of your life…to let go, to move on, to move forward…

◆

You may want to imagine doing some kind of ritual or ceremony or dance with your wise self…As you imagine this, you empower yourself, trust the future, let go…You evoke the deepest knowing of your being, of beingness itself…You are courageous and at the same time compassionate with yourself…Imagine performing a ritual with yourself, a ritual that acknowledges your life, expresses any rage you may feel…transforms any blame you may feel…acknowledges your power, all that you've done, letting go and moving on…You can create this ritual in your mind's eye in whatever way occurs to you—however you are inclined.

◆

You may want to take time to ask your wise self how it is you can be more comfortable in your body…How it is you can take charge of the life you do have…how you can create peace in your life now…If you're in pain, imagine your lungs bringing in lots of oxygen, your breath spreading through your whole body…your breath carrying relief throughout your whole body…Breathing…each breath massaging the whole of your body with relief, with calming comfort…Breathing…Send healing breath wherever your body needs it. With your wise self you may want to imagine creating a channel—a channel down into the ground to let the pain begin to drain away…Breathe out the pain…Expect it to lessen over time, expect it to be a little easier, a little more comfortable, as time passes…Tell yourself that this is the case…Breathing…breath brings comfort…Breathing through the areas that need attention, comforting them with breath. Breath carries space…Breathe space into the areas. Breathing space…breathing relief…breathing…

Notice what is needed for you to come to peace with yourself, with your life…Has anything been bothering you?…You may want to imagine transforming it; you may want to imagine it soaking into the earth…You may want to imagine doing something…taking care of something…allowing yourself to move forward. You may need to imagine doing something or saying something you never had a chance to…There may be something you need to ask for.

◆

Bring in loving kindness…Reside in the knowing of what is true for you…Knowing what you need to do to come to peace with yourself, with your life…

You may want to take time to simply remember your life…Taking time to focus on any concerns you may have…communing with your wisest self…Imagine yourself doing what is needed to feel whole…peaceful…to *be* peace…breathe peace.

◆

Go over all you've come to know in this meditation…Knowing that this energy is there for you always, that it transcends time and space…Acknowledge the support of your wise self, knowing your wise self is always with you, knowing your wise self is you…all you need to do is tap into your deeper self…This self stays with you always…Breathe peace. Be whole. Breathe…

Count Out

Go over in your awareness this sense of well-being…The whole of your body/mind functions harmoniously…It functions as harmoniously as the rest of the whole of nature. Know that every time you meditate you tap the harmonizing energies of the universe. They heal you, and you offer healing to the world.

Review the lessons and insights you gained, any symbols you worked with…Go over any agreements that you've made.

◆

Notice how acting on the knowing that you have come to in this meditation is going to affect your life…How it will affect your activities?…Now notice how it will affect those around you…Notice if any adjustments need to be made…if anyone needs to be spoken to…what support you have for these changes…what support you'll now be able to offer others.

Healing energy can be channeled from this state of awareness. Channel healing wherever you like. Imagine well-being. Hold yourself or another in the light of healing energy.

◆

Finish what you are doing. Re-center yourself with your breath…Know that it is an established fact that you are fully able to live in harmony…Feel how this is so, and it will increasingly be so as time moves on…Choose when you will again focus in on the well-being of your body when you meditate…Trust yourself, trust your body, trust your mind, trust nature. Trust life…

In a moment I'm going to count from one to five…At the count of five, you'll open your eyes remembering all that you've experienced…feeling refreshed, revitalized, and relaxed.

ONE—becoming more aware of the room around you…

TWO—coming up slowly now…

THREE—at the count of five, you'll open your eyes feeling relaxed, revitalized, and refreshed remembering all that you've experienced…

FOUR—coming up now, bringing with you your sense of well-being…

FIVE!—eyes open, feeling refreshed, revitalized, and relaxed, remembering all you have experienced…having brought with you your sense of wholeness—open heart and spirit…Healthy and resilient.

•8•

Making Your Life Work for You

There is a great elegance and mystery to the universe. It is as though *all that is* is woven together in a grand symphony of being—there is symmetry in constant flux from atoms to solar systems, from stardust to galaxies. Life is resilient; it self-regulates, it heals and recreates itself. Aware of it or not, we *are* held by the universe. It is in deep consciousness that we experience oneness. When we move with the unifying energy that runs through *all that is*, our lives become harmonious. Life is in alignment and there is a quality of grace present.

Western Rationalism has separated us from the whole, alienating us from the innate wisdom of our bodies as well as from the resilience intrinsic to consciousness itself. When we withdraw from the unifying life forces and constrict ourselves, we become rigid, disassociated, and unable to learn. Our lives become discordant—cut off from creative/healing energies. We are likely to act in ways harmful to ourselves or to others, for we have lost touch with the sanctity of life.

How often do we try to ignore the back pain, the uncomfortable relationship, or the tedious job because we just cannot see a solution? We all have problems; we don't make them up, they are quite real. They originate in the world we live in, the conditions of our lives, both past and present. Contradictions exist everywhere in spite of the connectedness of *all that is*—contradictions between our need to experience peace and the challenges we have to contend with in our everyday lives; contradictions caused by our unresolved feelings, ignored lessons, or outdated beliefs, or between the complacent and courageous sides of ourselves.

If we rely exclusively on rationality for solving problems, we compound them. Rational beta consciousness makes us feel as if time has speeded up, leaving no room for innerconsciousness to surface. Beta thinking categorizes, sorts, and separates. It would have us believe that only one side of a contradiction can be true, rather than both. Having a linear cause-and-effect orientation, it assumes that the key to making change is in discovering the origin of problems. This in turn causes a preoccupation with the negative; if we're not careful, we find that we put all of our attention on what we *don't* want rather than on what we *do* want.

Some people continually revisit the past searching for the origins of their suffering. They believe that in order to solve their problems, they need to understand what went wrong in their childhood. Looking back may make one feel more comfortable with current limitations, but it reinforces them rather than resolving them. Understanding why it is the way it is doesn't reveal how it could be different. I approach issues from the opposite orientation. Whatever the issue, suffering can be lessened if one asks oneself what one wants instead. We need a vision to strive for. Without one, the problem itself is the only point of reference, and therefore holds a monopoly on the issue. No matter how well one understands a problem, it gets replicated, acted out, because inner messages are the source of our behavior. Without a positive vision of the issue, there is no change for the better.

Working with the holistic aspects of consciousness is more effective in alleviating suffering than relying on rationalism; it opens the imagination and offers vision. You need the spacious awareness of the Inner Witness to reveal what is really taking place. The Inner Witness notices when you are beginning to shut down. And just as importantly, it recognizes insights and openings that emerge as the Active and Receptive Imaginations dance together. I believe that focusing on a vision of how you would like things to be orients you in a positive direction and will move you forward. This is the work of the Active Imagination. But this visioning process is not as linear as it might seem. When you work with a vision in the presence of the Inner Witness, you discover what doesn't quite fit or isn't plausible, or if the vision reverts back to the status quo, as well as witnessing how others respond. All of this is in the dance. *What is important is not the product of the vision, but the witnessing of the dance.* The imagination is multidimensional. It is the aspect of consciousness we employ to give shape to our aspirations and it is simultaneously the medium of psychic information. More than that, it is the stuff probabilities are made of. Appreciating all of this means that what we can and what we cannot imagine takes on profound significance. We both discover and create reality through witnessing the play of the imagination. Your Active Imagination (creative projection) is entwined with your Receptive Imagination (intuition and learning). It is not as though you work with one and then when you are done, you go on to the next. They operate simultaneously in a dance of creativity and intuition that is all played out in the presence of the Inner Witness.

As I indicated earlier in Chapter Five, the most profound work with inner-consciousness is witnessing what you *cannot* imagine; that is when what you project keeps reverting back to the status quo. This is crucial information. Contrary to the commonly held view of the imagination, in Applied Meditation, it is the window *into* reality. *How* it displays whatever you are working on metaphorically represents the current state of affairs and reveals both subjective and objective limitations. Use the story-making capacities of the Receptive Imagination to find where openings lie. In the process, your intuition will offer crucial information and you'll find that the Inner Witness catches it. The Inner Witness always grounds you in the recognition of what is taking place, and reveals what is needed to move into alignment with life force energies.

The Continuum of Change

Life is in a constant state of change. Because of our awareness of this, we know that things could be different. Change carries possibility. It is out of contradiction between the real and the ideal that all creativity emerges and the visionary within each of us is awakened.

The process of resolving problems usually occurs on a continuum. One starts by removing any blocks to creativity and intuition. If you are either preoccupied with the past or caught in avoidance, use Mental Housecleaning to create space for innerconsciousness to work. Change will take place either in your finding a new approach to the situation or in your discovering a vision that helps transform the circumstances. Cultivating either creates an opening into new ways of being, rather than shutting down and withdrawing. Whether you shift your attitude or discover a vision of a new experience, you then strive to embody it. As you endeavor to live into this different way, it becomes increasingly clear. At the point when the new way remains steady in your imagination, change is already well on its way to becoming your actual experience.

During the process, you continually witness how you imagine the embodiment of change. Watching this reveals where attention is called for. You discover what internal shifts will move you out of old patterns so that you don't collude with the very circumstances you are trying to overcome. And you will also find yourself with impulses to make particular changes in your circumstances. Change happens both inside and outside. What you discover needs to be acted on. Sometimes it is a subtle shift in your attitude or vision, sometimes a major change in your life—whatever is needed gets revealed in the dance of your imagination.

I stated in Chapter Five that what you focus on becomes the reality you perpetuate. This does not mean that you should *compel* yourself always to be positive. The act of forcing goes against the flow. Denial cuts one off from vital energy and it keeps intuitive knowing *out* of view. Only in openness can healing and creativity take place. One can't relax and deny at the same time because the festering problems needing attention naturally surface. Repressing negative emotions leads to compulsive behavior and addiction. Not allowing ourselves to face and come to terms with what is really bothering us, we drive ourselves to focus elsewhere. Not willing to be centered inside our selves, we compulsively eat, keep things clean, or constantly socialize (as if there is no choice), or maybe numb out with alcohol or television. The longer our problems go unaddressed, the more neurotic we become, and the original issues get buried under all the side effects of the compulsive behavior.

Consciousness, like the body, naturally heals when it is given space to do so. The gift of the Inner Witness is that it recognizes when we are beginning to shut down. This awareness is where our true freedom lies. The Witness offers space so that we have room to live *with* difficulties without shutting down. There is room to choose how to respond instead of simply reacting. Unlike beta consciousness, in spacious awareness, time expands out. In the space created, the Witness recognizes where imbalance lies; it catches flashes of inspiration and it hears the soft voice of intuition. We don't need to *do* anything for the Inner Witness to come forth, it is as natural to consciousness as breath is to the body. In fact, all we need to do is stop doing. Make space, take a deep breath, and relax into wholeness.

Sometimes you might find yourself having a hard time with an issue and creating a positive vision seems inconceivable and irrelevant. In meditation, simply sit *with* the difficulty. When experiencing pain, one usually reacts with tension;

yet in fact, breathing *into* pain is what alleviates it. Breath heals on all levels of experience. As you focus on breath, you find that it invites the Inner Witness. In the presence of the Inner Witness, just be with the situation as it is. Don't do anything with it; breathe and share presence with it. Breathe *with* it so to speak. Breathe; breathe space into yourself and into the scene—letting it be as it is; letting yourself be as you are. Listen deeply. Ask yourself what is good in the circumstance. Even the hardest of times have a good side; if nothing else, they carry invaluable life lessons. In the presence of the Witness, you'll find yourself able to learn and be at peace with the issue as it is rather than struggling against it.

To begin on the road of change, there needs to be a recognition that conditions do not *have* to be as they are. Here the Inner Witness recognizes that you can either shift your approach to or change the conditions themselves. This opens you to new possibilities. No longer in resistance and wearing blinders, instead you have expanded your view. The new realities you discover become the ingredients for your Active Imagination to conjure up a desirable vision, which may include a new attitude or a completely different circumstance.

In the beginning, your projection is likely to feel as though it is not quite plausible. It has an elusive feel to it, as though it is just beyond your grasp. Your vision keeps reverting back to your current experience. When you imagine the desirable experience, it might feel like wishful fancy. This is when your current experience is the only one that seems possible. Working in the gap between your vision and your experience is the heart of Applied Meditation. As you stretch your imagination into new possibilities, you'll be able to witness the nuances of how your imagination depicts your projection. This reveals exactly where attention is needed to cultivate conditions amenable to change.

Einstein tells us, "No problem can be solved from the consciousness that created it. We must learn to see the world anew." Engage with the Receptive Imagination whenever your vision is not plausible, or you simply have no vision because the difficulty screams too loudly. Imagine the situation itself becoming personified, that it has an intelligence of its own, and then converse with it. If tension arises, just go back to your breath and breathe through your tension, release it and simply witness. When you are ready again, work with the Receptive Imagination, let yourself be playful. With a really troubling issue, it might take many meditation sittings before you are able to work with the Receptive Imagination. Be patient and give yourself the time you need. The

Inner Witness provides a spaciousness in which the Receptive Imagination can play. To see the situation anew, shake up the scene; turn it upside down; imagine everyone switching roles, or displaying traits opposite to their usual way of being. Open up your imagination; shake it all up and see where it lands. Change is constant, play with the energy, and discover what might emerge. Intuition and creativity come through in openness.

Recently, I had many more responsibilities than I had time to carry out. I meditated on the problem. An image of an egg timer came into my awareness. This egg timer was squeezed not just in the center, but in four places. No sand could get through. As I sat with the image it transformed into a trunk of an old cottonwood tree from my childhood. When I was little, I used to go to this tree to commune with it and with myself. It always held a magical quality for me. In its presence, I had a visceral feeling of rootedness and a knowing that time would carry me rather than my running after it. In that meditation, I relearned the lesson: listen in and time opens out. As the day unfolded, I was able to move through it in a relaxed and effective manner.

As you work, you will have insights that are in alignment with your intention. When you act on the insights that you gain, you will find that either you have changed your original vision or that it has become increasingly plausible. You gradually see/sense more clearly what it would be like. You find that you are stuck in old patterns less and less. Eventually your vision no longer reverts to the past. When you get to the point where you can imagine your new reality vividly—believing that it is plausible and feeling what it would be like—change has already gained momentum. You no longer view your old experience in the same way. You are now expecting conditions to be different.

Witnessing the dance that takes place on the continuum of change reveals where attention is called for. Sometimes it is inside, sometimes it is outside, and sometimes it is both. *When you strive to focus on a desirable vision, whatever unfolds that obstructs it, is not a reflection of the limitations of your imagination. To the contrary, it is pointing to the very conditions that are blocking change, whether that is something inside or out.*

Beliefs Are Our Roadmaps

During the process of projecting a vision of the future, you might witness that messages get provoked like, "I'll get rejected if I do that!" The message is likely to be an old familiar one, as well as pointing out a way that you have been colluding with the limitations you are striving to overcome. This is where the past enters the scene. You work with it in this context because it blocks your ability to clearly imagine the future. Whatever messages you give yourself that discount the possibility of your vision are the messages that are keeping you from experiencing the new reality. Use the Receptive Imagination to personify the messenger and negotiate with it. You might imagine a cartoon character. Ask it what it is protecting you from. As you engage in the story that is unfolding in your imagination, you'll find new ways to take care of yourself. It is important to inform your deeper self that life has changed and that now a more open experience is available. Offer it a new perspective. Notice what you might *do* differently. As always, make clear agreements with yourself and stick to them.

We can be thankful that innerconsciousness is not critical. Our behavior is loyal to our inner messages and our innerconsciousness is accepting of the new messages offered. You will find that the old beliefs are amenable to change. This process may bring up the same issues that one seeks in classic therapeutic settings. Rather than scrutinizing and analyzing, take advantage of the fact that innerconsciousness is suggestible. You *transform* limiting inner messages. Explaining why you are stuck is irrelevant; what matters is the establishment of a new belief providing you with a new footing; this puts you on the road of transformation. It is a totally different orientation than going into the past in search of what is wrong. As you transform the obstructing inner messages, you'll find your original vision becomes increasingly clear. Or something may be revealed in the process that causes you to want to shift the vision.

Though you don't want to go searching into your past for what is wrong, you do want to be mindful of the messages you are continually giving yourself. Our beliefs are the various conclusions we have drawn in the past. Just because you drew a particular conclusion as a result of what has happened doesn't mean your conclusion still applies. Circumstances have often changed. If they have, then what may have been a good conclusion before is now a limiting belief. It is our beliefs through which we interpret all that comes to our awareness, and out of which we always act—they are the assumptions we operate out of. They shape what we anticipate and control what comes into view.

Beliefs are the maps we use to navigate our lives. You want to be sure that yours are not outdated. Only certain landscapes can be viewed from a particular road. Some beliefs are functional and constructive, while others perpetuate problems you would probably prefer to leave behind, in which case it's time to reroute yourself. Consciousness always moves along pathways paved by *habituated* beliefs. We act out of habit. That's fine if any particular path takes you in the direction you want to go, but if it's not, then you need to blaze a new trail upon which your consciousness can travel.

Outdated beliefs attract circumstances that you would probably rather not have. When you find yourself replaying the same old dramas, remember that they don't stop with you. If you have children, you pass them on and they cycle through from one generation to the next. If you find yourself caught in trying to distinguish between a belief and reality don't worry about it. Reality is constantly changing and you can influence the course of change it will take. Choose anything about yourself or the world you don't like—they are all beliefs, not reality itself.

Seth suggests:

In those areas in which you are dissatisfied, you feel that you are powerless, or that your will is paralyzed, or that conditions continue despite what you think of as your intent. Yet if you pay attention to your own quite conscious thoughts, you will find that you are concentrating upon precisely those negative aspects that so appall you. You are hypnotizing yourself quite effectively, and so reinforcing the situation. You may say, horrified, "What can I do? I am hypnotizing myself into my overweight condition (or my loneliness, or my poor health)?" Yet in other facets of your life, you may be hypnotizing yourself into wealth, accomplishment, satisfaction—and here you do not complain. The same issues are involved. The same principles are operating. In those positive life situations, you are certain of your initiative. There is no doubt. Your beliefs become reality.

Now: in the unsatisfactory aspects, you must understand this: *there is also no doubt.* You are utterly convinced that you are sick, or poor, or lonely, or spiritually opaque, or unhappy. The results, then, as easily and effortlessly follow. Natural hypnosis, in the terms given here, operates as well in one case as in the other.

What should you do, then? First of all, you must realize that you are the hypnotist. You must seize the initiative here as you have in other positive aspects of your life. Whatever the superficial reasons for your beliefs, you must say:

"For a certain amount of time I will momentarily suspend what I believe in this area, and willfully accept the belief I want. I will pretend that I am under hypnosis, with myself as hypnotist and subject. For that time, desire and belief will be one. There will be no conflict because I do this willingly. For this period I will completely alter my old beliefs. Even though I sit quietly, in my mind I will act as if the belief I want were mine completely."

At this point, do not think of the future, but only of the present. If you are overweight, insert the weight that you think is ideal for you while you are following this exercise. Imagine that you are healthy if you have the belief that you are not. If you are lonely, *believe* that you are filled with the feeling of companionship instead. Realize that you are exerting your initiative to imagine such situations. Here there can be no comparison with your normal situation. Use visual data, or words—whatever is most natural to you. And again, no more than ten minutes is required.

If you do this faithfully, within a month you will find the new conditions materializing in your experience. Your neurological structure will respond automatically. The unconscious will be aroused, bringing its great powers to bear, bringing you the new results. Do not try to overdo this, to go through the entire day worrying about beliefs, for example. This can only cause you to contrast what you *have* with what you want. Forget the exercise when it is completed. You will find yourself with impulses that arrive in line with these newly inserted beliefs, and then it is up to you to act on these and not ignore them.[1]

There is nothing mysterious or hidden about our beliefs, they're constantly present. When we make an effort to look, it is appalling how apparent they become. Years ago, I made a commitment to myself to discover my own racist attitudes. Aware that I had grown up in a racist society, I knew that there was no way that I did not have some racist assumptions. Our inner landscape is a reflection of the outer world. I found underlying attitudes that had been invisible to me because I had always taken them for granted rather than choosing to notice them. For example, I discovered that it had never been fully plausible to me that there were people of color who ran governments. It was an understandable attitude since my experience had shown me only white people in decision-making positions. It was subtle, but it was also obvious when I took the time to look.

Be mindful of your internal dialogue, for it is a continual stream of suggestions. Being aware of it will reveal all of your beliefs and attitudes, both positive
and negative. What messages are you giving yourself? As life is in constant
change, you can discover negativity by simply noticing if whatever you are
thinking or feeling is life-affirming. Is it moving or static? Is it open or constricting? Notice when your thinking is repetitive; when it is closed in on itself
there is no opening for insights to break the unsatisfactory cycle. Fresh perspectives are *excluded* by your belief and will go unnoticed. Typical of this kind of
thinking is having clarity about all the reasons why something is wrong, and only
focusing on why it is the way it is. There is no room to recognize positive qualities or possibilities. It's easy to discover these thoughts if you hear yourself using
all-inclusive terms such as "can't," "never," "always," "nobody," "every," etc.
Reorient yourself. Notice yourself saying "can't" and change it to "haven't been
able to." If you say "always," change it to "usually." If you say "never," change it to
"haven't yet." These simple changes will have profound results for they will
enable you to recognize new input, and you will find your situation becoming
flexible and amenable to change. You can also reveal negative beliefs by going
over the affirmations listed in this book and witnessing your responses to them.
Like working with projecting a positive vision with your Active Imagination,
affirmations provoke beliefs that you probably had been taking for granted.

Bring your negative beliefs out into the light and then use your Mental
Housecleaning device to transform them, thus enabling you to act in new ways.
When you are not *acting* out of the old beliefs, they simply become background
echoes, eventually fading altogether for you have withdrawn their lifeblood.
They only receive sustenance when you act out of them. *Without action they die.*

It is important to bring to light the beliefs that need to be updated. But don't
fall into the trap of only looking for what is wrong in your beliefs. It is at least
as important to notice positive resources that you would like to cultivate. For
instance, you have a complacent and a courageous side. Give your courageous
side a winning edge by cultivating beliefs that awaken it. Think of moments
when you have taken risks, stepped up to the challenge. What did you assume
at the time? Think of role models who you see as courageous, what beliefs do
you imagine they have? What if you look at the world through the glasses of
these beliefs? You can breathe even more life into them. What are your positive
resources, what do you love about yourself, about life, what makes you feel

graced? Here are beliefs that you might want to cultivate. Witness what happens when your Active and Receptive Imaginations dance with these beliefs. Listen deeply, what impulses arrive? Let it make your heart smile. When you cultivate positive, desirable beliefs, they take root in your life and their flowering will please you.

Materializing your imaginings takes a conscientious act of will—if you are not conscientious, you'll find yourself behaving in the same old way. We are creatures of habit; if we don't *choose* to act differently we simply behave in known familiar ways. Your consciousness will move along the well-beaten paths it is used to using. When you set yourself on a new path, with commitment, change happens. With an act of will, choose to start anew. Since beliefs are born out of experience, it is good to do something that is symbolically in line with the new belief. Remember, new actions create new experience that deepens your new belief. If you are trying to get over being shy *make* yourself strike up a conversation with someone, if you tend to isolate yourself, invite friends over for lunch or join an organization you would like to support. You can take a class, develop new skills, learn to tango! You have nothing to lose but your old habits.

At first, it is likely to feel awkward and unfamiliar, but with time the new path will become as familiar as the old, and you can move your creative will on to other more challenging areas. You now have enough experience to solidify the new beliefs and they will remain on their own. Action is the lifeblood of belief. If at times you find yourself sliding back into old patterns, don't interpret it as a sign of failure; quite the contrary, if you weren't changing you wouldn't notice the backslide. In the past, you took that behavior for granted and didn't see it. Give yourself a break, be patient—it all takes time. Whenever you discover yourself in old patterns just focus on the new patterns and choose to act out of their power. Let your Inner Witness be your guide.

Being Attuned to What Is True

Oftentimes, when you try to imagine a desirable experience, the obstacles that arise are actually a reflection of *objective* conditions to be overcome in order to make space for the ideal to be cultivated. Don't worry if what comes up is rooted in objective conditions or outdated beliefs. You work with it in the same way. Just as you do in addressing worries (described in Chapter Five), you engage the Receptive Imagination to find what is amenable to change. Witness which of the imaginings you are playing with does not revert back to the status quo. Again, the imagination is the medium of psychic awareness. Play with the scenes and see what images are constricting, and what images easily settle into a new configuration. This will both give you a vision you can then work with, and will point to strategies you can use in your life.

To illustrate, let's say that the ideal is to be calm and relaxed at work instead of feeling scattered, rushed, and stressed. You lie back and meditate, visualizing yourself fully relaxed at work, then you extend your vision to include the context of your workplace—suddenly an image appears of your boss bustling through the office, asking for a cup of coffee. Don't blame yourself for not being able to imagine yourself relaxed, your inner self is telling you that, in actuality, no matter how relaxed you get, your boss is going to disrupt your space.

When you employ the story-making capacity of the Receptive Imagination, you can imagine alternative scenarios in order to discover other ways your boss's needs might be met. Does your boss know how to make coffee? Imagine teaching him; see how he takes to the idea. In this process, you will be able to discern the potential outcome of any action under consideration. (A good idea when the problem is with your boss.) If you can't find a scenario that feels plausible, then the Inner Witness will enable you to come to terms with the situation. You will find yourself with a sense of knowing what feels right, whether it comes as a result of the work of the Receptive Imagination, or from sitting with the issue in the presence of the Witness. You will have moved out of reaction so that you'll be able to maintain your calm at work.

As I described in Chapter Four, intuition is not pushy, you have to *choose* to pay attention to it. *If you never shine the light of awareness into the area of concern, then intuitive knowing will not be revealed.* Engaging the story-making capacities of the Receptive Imagination in the presence of the Inner Witness provides the context for discovering the operative energies in any circumstance you choose to focus on. You'll gain insight into exactly what's needed to change your perspective or change conditions. In the presence of the Inner Witness, you recognize the answers. If you are unable to find an opening for a new configuration of energy, then you will be able to discover lessons needed to be at peace with current reality rather than struggling against it.

Have you heard the serenity prayer? "Grant me the serenity to accept the things I cannot change; to change the things I can; and the wisdom to know the difference." Witnessing as the Receptive and Active Imaginations dance together will enable you to do just that.

When you work with the Receptive Imagination, dialoguing with personified obstacles or beliefs, it is important to be mindful and witness your attitude. Are you coming from a clear, open, receptive place, or is an emotional charge present? Your intention and anticipation dictate what comes into view and what unfolds. Doing your meditation work in the presence of the Inner Witness will reveal if you have digressed into an approach that is shutting down or invested, rather than one that is opening up. Always work in the presence of the Inner Witness so that you can see when you are opening up and when you are moving into constriction.

In spacious awareness, you have freedom, you can choose, you can be true to your deepest aspirations, and you can come into full integrity with yourself and others. In wholeness, healing happens and great possibilities are illuminated. When you keep the Inner Witness present you safeguard yourself from getting caught in narrow self-interest that creates problems both for yourself and others.

When we open to deep consciousness, we move into alignment with the flow of life force energy. Compassion arises, healing happens, and creativity inspires us to join with others to create our world anew. Not at cross purposes with the resilience of life, we are open to the relations we are embedded in. In meditation we reconnect with *all that is*.

Induction

Focus on your breath...Let your breath be full and easy...And at same time, let your breath be very relaxed...relaxed as a sleeping baby. As your breath relaxes, bring to awareness your symbol for physical relaxation...Give your body permission to relax. Feel your body relaxing into the support of the earth...Ground yourself. With each exhalation, let go of tension...Breathe through it and feel it release...With each inhalation, draw up the sustenance of the earth.

◆

Bring into your awareness your symbol for mental relaxation. Give your mind permission to calm down, to be relaxed...Let the chatter begin to meander...As you inhale draw in the vast energy of the sky...Sense your mind as spacious as the sky...lots of space for whatever crosses the sky of your mind...open.

◆

When you are ready, bring to awareness your symbol for emotional relaxation...Give yourself permission to emotionally relax...Breathe out any feelings that are tugging at you. Let them soak into the earth...Feel your heart opening...Appreciate your goodness...Offer yourself some loving kindness.

◆

Now bring to awareness your symbol for your creative self-restoring center. Take a moment and appreciate the gifts of life...Remember and acknowledge what you are grateful for...Life is sacred.

◆

This is your creative self-restoring center where you will remain fully relaxed and fully alert...receptive, creative, and mindful. Your intuition is keen here, the inner visionary is present and full of creativity, the quiet knowing of the Inner Witness is here too. Here you discover what is so.

To enliven this space you now occupy, focus on your breath...As though your awareness were to rest on your breath...Breath carries life...Imagine all the molecules of air that you inhale into your body are vibrant and glittering...feel them bounce around in your lungs...Then they go into your blood and moving through every cell of your entire body, bringing life and vibrancy. Every cell in your body breathes...Experience your breath moving through your body, healing your body. Your breath renews you...Every moment breath brings life...

Now imagine your breath enlightens the mind, like a breeze that clears the air, breath clears your mind...enlivens your intelligence...Imagine breath moves through your feelings making them fluid, flexible...your heart opens up...Ride your breath, the breath of life, the spirit of life flows through you, through the whole of your being...renewing you, clearing you. It feels good to be present with your breath, your breath that constantly renews your being, every moment of your life...

You settle into your breath, as your breath settles into you. Let yourself be carried by the rhythm of your breath...Extend your awareness, imagine as though the universe was also carried by breath...Everything breathes...

Breath is universal...feel universal energy, the rhythm of the universe...the natural movement of the universe, all the planets moving around their sun, each atom of which you're physically composed, each atom with electrons that move around the nucleus, the order of the universe, the continuous, inexhaustible, changing order...

This order contains within it spontaneity. The universe is dynamic, within everything is contradiction. Within life is death which, in turn, gives life to another...There is no life without death—no death without life.

Focus in on what you imagine to be your vital, dynamic center...Focus in on that place within you that is very quiet...and potent at the same time...Your center, extremely peaceful and vital at the same time, excited yet quiet...Feel your center as though it is full of magnetic energy...a great concentration of energy that radiates out from your center, moves through the whole of your being...centering you, clearing you...returning you to your power...receptive in your power, open and focused...Imagine this magnet in the center of your being breathing in universal energy...You are in rhythm with *all that is*...Your dynamic center roots you in the ground of life...Feel yourself fully present grounded and open. Notice how that is; powerful and receptive, grounded and open. Sense the dynamism within you. Through the calm quiet, power from within emerges...Your mind is full of content yet it is receptive, ready to move wherever you choose...Discipline and order create channels through which artistic creativity spontaneously appears...

Feel the dynamism within you...the balance...the equilibrium. This magnetic center of receptive power within you enables you to maintain balance amidst constant change. Experience how this is so...Imagine a concentration within you of vital life force, the focal point of your life, whatever that means to you, the magnetic center of your being that roots you to life itself...imagine the tone, the quality, the colors of this center, your center...This center keeps you balanced through all the ups and downs of your life. The fulcrum of your life...your center that enables you to maintain balance amidst change...Whenever you pay attention to it, you bring yourself into the present moment centered, powerful, and receptive...

Affirmations evoke qualities and draw on powers attuning you to express their energies in the world around you. Feel the potential of the affirmations, pretend they are already manifest. Exaggerate the qualities. Feel yourself open to the powers. Feel them awaken themselves in yourself...

My life is on purpose…

I am acutely attuned to my intuitive impulses…

A spring of creativity continually flows through me and out into the world…

I am visionary and courageous…

My beliefs are grounded in the present…

I am aware of all that I say to myself and always move my consciousness in positive directions…

My attitudes are constructive, they enable me to be clear and open in the present situation…

I am in touch with my inner source of knowing…

I am open and learn the lessons I need to meet the challenges life offers…

I am continually learning. Everyday my wisdom deepens…

My feelings flow easily and clearly throughout my being…

I perceive the true source of discord both within and around me and know where to direct my energy to create harmony…

I always make clear choices…

I am grateful for the gift of life…

I trust my experience…

I maintain balance amidst change…

I trust the future…

Know that in focusing on these affirmations you have evoked deep powers. These energies will materialize in your experience. Take time now to focus on any of your own affirmations, or any symbols you have been working with. You might also choose to focus on positive beliefs you would like to cultivate. Experience how it is to embody the energies you cultivate. Take this time to do any inner work of your choosing.

◆

Know that in focusing on these energies you set clear intention and your consciousness will travel in these directions. This energy is magnetic and attracts resonant events into your experience…Trust that all of this is so.

Cultivating Your Best: Meet Your Potential Self

When needed, replace the feminine pronoun with the masculine or say both.
Now move your awareness deeper into your self…Sense a place where there seems to be an extreme concentration of energy, as though this energy is magnetic—it draws you to that place…In this place you'll find a descending staircase. This stairway is going to take you into a power spot within you—a very comforting place for you to be. It is in this place that your fullest potential resides…deep within.

Now I will count down from ten to one, and as I do, you will lower yourself down into a power spot, a place where you will be fully in tune with your power, with universal power. At the count of one, you will be very aware of your fullest potential lying hidden inside you…the source out of which your talents spring. At the count of one, you will be very aware of your potential, in fact, you'll meet your fullest potential as though she's another being. Ten, deeper…Nine, descending deeper into yourself…Eight, each exhalation carries you down the stairs, beginning to feel the strength surging up as you go down…Seven, deeper and deeper into the person that you are…Breathe in power, breathe out and go deeper…Six, very soothing very strong energy here…Five, down deeper still…very strong energy…Four, you can almost hear the power…Three, down into this very special, very powerful spot…Two, a very powerful, very special place inside of you. *One,* feel the energy of this place, the power, the vibrations around you. This place is full of potential…feel its resonance.

Imagine meeting your fullest potential as though she is before you; notice her, create her; she is fully dynamic...Imagine her...Sense her charisma...Create her...Let her inspire you; her strength, her creativity, her intelligence, her emotional richness...In her presence, she inspires a feeling of fullness...Let her inspire you...Breathe, imagine her in all her potentiality.

◆

Talk to her, what does she love? She may not answer you verbally, but you will find yourself knowing what is so for her...Notice where she finds meaning...What does she deeply care about?...What inspires her to come forth?...When has she surfaced before?...Sense how the two of you can begin to work, to play, to live together.

◆

Ask her about those aspects of yourself you don't like...What advice does she have for you? How can you make room for her in your life, so that her expression can dynamically come through you and clearly manifest itself?...What can you do so that you and your potential are the same?

◆

Decide if you are willing to do these things. If you are, imagine yourself doing so...Let yourself receive her power, your power, receiving it into the whole of your being, as though your potential power were to pour into the whole of your body...the whole of your mind...all of your feelings...your spirit...

And if any areas have trouble receiving the energy, the power that is yours, ask them what they need to receive the energy...to allow yourself to fully manifest your potential power. Decide if you are willing to give them what they need. Imagine yourself doing what you're willing to do.

◆

When you're ready, let yourself merge with her...Constantly living on the edge of a new frontier, the frontier of creativity, the frontier of new experience always pushing yourself and trusting yourself at the same time…always learning, always growing…Dynamic.

Notice how it feels to have her move through you. Let her be you, feel yourself, see yourself, experience yourself living out your fullest potential, continually expanding the experiences life has to offer you…continually extending that experience as though you keep pushing the horizons farther out, creating a larger world to play in, to explore in, to work in, to learn in, to grow in. Decide where you first want to exercise your fullest potential…make your best offerings.

◆

As you do all this, notice what kind of support you can now give others so that they may be able to lead lives expressing their fullest potential.

◆

Notice how it is that others can support you in expressing your potential. Notice how it will affect others if you live up to your fullest potential, what you need to do to make space for that in your life.

◆

Know that as you can imagine it, you can make it so. Take time to acknowledge your potential self. Tell her you'll be getting to know her, getting to be her more and more as time goes by. Know that this is so. Thank her…

Explore Your Life and Bring About Balance

Imagine you were to begin to float up above your body, above the roof and look down on a clear day…look down at all the buildings…and float a little higher up and look down on the whole area…the water, the shape of the land, and a little higher, seeing the layout of the land, the hills, the waterways, the roads, the vast ocean, the weather patterns. As you get higher, the land seems to be so small. Imagine that you even move out of the atmosphere of the earth, and as you move out, you can see the earth getting very small and you're immersed in the whole of the cosmos…Imagine the expansiveness of the cosmos. Open your consciousness to include the cosmos, surrounded by it, just as the earth is surrounded by it, let yourself be surrounded by it...As you experience the vast and spacious cosmos, draw into your awareness a sense of how vast time is, centuries and centuries of time...before us, ahead of us. Time is as vast as space...Experience your cosmic consciousness; it communes with the infinity of space and time. Awesome.

◆

Now, in your imagination, come back a little closer to earth...Know that with the consciousness you now possess you can witness the terrain of your life—terrain of the past, of the present, and of the possibilities in the future. Imagine your life symbolically translated into landscapes...You can see quite distinctly where the different aspects of your life are going. Just as if you were a bird, you flutter around and above different areas of your life and see how you are doing down there...what replenishes you...what drains you...where the concentrations of energy are. As you explore, remember to use your Mental Housecleaning device as needed.

Explore the emotional climate of your life...How is it in different areas? Notice the quality of energy...is it open or constricted?...Anything neglected that needs attending to?...Joys that can be appreciated more?

◆

Notice this in the different areas in your work life...your family life...your friendships...your responsibilities...your routine...your creativity...your leisure...your play...your health...Trust your experience. Witness what is so.

Notice if one area bleeds out into another...How is the emotional climate of your life? As you discover your feelings in the different aspects of your life, notice the beliefs behind them.

◆

Where is it stuck?…Where does it flow?…Notice if anything of the past is littering the landscape…Are there any aspirations calling attention?…How's the weather of your life?…Anything that needs some breathing space?

◆

If you find yourself getting caught up in any aspects of your life, breathe and go back into the sky, into the cosmos of timelessness and spaciousness, and you'll find you can see with clarity once again.

◆

Look down on the terrain of your life, notice the quality around your different experiences…How are you feeling about yourself?…Are you learning, or are you stagnant?…Are you complacent anywhere?…Where is courage to be found?…Are you living up to your potential?…Which aspects of yourself are active?…Are there gifts in your life that you might appreciate more?…Are there gifts you carry that you can offer more?

◆

Are there any greener pastures?…Are there aspirations you would like to step into?…Now be aware of how you would like things to be.

◆

Find the soft spot, where change is welcomed both within you and around you…Make change be within the realm of possibility…Create the probability.

◆

Trust your nature, trust nature…Celebrate the life that is yours, the life we share.

Getting Unstuck: Moving from Impasse to Insight

Now bring to awareness a problem you choose to work on for this meditation—an area in your life you would like to be different. Remember times when this concern has been present. Recreate these times…Notice the atmosphere in which this problem thrives…the qualities present…your sense of self, the current of energy…the motives present…which aspect of yourself is prominent…others that might be involved…Bring all of this to awareness in the light of the Inner Witness.

Now let the qualities of this problem coalesce into a symbol…Now put the symbol through your Mental Housecleaning device. Sense all the troublesome, tangled-up, heavy, stiff straining energy draining out—soon to be gone altogether…Expect it.

Now project yourself into a time of the future—don't worry about where or when it is, simply experience a time in the future in which you're living in a liberated way…liberated from that familiar concern from the past. Don't worry about how or when this comes about, just experience yourself living in a new independent way—this area of your life has become easy…What used to be the wished-for is now real. Feel what this is like…Notice the atmosphere of this time, the quality of this new time, your sense of self…Resolution has already occurred…pretend this is so, imagine it, exaggerate it…What does your life feel like?…Your routine…your relations…What does it all feel like? Give it more detail, more life, embellish on the feel of living in this liberated way…Create the scenes in detail. If your vision is inviting, be with it and ignore what I am about to say. Instead, experience this transformed time.

If the time is not so inviting, or you have not been able to imagine a time in the future that is liberated and problem-free, then recreate the scenes in which the issue comes alive. Turn it upside down, shift it around, imagine that people trade roles…Shake up the scenes, imagine the energy reconfigures…Talk to the characters…Invite the problem-symbol to enter the scene…Talk to it now, imagine it has personality and communicates with you. It may communicate with words or direct knowingness—trust your imagination. Ask it what it's doing…what it offers your life…what it is protecting you from…how it's feeling…what it believes…what it teaches…what it wants…Tell it how you're feeling, what you want…Negotiate so you can approach the issue in a new and open way.

◆

Bring your attention back to my voice…Harvest the energy. Create a symbol for this time of living in this new way, whether it be in the future or a new approach now, create a symbol. Create a symbol of this new way of being, an easier way of being…Imagine as though this symbol is charged with knowingness, knowingness of resolution. Imagine it hovering above your body and beginning to pour its energy into your body…however you imagine that…Breathe it in…Feel resolution-energy pouring through the whole of your body…re-educating the cells of which you are physically composed…If any area has trouble receiving the energy, imagine asking what it wants in order to open to this new way of being.

◆

Make agreements with the reticent areas of your body…Feel them receive as much of the energy as they are currently willing to…Feel your body empowered by the energy charged with this liberating energy…Feel yourself embody this new way of being…

Now let the empowering energy of the symbol shine into your mind. Breathe, feel the energy. As though you were breathing light, shine the light of this new way onto all of your ideas…onto all your beliefs…However you imagine this to occur. What does the world look like when you view it through this energy?…If any voices or ideas pop up, unwilling to take it in, sense what it is they want…Negotiate…Make agreements…Let the energy spread through the whole of your mind.

◆

Feel your mind full of resolution, believing in this new way…Now let the energy of the symbol spread through your emotional self. Breathe, open your heart to the energy…Breathe it into your heart…Immerse all of your feelings with the energy. If there is any feeling that doesn't receive the energy so easily, ask what is needed…Imagine doing what you are willing to…Let your heart smile, as it basks in this energy. Celebrate this new energy.

◆

Feel your whole emotional self charged with this energy…Now let it spread out and flow through your spirit, let the energy emanate from your spirit…The whole of your being filled with the energy. Breathe it…Your whole self vibrates in a new way. Imagine the energy sings and dances…

Now if you wish to gain further insights you can bring back one of the original problematic scenes, bring it back into your awareness…Now ask your solution symbol what to do about the situation. Let yourself know what to do to empower yourself, to change the quality of the situation…to move forward in new ways.

◆

Acknowledge what you have learned…Is there anything you needed to cultivate the energy?…Or to make room for the new ways of being?…Notice how your life will feel as you act on this new energy…Is there anything you want to do to symbolically root the energy in your experience?…Notice how all of this will affect others…Be aware of people in your life who will support you in this change.

◆

Give yourself permission to believe in change, to believe in yourself and your ability to change…The very fact that you have imagined these things makes them possible…The energy exists. It is possible; it is probable; it is your choice.

From Trauma to Wisdom: Making the Past a Place of Power

You are now in a very magical level of innerconsciousness where the limitations of time dissolve. You can become fully aware of the past, using its power to move into the future. Imagine yourself now to be a leaf on a tree in late fall—on the edge of winter. The leaf flutters down onto the ground; feel as though you are the leaf gently fluttering down…As you flutter down, your inner awareness becomes more and more aware of time, of your own personal time in your life, chapters in your life…You are moving down deeper now…You are about to land in a very special place where the limitations of time have disappeared. Feel yourself descending…a very magical space with lots of leaves that have fluttered down onto the ground…With each exhalation of breath, you can feel each layer of your descent down through time into this special place that exists outside of regular time…This is the autumn of time itself…Here you can re-experience and remake the seasons of your life. No matter what took place, the past holds positive power for you.

In this magical place, imagine a mantelpiece with a mirror towards the back of it. This mantelpiece is very special. Your imagination can use this mirror to reflect your life. If you look into it, you can see what's behind you…all that leads up to where you stand at this juncture in your life—the path of your life, the twists and turns of your past. You can see it like a movie.

If you choose, you can enter the looking glass, go back into the past and view it with what you know now…thereby learning more. Your current self can offer your past self the support she could have used at the time…This rearranges it so the energy that resides there is different and you'll find that you'll carry your past around with you differently…Know that by reviewing your past your wisdom becomes wider and wider, it encompasses more and more…You'll find that you move into the future with great foresight and deep wisdom…Know that this is so.

Now play back any particular time, event, or chapter of your past that you carry strong feelings about—that still upsets you. Breathe as you review. Breath releases any energies that may have gotten stuck there…Choose one particular time, and just watch it unfold in front of you in the mirror…scenarios of the past…Take a moment and watch them unfold, watch yourself in the scene. Imagine it as if you were watching a movie of someone else's life. Watch everyone, watch it unfold as it did unfold…If tension arises, breathe and release it…Replay the scenes in the mirror on the mantle of the past. Now choose any particular episode that you saw, that you're seeing, that you would like to work with. If there are several, choose one and tell yourself you will work on the others another time…Choose an episode that you need to fully digest so you can let it go into the past where it belongs and you can receive the wisdom it gifts you with…Know that now you are empowered to receive the lessons it gifts you with…and you can forgive and let go releasing it. The lessons empower you to live in wisdom…Breathe…breath transforms and releases.

Replay the scenes once again…Notice how you felt, what you believed about yourself…about others…what you believed was possible at the time…Notice which aspect of who you are was prominent…Remember what you decided at the time…Notice what choices you might make if you knew then what you know now. Watch, breathe. As you revisit the scenes offer your past self some loving kindness. Your past self did the best s/he could at the time. Offer the whole scene compassion.

◆

Breathe out and sense all the difficult feelings…as though they drop into the ground transforming into rich soil, offering rich soil for growth…Let yourself mourn the scene…let it go…Put any stuck feelings into your Mental Housecleaning device…Imagine the emotional storm beginning to dissipate leaving behind cleared, fresh, cleansed air. However you imagine this…send compassion back into that scene, compassion for yourself, for others…Know that you can heal your past, you can heal your memories. In fact, as you give compassion to this episode of your life, you are healing your past and you are enriching who you are in the present. Know that this is so.

◆

Acknowledge what you have learned from this chapter of your life. Appreciate the positive power it has gifted you with. Experience the positive side of this episode of your life. Imagine as though it were a gift, a gift to your pool of wisdom…Allow yourself for a moment to appreciate this time in your life…what lesson has it given you? Will you give yourself permission to accept it? Will you let it settle into who you are? Feel yourself embody the gift that this experience has given you.

◆

Now pretend that you are the choreographer…Let yourself remake this time…Let the dance be different, how you wish it had been…Change the quality of energy that transpired. Imagine how it would have been had you known what you know now. What understandings would inform the scene?…Imagine saying, doing, what you couldn't at the time.

◆

Now focus on what you learned from this time, how you can now grow from it, let this time add to your pool of wisdom…Breathe it in…Bring the lesson into yourself, into your whole self, almost as though it were to become cellular knowledge…Breathe it into your heart…Let it nourish who you are, gaining strength to move into the future. Bring lessons learned into the present. Notice if there is anyone in your life now that you would like to express what is true for you.

◆

Imagine your past as a golden thread of your life. Let your past weave a golden robe of wisdom…Immerse yourself in wisdom…Transform the weight, the baggage of the past into this golden robe of wisdom…As you let go of the past, embraced by the lessons it offers, you move into the future with grace, with ease, with wisdom, and foresight…Know that this is so.

◆

As you finish these rituals of letting go of the past, celebrate the lessons you've learned; feel the energy of the past filling up the whole of your mind, feelings, body, your spirit, filling the whole of yourself with strength and openness to create the space to move into the future with grace, feel yourself filled with the gift of the past…project this wisdom into the future…

As you do this, become aware of what needs to be done in your daily activities to carry this energy into your life…embracing the lessons…Let go of the past, creating space in the present to move into the future in new and liberating ways…What do you need to do to make room for this new way of being in your life?…Imagine yourself doing whatever you need to do to embody this energy in your daily activities. Feel yourself living by this newfound wisdom…Notice how it may affect those around you.

◆

Lessons change who you are…You change the future, moving forward in new ways, in grace, ease, with wisdom and foresight. Acknowledge your past for letting you know what you now know…Acknowledge change.

Liberating Yourself: Transforming Defeating Messages

Focus your energy now on this moment, right here, right now, your present reality…Realize that your present, on which you are now focusing, at this moment, this place, right here, right now, is your place of power…this present reality…Realize that you always live in present time…Focus on breath…It grounds you in this moment, in present time…Your energies are always focused through present time...this moment, this place, this present reality is continuous. It is inexhaustible. The present is your place of power...Each moment is gifted with the next. It is always your present moment where you effect change both inside and outside of yourself...The present is your place of power...Reside in the knowledge of this. Breathe...Right now, right here, is the accumulation of all of your past experience focused right now...all of your aspirations are also right here...Your power is always in the present...Feel the reality of these statements...Take full possession of your power right here, right now, where you can effect change both inside and outside of yourself...

You always act out of your inner messages...Realize that you can create messages that enable you to act the way you choose...shaping your beliefs as you would like them to be...You are about to create inner messages that say exactly what you want them to...Know that consciousness is fluid, flexible, amenable to change. It welcomes new pathways upon which to welcome life.

You are now going to work on an attitude—an attitude that you have about yourself or the world or both—that's limiting...an attitude that perpetuates a way of being that you know you need no longer carry...Knowing that things can be better than that outdated attitude allows, knowing that you can act in more liberating, free ways, knowing that you can be more open...As you hear the sounds of these words your consciousness is now adjusting itself to exactly that level where you can transform these outdated attitudes; you can change them and create new inner messages enabling you to act in new and emancipated ways...enabling you to act the way you choose...Your consciousness is now at a very creative dimension where you create new realities...Pick one particular attitude you would like to transform...Now bring to awareness the belief that you have chosen to change...Notice how this belief makes you feel...how it makes the world feel...

◆

As I speak to you now, the sounds of these words are evoking a specific episode from your past that was significant in creating this limiting attitude. If a number come to mind, pick one…Image stepping into the scene…Notice how you're feeling…Notice all the details of the scene…Notice the atmosphere…Now imagine as though the attitudes it engendered created stiff, armoring clothing…This clothing doesn't fit anymore. Take off the constricting garb, imagine taking off the belief…Breathe a sigh of relief…Put it through your Mental Housecleaning device.

◆

Breathe…Feel the release, the opening. Let your body, your mind, your feelings and spirit be released from the old belief. It is gone now…Feel how much more comfortable you are now…Now assure yourself that just because it happened that way before does not necessarily mean it will again. You can choose to reroute your consciousness…You can also change the magnetic atmosphere so different kinds of circumstances coalesce. Now, assure yourself that this old belief is not reality. That instead it was only an interpretation. Tell yourself that this is a belief about the past…Tell yourself that now is your point of power…that now things are different…This was an idea about reality, not reality itself…The present is different…The future is different…Know that this is so.

◆

In the present moment, you can repaint the past, you can recreate the future. Now is your point of power. Imagine whatever manner occurs to you, change the scene you've experienced so that it feels good, so it includes what you now know…Put on new clothing, create a comfortable situation that inspires you to realize your fullest potential…it inspires everyone in it to realize their fullest potential. Breathe new life into the scene…You might want to create an atmosphere that is the opposite of the one you felt earlier. Create the opposite atmosphere, the opposite emotional feelings…the opposite thoughts…Let yourself be expanded and opened by these feelings…Adjust the scene until it fits just right. What new beliefs are informing the scene?…There is a quality of freshness, openness now…Notice how this is…What happens now?…Change it so that it is empowering to everyone.

◆

If any other scenes arise from this old attitude, change them as you changed the first scene…Know that by changing the pictures of the past in your imagination…by changing those pictures you change the messages you give yourself, changing the way you relate to the world. You repossess your power…You claim your power in the present. In replacing constricting imagery in your consciousness you leave old patterns behind…You create space to act in new, open, and liberating ways. In doing so, you've changed the future. Consciousness is powerful, flexible, and fluid…Now is your point of power…

Keep transforming memories, thoughts, feelings of the past. As you do, also notice if there are anticipations of the future that need to be cleared out…Use your Mental Housecleaning device to make space for this empowered way of being…With your breath, each time you inhale, gather the empowering energy…As you exhale, direct the powerful energy of your new belief into the whole of your past…Fill up all the holes, the wounds, the gaps until you find yourself standing fully present on the steady ground of your new experience, now.

◆

Your new belief is fully rooted…Now experience this newfound self that you are now…Know that you have changed…How do you feel about yourself now?…Let your imagination move in the direction that this new belief causes you to go…How does life feel from this perspective?…What new kinds of things occur?…How does it feel?…What will you do?…What unfolds ?…How does it affect others?...Let yourself energize probabilities that can occur with this new belief in place. Breathe life into the vision.

◆

Now, create an image, a symbol representing this new way of being...This symbol will enable you to act in new ways that are fully coherent with this empowered way of being...You have left the old attitude behind; it is relegated to the past...Feel the liberation, the wholeness, the harmony, of this new self who you are now. Know that if ever you find yourself acting in old ways, you can bring this symbol into your consciousness, and it can bring you into coherence with this new way.

Now take time to talk with this symbol, personify it, create it as an independent being. Ask what specific things you can do to bring this new way of being into your life...What impulses are present that are congruent with the new energy? What can you do as an offering of good faith?...What will nourish and feed the new belief to take root?...Sense the answer. Trust your experience...See yourself doing these things...How, when, where, you will do them?...What support is there for these changes?

◆

Tell yourself that you will recognize impulses that arrive in tune with your new belief...Tell yourself you'll respond to these impulses further rooting this belief.

◆

Ask your symbol to come into awareness spontaneously whenever you need it...Know that this new way of being is soon to become as familiar as the old. Change has already happened. Thank your symbol, go over any agreements you've made and acknowledge yourself for making this change. Now all you have to do is act on it. Welcome change.

◆

Know that your consciousness is energy, energy creating realities. Know that you changed your consciousness, changing your reality...Energy moves in new directions. Know that in changing consciousness, your environment also changes; it conforms to this new way of being...new realities materializing. Know that the symbol will come into your awareness whenever you need it, bringing with it the energy that enables you to act the way you choose...Know that you have left your past behind and created the future of your choice, for now is your point of power...Know that this is so.

Stay on Your Path: Purpose, Choice, Habits

In the presence of the Inner Witness, invite in the different threads that offer your life meaning now. What motivates you...what is important to you.

◆

Take time to bring into view whatever you sense to be the purpose of your life right now...aspirations...commitments. What is important in your life now? Bring it all into view...Feel these greater purposes...Sense their meaning, their energy...Be your aspirations and commitments...Share presence with them...They are intimately familiar, be with them now...Experience the quality of purpose. You may simply feel energy, you may see yourself in different activities. Becoming more intensely aware of your purpose, the direction of your life, the changes of your life that are right for you to be in coherence...Feel yourself in alignment with your integrity...Feel yourself in alignment with the forces of the universe...Experience this energy, this purpose, the refinement of yourself, the refinement of your will, of your connections to the earth and everything on it, to the people around you, to your creativity. Feel the coherence with your purpose. Breathe it.

◆

Now imagine this greater purpose forming a symbol, something that represents your greater purpose. Imagine all the energy that you're experiencing, sensing, knowing, coalescing into a form…maybe a picture, maybe a light, a sound, maybe a being. Create it now…Know that this symbol of your purpose illuminates a path for you. It brings you into alignment with your greater purpose and enables you to easily act on your priorities. Keep this symbol in your awareness…Now focus on the concept of choice…choice…choice…You claim freedom when you claim choice.

Notice what part of you chooses…Witness what's doing the choosing in different parts of your life…your home life…What's at the steering wheel? Is it moving in coherence with your purpose? Which parts of you are making the choices in the different aspects of your life?…Your work life, what parts of you are at the steering wheel in your work life?…Take time now to look into your life…your daily routine, all the things that you do…all the aspects of your life…your work…your relationships…taking care of your body, your habits, your projects, all the different aspects of your daily routine. Witness what is at the steering wheel at different times in your life.

◆

Are your head, body, and heart all involved?…Or is one involved and the others left out?…Are you on the path illuminated by your purpose?…Are you sidetracked?…Witness if any areas of your life are not on the enlightened path of your purpose.

◆

Choose a particular aspect in your life that is off track to work with…What's doing the choosing in this particular area of your life?…What qualities are prominent?…Is there another part of you that is more suited to be at the steering wheel?…Bring to awareness your symbol of purpose and let it enlighten you. If there's another part of you that needs to do the choosing have that part of you talk to the part of yourself that has been doing the choosing...Imagine how the new part can take care of the old. Imagine what is the best place for the old part to make its true contribution...What does it offer when it is free from what it used to do?...Imagine all the aspects cooperating, and you are back on the right path...What does the other part of you need, if it's not going to choose—what will it do instead? What can you give it to keep it happy and occupied? What gifts can it give?

◆

Now what choices do you want to make in regard to this area of your life?...What do you have to give up?...What are you willing to do?...Focus on your purpose symbol, experiencing what it resonates with, so you can make a clear choice. And tell yourself about it. Announce it to all aspects.

◆

Feel, sense how this commitment that you have made reroutes you, breaking new ground that is in alignment with your purpose...What feelings are present as you move forward in this new way?...Notice what new vistas of experience are now available to you...How will your relations with others change?...Make adjustments if need be.

◆

How are you going to make time and space to honor your choice, to keep on this path and not get drawn off?...You must take care of all parts of yourself. If you neglect some they might take over at the controls...Take time to see to it that the right part of you is at the steering wheel...Notice what if anything gets in the way of this change as you move on down the path...if anything beckons you off course...Notice what needs to be done about it...Are there danger spots you foresee?...Does anything beckon you? Or do you ever find yourself behaving in old ways simply from the force of habit?...Witness if anything calls you off your path. If you find this happening, you may wish to do Mental Housecleaning, to recycle the old ways and make space to act on the new choices. Bring in the energy you need to inspire you to give you the determination and fortitude you need to stay on purpose, to stay in alignment with your choice.

◆

Feel the sense of wholeness as you walk this path…What does life feel like here?…As you experience this new direction, notice what supports you to stay on the path…It may be friends, it may be a symbolic act, it may be rewards you can give yourself…What supports this choice, your path, the one that feel right for you? Invite the qualities you need to accompany you.

◆

Extend your awareness to include all your life activities now. Keep your life purpose symbol with you. Imagine moving into your life; as you move on down the path of your life purpose, note what is a comfortable pace for you…so you can be relaxed and energetic…Having the activity that you need, having the rest that you need. As you choose to move on down the path, it may become clear to you that there are some things that you need to let go of, that there are some things that are simply baggage weighing you down, making your movement cumbersome, awkward…Notice what you might be carrying with you that you need to let go of, or carry differently, so that you can move through your activities more gracefully…What do you need to do so that you can be lightfooted on your path of life?…There may be ways that you can further facilitate ease and grace as you move down your path…What might empower you?…What new habits will make this path smooth-going?…Choose what you are willing to do…Tell yourself about it. Commit to it…Imagine carrying out this choice.

◆

Keep on going down the path until it's very familiar to you, noticing the kinds of experiences that transpire…Noticing how it feels good to be on this path— what bumps come on the path, what turns come on the path, what vistas come into view in this life that you're leading…You may notice particular occurrences that are likely to have happened as you've moved on down the path, that have made it easier to travel this path. Ride on down the path until it's very familiar and easy to be on this particular path, until it's such a part of your life that it becomes instinctive, it feels natural. It is your life.

◆

Now, go over any insights you have gained and agreements that you have made or need to make to follow through on the choice that you've made…projecting this energy into your life. Know that you do have the choice to be able to bring this energy into your life. Choose if you're willing to do that. Go over the agreements with yourself. Know that in imagining it, the change has already been set in motion…Know that whenever you bring to awareness your symbol, it will illuminate this path that is right for you. Tell yourself that when you bring your symbol to awareness you'll act in accordance with your purpose. When you have your symbol in awareness, you move into coherence with your highest purpose and you make the choices that are best. You act on your priorities, and make choices that are for the greater good…Expect all of this to be the case.

Count Out

As the energies you have been focusing on manifest in you and around you, notice how they will affect others…Make any adjustments that might be needed…Note if there is anything that needs to be communicated to anyone…Hold a vision that increases well-being for everyone.

Finish what you're doing and make yourself ready to come out to outer conscious levels by knowing that you'll bring with you all the energies you've contacted, going over any insights and commitments…Know that the very fact that

you have imagined these things makes them possible…makes them probable…The energy exists. You are fully capable of bringing these visions into your
life. Take a moment to acknowledge your gratitude.

◆

Knowing you can return to these dimensions whenever you wish…You may
want to project when you will again meditate…

In a moment, I'm going to count from one to five…at the count of five, you'll
open your eyes remembering all that you've experienced, feeling refreshed, revitalized and relaxed…and fully empowered.

ONE—becoming more aware of the room around you…

TWO—coming up slowly now…

THREE—at the count of five, you'll open your eyes feeling relaxed, revitalized, and refreshed, remembering all that you've experienced…

FOUR—coming up now, bringing with you your sense of well-being…

FIVE!—eyes open, feeling refreshed, revitalized, and relaxed, remembering
all you have experienced…ready to act on the energies you have
tapped…having brought with you your sense of wholeness—open heart
and spirit.

Receptive Imagination Offers a Gift of Insight (15 minutes)

Focus on your breathing...Let your breath be full and easy...each breath rolling through your body like waves caressing you into deeper and deeper states of relaxation...Bring to awareness your symbol for physical relaxation...Feel your body relax more and more into the support of the earth...

As your body continues to relax, bring to awareness your symbol for mental relaxation...Feel your mind relaxing into its natural state of spaciousness...Let your breath be like the breeze that clears the air...clear your mind...Your mind is as spacious as the skies...lots of room for whatever thoughts cross the sky of your mind...your mind relaxes...

As your mind continues to relax, bring to awareness your symbol for emotional relaxation...Give yourself permission to emotionally relax...Let all the feelings that may be pushing or pulling at you drop down into the ground by the sheer weight of themselves...Breathe them out...Let it all go down into the ground to be transformed in the soil...Feel your heart getting lighter...open...Offer yourself some appreciation...Tell yourself about your goodness...Offer yourself loving kindness...Feel your heart relax into its natural state of generosity and compassion, as though it smiles...

As your heart continues to relax, bring to awareness your symbol for your creative, self-restoring center...Acknowledge what you feel grateful about...acknowledge the sanctity of life...This is your creative, self-restoring center...In this place you're connected to *all that is*...In this place you can feel your connection to *all that is*...Here, your Inner Witness is present...your imagination is free...your intuition is keen...your creativity is ready...

As you hear the sounds of these words, you can feel yourself moving into an even deeper state of awareness...Feel yourself relaxing into an enhanced level of awareness with each exhalation...Feel yourself moving deeper into yourself, deep down where healing and creativity flows…Your consciousness knows just where it needs to go and is settling into that place now…Trust consciousness…

You are now centered at a deep level of awareness, relaxed and alert…This is where you can witness intuition speaking through your imagination…Here, your intuition is ready to offer you insight and knowing…Choose a specific concern you'd like to work on now, an issue that you would like to deepen your understanding of.

◆

Bring it to awareness…Remember the times when this concern has been alive for you…Replay these times in your awareness now…You may want to choose one and witness what happens…Replay the scene…witness the feelings that arise…the mood…Imagine the scene unfolding…just *witness* it.

◆

If tension arises, breathe through it…let it go down into the ground and transform in the earth…Witness the scene…Notice the quality of energy present…in you…If there are others there, witness the quality of energy in them…and between people…What intentions are present?…Where is energy moving?…Notice if it's stuck anywhere…If it is, breathe through it…

Now, imagine as though *all* the energy wrapped around this concern were to roll up into a symbol, a character, a representative of some sort…Imagine it…Make it up…This representative has an intelligence of its own and brings the gift of insight…Greet it…Converse with it. It has its own way of communicating…Listen…listen deeply…It offers a gift of insight by using *your* imagination to reveal truth…Imagine the representative's experience…What's the story here?…Imagine what this concern has to say…It may not communicate verbally…it may offer a quiet knowing, or it may offer pictures, or symbols—a metaphor.

Ask it what you would like to know...Notice what you experience *as* you ask, for answers are often instantaneous...What does the concern want?...What is it protecting?...What do *you* want?...How might you work together?...What might you each offer one another?...Appreciate the offerings...Remember, if tension arises, breathe it out and let it be transformed...be forgiving...See yourself in a positive light...See the concern in a positive light...Breathe through any constriction...Let it drop into the ground to be transformed in the earth...

What is the gift here...what is the lesson offered?...Feel yourself opening to the lesson...Feel yourself equal to the challenge...Appreciate the offerings...Trust your experience...Feel the shift of energy as you embody this knowing...Imagine what you're inclined to do...what offering you may make to the world...

Now, as you breathe, breathe out a sense of well-being...of peace...Channel this energy wherever it may be needed...Imagine acting on it...imagine it spreading...well-being...

Thank the concern for the gift it has brought you...Acknowledge any insights you've gained and choices you've made...Acknowledge how you may act on them in your life...Appreciate the gift of life.

◆

Make yourself ready to come out to outer conscious levels now, bringing with you the insights you've discovered, ready and able to act on them in your life, and knowing you can return to these dimensions whenever you like.

In a moment, I'm going to count from one to five. At the count of five, you'll open your eyes, revitalized, refreshed, relaxed, remembering all that you have experienced and bringing with you the energies you've tapped, ready and able to act on them.

ONE—coming up slowly now…

TWO—becoming more aware of the room around you…

THREE—at the count of five you'll open your eyes, feeling revitalized, refreshed, relaxed…

FOUR—coming up now…

FIVE!—eyes open, revitalized, refreshed, relaxed, ready and able to act on the energies you've tapped.

◆9◆

Spirit Lives in Relationship

Working Inside Out is a journey that begins in the world inside each of us, and moves out into the world we share. If you have been working with the first part of this book, you have likely begun to reclaim a sense of wholeness in your meditations. Now the challenge is to experience the wholeness in the world.

Western Raionalism has conditioned us into a mechanical, linear worldview so that we tend to think in terms of separate objects, individual personalities, and goals to be achieved rather than relationships; that is, the dynamic processes created *between* us. We find ourselves alienated in a dispirited world. Thinking of ourselves as isolated, we lose track of our connection to the larger picture. This way of seeing makes us oblivious both to healing energy and to the multiple currents that shape situations we face. Yet this separateness is only an illusion; there are alternative worldviews that embody a sense of both connection and completeness.

In Chapter Five, we saw that the world is animate, that energy connects us, and that we are related on varied and deep levels. One image that stands out for me is the robot programmed to move randomly spending an inordinate amount of time in the proximity of the baby chicks that were imprinted with it. This shows us that spirit infuses the inanimate world. The world itself is alive with spirit. This is the normal way of seeing for most indigenous societies, but modern cultures have lost sight of the presence of spirit in our everyday lives. We have been cut off from meaning. New developments in whole systems theory are changing this. As Joanna Macy describes:

By shifting their focus to relationships instead of separate entities, scientists made an amazing discovery—amazing at least to the mainstream western mind. They discovered that nature is self-organizing. Or rather, assuming that to be the case, they set about discerning the principles by which this self-organizing occurs. They found these principles or system properties to be awesomely elegant in their simplicity and constancy throughout the observable universe, from sub-organic to biological and ecological systems, and mental and social systems, as well.[1]

These principles reanimate our view of the world; they help us to focus on what is going on between us. Taken as a whole they allow us to see life as a dynamic dance of structure and process; to experience the unfolding of meaning from seemingly separate elements. Joanna Macy relates four characteristics that are found in all self-organizing systems:

1. Each system is a whole, irreducible to its parts. Its unique character derives from the synergistic interplay between its components generating "emergent properties" and new possibilities, which are not predictable from the character of the separate parts.
2. Through the flow of energy, matter, and information, open systems maintain their balance; they self-stabilize....This is how we maintain our body temperature or heal from a cut.
3. Open systems both maintain their balance amidst the flux, and evolve in complexity. When challenges from the environment persist, they either fall apart or adapt by reorganizing around new, more responsive norms.
4. Another word for "system" is "holon," which is whole in its own right, comprised of subsystems, and simultaneously an integral part of a larger system. Thus holons form systems within systems, fields within fields. Each shift in "holonic" level be it from atom to molecule, cell to organ, person to family—generates emergent properties that are non-reducible to the capacities of the separate components.[2]

This systems approach points to subtle connections that go beyond what we have been taught is normal. In Chapter Five we saw that conscious of it or not, we are psychically attuned to exterior reality.

Larry Dossey, in his exploration of the nonlocal mind, describes a particularly fascinating study that shows how anticipation mysteriously seems to impact outcome. Do you ever remember feeling you were being watched, and then you turned, and indeed someone from the other side of the room was looking right at you? How did you know? This question has intrigued researchers who performed numerous studies where one person in a room was stared at by others in another room who intermittently and randomly watched the subject on a closed circuit television monitor.

When researchers asked the subjects to tell them when they felt they were being watched, people proved to be fairly accurate at detecting when this was occurring. Then the research took an interesting turn. Investigators stopped asking those being stared at how they felt. Instead, they were hooked up to a computer that measured the electrical activity on their skin, which is an indicator of physiological arousal. These experiments showed that the people who were being stared at had heightened electrical activity in their skin during the very same periods they were being watched.

This line of research takes on an even more fascinating dimension. The experiments were repeated by two other investigators, one of whom believed in the existence of the nonlocal mind, while the other was a skeptic. The skeptic's experiment showed no evidence of nonlocal mind, and the other researcher's experiment proved that it does exist. These two scientists decided to collaborate on a study. They employed rigorous double blind protocol. They worked from the same location, with the same equipment, and the same pool of people. The only difference between the two trials was that they were carried out by investigators who expected different results. No one knew who was in which group. The subjects that the skeptical researcher worked with showed no change in physiology when stared at. Conversely, the group that the believing investigator worked with showed significant electrical activity in the skin during the periods of staring. Biologist Rupert Sheldrake has developed a theory to explain what took place:

The theory of morphic fields says that self-organizing systems, like social groups, have a field that links the members of the group together...Flocks of birds have morphic fields around them, which is why when the flock turns they can all turn practically simultaneously, without bumping into each other. You could think of this as similar to the way iron filings behave in a magnetic field.

I looked to see if where there were these fields you would see telepathic connections, because that would mean these fields would allow influences to travel at a distance. You can know about fields only through their effects: the only evidence we have for electrical fields is their electrical effects—the same is true for gravitational fields.

Fields are invisible—you can't see the gravitational field that connects the moon to the earth, but yet the earth pulls the moon and the moon pulls the earth, which is why is affects the tides. My theory is that there are fields around social groups and between people and their pets, and it's these fields that act as a channel for communication.[3]

Could it be that in the awareness experiments described above, a morphic field is created between each researcher and their subjects? I believe this dimension always influences us whether we pay attention to it or not. Engage with it and our experience of life and all our relations fills with much greater meaning; we feel both held by and able to participate in the unfolding of the universe. Life doesn't happen to us; we are part of *all that is*.

It is as though we are held by energy fields as real as the air we breathe. There is coherence between what takes place and what we anticipate. The chameleon changes color to merge with the landscape. Take a moment and imagine that the world is a chameleon in the environment of the mind—not each of our minds, but the sum total of all of our minds. What kind of energy field are we collectively creating?

Culture Is the Air We Breathe and the Water in Which We Swim

In the U.S., we are conditioned to believe we are separate and fully independent from one another. Many of us do not experience ourselves embedded in a larger community—instead, we feel we have to fend for ourselves. When we have problems we take the dualistic point of view and affix blame. Whether we blame ourselves or others, we have objectified and separated everything, thwarting our ability to see the full picture. When we blame others for our problems, we relegate ourselves into a powerless victim position or we blame ourselves and feel inadequate to make change. We do not experience the relationships we are embedded in, or the multiple dynamics that make our problems or can be employed to solve them. We are alone, striving to meet the fictitious images of what we should look like and own for a fulfilled life. Add the violence pervasive on television, in video games, and in the movies, and we have a lethal mixture.

Children are continual reminders of the joy of being alive. Watching a toddler in the midst of discovery will bring a smile to anyone. Childhood is the time full of pranks and play, magic and mystery. I believe that a society's quality of life is measured by the well-being of its children.

Witness: there have been more suicidal deaths by those five to twenty-five years old over the past ten years (approximately 50,000) than U.S. combat deaths in the ten-year Vietnam War (47,355).[4] The image of a child committing suicide horrifies the heart, but in fact, it is coherent with the larger context in which it is taking place. The U.S. Secretary of Health and Human Services tells us: "In our country today, the greatest threat to the lives of children and adolescents is not disease or starvation or abandonment, but the terrible reality of violence."[5] There are more deaths to children by homicide than suicide.[6] Family life doesn't look good—annually, there are nearly five million partner rapes and physical assaults against women by an intimate partner, and approximately three million perpetrated against men.[7]

This violence takes place in our private worlds, hidden away from one another with no extended family or community to turn to. In other times and other cultures people have turned to their elders. In the U.S., over one and a half million of our elders are in nursing homes.[8] Our grief is not heard; our wounds are not seen. The greatest threat to our well-being is not a terrorist living half way across the globe, but what we have become to one another on a daily basis. In fact we live in a war zone. When the violence is hidden in the privacy of strict, culturally imposed silence ("it is none of my business"), it is made invisible. There is no place in which the heart can act and we lose our ability to care for one another.

Caring is a natural reflex of the heart. When we see another in need we respond spontaneously. When faced with a major disaster there is always an outpouring of support. Witness the groundswell of response that happened after 9/11. People rise to the occasion. Everyone pitches in to help. There is a palpable feeling in the air when people see their fates tied together. Everything is seen in a larger context and pettiness falls away. People put their individual concerns aside. A generosity of spirit fills the air. Everyone counts. In such an atmosphere people relax and let down their guard. When everybody knows they belong—no matter what—buoyancy is created. People are relieved of having to expend energy to defend their place, synergy happens, and a convivial, caring, and cooperative spirit infuses the scene. People know they can count on one another.

We humans are intrinsically social beings. We *need* to belong. There are no conditions in which we thrive more than in loving family and community. I believe that when we are deprived of our natural habitat, we go berserk.

If the events of September 11, 2001, have taught us anything, we learned that we are not separate and immune from the rest of the world. What if we experience here in the U.S. what has taken place in Argentina, when the banks locked the doors and froze everyone's accounts? To whom would you turn to survive? Who would turn to you? If we can't answer this with "lots of people," we need to start building communities now—communities woven strong with the fiber of loving relationships. This is the way to achieve homeland security. For us to make community we need to break the silence and openly acknowledge what is taking place. With nowhere to turn, more young people die every year than the number of people who fell in the twin towers. We need to change this. Everyone's life counts.

When we are in an energetic field of violence, coercion, and control, we find ourselves in one kind of territory; if we are in an atmosphere of shared care we are in quite another. Love and care create energy fields we would all prefer to live in. What if we could rely on one another all the time? We are called to create community, move out of isolation, and connect with one another instead of fearing each other. Doing so not only will save children's lives, it will save our own. People who live in community, have intimate relationships, and serve the larger good live longer, and I might add, have more fulfilling lives.[9] We need to take the time for each other—our survival depends on it.

The question becomes—how do we create fields of energy that lift all of us up? This is challenging given the condition of the world. Just like pain, our first reaction is to pull back. Hearts are soft, sensitive organs; we put up shields to protect ourselves. We don't share our vulnerabilities. The problem is that it is this very sharing that opens the heart. Peace is more than the absence of war.

Over the past decade, I have consulted with many organizations seeking to become multicultural and more equitable. I have worked closely with agencies that provide support for victims of domestic violence. This is heartfelt work that addresses a great need—as you might imagine from the statistics above. The sobering paradox is that I have found more distrust among women in this arena than in any other setting. In one organization, when we conducted our initial interviews, we asked people to describe the agency's culture. Women used terms like: "the Gestapo," "people being disappeared," or "getting chewed up and spit out." This was not a description of the conditions that battered women had to contend with, but their description of relations inside the agency! I believe that unless we are very mindful, we take on the energies we are immersed in, on a daily basis. It is difficult to maintain a belief in humanity when picking up the wounded in battle after battle. But this is exactly what we need to learn to do.

It is equally a challenge to keep an open heart when faced with inhumanity. Denial causes us to shut down, dissociate and deaden ourselves; we cut ourselves off from fullness of being. The opposite holds the promise of healing. What we need to do is create energy fields that glow with authentic loving energy. The Inner Witness will be of great help because in spacious awareness we can both hold the enormity of suffering and continue to keep the heart open. Whether we experience violence directly in our lives or not, we need to create a fresh atmosphere of truth in which our culture can breathe.

Occasionally in meditations, we are asked to go to an imaginary place that is peaceful and serene. Usually people imagine being in a beautiful natural setting. For most of us, when we imagine a peaceful place, there are *no* people there. It is time for us to turn this around; create peace *with* each other. Imagine fierce peace—so enticing that people are inspired to join in, rather than challenge it.

It doesn't take rocket science to figure out what we want. Ask yourself which moments that you have shared with others have made your heart sing. Even if they have been few and far between, what is important is not how many you have had, or how long they lasted, but to recall how it *felt* at the time. What was true about the setting? For me, there is a spontaneity and joy present. There is a fluid nature in our interactions, a shared vulnerability and appreciation of one another. When we look deeply, we can discover what kind of atmosphere made it possible, focusing on what took place *between* people. These are the environments we want to create. They teach us how to weave strong webs of connection. The process itself will create community. The solutions to our malaise are not private ones. We are called to act together.

We are all equipped with what it is going to take: hearts—big hearts. It does not take new technology, but it does take commitment, time, and patience. The reward: wholeness, authentic relations with ourselves, our families and our communities—and saved lives.

Circles Cultivate Big Hearts and Weave Strong Communities

What we focus on is what we get. We need visions from which to draw—visions that affirm our common humanity, otherwise we will reproduce the same patterns. As with all work with innerconsciousness, one needs to find positive points of reference. We can create contexts that inspire the heart. One way is to host a gathering for people who would like to share stories of what matters to them.

I suggest that you invite a few friends, your family, or even a few families from the neighborhood to come together and share. Intergenerational groups are great. An ideal number would be five to seven people, though more or less works fine too. Explain that the reason to get together is to enjoy one another, get to know each other more deeply, and have meaningful connections. For those who have been meditating with others, expand your practice to include sharing heart stories as described below.

Sit in a circle together—in a circle everyone is equal, all voices count. Then go around and take turns sharing stories of positive moments in your lives. They needn't be particularly profound, just moments that have made the heart smile—short stories or long ones. Stories open the heart. Share moments that made your heart smile in regards to your children or other loved ones; share stories about someone in your life you consider a role model—someone with a great big heart. Stories have their own pace to them, so these stories are for the sharing, not to get to the point or punchline. These stories take listening with heart. Usually five or ten minutes is an ample amount of time for each person. Some circles choose not ever to interrupt, others may prefer to be able to occasionally ask questions that elicit more details, further drawing out one another's stories. For instance, ask, "What was that like?" "What was the atmosphere like?" "What do you suppose people were feeling that made them able to be that way?" or "What kind of connection did people have?" Don't respond to other's stories with your own opinion or experience. Listen—soak in the stories, feel them in your heart. Let them just hang in the air. Bear witness to them. Keep the storyteller the focus of attention. Discussions create a different kind of energy field.

You can share stories about receiving or offering kindness, or stories of courage, or reconciliation, or love. You want stories, not reports. Tell about times that depict the best of what it means to be human. These stories will lift everyone's spirits and build a positive field. They will also offer much needed hope in these perilous times.

If the group is larger, or the stories longer than the evening can hold, break down into smaller groups so that everyone gets time to tell their whole story. Then come back as a full circle and share the shining moments and the hope they inspire. People will feel uplifted after hearing these stories. The room will fill with lots of positive points of reference.*

After the stories, do an Energy Circle in which each of you can ask for the specific qualities you would like to cultivate in your lives now (see Chapter Six). This will enable you to begin to live *into* the changes you want to make. Before you know it, these changes will manifest in your life both in how you are in the world and in what happens to you. While in the Circle, remember to channel energy to people and places on the planet that could use some healing.

When we surround ourselves with these stories, they create another kind of energy field, one in which we can cultivate new habits of the heart. If you keep meeting with each other in this way, you will develop deep bonds. These are the kinds of relationships that get strong enough that you'll come to trust that you are there for each other when the going gets rough. The energy field you create with this kind of sharing is durable. It will weather the storms. It invites deeply honest communication. There is room to share our vulnerabilities and space to work through conflict. In these settings you can reflect together on bigger questions that we all face (see Chapter Eleven).

In addition to creating contexts that build life-affirming fields of energy, I believe it is also necessary to take a close look and reflect upon the cultural norms we in the U.S. may have taken for granted. Reflecting on the codes we live by, that is the values beneath our actions, will show if they are grounded in a spirit of mutuality. As we have seen in earlier chapters, negative beliefs that go unnoticed produce experiences that we do not want. When they are brought to the surface we can do some Mental Housecleaning. And with mindfulness, we can withdraw their lifeblood by simply not acting on them.

---

* If you would like help connecting with others in your area for doing Circle work, please contact us at circlework@toolsforchange.org.

The Corrosion of Our Relationships

The very fact that we are endowed with life means we are embedded in a web of mutually interdependent relations. We each have our place in the web. However in mainstream culture instead of experiencing mutuality we often find ourselves feeling as though we are up *against* one another—having to fend for ourselves. Competition renders us oblivious to the web of relations we are all embedded in. It acts like acid on the fabric of our culture, eating away at the bonds that connect us. Instead of encouraging generosity, competition fosters an attitude that individual well-being is attained *despite* one another, not because of one another.

Trust has become an alien feeling for many of us, and alienation itself is now an experience that has become as American as apple pie. It is clear that our connections are fully corroded. Our interactions are filled with put-downs and manipulations. Suspicion and intimidation fill the air. We protect ourselves from potential humiliation and try to find a unique angle that will give us an edge over others. We vie for special praise and prestige. Is it any surprise that stress-related illnesses are the number one killers?

We live in a competitive society, relegated to being "out there," fending for ourselves, trying to survive—to make it. As a result, deep down inside each of us, there inevitably resides a gnawing sensation that tells us, "I am not good enough." We feel that we must constantly prove ourselves in order to justify the life that is already ours. Competition does not, in my opinion, create an atmosphere conducive to individual expression and creativity. Out there alone, fending for ourselves, we don't take risks. The great irony is that competition creates conformity. We can't trust ourselves; we can't trust each other.

The depth of our isolation is proportional to the depth of our separation from our own nature, from one another, and nature itself. We've traded in our relationships for plastic substitutes. We let TV fill the gap created by this separation, numbing our pain while it insidiously implants an insatiable appetite for the ultimately depleting pastime of consumption. We get doubly caught. We find ourselves motivated to purchase the latest and the best for show—proof that we are good enough. We insult our own worth when we believe we have to prove it through appearances. This may fill the pockets of the rich, but it bleeds the earth and buries the rest of us in debt. It puts stuff between us; our mutuality gets buried too. We deserve more meaningful lives together. Life offers more. When we feel part of the human condition rather than apart from it, we naturally take on social responsibility, and our lives are filled with meaning.

Competitive conditioning has penetrated deep into all of our psyches. Our thoughts are riddled with either/or oppositional thinking that is perpetually preoccupied with comparisons, striving to answer the eternal question: "Who is the best?" None of us who grew up in the U.S. have been lucky enough to be unscathed. We all make up the social fabric of our times; we are as determined by it as it is by us.

The world around us is mirrored within us so we need to examine those values and attitudes we tend to have which have particularly adverse effects on our relationships. What is fundamental is respect for the integrity and dignity of all life. That means changing the "me-first" attitude most of us have been taught, to the reality of "me-as-a-part-of-it-all." Watch yourself for feelings that tell you that you are better than someone else or not as good as another. If you prefer tulips to daisies, does this mean that a tulip is better? Each lives on the earth; it is presumptuous to decide that one is better than another. This competitive thinking is so pervasive we tend not to recognize it when we see it. How often have you been at a meeting or in a group where someone gets up (after a particularly impressive statement) saying, "That's a hard act to follow." This statement is rooted in the assumption that everyone is being compared to one another. Being alive by definition means one belongs.

Being mindful and witnessing what beliefs are shaping our interactions and consciously choosing the values we want to live by is essential. When we stop and look deeper, it is clear that many interactions are simply rooted in social conditioning. Programmed behavior is routine—remember you're acting out of your inner messages. If we take social codes as facts of life and they are not serving us, they become invisible bars that imprison us.

All ideas lead somewhere. The eternal question is, are they taking you where you want to go? Be mindful of the choices you make. Notice if they move you into connection with people or farther away from others. What values are they rooted in? What motivation is driving you? Do they open the heart or try to prove something? Being mindful will reveal shifts that you can make. Notice which orientation opens the heart to shared concern and mutuality and which leads you to ignore others in pursuit of your own agenda? Notice if you believe that your words are more or less important than what others say, or when you get caught up evaluating others. Witness whether thoughts and feelings are moving toward increased isolation or connection. Note precisely what is motivating you, and if the aims serve the common good. Observing when we constrict ourselves—and/or censor ourselves—will reveal the areas that need to be examined. And always moving from looking for what is wrong with each other—if instead we look for and express what we appreciate, we will find ourselves opening to and celebrating one another rather than having to be perpetually on guard.

When we cannot express our wholeness, everyone loses. Ask yourself: "Why am I tense, what am I protecting myself from?" "What do I need in order to relax?" "What if I said what I really think/feel?" "If I can't be fully honest, what might make it safe?" If you find yourself moving away from, rather than toward others, stop and breathe, remember your connectedness in the web. Like working in a circle, the answers are not high tech. They just take time and commitment.

Again, meditation will be of great help. Sitting in the quiet of meditation, bring yourself back to your own self. Doing so will enable you to discover what is true for you and not just how you are conditioned to behave. Breathe, be with yourself, and offer yourself kindness. When we slow down, stop striving, stop trying to prove anything, get anywhere, just stop and breathe, life opens out into wholeness. We accept ourselves; we accept others. Further, we welcome each other. When we start there the only place to go is curiosity, creativity, and celebration.

From Denial of Feelings to Authentic Relations

Love is a relational experience. In my opinion, love and power *over* relationships are antithetical. In the latter, we dissociate from ourselves and one another. We vacate, doing great harm to ourselves and others.

In this country, we have inherited a culture born of bloodshed. The wealth we have amassed has not been born out of fair deals. People were killed, stolen, exploited—the heart does not take well to these kinds of scenes. It shuts down, pushing us into denial; genocide and slavery are covered over with terms like "Manifest Destiny," "the American way of life," and "progress." I don't believe those who were on the receiving end consider it "progress." No one likes to acknowledge that their comforts have been made possible through the suffering of others. We in the U.S. have inherited a culture that denies us the freedom to be real, real in the expression of whatever we are feeling—joy or sorrow. It is not that this is conscious, but it is in the field. Mainstream culture shapes what is considered appropriate to express publicly and what is considered private (no one else's business).

To show caring is to risk being labeled sentimental, to be principled is to be called impractical, to be honest is considered vulgar, to have humor is seen as a betrayal of authority. Mab Segrest, in her book *My Mama's Dead Squirrel*, tells a story that depicts the U.S. culture of denial.[10] She describes a time when her mother gave a tea party. Unbeknownst to her mother, there was a dead squirrel right in the middle of the living room couch! The party continued on for hours, no one said or did anything about the squirrel. Image has replaced authenticity. We are expected to behave: be polite, be nice, and stay cool, calm, and collected—hide vulnerabilities, cover over mistakes, and be sure to act as though we know the answer. It's a real challenge to have meaningful and healing relationships in a culture such as this.

Taking the risk to be authentic with each other, the heart comes out from behind the wall. Whether we are with one person or in a group, we can consciously set the intention to encourage patience and a space for emotions as well as thinking. It is the intention that we bring to communication that is the most important factor. When things get confused or sticky, stop for a moment and breathe together. When beta consciousness is no longer at the controls, a tremendous sense of freedom supercedes the fear of being judged, and our individuality spontaneously comes forth. Compassion arises naturally when the heart is in the forefront. Residing in our larger humanity, we remember our own fallibility and have empathy for others, even those with whom we disagree.

In the same way that you strive to be mindful of internal constriction, strive to be mindful of what you pull back from in relationships. Sit with it and allow insight to arise. In meditation, put yourself in the other's shoes. What happened that brought about this response? Invite your Receptive Imagination to play with the situation to learn what it has to offer. Innerconsciousness can provide clear understanding, which inspires empathy. Notice what happened and what you think, feel, and want regarding the matter. The heart doesn't rush. Patience enables us to slow down, take a full breath and take in the whole of a situation. Widening horizons, wisdom emerges. Creating space for truth to come forth makes the field open to heart talk. Then our relations fill with meaning, love, and laughter.

The heart lives in connectedness; it is forgiving. We no longer need to play out roles or defend our positions. We are not trying to prove anything or be anybody; we can just take pleasure in one another. Deep listening and being heard invite having everyone's experience honored. We don't need to analyze, or fix anything—just witness one another with compassion, making the field open to heart talk. When we do, we weave a caring field and develop enduring relationships.

How do we apply all this when differences arise in our daily interactions with each other? I have been conducting mediations for conflict resolution for many years. I always begin with a centering exercise (my way of naming what we are doing without using the term "meditation"). I simply ask people to settle into themselves and find that place inside where they sit in their truth, while at the same time they can listen openly to the other. The rational mind cannot do this, it is hardwired to either/or thinking. But innerconsciousness can, for this is the place where the heart lives.

Stopping long enough to breathe enables us to be mindful; what is true becomes apparent. Take a moment and reflect together. If you have a regular meditation practice, it is easy to let go of the striving and sink into the present moment. Your own truth can be found here as well as the openness to listen to the truths of others. In any gathering, start with a few moments of shared breathing—this will establish a common energy field. As you have discovered by now, when we sink below the chatter of beta mind, clarity is there.

In the quiet, notice what actually is happening for you. Through what beliefs are you viewing the situation? What feelings are present and what do you need? Imagine what is so for the others involved, and what they are likely to believe, feel, and want. Wherever you have come across tension in yourself or others, breathe compassion into the scene.

When we constrict our energy, fear is present and often anger is there right on top of it. These energies bring dissociation, alienation, and separation. Stopping to focus on the breath and being in the presence of the Inner Witness will make space for the experience of wholeness to return. In spacious awareness, compassion will emerge and you'll find courage to stay present with what is taking place. You will make room for your feelings and have empathy for others who are involved. In spacious awareness, instead of reacting by withdrawing or lashing out, we can continue to be connected with others. In fact, we find ourselves inspired to move into deeper connection. Where you have fears, express them and let people support you. Though you might feel alone, in fact you are not. This is an act of bravery that often gives others permission to share their fears. In vulnerability, our hearts touch.

When you are meditating on a distressing situation and tension comes up, think of something that makes your heart sing. Flowers do it for me. I think of them and my heart just smiles—I can't help it. For you, it might be your grand-mother, a song, or a run in a park with your dog. Whatever makes your heart sing, bring it to awareness. Let your singing heart help you stay present with the situation you find distressing. Breathe and be with it. In the same way described in Chapter Eight, find what is good in the person(s) with whom you have been finding difficulty. Sit in a place of openness, of inquiry. In openness, new approaches emerge.

Meditation opens the heart; lets us bring the openness into those places in our families and communities—indeed into the world—that are wounded. In the act of healing, we all get to return to wholeness. In the words of the great Buddhist monk and peace-maker, Thich Nhat Hanh:

> To understand ourselves, we must learn to practice the way of non-duality. We should not fight our anger, because anger is our self, a part of our self. Anger is of an organic nature, like love. We have to take good care of anger. And because it is an organic entity, an organic phenomenon, it is possible to transform it into another organic entity. The garbage can be transformed back into compost, into lettuce and into cucumber. So don't despise anger. Don't fight your anger, and don't suppress your anger. Learn the tender way of taking care of your anger, and transform it into the energy of understanding and compassion.[11]

I am not saying it is easy. I get caught in the mire of conditioning more often than I like to admit. But I am saying that the answers to the malaise in our culture lie inside each of us, all we need to do is bring out the answers and share. Look for the positive, be honest about our troubles and share care. This, too, is not rocket science, nor is it a quick fix. It is not a new technique; it is slowing down and being together in our nakedness.

In Wholeness We All Belong

As we can witness wholeness in our meditations, we also can in our lives. Just what does "wholeness" mean? There is no dissociation; there is forgiveness of self and others. Everybody matters, everybody counts. All that is, simply is. In wholeness, there is no scapegoating, no blame, no shame. There is honesty, there is integrity, there is respect for the sanctity of life. Wholeness means we each are good. It means you are already good enough, it means we each belong.

Wholeness means diversity of life experience, of cultural background, of physical ability. Wholeness includes you, me, and everyone. In inclusion we can share our vulnerabilities. Wholeness means it is *all* of our business, not *none* of our business. It is exactly the opposite of the competitive spirit, not separating out the "good" from the "bad"—war does that. Peace makes wholeness. Wholeness makes peace.

The world is not organized as yet in terms of wholeness—exploitative relations are nearly everywhere we turn. Others have real power over our lives and well-being. Institutions eat us up and spit us out. We need to practice developing very big hearts—gigantic hearts—for only in that can we truly witness the world as it is today, and join in heart connection to heal the future.

Induction

Focus your awareness on your breathing...breathing with your belly. Bring into your awareness your symbol for physical relaxation...Feel the whole of your body relax. Give your body permission to relax...Breathe through tension...Release it into the ground...Ground yourself...

When you're ready, bring into your awareness your symbol for mental relaxation...Feel your mind relaxing into spacious awareness...Lots of room for whatever thoughts cross the sky of your mind...Bring through the energy of the sky...Feel your thoughts become easygoing...watch them begin to meander through all the space of your mind.

When you're ready, bring to awareness your symbol for emotional relaxation...Give yourself permission to relax emotionally, let all the "shoulds" soak into the ground...Acknowledge you're good heart...Pay attention to your feelings, and if there are any feelings that are calling for your attention, take care of those feelings in whatever way occurs to you. Give yourself permission to relax emotionally. Let go of any feelings pushing or pulling at you. Breathe them out...Take a moment to offer yourself some loving kindness...Feel your heart relax into its natural state of generosity...Feel your heart open...Feel compassion.

Bring to awareness your symbol for your creative, self-restoring center...Take a few moments to bring to awareness what makes your heart sing or maybe quietly smile...Bring to awareness what makes your heart open...Feel your gratitude to be alive...Sense your whole being open...You are in healing space, sacred

MEDITATIONS

space...receptive...creative...mindful...alert...relaxed...In this quiet inner awareness, you experience connections to *all that is*...This is the energy that heals. Here you experience your connectedness to all life...

Bring to awareness loved ones in your life. Invite them to join you in this meditation for a few moments...You may want to bring in others too...Take a few moments to share presence with each other...Send them some loving energy, however you imagine doing this, with color, light, music, or simply good intent...Fill the space between you with generosity and loving energy...Imagine that there are vibrant ribbons of energy that move between you...You are all held up in a great net of vibrant loving energy...Lives entwined in loving energy...Imagine it...The energy connects with others too...Feel it. Breath carries connection from one to another. Love connects from one to another...Imagine it.

◆

If you find you're in resistance to any of what unfolds for you in this meditation, witness what is true for you. Witness what is inside the resistance. Listen to what it has to say to you. Ask yourself what is true in your heart...Give yourself permission to believe in your vision. Mental Houseclean what ever you need to, making room for your vision to take root...

I am now going to suggest a number of affirmations. If you wish to affirm them, repeat them to yourself after me, feeling as though they're fully true. Know that in focusing on affirmations you create patterns of energy that move out into your life, materializing in your daily experience both within and around you...

I honor the integrity of all people and all life itself...

I honor the heart...

I open my heart to others...

I listen deeply to others...

I trust my experience and tell my truth...

I believe in myself, I believe in my family and friends, we believe in our community; there is a free flow of support among everyone...

We reside in the care we have for one another...

I feel my connections to those around me...

I am a cooperative person...

There is an abundance of love in my life...

I communicate clearly and comfortably...

I am honest with myself and others...

I weave strong community...

I take time to tune into myself and others, responding to all situations with clarity...

I am sensitive to the needs of others...

I am compassionate...

I am assertive and respectful...

I express all my feelings in constructive ways...

My increasing personal power is for making this world a more harmonious place to live for everyone...

I maintain balance amidst change...

And contribute my best to making peace...

I trust the future...

Know that in focusing on affirmations you have created patterns of energy that will manifest in your life both within and around you. You will find yourself acting in accordance with the affirmations.

Now imagine yourself being in a place, a mountainous place, a meadow in the mountains with a lake in the center of the meadow. Imagine being by a mountain lake in a very peaceful meadow. You can see the sky reflected in the lake, the trees, the mountains reflected in this lake. A very peaceful crystal clear mountain lake…If you like, you can invite others to be with you in this beautiful place…

Feel the welcoming quality of this place…It welcomes you, others, spirits; this is a welcoming place. Imagine the scenery around you…experience the sights and sounds…the colors and smells…textures, the quality in the air…the silence, the movement, the freshness of this place…Imagine all the plants that grow here, the animals and insects that live here—all a part of this place…aware of the water, the mountains around you, as though the meadow were cradling you. Notice that the lake is very still and very quiet—crystal clear.

You can look down into the lake and see the bottom of the lake…This is a very magical lake. It can help bring peace in your life and relationships. It will clear you and refresh your life. To work its magic, gather up all of what has been going on in your day-to-day activities—all that makes you spin your wheels…As you inhale gather it…Symbolically roll it up, and as you exhale, toss it all into the water and the lake will transform the energy…It will all disappear into the lake to be transformed…All the different things that stress you out and make you spin, keep throwing them into the lake…Symbolize them and throw them into the lake. Responsibilities that you have…feelings that you have…relations with friends, family…things that you have done…things that you haven't yet done…throw it all into the lake to be cleansed, transformed…Each time you toss something into the lake, you'll find yourself feeling lighter and becoming more and more present…Feel the relief…Watch the splash as it hits the surface of the water…Watch the ripples of the water rolling out over the surface of the lake…Watch all that you throw in dissolve and disappear into the depths of the lake.

◆

After there is no more to throw in, watch the surface slowly come to a very quiet state once again. Know that as the lake becomes calm, at the same time, the whole of your inner dimension becomes calm and quiet and as clear as the water of the mountain lake...Know that your relationships invite peace and clarity now...You'll be able to see into the depths of yourself, into your relationship, into beingness itself, as clearly as you're able to see into the depths of the lake. Let this calming process occur. Breathe calm, each breath clears you.

◆

In tune with the clarity and peacefulness of this mountain lake, imagine the same quality of peacefulness and receptive reflection residing inside of you...Breathe it in...so peaceful you reflect clearly. Feel that peace within you...Know that as you feel this peace within you, you're able to be fully receptive and perceive clearly whatever is going on around you. Just as the mountain lake reflects clearly, you can listen, see clearly...a very accurate reflection of what's going on around you is created in your consciousness. Notice the quality within yourself as you are able to listen receptively, and your reflections are clear and acute, true reflections. In this place, you can truly appreciate others in their full being.

When you're able to be quiet in yourself, quiet as a mountain lake, you can be aware of the needs and offerings of those around you...of the needs and offerings of the environment around you...you can hear them...and be aware of your own needs and your own offerings. Aware of the great exchange of energy that is always moving.

Integrity of Life

This mountain meadow is a very quiet and peaceful place, yet full of life, thriving, teeming with life...the meadow is full of life, the lake is full of life, even the air is full of life...Imagine all the life in this place, the pulse of life, all the different plants and animals…all the different kinds of life forming a web-work of relationships, all relating to one another. Awesome. Feel the quality of energy that vibrates out of the different forms of life here, each unique, each with an integrity of its own, each life, each being distinct in and of itself, yet part of the whole…Life is breathing in all that lives here.

◆

Imagine strands of luminous energy that connect each life form as it is in relationship with others that live here…So many strands of energy exchange that all is held up in this web. And all provide some of its strength. Each has its spot in the web.

◆

Now, draw your focus into yourself. Let your awareness move deeper and deeper inside yourself. As you breathe, become aware of the quality of energy that emanates from your center, the very essence of who you are, the tone of your personality, whatever that means to you, just as other people seem to have a tone, imagine yours…Be very receptive and listen to the tone of your being. However you sense this…Listen…Feel. Be aware. It may be color, it may be sound, it may be qualities, vibrations, whatever you imagine it to be…Experience the very tone of your being, the center out of which all your life force energies spring.

◆

Experience the integrity of this quality. Acknowledge the dignity of your being, just as every form of life has an integrity of its own, so too, your being has an integrity of its own…Life breathes in you…Honor your integrity, appreciate yourself, believe in who you are. Love yourself as you love life itself…Know that the person you are is fully complete, whole, you are enough being who you are. You are so uniquely who you are, the tone of your being is so you that it can't be compared with anything else. To compare it is fully irrelevant, it simply is what it is...Acknowledge the dignity of your own way of expressing life in the world. Not another form, not another person, nothing expresses life as you do...Just as a flower does not question its self-worth, you need not either. You simply are, only you have this particular tone, this particular quality...only you express life in this way. Feel the integrity of your energy...Feel the integrity of life being expressed through you, as you give it form, as you give it shape in your own characteristic way. Honor yourself, honor the life breath brings.

◆

Trust yourself, knowing that you are a complete, full being, you are enough...Nurture yourself with this sense of fullness. Imagine that this sense of fullness, the tone of your being forms waves as you breathe...Feel them roll through your whole being, returning you to yourself. Breathe...Relax into the being that you are.

◆

Imagine that these waves roll through any areas in your life where you felt you were not good enough, where you felt inadequate...Fill up these areas and as they fill notice yourself feeling whole again. Imagine yourself feeling whole in these scenes...Let the waves roll through you however you imagine that, let them fill any holes within you, and fill any holes in your life, returning you to your sense of wholeness...The integrity of your being, the tone of your being shines out.

◆

Now extend your awareness to include the other people in your life. Focus in on one person at a time and be aware that they, too, have a tone to themselves that is uniquely theirs...Each person has a quality that is uniquely theirs, just as you do. Life is being expressed through them in their own way...Each person has integrity of their own. Each person is different. To compare one tone to another is fully irrelevant, like comparing one particular musical note to another. Acknowledge the integrity of all the different people in your life.

◆

Witness the wonder when you put everyone together...What gets woven?...Everyone has a place on the web...all connected.

◆

Now extend your awareness to include all the different life forms. All the diversity in life on the earth...each form of life has integrity of its own. Each entity by the very fact that it's alive has integrity of its own...giving shape to the life flowing through it, giving shape to life itself...The very fact that it's alive means it invites respect, it holds its place in the world...You needn't question your value, the very fact that you are alive gives you value. All that lives is sacred...

Bathe in the knowingness that your life deserves the space that you have on the earth. By affirming your integrity, you affirm the integrity of all life, of each form of life, of each entity alive...as you deserve the space you occupy, your life deserves to be respected for the integrity of life itself. Let yourself fully occupy the space that is yours...Breathe. Take up your space on the web...Don't occupy more space than is yours, crowding others, but don't shrink from the space that is yours either...Fully occupy your life, in this time in this place, honoring the integrity of who you are...As you do, you inspire others to treat you with integrity...Honor the integrity of your life...Honor your intelligence, let yourself be confident. Know that the integrity of your life in and of itself is justification for the expression of who you are. You needn't be a particular way, your life is expression...Residing in the dignity of who you are, you defy manipulation. Experience yourself moving through the activities of your life filling up the space that's yours...Imagine expressing life through your own unique tone and quality, different than anyone who ever has been or shall be, your life has integrity of its own...Only you can express life the way that you do.

Just as the sun radiates light, heat, warmth, let your center radiate who it is that you are, creating your space in the world, contributing your gift to the world...Only you can fill the space...Only you offer this gift.

◆

Know that there is a space for everyone to fill, for everyone has a unique quality. Honor the integrity of all those with whom you come in contact...each person...each form of life...Feel yourself, see yourself moving through your activities with respect for others, fully respecting yourself as you respect others. Manipulation ceases to exist in this atmosphere, for no one is ever more important or less important than another...People celebrate one another. Integrity has no value, it simply is. Bathe yourself in this knowingness...Nurture yourself with this knowingness...

Equalizing and Enriching Relations

Residing in your reflective, receptive power, feel your power, feel your openness. Let yourself be open and powerful at the same time...Breathing in power, and as you exhale, feel yourself opening up.

From this place of receptivity, of reflection, imagine being in a room with lots of people, some kind of gathering, meeting, or event, with lots and lots of people present.

◆

Now be aware of the people who are in this room, and whatever seems to be missing in terms of the elements of humanity, then bring in the people who are part of the missing elements...Let the people in the room be as diverse as all of humanity...all different ages, all different races, different cultures. Let the room be full, enriched with the vibrancy and diversity of humanity...different cultures, different sexes, different sexual orientations, different classes…People from all kinds of walks of life…Imagine beginning to interact with everybody.

◆

Witness as you relate to different people—those in the room and those in your life—when subtle or more obvious feelings of different worth come up. In the quiet of imagining the different people, simply witness what comes up for you…Notice what judgments come up…Sometimes you may feel better than others. Sometimes you may feel they are better then you…maybe because of knowledge…or capability…or money or power…or friends and connections…for whatever reason…because of size or age…for whatever reason…Notice when judgment of yourself or of others tends to arise in relation to the people in this imaginary room…What comes up as you imagine your relation to them? Witness.

◆

Does anyone not take you seriously?…Does anyone belittle you, trivialize you?…Or maybe someone gives their power over to you. Notice if any people admire you at the expense of their own self-respect, taking you more seriously than themselves. Witness.

◆

Now put all of this competitive energy into your Mental Housecleaning device, or let it soak into the ground…Breathe it out…Bring heart into the scene…The heart doesn't judge. In the presence of heart, dignity, integrity, and appreciation fill the air…There is no one better than another. People simply are…Infuse all the situations you've become aware of with heart, respect; appreciation for the value of life percolates through everyone…Go over each of the relations you discovered earlier in which you felt you were one-up or one-down and change your feeling to one of mutual support and respect…Breathe heart into the scenes…Notice what needs to shift in the scenes for heart to breathe…When you run across particular attitudes in need of transformation, Mental Houseclean them.

◆

Feel yourself able to respect your own integrity, being of equal value to all of those around you, believing in your own experience and able to respect others' integrity...believing in their experience, knowing they are equal to yourself...Everyone has something to offer...We are all intelligent, feeling, spiritual beings...Infuse all of your relationships with the mutual respect of common dignity. No one has to prove anything. Let heart replace the old patterns of judgment—feel compassion for yourself and others.

◆

Feel trust emerge. Feel the exchanges moving from separateness to connection. Feel hearts opening...Create an atmosphere in which everyone is fully interested in one another, cares for each other and listens—listens openly, listens deeply...Simple appreciation of each other fills the air...

We can appreciate what we have to offer to those around us and what they have to offer us...having relationships of equality and cooperation.

◆

Now, imagine the sun shining down upon us, shining within us, the vibrance of the sun, the radiance of the sun...Imagine as though there was a tiny sun inside each of us, radiating out from our hearts, warming ourselves and those around us...Feel that soft, warm place within you...the place that smiles at the warm spots inside others...Imagine residing in this quiet, warm, soft center...smiling inside...As you reside in your warm center, you can open and allow yourself to connect with others with warmth...moving below the surface and sharing...having the courage to reveal yourself. Everyone connecting to warmth, sharing our hearts...expressing what is felt...Imagining yourself in different life situations grounded in your heart, centered, real...vulnerable, your power emerging out of openness.

◆

When you come from your center, feel yourself easily connecting to others, sinking into realness, richness...connections vivid, rich, and real. Each inspiring warmth in the other...expressing appreciation of one another.

◆

Feel life expand as the meaning of human connection penetrates through your life. Life is enriched with meaning, with love...We care for one another. Feel the care we share...When we care, we take care of one another...sharing our good times and our hard times...we work and play together. The emotional climate of our lives is rich...Notice how in this climate our commitments are born...Let yourself receive from those around you and give your offerings.

◆

Be aware of how you can move this energy into your life...into your family, work, and community life...Imagine appreciation for one another becoming infectious...trust developing, deepening...heart sharing...Imagine the little things that awaken the heart...Imagine specifically with the different people in your life, how together you can awaken the heart...Imagine ways of being that inspire appreciation of one another...

Decide what you are willing to do to honor heart in your life, to honor the people in your life. Imagine how you want to express your appreciation...

Choice Patterns

Bring to mind your life of late...the situations at home, with your family, with friends, what's been happening at work, what's happening in your community...let the whole of your life be present with you now, as you reside in this peaceful reflective space...let your life parade through your awareness.

◆

Remember decisions you have made at home…with friends at work and in the community…choices you've made about what to do…or not do…or things to change…or let be…choices on how you spend your time…what to share with others…what not to share…Bring to awareness different choices you've made in the arenas of your life…simply be aware of them. Witness.

◆

With each of the choices you've brought to mind, taking one at a time, ask yourself how you came to choose the particular course you did…why you did what you did…Witness what you were aiming at when you made your choice…or maybe there was something you were avoiding. Witness what was motivating you…what your intention was. Witness this for each of the choices you have brought to the light of awareness…Without judgment, notice what you believe in each of the different scenes…What policy were you operating out of?…Where was your heart?

◆

Did you take others into account with the different choices that you made?…Were you sensitive to the needs of others? Did you remember your own needs? Did you include others in your process?…Did you move into connection or isolation?…Reflect on these questions as you review the choices you have made.

◆

Notice all that makes up the basis of your choices…What quality of energy is present?…open or shut down?…trusting or anxious?…connected or alienated?…Which aspect of yourself makes the different choices?

◆

Now look at the choices other people in your life make…How come they do as they do?…Notice the patterns…What kind of social fabric do all of you weave together?…Is it strong, supportive?…Is it brittle or soft?…Is it cohesive or moving every which way?…Are there frayed edges?…Can you count on each other?…Are some areas weak while others may be reliable and durable?…What kind of ties do you share? What bonds you?…Reflect on the social fabric of your home life, your community life, and the life of your workplace.

◆

Ask yourself how it could be better…more cooperative…energy flowing easily…Make any adjustments or repairs that might be needed to create strong, nurturing fabric that supports everybody's needs. Everyone supported, yet doing their part in keeping the fabric strong, doing their part to help keep it all together…everyone being able to count on one another…supported and supporting the fabric that weaves your lives together. Imagine loving, caring energy moving through the threads.

◆

Notice what you would like to do to bring this energy into your life…Notice if there is anything you need to communicate with anyone in particular…

Crystal Clear Communication

Know that this reflective mountain lake is like a crystal ball—you can watch whole scenarios unfold in it. You can observe scenarios unfold before you, as you do, they will become crystal clear. Just as water reveals the true colors of a stone, you can now discover the true colors of any relationship…Choose one particular relationship you would like to work on, a relationship that is troubling you, that bothers you, something that is going on between you and another person that concerns you…

Replay particularly significant scenes that took place between you…let the lake reflect them back to you…Witness the interactions as they replay before you…Watch them as though you were watching a movie of somebody else's drama…Notice the atmosphere between you, all the details of the scene, as though you have control of the film and you can rewind it. Go back and freeze the frames in which the particular things that happened bothered you. Just make note of those things…exactly what took place that bothered you.

◆

Now focus into your own self. Witness what feelings surfaced in you as all of this unfolded…Witness the feeling…Notice the feeling—open, closed, fearful, angry—the raw feeling…Now focus in even deeper, notice what you are telling yourself about the situation that provokes these particular emotions…What is it that you believe about the situation that makes you feel this way?…Is there anything that has happened in your life before that seems like it might happen all over again?

◆

Breathe. Bring yourself into present time…Bring wisdom to the scene, breathe out reactivity…This time is a different time; it is not all the same as before…Notice what you might be doing that is contributing to the situation…Witness. Acknowledge what you need…Acknowledge what you might offer to transform the situation.

◆

Imagine putting aside your experience for a moment. Release it. Breathe…Clear yourself, re-center yourself…You can see the depths of the lake clearly—crystal clear…Again focus on the magic of the reflective lake and let it reflect what you imagine to be the experience of the other person(s) in the interaction…Rerun these same scenes and witness what unfolds from the other person's perspective…Whatever you imagine that to be, imagine what is true for the other(s)…If there is more than one other involved, focus in on one person at a time and witness what is true for each. Put yourself in their shoes…Watch the scene through their eyes…Replay it, and note the frames that bothered the other from their perspective...Notice the feelings that arise...What makes these feeling arise?...What does this situation remind the other of?...Imagine what is true for the other...Sense what is in their heart. Focus in on each person involved and discover what might be true for them. Listen with your heart.

◆

Imagine what the other(s) would like in order bring about well-being.

◆

Now imagine each of you replaying the scene with a very clear awareness of one another. Imagine there being room to take into account everyone's feeling and beliefs...Witness this.

◆

When you see it unfold in a way that feels good to each of you, imagine entering into the scene. Imagine you being the person you've been watching yourself be...Fill the scene with respectful, clear communication...Deep listening. Heart caring...Sense how it is to be in it, to experience it...Imagine cooperating, each of you having room for your choices and respecting the other...See if compromises need to be made...How does it unfold?...Feel what it's like.

◆

Notice what you need to do to bring this vision into the interactions. Take note of what you need to remember, to communicate, and act on to carry this harmony out into the situation.

Anger Yields Justice

In this peaceful reflective space, become aware of whatever you sense to be your own greater purpose; if you have a symbol for this, bring it to mind. Reflect on your sense of purpose, maybe specific activities—it may be living out a sense of yourself, an exploration of life itself, bringing a quality of being into the world...Sense the greater purpose of your life now...Your purpose may change from time to time. Be aware of your purpose in this particular chapter of your life...However you sense this to be, trust your experience.

Take the quality of this purpose, this sense of yourself, of your life, of your dignity, take it into your activities and see the little things that you do, day in, day out, enlarged by your purpose...Feel yourself continue to be in accord with your purpose as you move through your activities, day in, day out.

◆

Imagine you have an umbilical cord continually attached to your greater purpose as you move through the affairs of your life from moment to moment...day to day...situation to situation...continually aware of the greater purpose of your life, life itself. Make the cord that attaches you to your purpose very flexible, so that energy can freely flow from your greater purpose into your situation wherever you are. However you imagine this.

◆

Notice when you, your sense of purpose, your dignity, your integrity is violated, whether you personally, or your deep sense of the integrity of life itself, of social justice, is violated...Be aware of the different situations in life that cause you to feel violated, to feel anger, or even rage.

◆

When you find yourself angry, be sure you keep the cord to your greater purpose clear and open, energy moving back and forth between you and your purpose, continually re-sourcing each other as your purpose grows, as you become stronger.

◆

Pick one particular situation in which you were angry...Feel if the anger creates any knots inside...Let them loosen up...Drain the hardened energy into the ground...Let yourself be flexible and strong instead.

◆

Let the anger fuel your convictions, opening the cord to your greater purpose, giving you strength...Imagine the opposite of the injustice, and imagine how your angry energy can fuel its creation. Give yourself a vision to strive for...Notice what the anger wants you to do...Bring compassion into the scene and let it hone your anger into a powerful energy of transformation...transforming you and all that it touches.

◆

Decide if you want to do that with your anger...or if you want to take it elsewhere...Scan your life and notice where you can take this anger. Scan the community, notice where you can take this anger, and let it work *for* you...*for* the community...Create a positive channel for it to move out...to bring about justice.

◆

Reflect on what within you exacerbated the situation. What was your side?...Were you keeping your power? What were you doing that made this possible? Let the whole situation teach you...Have compassion for yourself and others.

◆

Now you can explore your greater purpose in other situations where negative feelings are present...Scan your life and notice where you may harbor anger, or bitterness, or cynicism...or hostility...or hatred or depression...Choose any situations or feelings you would like to work on, working in one area at a time. Breathe through the energy. Bring heart to the scenes.

◆

Notice what needs to change within you so you can express your feelings creatively...expressing what is so for you.

◆

Finishing what you are doing...reviewing all that you discovered in this meditation...Noticing what you need to do to act on your discoveries...Imagining doing what you choose…always in tune with your greater purpose in all the different circumstances in your life…all your feelings being creative forces in your life.

Family: Healing the Past and Creating Loving Present

You are now in a very receptive, reflective place where you can receive insights, you can adjust energy patterns. You can shift how you carry experience. You can heal and open your heart. Now, let your imagination return you to your childhood home. Remember where you grew up…Bring your family into the scene, exploring your childhood family…re-experience your relationships with your family, parents, siblings, extended family…witnessing yourself interact in your family. If you had more than one family or more than one home, let your imagination revisit each. Witness how it was. Let memories float through. Witness.

◆

If tension comes with any memories, breathe, breathe through them…The time has passed, it is time for healing now…When loving times return to mind, let them expand your heart all over again.

◆

Take time to explore each of the relationships that you had…One at a time, witness what it was like…As you watch, you can see your own perspective and you can also see the perspective of each of the members of your family…how they experience the family, your family. Take time to experience the different scenes from different perspectives…What bonds you? What binds you? Witness.

◆

Have compassion for yourself…Breathe compassion into the scene…Have compassion for each person…

◆

Wherever changes may be needed, imagine as though it happened differently...Shift it in your imagination...Feel shifts take place inside yourself...Imagine the patterns of the family unfolding in such a way that love is in the air...Everyone's needs are met...Everyone is cared for and everyone is respected...Everyone shares...Everyone cares...Imagine this occurring. Imagine patterns being set up that are nurturing and empowering. Pretend. When this was *not* the case, imagine what it would have been like if it had been the case. In the quiet of this magical receptive space, imagine what it would have been like. Imagine what opens the heart...Imagine what opens your heart.

◆

Notice what you need to do in your life now to feel good about your family; maybe you need to communicate something in particular...When you discover what you need to do, imagine doing what you're willing to.

◆

You may wish to create a symbol of this loving, supportive family that you have now experienced. Know that you can use this symbol whenever you are with your childhood family to help you bring these energies into the scene. The fact that you can imagine it makes it possible...When you are ready, acknowledge your mutual love and say good-bye to your childhood family...Let them leave the scene. Know that new patterns of the heart have been established.

◆

If you have a new family, bring this family in; if not, you may wish to create an imaginary family...Explore the patterns of interaction—what bonds you...what binds you...notice the quality of sharing...notice if there are any residual patterns left over from childhood that are no longer appropriate...If you came across any old patterning, talk to your deeper self, assure yourself that life is different now...Now notice how it is to be an adult with children this time around.

◆

Take time to create the quality family you'd like to have now and in the future. Love in the air. Hearts open. Care shared…Work with your current family, and if you have no family now, create one from your community, with people you know or maybe with people you would like to know. Feel family in your life now…the sharing of support, love, laughter…Imagine everyone being able to express both negative and positive feelings in this atmosphere of support…Experience how your family lives…how they connect—with you, with each other—where you're intimate, what ways you share support, what struggles you share, good times, bad times…your commitment to one another…the community your family is within…Notice what the others are doing, notice all of you affecting each other. Notice each of your perspectives…Notice your responsibilities to each other…Notice how you enjoy and play with one another, festivities you share.

◆

As you experience family now in your life, notice what needs to be done to cultivate this loving energy in your life…Notice if there is anything that needs to be communicated…Imagine yourself doing whatever you're willing to do, to bring this quality of family into your life…

Acknowledge yourself and each of the members of your family…Notice what in particular you especially appreciate about the different people in your family…Imagine how you might express and show your appreciation to them in your regular life.

◆

Imagine ribbons of loving energy moving from heart to heart, weaving your family together…Imagine that these energies touch the hearts of others in your lives…Love shines…heart to heart…Holding everyone in a loving light…

Thank each family member for all these energies you've connected with, acknowledging all of you for the support and love you share.

Count Out

Finishing what you are doing make yourself ready to come out to outer conscious levels.

◆

Before returning to an outer focus of attention we are going to breathe healing into our hearts and world. Take a few moments and generate loving energy in your heart. You may do this by remembering loving moments, or drawing on the quality of compassion...However you are inclined, imagine that your heart opens to love and compassion...

Now breathe them out and channel them wherever they may be needed...With each exhalation, breathe them out and offer them wherever they are needed...Cultivate fields of this wonderful energy in your family...in your community...in the world...wherever they are needed...Healing happens...breathing compassion, love, generosity...Imagine it sings, it shines.

◆

Acknowledge the fact that the very process of your being able to imagine all that you have makes it possible...makes it probable...Let yourself believe in the goodness of people.

◆

Go over any choices you have made...energies you have become attuned to...Tell yourself you will intuitively act in accordance with these energies.

◆

In a moment, I am going to count from one to five...at the count of five, you will open your eyes feeling revitalized, refreshed, and relaxed...remembering all that you experienced...ready and able to act on the energies you've evoked...heart open and strong.

ONE—coming up slowly now…

TWO—becoming more aware of the room around you…

THREE—at the count of five, you'll open your eyes, revitalized, refreshed, and relaxed…

FOUR—coming up now…

FIVE!—eyes open, feeling revitalized, refreshed, and relaxed, remembering all that you have experienced, ready and able to act on the energies you have evoked.

Heart Song

Track 5

Focus on your breathing…let your breath be full and easy…Bring to awareness your symbol for physical relaxation…Tell your body it can relax now…Feel your body relaxing more and more with each exhalation of breath…Send your breath through any areas of tension…feel them releasing…Feel yourself relaxing more and more into the support of the earth.

When you're ready, bring to awareness your symbol for mental relaxation…Let your breath be like the breeze that clears the air…Let your breath clear your mind…and your mind relaxes into its natural state of spaciousness…As spacious as the skies…lots of room for whatever thoughts may cross the sky of your mind…Your mind opens…is relaxed and alert…

When you're ready, bring to awareness your symbol for emotional relaxation…Breathe out and release any feelings that are pushing or pulling at you…Breathe them out…let them drop down into the ground and transform in the earth…Give yourself permission to emotionally relax…Take a moment to appreciate your goodness…Offer yourself loving kindness…Feel your heart opening…Sense your heart relaxing into its natural state of generosity and compassion…

◆

Bring to awareness your symbol for your creative, self-restoring center…Take a moment and appreciate what you hold sacred…what you cherish…Remember your gratitude…Life is sacred…This is your creative, self-restoring center. Here, you're held in vast awareness…The Inner Witness is present…receptivity is present…creativity is present…Here, you tap healing energy…you can channel this healing wherever you choose…This is your creative, self-restoring center.

Now bring to awareness whatever makes your heart sing…It may be music…it may be a loving moment with another…it may be a place…it may be a moment of creativity or inspiration…Moments of generosity…It may be a child…Bring to awareness what makes your heart sing, or quietly smile…Whatever makes your heart sing or smile, bring it to awareness now…Let it all dance in your awareness.

◆

If there are any scenes that attract your attention, focus in on one…Recreate it; remember the details…Let it make your heart open wide all over again…Breathe…breathe all of this into your heart…Fill your heart with this energy…Breathe it in…Let it open your heart…your heart smiles, sings…opens wide…

Now, bring to awareness what in particular has been distressing you of late. If there's a person or situation that's been distressing you or maybe a feeling inside that's come up for you lately…Remember a scene in which it is present. Recreate it now…imagine it…If tension arises, breathe through it…Release it into the ground to be transformed in the soil…Remember the good energy in your heart…breathe heart energy…breathe your heart song into the scene…Breathe out the tension and breathe heart energy right into the scene…As best you can, fill the scene with heart energy, however you imagine doing this…If tension arises, breathe compassion into yourself…

Breathe compassion into the scene...Keep doing this until you can keep your heart open and witness the situation with compassion...Breathe...Release tension into the ground...Breathe...breathe compassion for yourself...for others...Be in peace...Be in peace *with* the scene...Let yourself breathe and be with the situation...Offer loving kindness to the situation...See yourself in a positive light...Be forgiving...

Look deeply into your heart...Witness what you really need...Reassure your whole self...Offer each aspect of yourself loving kindness.

◆

See others in a positive light...Be forgiving...Have compassion for everyone...What is the gift of the situation?

◆

Breathe...let your heart sing again...Notice what might open the situation up...What you might say or do...Imagine it...

Make heart connections between you and any others present...Make the connections from heart to heart...make them be filled with loving energy...Weave loving energy between you...Imagine it...intend it...feel it...

◆

Breathe this energy into your life...Imagine what you may want to do or say...Imagine doing it...saying it...Sense the shift of energy...

Breathe loving energy wherever you'd like to channel it...wherever it's needed...in the world, in yourself...healing...Channel it where it's needed.

◆

Acknowledge and appreciate the gifts of life...what makes your heart sing...

Make yourself ready to come out to outer conscious levels...In a moment, I'm going to count from one to five. At the count of five, you'll open your eyes, revitalized, refreshed, relaxed, your heart open, bringing with you all the healing energies you've tapped, ready and able to act on them in your life, and knowing you can return to these dimensions of awareness whenever you choose…Heart singing.

ONE—coming up slowly now…

TWO—becoming more aware of the room around you…

THREE—coming up now…

FOUR—…

FIVE!—eyes open, revitalized, refreshed, relaxed, ready and able to act on the energies you've tapped, your heart open, your heart singing.

·10·

The World We Live In

In Openness Resilience Arises

Every day we are assaulted by news that takes our breath away, news that causes us to recoil and pull into ourselves. Although in the past people have felt that the world was coming to an end, ours are the first generations to live with the possibility that we might annihilate all life whether it be from nuclear holocaust, global warming, pollution, or over consumption. The possibility that there may be no future is an awareness that is hard to hold. It is a possibility so painful to contemplate that we try in thousands of ways to blot it out. Like children pulling blankets over our heads, hoping to be invisible to the things that frighten us, our instinct is to hide. But the degree to which we shut down is the degree to which we are not alive.

Breathing into pain opens space for healing and deepens understandings. Breath grounds us in the present, and we find a pathway to peace, to truth, and to what needs to change. Mindfulness reveals when constriction takes hold so we can then choose to open. This opening is not a process of pushing, pulling, nor quick-fixing—it is emergent. The solutions become apparent as we open and respond to the truths of our times. Meditation allows us to move out of reactivity—rather than turning away and shutting down, we expand into wholeness.

Opening to the state of the world, we come alive and become resilient. This is no small task when the planet itself feels as though it sits on a precipice, and information comes at us at such a fast speed, in such great quantities, it gums up the works of intelligence. Rather than being empowering, information overwhelms us, dumbs us down, and finally it numbs us out. As we stop and breathe, we awaken our own ability to respond and invite healing to surface.

Western culture's emphasis on rational thinking has led us to act as though we are separate from one another and the rest of nature. This false dualism has wreaked havoc on the world, splitting the self from nature, from the body and from others and has allowed economic growth to be the sole indicator of success.

My purpose is not to overload you with the gravity of the world's problems but to encourage you to use meditation to bear witness on the reality of the moment we share. As you read this chapter, breathe, reflect, and keep your circulation going. Open your heart to the bleak picture we face and vision how you would repaint it. For example, imagine the opposite state of affairs and what might support that possibility. The world sits in such a delicate balance that the acts of any one of us might tip the balance. This is a time that is full of opportunity to create ways of living that hold the promise of sustaining humanity and the planet through millennia. The choice sits with the generations alive right now—that is us, all of us.

Be mindful as you read; stop after each paragraph and breathe. When you are upset, pause. The fact that you are upset means that you believe it should be another way. You may want to run energy as we talked about in Chapter Six, find the deep capacity that we have to witness the state of the world without holding the energy. Vision how you would like the world to become instead. It is vision that provides guidance and inspiration as we each do our part in turning the tide. As you read, close your eyes, breathe, and let your deep self hear. It is our deepest selves that can get us through these times. Breathe, feel yourself alive, part of this great living earth that offers us home; part of humanity in all its great diversity. Feel yourself belonging.

The Destruction of the Natural World

There is nothing excluded in wholeness, but working in beta linear consciousness, modern economists have coined a term that allows economic activity to be split off from its consequences. "Externalities" refer to the "side effects" of making profit in any particular venture. Externalities are not included in calculations of profit and loss—be they environmental or human costs. In fact it is a fancy term used to avoid responsibility. As long as we think of the following consequences of industrial society as "externalities" we abdicate our ability to secure the future. Only in wholeness can we act with integrity. People brought about the following conditions, but it is not too late to turn the tide. People make history; in wholeness we can act with integrity to remake it.

Some say that the trees are the lungs of the earth. If externalities are counted, then just one ninety-nine-cent hamburger costs fifty-five square feet of rainforest.[1] Imagine standing next to a big empty football field; notice its size. Now fill it with tropical trees, and birds, and all sorts of critters. Imagine the sounds of the forest and the moisture in the air. Feel the breath of the earth. Now double its size, two football fields full of birds calling, monkeys swinging, vines growing. Now let your heart know that every single second all this life is destroyed in the process of turning forests into grassland for cattle.[2] We are losing our farmlands too; it takes nature three thousand years to create the soil needed to plant a crop. Fertile lands are disappearing while the deserts grow at the rate of ten million hectares every year—about the size of 17,000 football fields![3]

The coral reefs are dying, taking with them all the glittering life that makes its home there. If global warming continues, all the reefs will be dead in twenty years.[4] Glaciers melt and the oceans rise. By the end of the century all glaciers will be gone; islands, and coastline everywhere will be swallowed by the sea.[5]

The web of life is under assault. Species are disappearing one thousand times faster than their natural rate of extinction. The fabulous diversity of species that share this wondrous planet that gives us home is under assault: birds' songs will never be heard again, flowers will never be seen again, insects and whales will be gone forever. Frogs and tigers may come to live only in fairy tales. At the present rate, every year 50,000 species lose their hold on life.[6]

And humanity is not faring much better. As biological diversity is being destroyed, so is cultural diversity. Of six thousand languages currently being spoken around the world, only three hundred are being taught to the children. Within a generation or two none of the people from those cultures will have a direct connection to their history.[7] With the languages gone, the cultures disappear. McDonald's, Nike, Coca Cola, Microsoft, and IBM are now the most recognized names on the planet.

Gross Profits Produce Poverty

The current economic system concentrates wealth, a process that makes for fewer and fewer rich people and more and more poor. A fifth of the world's population lives on less than a dollar a day, without the means to purchase basic necessities such as food, clean water, and health care.[8] On the other side, the richest 20 percent of the world's population consume 84 percent of its resources.[9] The assets of the three richest people in the world are equal to those of the 48 poorest countries.[10] Despite being the richest country in the world, at the turn of the millennium, the U.S. Census reports that one-fifth of our citizens also can't meet basic needs.[11] The top 1 percent of households in the U.S. owns more wealth than the bottom 94 percent combined. Compensation for CEOs has skyrocketed, while real wages have fallen for wage workers. For every dollar the company worker makes, the CEO gets $400.[12] As layoffs multiply, Manpower—a temp agency—has become the biggest employer in the U.S.[13]

Growth and "progress" are used as justification for these "externalities" but in fact the economic system creates more wealth for a few and scarcity for vast numbers of people. The imbalance causes more and more instability as this tendency accelerates. Cancer grows in total disregard for its environment. Do the transnational corporations operate any differently? The profits of the transnationals hide the gross imbalances being generated. Economic globalization rests on concepts that can only hold meaning to cold, calculating linear (beta) consciousness. Economic profits have become the sole criteria of success. In the name of progress, the self regulating and self-healing processes of our societies have been stripped away.

But the heart has a wider view. The earth suffers while fewer and fewer get access to more and more, as the rest of us lose what little security we had. The current system is clearly stressing the self-correcting and healing systems that have kept the earth in balance for millennia. Nature creates equilibrium; it is self-balancing. The gross iniquities I have described above can only be perpetuated by coercion and manipulation. The vast majority of people on the planet would not choose this state of affairs.

This-profit driven system maintains an awesome apparatus of propaganda which generates false needs; a legal and regulatory infrastructure that now makes it against the law to meet your needs if it cuts into corporate profits; and military might that is used when the first two strategies fail. It thrives on economic blackmail or plain bribery—if your livelihood is at stake, you tend to play by the rules of the game. This is as true for individuals and communities as for nations. The game is not new. In 1935, General Smedley D. Butler testified before a congressional committee regarding his thirty-three year Marine Corps career:

> I spent most of my time being a high-class muscle man for big business, for Wall Street and for the bankers. In short, I was a racketeer for capitalism...Like all members of the military profession, I never had an original thought until I left the service...I obeyed the orders of the higher-ups. This is typical of everyone in the military service. I helped make Mexico and especially Tampico safe for American oil interests in 1914. I helped make Haiti and Cuba a decent place for the National City Bank boys to collect revenues in. I helped in the raping of half a dozen Central American republics for the benefit of Wall Street.
>
> The record of racketeering is long. I helped purify Nicaragua for the international banking house of Brown Brothers in 1909 to 1912. I brought light to the Dominican Republic for American sugar interests in 1916. I helped get Honduras "right" for American fruit companies in 1903. In China in 1927, I helped see to it that Standard Oil went its way unmolested. U.S. military power was used to establish the ground rules within which American business could operate.[14]

In the second part of the twentieth century, the game continues with new intensity. Chile, Congo, Haiti, and Guatemala and sixteen others have had freely elected democracies that fell victim to U.S. intervention (often carried out by the CIA).[15] Military regimes were propped up in their place. Phillip Agee, ex-CIA operative has said, "There have been more than one million killed—direct victims of the United States' harsh policies. This organization ranks literally on par with the Gestapo.[16] In the last hundred years, there have been over a hundred military interventions.[17]

Thomas Freidman lays out the relation of militarization and globalization:

> To ignore the role of military security in an era of economic and information growth is like forgetting the importance of oxygen to our breathing...Indeed McDonalds cannot flourish without MacDonald Douglas, the designer of the U.S. Air Force F-15. And the hidden fist that keeps the world safe for Silicon Valley's technology to flourish is called the U.S. Army, Air Force, Navy and Marine Corps. And these fighting forces and institutions are paid for by American tax dollars."[18]

In the year 2000, even before the tragic events of September 11, 2001, $343 billion was shoveled into the U.S. military—more than twice as much as all of our allies put together and more than that of the next five highest spenders combined.[19] Over half of each U.S. tax dollar goes to support the military machine. Economic might and military power enable the U.S. to act in the world without regard to consequences for others.[20]

Acting like the biggest bully on the block, the U.S. has walked out on agreements the rest of the world wants to abide by: In the past five years the U.S. has walked away from or tried to scuttle treaty after treaty including the Biological War Convention, the Kyoto accords, attempting to slow global warming. Under the Bush administration, the U.S. announced it was abandoning the Antiballistic Missile treaty, once hailed as a major step in slowing the arms race. The U.S. refuses to be held accountable to world bodies such as the International War Crimes Tribunal. It hypocritically refuses to accept international inspections of American facilities that produce biological weapons. From conventions banning anti-personnel landmines to those on the Rights of the Child, and even the Framework Convention on Tobacco Control, the U.S. stands apart from the rest of the world. The trail of broken treaties, begun with the first nations on this continent, continues today. The U.S. government won't even acknowledge that children have rights.[21]

The costs of the global corporate agenda, which places trade and profit above human or environmental needs, have been brought back home to the U.S. as budgets for human services get cut and environmental regulations get slashed. In the U.S., prisons are popping up everywhere as school budgets decrease. Police are immune to prosecution if they kill innocent people and incarceration rates are skyrocketing despite the fact that crime has gone down. Over 1.8 million people are currently behind bars in the United States. This represents the highest per capita incarceration rate in the history of the world.[22]

Citizens are being asked to give up our rights in the name of the "war on terrorism." Untold numbers of innocent people are detained or killed both inside the country and out in this mistaken approach toward assuring security. One month after September 11, 2001, Thich Nhat Hahn's words spun around the Internet appealing to our highest sensibilities:

Terror is in the human heart. We must remove this terror from the heart. Destroying the human heart, both physically and psychologically, is what we should avoid. The root of terrorism should be identified so that it can be removed. The root of terrorism is misunderstanding, hatred, and violence.

This root cannot be located by the military. Bombs and missiles cannot reach it, let alone destroy it. Only with the practice of calming and looking deeply can our insight reveal and identify this root. Only with the practice of deep listening and compassion can it be transformed and removed.

Darkness cannot be dissipated with more darkness. More darkness will make darkness thicker. Only light can dissipate darkness. Violence and hatred cannot be removed with violence and hatred. Rather, this will make violence and hatred grow a thousand-fold.

Only understanding and compassion can dissolve violence and hatred...Acting without understanding, acting out of hatred, violence, and fear, we help sow more terror, bringing terror to the homes of others and bringing back terror to our own homes...

Everyone has the seed of awakening and insight within his or her heart. Let us help each other touch these seeds in ourselves so that everyone could have the courage to speak out.[23]

What if we changed our priorities and decided that a better way to establish true security would be the way of the heart? The concepts of freedom, democracy, and justice that inspired the formation of the U.S.—though not realized fully—have been a beacon for people around the world. Millions have come to these shores for the promise of freedom and a better life. The challenge for the U.S. is to fulfill these great ideals within the country and to stand for them everywhere in the world. It is a challenge that can be met.

We hold these truths to be self-evident; that all men are created equal; that they are endowed by their Creator with certain inalienable Rights, that among these are Life, Liberty, and the Pursuit of Happiness—That to secure these Rights, governments are instituted among Men, deriving their just Powers from the Consent of the Governed; that whenever any Form of Government becomes destructive of these Ends, it is the Right of the People to alter or to abolish it, and to institute new Government, laying its Foundation on such Principles, and organizing its Powers in such Form, as to them shall seem most likely to effect their Safety and Happiness.[24]

Two hundred years after these words were written, African-American theologian Vincent Harding calls for a new U.S. He ends with ringing lines from
Langston Hughes:

> We can now understand that the first constitutional creation of the American
> nation was like a poorly attended dress rehearsal, with most of the rightful and
> necessary performers and creators barred from the stage. Women were locked in
> homes, black people held in thrall in both South and North, Native Americans
> harassed, destroyed, and driven from their land, and poor people of every hue
> taught to let their propertied "betters" make the crucial public decisions for
> them. Now, nearly two hundred years later, all the hidden, driven, enslaved
> improvisers are thronging toward the stage, walking on it, creating the drama,
> reshaping the sets, reflecting the realities of the modem world. Of course, many
> of the old-line actors think that the show is still theirs, that they are at least in
> charge of saying which of the "newcomers" will be allowed to participate and
> how; they believe that their access to the levers of destruction gives them ulti-
> mate power to deny new creation. But I am certain that they are wrong. The
> making of the United States—like the making of the modern world—is begin-
> ning again...
>
> O, let America be America again—
> The land that never has been yet—
> And yet must be—[25]

The U.S. now has the opportunity to step forward to complete its commitment to those great principles both at home and abroad. We can share the
earth's abundance in equitable and sustainable ways that honor the natural
world. The U.N. Human Development Report tells us that $210 billion would
be enough both to solve the world's most pressing environmental problems
($140 billion) and to eradicate absolute poverty worldwide ($70 billion).[26] We
have the money and the know-how, we just need the will.

The World Reflected Inside

The pseudo surplus of capitalism leaves us unfulfilled. Competition and
advertising combine to create needs that can never be satisfied. We continue
to pursue the bigger and the better in an unending effort to fill the void. Yet,

in fact, we become enslaved by the need for more stuff, more excitement, more love. Those of us who have credit go deeper and deeper into the hole; those of us who have jobs become afraid to leave them. The stuff itself becomes a trap.

Freedom has come to mean we can get whatever we want and to do whatever we want. In fact, the more we have, the more we become paralyzed. We get trapped by our fear of losing what we have; and build walls around our houses. We are afraid of losing our jobs for fear that we won't be able to keep those houses. This ensnarement was obvious as long ago as 1820 when Big Soldier, an Osage chief, politely refused to become a part of "American Civilization":

> I see and admire your manner of living, your good warm houses; your extensive fields of corn, your gardens, your cows, oxen, workhorses, wagons, and thousands of machines, that I know not the use of. I see that you are able to clothe yourselves even from weeds and grasses. In short, you can do almost what you choose. You whites possess the power of subduing almost every animal to your use. You are surrounded by slaves. Everything about you is in chains and you are slaves yourselves. I fear if I exchange my pursuits for yours, I too should become a slave.[27]

In the U.S. we have all been conditioned to think of ourselves as autonomous, independent, and "free." Collectivity is seen as standing in the way of the individual. In consequence, one experiences isolation rather than connectedness. We fool ourselves, we don't really do anything independently, but as we have seen when we act as though we are we create havoc. We don't live in isolation; we only feel isolated or, more precisely, alienated. We forfeit the experience of the inherent relatedness of everything.

Felix Green observes the impact of individualism and exploitation:

> The exploitative system is now tearing apart the whole fabric of civilization. The will to "succeed," the will to outsell, outwit, outdo and if necessary outgun others kills the intuitive, instinctive sympathy and relatedness which we would otherwise feel towards each other, and it is these that form the invisible, essential bonds which hold societies together. As individuals, a "me first" system makes us hard, calculating and lonely.[28]

Out there, alone, fending for ourselves, we cannot afford to be disapproved of, or to be exposed. Our individuality never gets expressed as we squelch anything we think or feel that is out of line. In school and work, our creativity and spontaneity never get a chance. Our values imprison us, and our fear of disapproval is the guard that keeps us in jails without bars. *We have traded in subjective autonomy for the American myth of objective autonomy.* When we remember our connectedness we can relax into the web of life which holds us all. We can raise our voices and claim our passions.

A common deception rooted in individualism is that if everyone becomes self-aware and self-responsible, then society will no longer be askew. Again the sole focus is on "me." We need to move our attention out and become aware of what is taking place around us. Narcissistic focus comes from the same mentality as the corporation's narrow focus on profits. Individualism is a cancer; it makes us oblivious of the relations in which it we are both embedded and dependent. We have all been indoctrinated into the system.

When we relax and meditate, our natural connectedness arises and we remember our gratitude. The paradox is that the more we are able to be in deep connection with ourselves and others, the more we are able to become autonomous.

This conditioning runs deep. My process of overcoming my individualism continues to evolve. As I meditated on my individualism, more layers of the onion peeled away. Remember from Chapter Three the sailboat symbol I created to help me overcome impatience in groups? The sailboat utilizes natural forces to get to her destination. I realized that the sailboat had represented getting to *my* chosen destination all by myself—not a very collective frame of mind, though an improvement at the time. A new symbol came to me; I'd seen a jellyfish in an aquarium that moved in the most graceful ways—all the different parts of it dancing in the water. What struck me was that it actually was not one organism, but a community sharing a common destination. I use that symbol to help me keep both patient and connected. Now, I feel a deeper trust and can relax into the whole.

Holographic Life

When we find ourselves upset about what is taking place in the world, it is a reminder that we are, indeed, interconnected. Though we may feel isolated, overwhelmed, or disconnected from what is taking place, whether we acknowledge it or not, we are each a part of the whole, and there is no escape. When we shut down, we weaken the whole. If reality is an intricate, interconnected hologram, then we cannot turn away from any one part of it without damaging its integrity. Conversely, as we open, we facilitate the circulation of energy, making room for the self-correcting, self-regulating, healing processes intrinsic to open systems. When challenges persist, open systems either evolve or fall apart. It is truly awesome to think that by cultivating a generous heart we not only feel better, we impact the whole world. Even relaxation is not a private experience! Open and you heal the world—what great powers reside in each and all of us!

Yet relaxing without going into denial, when focused on the state of the world, is a daunting task! It is as though we are being asked to be open in the face of our torturer. This takes a gigantic heart; I have to admit, a heart bigger than I possess. It is like working with an affirmation. You wouldn't need an affirmation if it were already true; an affirmation simply orients you to a desirable direction. Mindfulness helps us move into openness and we can witness suffering without withdrawing and shutting down. In receptivity, we talk to the issues facing us; we don't turn our back to them instead we imagine the stories that might carry us through.

We are called to bear witness: to bring peace to a war zone means keeping a peaceful heart in the midst of the fire. The times call us for to step into the fire. This is an immense challenge, and a great act of courage. Visioning peace in a quiet natural setting is not such a difficult task. Visioning peace when you are informed of the issues that are fueling war is not at all easy.

If we believe that we are victims, we abdicate our power and feel as though life happens to us. Victim mentality dwells on hopelessness, sometimes with a righteous tinge. We have been socialized to think that we are separate, that problems are "out there" or of our own making. In either case, we are expected to solve them on our own—no wonder it is so overwhelming!

But we are not separate. We are deeply connected, and our fates are entwined. We cannot deny the devastation. The good thing is that as we feel it, we come alive to our interconnections, and we open to awesome powers. The key is to feel what is true and align with the resilience of life to turn the tide. We can call on feelings as fierce as a mother who protects her young.

Some people believe they cannot contribute to the world until they have "gotten themselves together." Others believe that they cannot attend to themselves because the world itself is in such dire straights that it needs all of their waking attention. This individualism causes us to fragment and we become disempowered. We cannot "get ourselves together" separate from being in the world anymore than we can help the world while ignoring our own needs. Just as we breathe in and out; we work on the inside and we work on the outside. One cannot breathe in one direction.

Our hearts have been torn by individualism. To come to sense our interbeing is the most powerful way I know to heal the rupture. This potent word is one that Thich Nhat Hanh uses to name our true state of interconnection and interdependence.[29] Meditate on interbeing: life is woven together, as we breathe out, the trees breathe in. Follow your breath into the air and through the plants, follow the water you drink though your body and back into the body of the earth, witness the food you eat—its growth, the soil it came from, and the many hands that brought it to your table. We live interbeing with each breath. With others, contemplate interbeing and share your sensations and visions; you will gain a wealth of alternative points of reference to supplant the limited ideas we have of ourselves as isolated beings.

We have been conditioned to think there is no point in embarking on a course of action unless we know that we will be successful. The scientific rational approach instructs us to carefully inspect all ideas and not to proceed until there is no doubt and the efficacy of the approach has been proven. All ideas are suspect until they have weathered thorough debate. The heart, however, does not function this way. It moves us to action when whatever we care about is in peril. It needs no proof or deliberation. Whether we are successful at turning the tide is not the question to be asked, for we cannot know. We only know that we have an invitation to come alive. Responding to the call that lives in our hearts, we join with millions of others; that is the gift itself. Answers emerge as we walk together.

Signs of Hope

Behind the headlines, breaking news, and litany of disasters, a new way of living is emerging. Signs of hope are everywhere. Every day, people love, give birth, plant gardens, sing, dance, create, play, take time with one another, pause in a busy schedule to watch a flight of birds. When we take the time to breathe, life pulses around and through us. Every day, people act on faith and hope. The decisions to embrace life, one moment at a time, are steadily moving all of us toward the possibilities of new ways of being with one another and the earth.

This sense of a new time emerging is being felt by so many. For some, it is captured in the phrase "paradigm shift," for others it is a new awakening. Recently, some have said it is the rise of creativity over control. Joanna Macy calls it "The Great Turning." She says that a revolution is underway as people begin to realize that all of our needs can be met without destroying our world.

> We have the technical knowledge, the communication tools, and material resources to grow enough food, ensure clean air and water, and meet rational energy needs.
>
> Future generations, if there is a livable world for them, will look back at the epochal transition we are making to a life-sustaining society. And they may well call this the time of the Great Turning. It is happening now. Whether or not it is recognized by the corporate-controlled media, the Great Turning is a reality. Although we cannot know yet if it will take hold in time for humans and other complex life forms to survive, we can know that it is under way. And it is gaining momentum, through the actions of countless individuals and groups around the world. To see this as the larger context of our lives clears our vision and summons our courage.[30]

There are three dimensions of this Great Turning: The first is holding actions that slow destruction of the earth and her peoples, The second aspect is making structural analysis, and beginning the creation of life sustaining institutions, and the third is a profound transformation of consciousness.

Actions to slow the damage to Earth and its beings are perhaps the most visible expression of the Great Turning. These activities include all the political, legislative, and legal work required to reduce destruction, as well as direct actions—blockades, boycotts, civil disobedience, and other forms of refusal.[31]

Around the globe, people are resisting destruction. Mothers who lose children to violence organize to provide solace to one another whether in Detroit or Buenos Aires. People band together to defend forests from untrammeled cutting, to keep farmland from being flooded; and to protect the earth from being scarred by toxins, coal mines or nuclear waste. In cities and towns across the country people working for environmental justice are planting grasses to clean toxic soil, documenting the use of lead in paints and pipes of local schools and battling waves and winds to clean birds and wildlife suffocated by oil spills.

In India, five hundred thousand farmers protested against Cargill to protect their traditional way of saving seed from one year to the next—an ancestral practice that secures each generation's survival.[32] This has grown into a huge national movement to protect the rights of village farmers. Women around the world hold vigils for peace, inspired by the courage of Latin American, South African, Israeli and Palestinian women, Women in Black and the Mothers of the Disappeared. Their powerful but silent presence bears witness to alternatives to war.

The persistent and imaginative protests against the World Bank and the WTO and other trade institutions are among the most visible of these kinds of activities. Less dramatic, but equally courageous are the people who have come forward to testify about the corruption in corporate America and in the U.S. Government.

The analysis of structural causes and the creation of structural alternatives, says Macy, is the second dimension of the Great Turning, and is equally crucial.

> In order for us to free our selves and our planet from the damage being inflicted by the Industrial Growth Society, we must understand its dynamics. We must understand the tacit agreements that create obscene wealth for a few, while progressively impoverishing the rest. What are the interlocking causes that indenture us to an insatiable economy that uses our Earth as both supply house and sewer? It is not a pretty picture, and it takes courage and confidence in our own common sense to look at it with realism; but we are now demystifying the workings of the global economy.
>
> When we see how this system operates, we are less tempted to demonize the politicians and corporate CEOs who are in bondage to it. And for all the apparent might of the Industrial Growth Society, we can also see its fragility—how dependent it is on our obedience, and how doomed it is to devour itself. In addition to learning how the present system works, we are also creating structural alternatives. In countless localities, like green shoots pushing up through the rubble, new social and economic arrangements are sprouting. Not waiting for our national or state politicos to catch up with us, we are banding together, and

taking action in our own communities. Flowing from our creativity and collaboration on behalf of life, these actions may look marginal, but they hold the seeds for the future.

Every spring, hundreds of thousands of people inside our nation's cities plant gardens, restoring the earth and their own sense of self-sufficiency. Young people are challenging car culture by critical mass bike rallies and converting old school buses into bio-diesel transport. Alternatives ways of living are emerging around the world: In Columbia, Gaviotas is a community that is a hotbed of inventions for sustainability. For three decades, Gaviotans—peasants, scientists, artists, and former street kids—have struggled to build an oasis of imagination and sustainability in the remote, barren savannas of eastern Colombia, an area ravaged by political terror. They have planted millions of trees, regenerating an indigenous rainforest. They farm organically and use wind and solar power. Every family enjoys free housing, community meals, and schooling. There are no weapons, no police, no jail. There is no mayor.[33]

In a small German village called Stuyerburg, Lebensgarten, once a slave labor munitions factory for the Nazi regime, has been converted into a multigenerational ecological village. In Detroit, neighborhood groups are turning abandoned houses into homes for teen mothers, using principles of sustainable architecture. Neighborhoods in Argentina form cooperatives in the wake of a collapsed economy. These cooperatives produce food, medicine, and goods necessary for daily life. In the U.S., urban communities form direct relationships with small farms, creating community-supported agriculture, bypassing the distribution channels of mega-agribusiness.

These activities are happening in backyards, village squares, bus stops and on the internet where people make connections that are reshaping our world. New sources of information flow around the mainstream. Independent Media Centers have sprung up in cities and communities around the world.[34] They and other media and technology initiatives provide an infrastructure for news that is more global and unfiltered than the mainstream media.

These alternative flows are potent. A small Canadian NGO found out about the devastating implications of a secret pact called the Multi Lateral Agreement on investment, and puts the text on the Internet. Within two years, the agreement, seen as key to implementing the new world economic order by the corporations and the main economic powers, was defeated by thousands of grassroots organizations cooperating through e-mail and trust. This sense of cooperation has led to more and more connections, collaborations and inter-weavings in challenging the World Trade Organization (WTO), the World Bank, the International Monetary Fund (IMF) and other global trade institutions [35]

Restorative Justice is taking root in many of our cities as a community-based way of dealing with people who commit criminal acts.[36] Alternatives to Violence,[37] The Freedom Project, and the Zen Peacemakers work with prisoners to create peace within the prison system and to support people when they get out. And in the Indian state of Kerala, for nearly forty years almost three hundred murderers have lived in an open prison, without fences, armed guards or surveillance towers. In all its years of functioning, there has been only one repeat offender and one escapee.[38]

Grassroots and indigenous leaders are meeting around the globe holding council. Indigenous people share culture and politics as they develop a vision that is global in scope and local in character. People from all over the world are gathering in Puerto Allegre, Brazil under the banner, "Another World is Possible."[39] In the second year, over 65,000 grassroots activists came together to envision and implement sustainable ways of living.

These structural alternatives cannot take root and survive without our adopt-ing values to sustain them—this is the third dimension of the Great Turning.

They must mirror what we want and how we relate to Earth and each other. They arise as grief for our world, giving the lie to old paradigm notions of rugged indi-vidualism, the essential separateness of the self. They spring up as glad response to breakthroughs in scientific thought, as reductionism and materialism give way to evidence of a living universe. And they come to pass in the resurgence of wis-dom traditions, reminding us again that our world is a sacred whole, worthy of adoration and service.

Systems thinking, deep ecology, liberation theology, Creation Spirituality, shamanism, ecopsychology, and earth-based spiritual practices are all palpable evi-dence of this shift. There has been over the past century an influx of Eastern reli-gious thought, and by now a real groundswell of Buddhist practice in the West. Within Judaism, Christianity, and Islam, underground streams are emerging that express devotion to the living Earth. Everywhere, people are embracing holistic health, spiritual healing, and w ays of understanding that harken back to times before classical Western science.

The Great Turning is built on trusting our true inner natures and *all that is*. This book and the work of Applied Meditation is about bringing the great powers that live inside our hearts and spirits out into our world and our work so that the "New World Order" turns out to be a passing fad and we secure the future for the whole millennium and more.

Induction

Breathing with your belly, bring to your awareness your symbol for physical relaxation and feel the whole of your body relax…Breathe through tension, release it into the ground…Relax into the support of the earth.

◆

When you are ready, bring to awareness your symbol for mental relaxation. Extend your awareness to include the vast reaches of the sky, the sky that extends out forever…Feel your mind relax into its natural state of spaciousness, as spacious as the skies.

◆

Now bring in your symbol for emotional relaxation. Let go of the "shoulds." Nurture yourself with a feeling of connectedness. Feeling supported by all the life around you, supported by life itself. Just as you can relax into the support of the earth, you can relax into the support of the community…Relaxing into the web-work of life, the net of relationships of which you are a part, supporting your life…Imagine that your heart relaxes into its natural state of love and compassion. However you experience this, breathe love and compassion. As you relax emotionally, your heart opens…love and compassion arise.

◆

Bring to awareness your symbol for your creative, self-restoring center, where your expanding awareness flows. Here you are receptive to energy and information beyond the ordinary limits of space and time. Here your heart opens and deep knowing grows…Here you can listen to the whispering of spirit…Here you can bear witness to what is true…This is where visions are born. And you can join in creating the world anew…This is where healing and creativity arise…Here you discover the energies, information, and courage you need to heal and create the world anew…Take a moment to honor what you hold sacred…Remember your gratitude for the gift of life…It is a gift to be alive…part of the whole and the whole lives inside…held in interbeing.

◆

If you would like, you can invite spirits to accompany you in this work…beings of the past or future, or beings who occupy different life forms…If you would like, invite them to accompany you…Welcome them.

◆

Feel your heart and spirit ready for the work you are about to embark on.
I am going to suggest several affirmations; if you wish to affirm them, repeat them to yourself after me, feeling as though they are fully true.

I believe in myself, I believe in my family and friends; we believe in our community; there is a free flow of support among us in creating change…
I am honest with myself and others…
I remember our interconnectedness…
I relax into interbeing…
I am grateful for the gift of life…
I offer my gifts to life…
I am aware of the impact of all of my actions and I act responsibly…
I am open and generous…
I help my community come together…
I trust the support of others…
I am compassionate, my heart opens more each day…
We maintain balance amidst change…

We gain strength from our connection to the peoples of the world…

We have confidence in our ability to care for the world…

A spring of creativity continually flows through us and out into the world…

We believe in life, we are dedicated to protecting life…

We trust the future, we work to bring about a positive future…

Know that in focusing on affirmations you evoke powers from the depths of beingness itself, powers that manifest both within and around you. In focusing on affirmations, you cause yourself to align your energies with them, and you will discover yourself acting out of these very powers you have evoked…

Listen very carefully to all that is said letting the words draw up your deepest knowing, knowing from the depths of life itself.

From Holding On into Openness

Feel that as you are relaxed, you are open…your body opens…your mind opens…your feelings open…Let yourself enjoy this open state…Breathe out and feel openness…Find that place within you where you feel very wise, very strong, and yet open…fully receptive in your strength…receptivity being your strength. Let your awareness ride on your breath, your breath brings release, you open…Breathe. Feel openness. Experience this openness…In openness you experience wholeness…With each exhalation, feel yourself relaxing into your natural state of wholeness…openness…

Now imagine yourself being a little seed, all enclosed…Imagine that you're planted and you're watered…slowly you develop, then you burst out of your shell, you grow up towards the sun, you reach out towards the sky…You get bigger and bigger…And then you create blossoms that start out being enclosed buds…just as you used to be an enclosed seed…Then they open up…Feel that the process of growth is a process of opening.

◆

Experience how openness allows movement through you…Breath is easy…in openness there is fluidity…fluid motion moving through you…welcoming newness…It's this fluidity that gives you strength…supple…Know that it's as soon as you shut down and become rigid and brittle that you become vulnerable to being broken—for the energy can no longer move through you. As soon as you constrict and turn away from your experience, you fragment and weaken yourself—energy no longer flows through. Feel the power of flexibility…Wholeness is not static, it is always in motion…moving with *all that it is*. In mindfulness, witness when constriction arises…All you need to do is breathe through and openness returns. Experience how this is the case.

◆

As long as you're supple and open, movement carries you. You are carried by life force energies…Breathe, feel that you can open further as you breathe. Breath always opens you…Feel opening throughout your being…Breathe and feel your life open…Breathe life energy into any aspects of your being that have gotten rigid…Breathe life into those places that need it…Nourish them with breath. Feel them breathe and become open, supple, fluid again…Let go and life carries you…No effort, just openness.

Experience how life itself is fluid, constantly moving, moving all the time…Tune in to your body and notice if there are any holding patterns…Send breath there…Breathe through and opening happens. With intention, aim your breath wherever you like. Feel opening happen. Breathe. Wholeness is a natural state.

◆

Extend your awareness to your environment, to all that is around you…Extend this openness to the life that is around you…Watch your breath roll through you and into the trees…Out of the trees and into other beings…Breath weaves life. Interbeing.

◆

Sense the many relations that connect you to your place on the web…Family…Bring to awareness the food you eat…those who worked to bring food to your table…You might want to tune to one kind of food…Imagine it alive and growing in the place from which it came…What it ate to grow into its being…Imagine all that took place that brought the food to your plate…the hands it has passed through…Community, exchange of energy…Interbeing. Witness it.

◆

Imagine the different things that you do moving out and touching others on the web…Just as breath weaves life, all activity contributes to the weaving of being…Awesome. Breathe, feel openness, feel generosity and energy move even more openly, more powerfully…All held in the web…All making the web. Imagine letting go into the web.

◆

If you come across any tension breathe through it…Breathe. Feel your body softening, letting go of your private position of holding on, and relaxing into the support of community…Feel yourself getting stronger and stronger as you relax into interbeing.

◆

Become aware of your mind. Witness what spontaneously pops into awareness as you survey your mind. Notice if you have any beliefs that have become rigid, or dogmatic, beliefs you hold onto tightly…If you come across any, breathe through and release them, Mental Houseclean them…Plant beliefs that inspire opening and trust…Notice if you have cynical ideas that say nothing will change anyway…Notice any beliefs that tell you that you have to fend for yourself, you have to defend yourself...Beliefs that tell you not to trust your own nature...not to trust nature...Breathe them out...Remember the intelligence intrinsic to life itself, trust it, know that this intelligence moves through you too.

◆

Send to your mind opening energy. Let your ideas be supple, not stiff and stubborn, but resilient and strong...Remember times you have felt most open and blessed to be alive...Breathe in this energy...Feel it infuse your whole belief system with connectedness, gratitude to be alive.

◆

Let your beliefs welcome learning. Feel the climate of your mind be open and relaxed, resilient and strong...more so with each breath you take. Your beliefs are supple. Imagine that your ideas grow and reach up to the sky...Feel curiosity awakening...Openness that welcomes insight to appear. Intelligence is like a flower that blooms in the sunshine.

◆

Now become aware of your feelings, the emotional climate of your life. Notice any feelings in your emotional life that are tight, constricted, alienated...feelings of separation or loneliness, areas in your emotional life that have become parched and dry...or brittle and bitter...or cold and icy. Scan your life and notice if any of these feelings come out in the different circumstances of life...feelings that no longer receive the nurturance of others, of life itself, feelings that close you off and move you into further isolation, feelings that are dense, hard...Breathe through them. Offer yourself loving kindness...Feel your heart breathe. Remember times that have inspired your heart to sing...Feel your heart open.

◆

Remember the flower that bursts out of its bud, opens in the warmth and light of the sun...Find a warm soft spot inside you somewhere, and let it come to the fore, and spread like the sap that carries life through a tree, reaching up to the sky. Let your feeling reach to the openness of the sky...Let the light of the sun in...Let the warmth in. Give yourself permission to be warm-hearted, to be light-hearted...If any beliefs crop up that stop you from warming up, lightening up, transform them as you did the others earlier.

◆

Everyone has warm spots inside them. Give yourself permission to touch the warmth of others, to receive the warmth of others...Feel yourself soften, relax into the simple satisfaction of human connection...Fill the hardness with softness...Fill the darkness with light...Moisten the dry spots with the love of life itself. Fill the separations with human connection...let yourself be emotionally open to life, to others...As you open, you move into a feeling of wholeness. Know that as you open emotionally your feelings become fluid, ever changing as life changes, enriching your life...filling your life with color, with meaning, welcoming the gift to be alive.

◆

As you open, your spirit lightens. Feel the spirit of life percolating through. Let your spirit be open too...

Let the openness extend to include all the people in your life...Let yourself be supported, flexible, a part of the life of the community you live in. Just as your heart pulses with life, feel the heart of your community pulsing with life...Alive. Like breathing in and out, you receive from others and you give to others, life holds all...Energy lifts us all...Feel yourself softening, flexible, connected. Each of those dense spots you found earlier, flood them with the energy of trust and connection, a sense of community...Flood yourself with the good feelings of community life...Letting go of separation, replacing it with the strength of connection...Feel the resiliency inherent in all of the connections of life itself.

◆

Now look out into this coming week. Imagine the events unfolding…Witness if you tighten up, hold on, alienate yourself, or separate yourself anywhere. Witness your tendencies.

◆

Breathe the quality of openness into the scenes…into yourself in the scenes…Let the energy remind you of interbeing. Trust yourself. Trust life. Feel resilience emerge as you breathe openness into these tendencies. Witness transformation. Reassure yourself…Relax, let go into the support that exists for you.

◆

Notice how in doing so you find yourself with more energy, no longer expending it to hold on…as you open creativity, curiosity, and compassion all have room to come forth…generosity of heart and spirit. Interbeing, exchange between you and community. The web is strong.

◆

Notice how it is you can remember to allow this to occur, remember to get your strength from your community, no longer using up your energy in separation, instead feeling openness and connection…The spirit of life is everywhere.

If you would like, create a symbol for this experience and tell yourself you'll remember to bring it to awareness if ever you find yourself shutting down. In doing so, you open to the resilience of life and it lifts you up.

Regaining Honesty and Trust

Witness your breath…Breathe, feel breath rolling through…Feel the sensations of breath moving through your body…Breathe…It feels good simply to be with yourself, present. Grounded in your body…your mind present…your feelings present…your spirit present…Whole…As you breathe, feel yourself relaxing deeper and deeper into yourself…relaxed and aware. As you relax, you open into wholeness…deeper and deeper. Relaxing into wholeness…Feeling yourself open to your own self…to life itself…just being…breathing…in the quiet being…just being. You are as you are. Life is as it is. Relax into this moment. Fully occupy this moment…Breath grounds you in the present. Witness breath.

◆

Feel the quality of wholeness, whatever that means to you…Sense your whole self settling in…comfortably present with yourself…as though breath soothes you and energy opens up within you like very soft soothing music. Here you can listen deep…Here, in wholeness, you can hear the whispers from the widest reaches of the universe. In wholeness *all that is* is present. And let the music of the universe soothe you, return you to your wholeness…From this place, give yourself permission to be fully receptive…Quiet in yourself…receptive and whole. Integrity lives in wholeness. Experience the integrity of being…Experience the integrity of your being.

◆

Honesty lives in integrity…*honesty*…Fully experience the word *honesty*, what it means…Bring through all the associations you have with honesty.

◆

Notice what aspects in yourself and in your life harmonize with the quality of honesty…Imagine scanning your life and witness how the quality of honesty resonates with the different activities you are engaged in…Witness how honesty resonates in different relations in your life.

◆

Witness where it comfortably resides in different aspects of your life. As you explore, notice if you come across any fields of resistance…like a negative force field between honesty and that particular aspect of your life…Witness.

◆

Notice if honesty is wholly present as you think about yourself...about others...about work...about leisure...about the world. Explore, discover where the quality of honesty resonates and where it doesn't. Just witness what is the case.

◆

Now survey your principles. What values do you hold in your heart? Bring them to the forefront of awareness.

◆

Witness what values you put at the steering wheel in the different aspects of your life...family life...work life...career...community life. What values do you go by?...Witness which values you use to navigate through your life...Notice what motivates your choices...What are you aiming for?...Witness what is the case...Notice if you are true to your principles.

◆

Is it your principles that guide your choices in the different aspects of your life?...Maybe in some places you haven't been able to enact your principles, because you do not have the power...or you are only letting a part of you be at the steering wheel—you have left wholeness behind...Have compassion for yourself. Breathe, let yourself reside in wholeness...If there are any places you have compromised your integrity, witness what can be done to heal.

◆

Let yourself know what is so in the different aspects of your life. Shine the light of awareness into any areas of avoidance...Allow the light of truth to illuminate your whole life...letting your life be whole again...Scan your relationships and notice if they are true to principle...Is there anything you are avoiding?...Anything you are hiding?...Is there anything you don't want to acknowledge?...Do you ever say one thing and do another?...Have you any secrets?...Give yourself permission to see the parts of you that you may prefer to avoid...the parts of you that you deny—but they are there nonetheless...Know that in so doing you heal yourself, you become whole again...Be compassionate with yourself, honor yourself, love yourself, and be honest with yourself. In wholeness you open to being fully alive.

◆

In the privacy of your own awareness, witness who you are, become aware if you ever find yourself ignoring what you know, what you believe, just to keep the peace...or do you ever subordinate principle to take advantage of opportunity?

◆

Offer yourself loving kindness...Be forgiving...What can you do to be true to principle?...To be honest?...To be genuine?...Are you willing to do this?...If so, imagine doing so and feel your integrity getting stronger and stronger...whole again...your whole self residing in the light of truth...Your humanity is animated...Feel yourself returning to your sense of wholeness.
Bring kindness, compassion, integrity into all your relationships...Feel this heal divisions in your relations. Know that where the quality of honesty is present, it creates ground for trust to grow...As you are whole, you inspire integrity in others. Hearts connect. Truth is magnetic...Feel it now, as honesty spreads, trust grows.

◆

Make any adjustments that you need in yourself, in your heart, in your life, so that trust can grow...or protect yourself when it does not flow through others in your life...As you are trustworthy, as you are honest, you create trusting relations with your family, your friends, and with your community. As trust grows, let it flow...Let it be like a river carrying you...Feel the support that you receive when trust is fully present...Feel the support that you give others...Imagine the whole community carried in the current of mutual trust and support...Feel the energy flow, carrying you, carrying others, supporting all of you, trusting energy…Uniting you with yourself, uniting you with your friends, uniting you with your family, with all who are around you…all in wholeness, all part of the whole…This energy is food for the soul…As the energy flows, notice how you can fully trust the process, letting it flow…letting the energy flow…Feel the energy flow through you, flow around you, yourself a part of it all. Wholeness…as the energy flows, let it flow into the whole of yourself, your body, your mind, your feelings, your spirit, the whole of yourself.

◆

Let it move out into the activities of your life, inspiring all to be honest and trustworthy…Everyone has an underground spring of humanity, imagine everyone's spring drawn up into the mighty river of trust, honesty, support…the river of humanity, it carries us all…It is the Great Turning. As this energy spreads, it exposes deceit and clears the ground for only trust to grow.

◆

You may want to create a symbol for this honesty, this trust, this flow of supportive energy within and around you, the humanity of us all. Whenever you bring this symbol to awareness, it will tap the great power of humanity that supports us all, it will enable you to be fully honest with yourself and your friends, fully trusting, and know that it will also reveal deceit, for you will clearly feel the discordance when your symbol is present.

◆

If you have any concerns, you may want to imagine talking to the symbol…in talking to it, you will come to know what you need so as to be true to your integrity…Or you may want to shine the light of the symbol into situations to discover what is discordant.

◆

Imagine how you will carry this energy into you life…In wholeness, you open to the gifts of life.

Towards a Balanced World: Distinguishing Between Cravings and Needs

Feel yourself in a very quiet place inside of yourself. Be in your own presence. Breathe…Reside in your own energy in this moment, breathing quietly…Simply be present with the whole of yourself, acknowledging yourself…being present with yourself…here in this moment…

Acknowledge the full range of your feelings…all of the feelings—some say one thing, some say another—they may contradict one another…Let yourself acknowledge and be present with all the feelings that move through you…Give yourself permission, full permission to feel your feelings. Be aware of all your feelings of desire and all your feelings of satisfaction…Let your feelings flow through you, all of them flow through.

Notice what you're wanting in your life…Notice if you crave anything…if part of you wants something and part of you doesn't…Look out over the landscape of your life, over the terrain of your relations, of your work life, of your home life, of your habits, of your aspirations, how you maintain your health and nurture yourself…what you do or want to do to enjoy yourself. Look out over the landscape of your life and notice the things that you like to do or want to do…Notice things you want to acquire, note what your wishes are.

◆

Now let the desires, the "shoulds," "coulds," all of them, soak into the ground…Let yourself relax into the life that percolates through you…Become aware of the resilience of life…the continual renewal of life…transforming energies constantly, the resilience, the renewal, the transformation…Let yourself relax into the trust of life itself…Experiencing the intrinsic knowingness of life, the self-clearing, self-healing capacities intrinsic to all life…Sense that your consciousness embodies this clarity, this self-clearing knowingness of life itself…Sense this self-healing intelligence inside you…Trust it.

◆

Now bring back to your awareness those things you discovered as you scanned the landscape of your life. You are now going to use the knowingness of life itself to distinguish between your wants and your needs. With this knowingness, you'll discover what is good for your life, for life itself, and what is not. Bring to mind one desire, be it a food, a thing, a type of relationship or activity—choose one desire or habit to explore. Bring the desire into the light of awareness. Witness. Notice its dimensions.

◆

Witness where your center is…Now notice what kinds of feelings resonate with this desire…Notice if this resonates with your integrity or with external pressures…With knowingness, notice the quality of the feelings involved…Do they clamor or are they soft?…Imagine their shape, are they round or sharply edged?…Does it connect you with nature?…Or does it distance you from nature?…Witness what is so with this desire.

◆

Cravings usually have a hardness to them. If you discover that it is a craving, the energy that takes you further away from your integrity, from the integrity of nature, imagine cracking off the shell, for inside of the craving you'll discover a true need…Within every want is a true need that may be completely different than the original want, but can be satisfied in a healthful manner.

◆

How does it resonate with your integrity?…With the integrity of nature?…If you discover greed, nurture the place out of which it springs…let it soften…Feel yourself relax, let the greed soak down into the ground…If you discover envy, let it be healed with the richness of life itself. To bring wholeness into the scene, remember the qualities of generosity and gratitude…times these qualities have been present in your experience. Experience these qualities now. Generosity… Gratitude.

◆

Breathe these qualities into the scene…Imagine the feelings and situations that have been present absorbing the qualities of generosity and gratitude…See what transformation takes place…Witness. Generosity and gratitude.

◆

Witness how what you have been focusing on impacts other life. Broaden your view and witness what is the case…Notice where balance is found and everyone's needs are met…the earth is honored.

◆

Now look out over the rest of the landscape of your life, notice the difference between your cravings and your needs.

◆

Transform the cravings and honor the needs…Notice what part of yourself is desiring things. If it resonates with life, if it is a need that feeds your life, or if it is a craving in compensation for disconnection…If you run across craving, let it be transformed by going through its surface and discovering what is inside…what true need is inside…Honor your true needs. Let go of the cravings. Bring in gratitude and generosity, these qualities heal. Mental Houseclean and let the bad habits be transformed. Know that in doing so you are creating space for you to be even more attuned to what is healthful for yourself and others, for life itself.

◆

Life becomes simple and satisfying with generosity and gratitude. Know that you fully deserve to have your needs met…Notice how as you honor your needs, you feel more connected to all the life within and around you…You can relax into the support of the web-work of life itself…

Become aware of the choices that you can make to honor your true needs, to honor life and relax in the web-work of life. In doing so you let go of the alienated wants; let the cravings soak down into the ground to be transformed…You deserve to have your needs fulfilled…Notice the choices you can make to honor your needs. Imagine a daily routine based on these choices. Honoring your needs, do your part in keeping the place you occupy on the web strong and resilient. Your place on the web.

◆

Honor life itself…honor the earth…Feel gratitude to be alive. Know that in honoring only your needs you create room for others' true needs to be met too, for you have taken only your fair share.

Keeping the Faith

As you hear the sounds of these words, you'll go deeper and deeper into the universal realms out of which all life springs…You'll feel yourself relaxing into the resilient support of the web of life. With each word you hear, you'll become increasingly attuned to the connectedness of life, the mutuality of life. With the sounds of these words moving through your awareness, your consciousness will expand from your usual individual awareness into cosmic consciousness. Give yourself permission to enter into your natural state of fluid connectedness, supported, supporting life, supported, supporting humanity.

Feeling the rhythms of life percolating through you…the pulse of life, the breath of life, the hum of life…Knowing life percolates through all creatures, through all people…

Sense the universal breath—what we breathe out, the plants breathe in, what the plants breathe out, we breathe in. Energy constantly supporting, transforming, moving—universal breath interweaves all that lives upon the earth…

Feel the great synchrony of the universe. The movement of electrons, the movement of planets, all in synchrony...Let your tensions be washed away by waves of universality; feel yourself sinking deeper into the support of life itself...

Experience the fluidity of life...everything moving, carried by time...day into night, season to season, year to year. History is alive...Each generation gives life to the next, generation to generation to generation...Each generation dreams and struggles for a better life for the next, history in the making...

Remember those who passed before who cared...living, breathing beings devoted to life, dedicated their lives to the struggle for humanity...Remember them now.

◆

They live on in the spirit of humanity...Summon up the courage of those who passed before...Breathe in courage...empowering ourselves, the spirit of humanity lives and breathes in us now...Let our ancestors rejoice in our rising to the times...Aroused, together we take up the call, make history, create the future...Feel life percolate through everyone; life regenerates itself. Life endowed us with life; now we are called upon to preserve life itself...We are part of the Great Turning, the great healing...

Give yourself permission to experience the fullness of your devotion to life, feel it in the depths of your heart, your soul, your whole being...Allow yourself to care...Remember the special moments in your life, times where your heart was warmed...celebrations...shared joys...shared love...majestic landscapes...the wonder of life itself. Remember what makes your heart sing...Feel your passion for life.

◆

Let your feelings merge with the feelings of others who have a passion for life...passion ignites passion...ever-widening passion for the protection of life, everyone caring...forming a great wave of humanity to change the course of history; history is alive within us...Together we have great healing powers, together we transform ourselves and the world...We make room for healing to happen.

◆

Remembering the powers, the power of people united, the power of life itself...healing powers are all around and within us. Life is about transformation...Let all the pain, the rage of yours, of the earth's, let it transform itself into a great healing force, a force as fierce as a mother protecting her young.

◆

Let the power of life surge through you. Breathe it...Feel it in your heart...pulsing life...empowering you. Feel it uplift you...arousing you...Aroused, humanity forms a great moving wave...Passion for life carries us, empowers us to emancipate life itself...to create a future where the dignity of all life is respected...where the life of every single baby of every kind is honored. Our ancestors rejoice as we answer the call of history, protecting the claim of life itself...

You have your life to offer, you can make a difference. The passion, the power of life lives within you...Feel yourself a part of the great struggle, healing powers move through you...Listen to your heart...Listen to your convictions...Listen to your instincts...What cries out to you?

◆

Give yourself permission to struggle for what you believe in. Remember, there are many who share your cares...joining together, feel how much more powerful you are, everyone is, as we're joined together...together we can make a difference...Believe in our power. Feel it...Together we can make a difference...We are making a difference already...Life always wins in the end, grass grows up through concrete and reaches for the sky...Life regenerates itself, life always wins in the end...

Feel your connection with life itself...with other creatures...with the plant world...with other peoples...We all create a great wave of life protecting life, securing it for the next generations...Feel yourself held by the web, opening to offering your gifts to keeping it strong...Imagine that humanity pulls through, the spirit of humanity lives on and each generation continues to dream and to struggle for the next generation...trusting the future, keeping the faith...Let yourself be empowered by life itself...Let yourself be inspired by life itself and we'll heal the future.

Count Out

Begin to finish what you are doing and go over all the insights you have had and choices you have made in this meditation...Breathe out, and project these visions into your life. Set the stage for action.

◆

Know that the very fact that you have imagined this makes them possible, makes them probable, makes them real...Breathe and draw in these powers. Embody them...Live into the changes you are making...

◆

Tell yourself this now...Acknowledge the collective power we share.

Appreciate all the energies, spirits, and your own good will for accompanying you through your inner work...Thank you for your inner work.

Make yourself ready to come out to outer conscious levels...

In a moment I'm going to count from one to five...At the count of five, you'll open your eyes, remembering all that you've experienced...feeling refreshed, revitalized, and relaxed, having brought with you the energies you became attuned to, ready and able to act on them.

ONE—becoming more aware of the room around you...

TWO—coming up slowly now...

THREE—at the count of five, you'll open your eyes feeling relaxed, revitalized, and refreshed, remembering all that you've experienced...

FOUR—coming up now bringing with you what you've experienced...

FIVE!—eyes open, feeling refreshed, revitalized, and relaxed, remembering all that you've experienced, feeling a sense of well-being, ready and able to act on the energies to which you've attuned yourself.

·11·

Reclaiming Wholeness in Our World Secures the Future: Circles Are Our Safety Nets

I visualize wholeness as round; it is not a pyramid or a square, but a sphere or a circle. Black Elk, an Oglala Sioux medicine man, tells us, "The Power of the World always works in circles, and everything tries to be round...The sky is round, and I have heard that the earth is round like a ball, and so are the stars. The wind, in its greatest power, whirls...and so it is in everything where power moves."[1]

We need circles, literally and metaphorically. In a circle, each person is needed to make it whole, and each is held by the whole. Circles create relationships where energy moves and spirit comes to life. In Circle, we take joy in one another and hold each other in our grief. We feel connected, able to reach beyond our isolation. We think together, envision together, and offer one another courage to bring our values into our work and community lives. In wholeness, we cannot separate our personal from our political selves. In Circle, we weave new ways of being and find ways to reclaim ancient wisdom to struggle against the forces that threaten life.

In meditation, we experience our connectedness to *all that is*. Meditating together, we create an energy field that lifts us all up. As we began to see in Chapter Six, meditating in the sacred space of the Circle makes that field exponentially more powerful. If you have been doing Circle work and began incorporating telling heart stories, you probably have gained a feel for what can be done to make a potent field. Regularly doing so creates a buoyancy that carries us. It also makes our life go smoothly. As Harrison Owen says:

When the circle of caring people is established, emergent order manifests, automatically, no problem, on cue. And the circle is important. Good stuff simply doesn't happen in squares and rows, or if it does, it is much slower and less satisfying.[2]

Working with Applied Meditation can create openings that touch the heart and help us to cope with the issues that arise. With mindfulness, we can let go of the turmoil of the day and be present. The strength of other people's compassionate Witnesses and their intuition helps us to face issues that are especially charged. We can unravel patterns of energy as we engage the Receptive Imagination and catch those flashes of insight that we might otherwise have dismissed. We ascertain how to overcome our limitations and move into a more liberated way of being. In Circle, we discover patterns of energy in the stories that people "make up." When we see the same patterns emerge, it is difficult to dismiss. We build faith in the efficacy of inner knowing.

Bring a decision you face to Circle and everyone can take an imaginal journey exploring the different paths you are considering. They will offer pieces of information that bring your options into clearer focus, making your decision much easier. We can explore the ripple effects together. Use the meditations in this chapter as doorways into discovery. Then when you have chosen a direction, you can work with the Active Imagination to both increase the probability of it coming to pass and to set clearly-aimed intention. Remember that people in loving relationships or cohesive groups are most effective at influencing possibilities (see Chapter Five).

Circles can help us to reconnect to the natural world. Taking regular imaginal journeys together through inner dimensions can bring us into a deeper rapport with what we usually see as without consciousness. Maybe a tree on the corner is having a hard time growing. In Circle, you can go in, channel positive energy and sense what might help. Alone this feels crazy; together, you will find patterns in your imaginings that reveal what will help.

Circles can also help us reweave community on very practical levels. For example, if your neighbors have been violent, in Circle, you can meditate, channel healing, and imagine what might be said or done to help shift the energy. Now you might decide to accompany each other to talk with them. The world is a hologram—going inside helps us be tuned and better connected on the outside.

We live longer, happier lives when we are surrounded by many loving relationships. But love doesn't appear on command. Working with meditation, story, and truth-telling in Circle creates a field that invites love to develop. Re-patterning our consciousness, we connect heart to heart and claim the world together. In Circle, the solutions to the challenges we face become clearer, be they personal, social, or political. We develop the kinds of relations needed to accompany one another through life's celebrations and struggles—going to the doctor or the school board together, or to the house down the street from which we have heard screams. We can take care of each other even when we are in despair.

One of my students from Arizona who leads a Circle called me recently to share the joy that she and members of her community had experienced. She told me how upset they were about the constant threat of coming war and the nightly roar of military jets overhead on their missions. Wishing for a place to share their fears and feeling a need to express this in a peaceful way, the community gathered together and walked silently through town to the Colorado River. There they formed a Circle to draw on the power of peace. She described the ethnic diversity of group, the children, and the elderly. When they were invited to share their feelings, songs began, poems were read, and people spoke of creating peace in their own hearts and communities. One elderly woman spoke softly about her fear for the world and about her own loneliness. When all had spoken, the children released doves into the air and the group made agreements to continue to find ways to create peace in the world.

The local news announced with interest that the Peace Walk would be a yearly event—this in a town where the military was the prime employer. Everyone in the group was energized and amazed at the palpable strength and love that was present. They had planted seeds for the future in the sacred Circle.

Circles are popping up everywhere.[3] As the institutions that supported us in the past crumble, we turn to each other for sustenance. We are one another's security. In Circle, we hold each other day to day. If we have Circles, when crisis hits we can turn to one another. I believe that more than any other kind of Circle, we need ones that bring people together across lines of difference. These are the Circles that will hold the strongest and come up with the new ways of being. The times are calling for a weaving of Circles. When they interlock they create a living safety net. Circles may be what offer the most promise for securing the future. Rather than watching "life" on television, let's knit Circles, sit in council,[4] meditate, share heart stories, and grapple with what to do about a troubling situation, study together, or conjure up public actions to take. In Circles, we are carried by and carry the Great Turning.*

Morphic Organizing

We engage in the Turning with each act that breaks the mold. In fact, each individual and small group that begins to transform their lives, and each new experiment in social relations has ripple effects that spread far beyond the immediate situation. Earlier in this book, we have seen the way that consciousness has nonlocal impact on health and well-being. According to Sheldrake, each holonic level from the cell to the group to the culture, has a morphic field. The morphic fields that surround living and social systems seem to have memory or resonance that holds things in place. The wonderful thing is when the right chord is struck, the morphic fields can communicate social successes very rapidly, and shift the ways things are more quickly than we could have imagined.

Work together on the inside by meditating and work together on the outside to create change; each empowers the other. With our Active Imaginations, we can carve new grooves through which energy moves. Let's say there is an important City Council meeting coming up. In Circle, you can meditate about it. Working with the Receptive Imagination, you intuit where the spots of flexibility lie. You will discover a good approach, one that is likely to be exactly that which will sway people. Then, with the Active Imagination, everyone can energize that strategy. I recommend that everyone imagine bands of energy moving between those who are going to the meeting—picture bands of energy that move to and from each of your hearts and minds. Assume that these bands carry information, weaving a web that supports everyone. Imagine it. Set the intention that these bands of energy will be present when you are at the Council meeting. This sets up channels of communication in advance so that you are fully attuned to one another when you are at the meeting. During the council meeting, you'll find that you have an uncanny way of knowing what one another will say before saying it. Running energy like this creates power.

The combination of setting clear intention beforehand and the psychic rapport that you have established through meditating together makes a potent combination. I think of it as moving intention up a holonic notch. The Circle operates as a whole, not as separate individuals. You become synergized and the

---

* If you are interested in finding others in your area working in Circles, write us at circlework@toolsforchange.org

collective mind you create is brilliant. You become one coordinated body in a great, choreographed dance. Not that someone else is choreographing your dance, but that you are so finely tuned to each other that you are unified—what athletes sometimes call being in the "zone" together, or "in flow."

You can increase your effectiveness by setting another intention. Imagine that there are bands of energy moving from the hearts and minds of those who sit on the City Council to the innerconsciousness of each of you. Then imagine that the energy bands are moving from your innerconscious to your conscious mind, then through your words back to their hearts and minds, and continuing to circle through this way throughout the meeting. Intend compassion and clarity to be the currents that are moving in these bands. This sets up a way for each of you to intuit what is true for those you are trying to persuade. You will find yourselves able to voice your remarks in a manner that is most meaningful. This is not about manipulating people, but being sensitive to the truths people hold, and then expressing yourself as effectively as possible. Like the technique of running energy, this may feel like an inconsequential story you create in your imagination, but it will have miraculous results.

I do this whenever I am speaking publicly or doing facilitation work. I find that I use examples to illustrate my point that had never occurred to me before. And later, I find that the example is the same experience that the listener has had. Recently, I was leading a colleague though a meditation to help her get ready for the challenges she was facing. I suggested that she sing to the cells in her body and that her song be carried into her body by her breath. I elaborated further, suggesting that she imagine ribbons of color were also carried by her breath. (Innerconsciousness never seems to be bothered by mixed metaphors!) I had never used this particular imagery before. After the meditation, she told me that whenever she needed to calm herself down this was exactly what she did. The imaginal world is somehow mysteriously hard-wired into what will and has already taken place.

The inside and outside worlds constantly mirror and dance with one another. I once was at an organizing conference; we were in a late-night conversation about the influences that were impacting our work. One woman, using the common metaphor from Alcoholics Anonymous, said that there was an elephant in the room. Literally the moment she said it, someone we didn't know walked into the room carrying a big stuffed elephant in her arms! Occurrences like this make the work we do feel enchanted. At this same gathering, I was telling a story to a friend about how elk had appeared in a meditation. I said that this vision represented the constant vying for being the head of the herd that was impeding the work. After the conversation, we turned to leave, and saw that a car had just pulled into the parking lot right next to where we were. The car had these huge antlers wired onto its radiator. Soon after that, we were invited to come hear an all-woman band that evening called "The Elktones." Working with spirit synchronous unfoldings become common; reminding us that we are part of a wondrous whole and telling us if we are on the right path, moving in harmony with Spirit. Our rational minds dismiss these events out of hand, but our hearts find them reassuring.

The challenge for us is to sense the energy currents and work with them. Think of this as morphic organizing or working magic. When we meditate on actions we want to take together, we create a field of energy where we come into deep resonance with one another. This field also makes for hearing the quiet whispers of spirit—even in harrowing circumstances.

In 1999, when the WTO was coming to Seattle there was a groundswell of local and international organizing that took place. My friend Ruby Phillips and I got together and wrote a meditation to empower people to be better able to stand strong in a field of shared intention. We then trained people to take ten minutes to explain and lead it in meetings throughout the city. The flier that introduced the meditation said:

> We are poised at an important moment; the possibility of changing history is upon us. The WTO times will be intense. The danger of provocateur-inspired violence and police/media reactions are high. How do we effectively express our outrage at the fact that the planet and all of her critters (including humanity) are careening down a path of destruction? Much is at stake—we do not want martial law and we do not want to provide an opportunity for the media to discredit us. With shared intent, we hold strong and offer a powerful presence and message to the media, the public, and those we oppose. Police, provocateurs, or reactive people among us may attempt to throw us off. We do not want to lose our collective power and become distracted from our purpose. Tapping into and maintaining the strength of our collective intention makes us infinitely more effective (and safer).

The meditation was simple. It invited people to remember what was at stake, why they were doing the work and the fact that there were thousands who stood with them. At the end of it, people created a symbol to represent what they were in touch with. We gave a short lesson in using symbols.

The evening after the first day in the streets, when we successfully kept the WTO from convening, about a thousand of us met back in a warehouse that was one of the main organizing sites. People shared stories of how they held strong even when being sprayed with tear gas, pepper spray, or when horses were coming toward them. It was inspiring to hear all the stories! Many who had done the meditation and had practiced working with their symbols, told us it was of great help to them in the high tension moments when they were confronted with abusive police.

Throughout the evening we kept hearing reports that tear gas wielding police were coming closer to where we were. People were exhilarated, exhausted, fearful, and awed at the amazing success of the day. And there was a lot of controversy over actions for the day following. In the midst of the turmoil, I led a meditation using a bullhorn to be heard. If that many people can meditate under circumstances such as these, we can meditate anywhere!

We became empowered that night to go back on the streets in the face of martial law being declared and even more police being brought in. The WTO meetings ended in failure due both to the protests on the outside and the fact that the less developed nations stood together to resist parts of the globalization agenda. Some of the delegates said that they had been given strength to stand up by the protesters outside. There is an Ethiopian proverb: "When spider webs unite they can tie up the lion."

I dream of a time when working with reflection, imagination, and mindfulness are all publicly shared activities—bringing wholeness back to our world. Together, we can fine tune our consciousness to one another, to the issue, and to anyone else involved. The energies we tune into in the imaginal world are elusive and hard to catch, but when we engage together, we see the patterns that exist and the shape of the energy fields that bind us. We can weave our visions together in new patterns, creating strong webs of intention and unified action.

Power Is Present: Overcoming Habits of History

These are extraordinary times full of great danger and great possibilities. We need extraordinary ways to address the challenges we face. Imagine that we move up a few holonic notches and work from there? Some spiritual traditions tell us that *all that is* exists in the present moment. I have to admit that I do not find it plausible that with a sweep of a very broad imagination one can change history. But I do believe we can change how we carry the past, and how it affects us. On a personal level, working with Applied Meditation, one can go back into one's past and rearrange the scenes that were wounding. Doing this changes the emotional charge that is carried. It begins the process of freeing us from repeating our history. On a societal level, I believe that when we as a people begin really to engage in efforts of reconciliation, we do not change the past itself, but we shift the hold it has on us. This is a great safeguard from repeating history and frees us to find new ways of being.

Our power lives in present time; we hold the past and the future inside us in this same moment. In meditation, we widen our Circle in ways that stretch our imagination. We can call on our deceased grandmother and a grandchild yet to be born—the possibilities are immense. Traditional cultures communicate with their ancestors to find wise ways to approach the challenges they face, and they take future generations into account when making important decisions. The trickster, the fool, and the shaman/healer, through their "craziness," cross boundaries or shake things up so they can settle into different patterns. Through their mischief, truth is revealed. When working with the Active and Receptive Imaginations become a collectivized activity, there is no telling what genius we might cook up!

In Circle, we can expand our sense of ourselves. As Joanna Macy says:

Act your Age. Since every particle in your body goes back to the first flaring forth of space and time, you're really as old as the universe. So when you are lobbying at your congressperson's office, or visiting your local utility, or testifying at a hearing on nuclear waste, or standing up to protect an old grove of redwoods, you are doing that not out of some personal whim, but in the full authority of your fifteen billion years.

Dare to vision. Out of this darkness a new world can arise, not to be constructed by our minds so much as to emerge from our dreams. Even though we cannot see clearly how it's going to turn out, we are still called to let the future into our imagination. We will never be able to build what we have not first cherished in our hearts.[5]

There is an image that has haunted me for a long time. Every summer there is an exclusive, invitation-only, all-male gathering in a place north of San Francisco called Bohemian Grove. Bush (father and son), Cheney, Clinton, Rockefeller, and Kissinger have been among the hundreds of bankers and corporate and government heads who gather in the redwoods. These meetings have been taking place for over a hundred years. It is said that the Manhattan Project, which brought the world the atomic bomb, was conceived there.[6]

Each year a ritual is held there called "The Cremation of Care" in which the participants burn care in effigy. What is the effect of this on the morphic field? Does this fortify callousness? What possibilities are there to rearrange the energy—to breathe space into it, to make compassion be what rises up rather than care going up in smoke? For many years, people have demonstrated outside the gates, to let the men know they are being watched. Last year, to generate a counterbalancing energy field, demonstrators created an alternate ritual: "The Resurrection of Care."

What if as a people we change how we carry our memories? What if we could change the fields of energy that dictate our cultural habits? This is all intangible, but that is the nature of working with spirit—it is profound and ineffable. If we take into account that traumatic events enter at theta level of consciousness and grip memory, then the task is formidable—some may say unrealistic. If we are to be realistic, we have already lost. The Great Turning's success may depend on our "fantasy."

In our lives, we are often called to do something larger than we have been doing. It is as if the world organizes itself in a way so we that can begin to move in unison. We may not even know that we have it in us to be ready to move. When we are connected heart to heart we can perform great feats. We hear of a woman who lifted a car off of her granddaughter, there are many such stories of individual heroism. In a similar manner, as everyday people, we can become engaged. What if we develop strong intention and the world is chameleon to the environment of mind?

In World War II Berlin, families of mixed heritage—Jewish men and Gentile women—were allowed to stay together during the early part of the war. Then the Nazi bureaucracy decided to round up the men for deportation to concentration camps. Seven thousand were captured one night and brought to a central prison. *Spontaneously*, the next day, a thousand women gathered at the station without organizing and started chanting, "We want our men back! We want our men back!" They would not stop for three days. The Nazi police and Gestapo couldn't make them stop even at gunpoint. Eventually, the commanders realized they had to let the men go—all of them, or else a revolution might start that would sweep Germany.

Sometimes changes seem to spring out of nowhere, the years of suffering and endurance and hard work existing below the surface. We often don't know the impact of our daily work for change. Then suddenly, waves of change crest and echo across national boundaries and shift the ways of the world. You can see this in the multiple stories of movements for democracy in Eastern Europe, Asia, and Africa over the last sixty years. The image of who we are as a people transforms, a new sense of possibility emerges, and people become courageous enough to stand together.

For example, in Poland, while there had been labor struggles for good working conditions and fairness during the early 1970s, they had been crushed. In 1979, there sprang up a small organization of twenty people—Solidasnosk, or Solidarity. It had the unique idea of democracy by workers, neither socialist nor anti-socialist. Within a few short weeks, its number swelled from twenty to 20,000 and by the next year it swelled to nine million. This movement became a foundation of change that eventually swept through the whole of Eastern Europe and the Soviet Union.

In the last thirty years of the twentieth century, the forces of globalization were proceeding according to the corporate agenda. Each plank of the plan seemed to be put in place with impunity; there was little or no recognition of the ongoing resistance from below by poor and indigenous people, labor, or the environmental movements around the world. Free trade agreements, the operations of the world monetary system and the untrammeled power of the major economic players seemed inevitable. In the words of Renato Ruggiero, Director General of the WTO, "We are writing the constitution of a single global economy." Then in 1997, as we saw in Chapter Ten, a world grassroots movement sprang up, first stopping the MAI in less than two years. In short order, the WTO was challenged in Seattle, the World Bank and IMF in Geneva, Washington, and

Jakarta, and the anti-globalization movement was forged. For those who are paying attention, there is a major protest happening somewhere in the world every week. For the first time, these individual struggles are beginning to weave together in all of their particularities.

And—the movements for creating alternatives are growing by leaps and bounds. There are more and more stories of people getting involved not simply to protest against injustice, but to create visions of a new world.

None of the actors in the above stories were concerned with being realistic. Perhaps we need to go beyond the "realistic" to loosen up the existing order. The challenge on a grand scale is how to go about changing the way we respond to the habits of history. Sheldrake tells us, cultural morphic fields are inherently conservative.[7] I think of habits as well-worn ruts in the road. With mindfulness we don't need to fall into the same old ruts. The question is, how do we see the contours of the ruts? And further, how do we create a vision of what we want instead? Remember, without a vision the problem itself dictates our behavior by default.

Looking inside at our own consciousness by itself will not show us the particular cultural habits that need to be transformed. This was made clear in a meditation workshop I taught some years ago. One of the participants was a well-meaning bank executive. We did a meditation where everyone created an inner sanctuary and invited spirit guides to join them. Afterwards, the bank executive described his guides as a black man who took care of the grounds outside his sanctuary, and a woman who took care of the inside. His perception of his guides in subservient roles was normal to him. Psychic perception is not mediated through eyes, ears, or touch, but through the thought forms already residing in the mind. This is the clothing the energy uses to make itself visible. Memories provide the vocabulary of imagination. As I said in Chapter Five, working with positive projections of the Active Imagination, if you have no flour in the pantry it places severe limitations on the bread you bake. This is equally true for receiving insight with the Receptive Imagination. I have yet to meet a man who discovered sexism by looking within.

Each one of us tends to take our own thoughts and beliefs for granted. Groups, organizations, communities, and nations all have sets of unexamined assumptions and beliefs that hold injustice in place, keeping us from being fully human. If we are to carve new cultural grooves we have to work with each other in diversity. We each bring different memories and different perspectives to the mix. We need Circles to include both the CEO and the young mom who works at McDonalds. When we tell our stories, put our experiences together, and meditate together, we can weave new fields. But this is no easy task.

This makes for a situation in which we continually examine assumptions. With each others' perspectives we see what needs to be transformed and make room for visioning new ways that are informed by history. This can only work if we protect the integrity of the Circle. In Circle, everyone contributes. Most of us have little experience of this kind of reciprocal relationship. People in positions of power are the least informed about issues of oppression. CEOs are used to being listened to, not listening. Their experience is that people treat them as though their words are very important. The worker at McDonalds, on the other hand, has the opposite experience; she is used to being ignored. Her experience tells her that to speak is to risk getting in trouble. These habits are deeply ingrained, and we duplicate the patterns if we are not really careful. The dynamic of who dominates the air time is not an issue of personality but social power. If we do not set up ways of interacting that consciously shift the cultural currents, the familiar patterns of domination and compliance replicate themselves despite our best intent.

Making things worse, the habituated pattern of the CEO is likely to be the dominant assumption about what is important. The center of gravity in the discussion moves to being problem-focused and relying on the facts as established by experts, then determining the best fixes. If several perspectives are put forth, the conversation shifts into a competitive banter. Whichever one best weathers the argument, wins. This certainly keeps heart, intuition, and creativity out of the picture..

We need to turn this dynamic on its head. I believe that it is the particular aspects of our experience which undermine the status quo that we have been obliged to leave at the door. The challenge is: how do we create ways of being in Circle that enable us to be whole and share our experience fully without provoking guilt, shame, or blame, and without feelings of anger, arrogance, and inferiority? A tall order, but I know that it can be done.

Weaving Trust: Leveling the Playing Field

Most of us have aspects of who we are that have been looked down upon by mainstream culture. It may be our sexual orientation, religious affiliation, race, gender, class, disability, or other aspects, and if we bring this part of our experience forward, we risk being trivialized, pathologized, and locked out. Surviving contemporary norms usually requires leaving behind these parts of ourselves. Over the last couple of decades, we gathered in groups, caucuses, and conferences of shared identity. We came together to share our stories and understand that our experience is not isolated, but others have been there too. As a result of the validation we offered one another, we came to trust our own experience. In these separate spaces, we didn't need to leave a part of our experience at the door. We got to be whole without having to explain ourselves. Often we have come to understand that these same aspects of ourselves that marked our difference from the mainstream were, in actuality, gifts that enlarge humanity and illuminate ways the wider society might be together in wholeness. These spaces allowed us to heal our wounds, and both reclaim and weave new identities. We have come out strong.

The challenge now is to call upon these strengths to create a new cultural force. We need to resist the pressure to regress into hiding some of our selves, to resist the all-too-familiar habits of "passing" (assimilating). When we make our particular differences invisible, it only puts the dominant norms back in control by default. It is the very aspects of our experience that we have had to leave behind that are the ones that will get *all* of us through.

The grooves of homogenization are deeply cut, but as we consciously create different ways to come together, we open great possibilities. Set things up differently and people don't fall back into habituated patterns. For example, when you hold a gathering or start a Circle, don't begin with the usual round of introductions where people share their name and what they do for work. Instead, ask them to name their grandmother and tell a story about her, or ask for the name of a child for whom they want the world to be safe. This opens the context for story, heart, and the weaving of the powers of our pasts and futures.

As part of a national initiative of grassroots think tanks sponsored by Spirit in Action,[8] Tools for Change organized a Circle of a dozen people that was the most diverse group of its size I have ever been in—men and women ranging from their twenties to their sixties, who were heterosexual, bisexual and lesbian, and some with disabilities. We included Chicana/Indigenous, African-American, Puerto Rican, Shoshone, Jewish, white, Chinese, and Filipina. Among our religious backgrounds and current practices were Pagan, Buddhist, Catholic,

Mormon, Jewish, atheist, and Baha'i. We occupied different class strata, from secretary to surgeon, and housepainter to government consultant.

The diversity made for a curiosity in the room that was palpable—deep listening was our norm. Since we were not homogenized, our horizons were stretched time and again. We always started with meditating or sharing stories, perhaps about a comfort food growing up, or a metaphor that illustrated how we each were feeling at the moment. We aimed to avoid doing anything that would awaken a competitive edge. In fact, we went for twelve weeks before we shared with one another what we did for a living and what kinds of social change work we were involved with. In addition to meditation, we worked with Appreciative Inquiry[9] to search out our own stories of liberation. We shared our grief using the Truth Mandala ritual,[10] we envisioned how it would feel to always belong. We drew and shared "spirit maps" of our life journey as it had unfolded.[11] We took great joy in discovering one another. Every week we came together, shared food, and delved into what spirit meant to us, what was happening in the world, our grief, our yearnings, great moments and difficult ones in our lives. These were times of truth-telling. We told stories, brought pictures of our families, and invited the ancestors to join us. We were able to relax and just *be* with one another in our fullness. None of us felt as though we had to prove or defend anything. We wove our voices together and built a strong field, one that still survives despite the fact that we all have busy lives. The experience confirmed to me again how crucial diversity is. The relationships that we built over the months of our formal meetings have endured, and we still meet together, share our lives, and help each other as we can.

After some storytelling and sharing, in the second session we asked people what they needed from the Circle and one another for the Circle to work for them. We avoided using the word "safe," which is a culturally loaded term. Some people never feel they are really "safe" and believe it is a construct that comes out of a privileged world view. Making agreements together created a sense of ownership early on. People came up with a simple list of agreements; we didn't spend endless hours crafting it and discussing how to best word it. It was a conversation that lasted about fifteen minutes, but we established norms that allowed for us to bring our full selves into the Circle. It formed the intention for which we were collectively mindful—not as control patterns, but as ways of noticing when constriction arises.

We shared commitment of time together, establishing sacred space, meditation, positive orientation, food, and exercises that opened the imagination. We had an altar complete with flowers and candles. All of this made for establishing a field for weaving both ancient and new culture. We usually started with a short meditation which allowed us to sink easily into a deeper place with each other. We knew that everyone mattered, that if anything came up that was troubling, we would go there together, we would not leave anyone behind or banter accusations or defenses back and forth—we knew we would speak from the heart. And speak from the heart we did. We all had a glimpse into one another's souls—it was truly a sacred time we created together. It is in contexts like this one that we can unravel the cultural habits that bind us and can weave visions that inspire everyone—visions that haven't left out whole communities of life on this planet—and most importantly, build the trust to work to make our visions manifest together.

Some of what made for such a rich experience was having clear commitment and intention for what we were doing together. We would mark our opening and closing with the lighting and blowing out of a candle. Doing this small ritual sets boundaries, invites reverence, and begins to build a positive energy field. We always opened with meditation, a song, prayer, or poem. Rituals like this invite people into a sacred space so the field in which interaction takes place is not primarily informed by unconscious habits. Reverence makes for mindfulness and gratitude. Another vital aspect is bringing all voices into the field. After our opening and frequently at other times too, we would speak in round format. This sets a pattern that makes it a little more difficult for the default of social power to perpetuate the status quo.

Because there was an overt acknowledgement of issues of oppression, it went without saying that if they came up, we were willing to talk about them. We developed trust quickly. It helped that there was not an atmosphere of "who is right and who is wrong." We weren't looking for problems, but felt secure that if any came up we would sort out what was happening together. In many groups, people either avoid the issues or won't let them go. This dynamic often occurs in the same conversation, and can cause a lot of confusion and frustration.

My organization, Tools for Change, has been doing trainings on issues of oppression for many years.* Certain dynamics show up again and again that

---

* I have coauthored two pamphlets which grapple with power, culture, and history. They offer approaches that help people and communities establish settings in which we share power and are truly multicultural. See pp 426, write us at Circlework@toolsforchange.org

hinder the creation of truly multicultural contexts in which power is shared. In Circles, if we are aware of them, we can avoid falling into bad habits of history. The more assimilated we are, the more we tend to think of difference as the problem, as though difference was what is causing a fracture (dualism). When someone raises anything that is particular to their social group, it is often met with: "We are all human, let's not focus on our differences." But it is this attitude that is causing great problems because it obliges people who have been rejected to have to split themselves in order to be accepted into the fold. Wholeness is what holds diversity. Social inequities crisscross through our relations and are continually informing the field. In my opinion, if this isn't acknowledged, it is fracturing the field.

Privilege means being given more options without having earned them through any of your own efforts. Imagine that you are swimming downstream. You feel that swimming is easy. Then you come across someone swimming upstream; they are having a difficult time making any headway. You might give them some pointers about how they could improve their stroke to make things easier. You are oblivious to the currents that carry you and are causing problems for your fellow swimmer. You don't understand why they weren't happy to receive your good advice. It is crucial to understand that privilege is usually invisible to those who have it, and that oppression is pervasive for those who don't. As a result, those with privilege, however well intentioned, operate out of stereotypes and assumptions that further entrench inequity. At the same time, those who are oppressed often assume that the others are operating out of premeditated power plays, "How could they not know something so obvious?!"

Most of us have plenty of opportunity to be on either side of the dynamic given the multiple levels in which oppression operates. This is true if we are looking at issues of gender, class, race, ability, etc. If we are not careful, the schisms between us widen. What often happens is that if one in a position of oppression points out misinformation, they are usually met with a defense of good intentions. Since in mainstream competitive culture image is paramount, people often take feedback as a personal affront. Another result of privilege is the more you have it, the more you are in the habit of seeing yourself as an individual devoid of social context. As a result, you take everything personally. When defensiveness takes center stage, we never actually get to look at the impact of the attitudes and behaviors on the situation and the wider society. Intention becomes the topic of conversation, and consequences never enter the discussion. This, in turn, makes it likely that the person who raised the issue will feel frustrated and may get angry. A rupture happens and learning never takes place. We fail in building trust or making justice. It is no wonder that many of us prefer to be in homogeneous settings.

U.S. history and current circumstances are so riddled with denial and abuse that meditation, song, and heart-sharing are vital to create a field that is strong enough to hold the truth in diverse settings. When these forms set the tone, we don't fall into the ruts of assessing who is right and who is wrong. Instead, we can hold one another in our humanity. We need stories because they bring our history into the field. It is good to ask questions that bring out our diversity of experience. Questions that people can answer with a story are especially good to use in circle format. This tends to open the heart and gives people an understanding of the larger context out of which someone is operating; plus, one cannot argue with story.

When there is tension in the room, like breathing through pain, lean in. Breathe together, meditate together, and tell your truths. We can delve into the mistakes that we have inadvertently made—mistakes we will always make. Whatever ways we hold privilege we have not had to think about the conditions others are contending with—that is what privilege is. Mistakes are inevitable; what is key is learning from them—not defending an image with endless discussions on intent. Instead, we can reflect on what is taking place between people, and think relationally, not in terms of personality. There is not a right person or a wrong person, but there are beliefs and behaviors that have consequences. When we separate intent from impact, we can discover what will bring healing and empowerment for all concerned. With a generosity of spirit and a shared commitment to each other, we can sort it out together. This is the hard work that enables us to become deft at recognizing the ruts in the road before we fall into them. We learn, we discover how to weave the relations that are enduring and trustworthy, relations that weave us all in.[12]

Circling

As with meditation, we each need to be mindful and notice when we are withdrawing and when there is something we are thinking but not sharing.

Otherwise, we move into dualism; we fracture the field when there is something that we are holding back. We have learned our survival lessons well, sometimes we have to continue to remain silent—but if we have to censor when we are in Circle, it becomes weaker. If you find yourself thinking or feeling something that you are unable to share, ask yourself what understanding you would need everyone to have if you were to feel safe enough to share this part of your experience. This will help you focus on exactly what you might ask for to pave the way for you to bring your full experience in. For maintaining well-being of the Circle, it is a good idea to regularly meditate on where you might have held back or what bothered you, as well as what the great moments were. Share this with each other and you will know what, in particular, can be done that will further strengthen your Circle.

I believe that we need to pay at least as much, if not more, attention to the questions we ask as to the conclusions we come to. The times call for good questions, not quick fixes. In our country, we have been conditioned not to speak up or question unless we already know the answer. The prevailing cultural currents keep us in patterns of looking for right and wrong, having the correct answers and never sharing our dilemmas or vulnerabilities. When we fall prey to these patterns, we get stuck in the same old ruts. *Starting a conversation with a conclusion only takes us where we have been before. But questions take us to uncharted territory. They invite us to listen to what is emergent, what is in the field at this very moment.* Questions carry us into new experience. They awaken curiosity and wonder; they move us into greater states of openness that bring wholeness.

People who meditate often move in and out of meditation with ease. As a group starts to work together in this way, it will be able to call on intuition in thirty seconds. Cultivating an ease in moving in and out of deeper consciousness will greatly widen the parameters of discussion. It is one of the most effective ways to banish the game of competition, and the defensive/offensive bantering that so often dominates public conversation. When we enter into conversation through the door of calm connectedness, through an appreciation of the web we are part of, then the quality of exchange illuminates our connections. The space between us lights up with insight and collaborative creativity. We can build on one another's ideas rather than getting caught in the trap of convincing and debating each other. When we have a different view, there is an understanding that multiple perspectives coexist, and it is not about deciding which one is best. We weave together our perspectives and something different for each of us emerges.

Circle work is about making reflection a collective activity. We can use our Circles as a place for questioning. Look at history, look at who controls resources, and who might be allies, look at issues of consequence, envision the future, listen to spirit. All of this the Circle invites us to do. We are so used to thinking only in terms of problems, personalities and individual rights that we often miss the most important pieces to the puzzles we are trying to figure out. Use the meditations as an entry into exploration by working with the questions embedded in them. We need questions that open our imagination, that bring our full history and inspire vision.

We each have a particular piece to the puzzle. When we each bring in our own ancestors and visions, we have the ingredients for strong web-weaving. I believe we have to go against the currents of assimilation. No matter how homogenous your Circle appears, find the ways that you are different—this is what broadens your views. Circles are about opening up and bringing out the nuances of difference. Patterns of assimilation and rationalistic thinking both tell us there is only one correct way of being, causing us all to scramble to find it and fit in. Whoever discovers or proves it first, comes out on top. But it is diversity that holds us all and gives the web of life its strength. Difference is about discovering the multiple ways of experiencing the world. It is difference that fortifies the web of community.

To develop trust and contribute to the healing of our world, I recommend taking on projects together. Clean up a street, go to a demonstration, make a community garden together; the possibilities are limitless. Doing projects together so that you come to know one another in deeper ways will empower your Circle and offer needed service in the world. Circles are training grounds to change the way we do things in the public sphere. As Black Elk reminds us, power always moves in circles.

Respiriting Public Life

Working personally with symbols reorganizes your own morphic field. You realign your energies and resonate with different circumstances. The telling of heart stories, collective reflection, and visioning realign the fields in our interpersonal lives—fields of energy that ripple out. As we begin working inside out, we reclaim public life, and create fields that inspire what is best in us to come forth. We open our imaginations, we celebrate one another and expand our care, moving it out from our personal lives to create a field that inspires everyone.

In Tools for Change, we believe it is essential to reclaim public life—make it whole—make it accountable to our ancestors and to future generations, filling it with the stories of our lives—stories that are not individual but are part of the great patterns of history. We are not separate, our histories and our fates are entwined. Untangling our frightful past builds trust and enables us to look power squarely in the eye so we can build a world that honors us all. Securing the future is not a question of who wins.

When we trust each other, we move from feeling that we are up against one another, into knowing that we are all in it together. (Which deck your quarters are on makes no difference on the Titanic.) Only in trust can we move up a holonic level and work with greater power.

Affinity groups have provided the strength of much of the activism over the last few decades.[13] They are based on building trusting relationships and consensus, with the intent of supporting each other in political action. An affinity group could be a week-long relationship based around a single action. Being small, they allow people to know each other in deeper ways. Affinity groups are organized in a way that includes all voices. This makes us strong, and helps us to all become leaders. If you have a Circle, transform it into an affinity group and join others to act together, moving up holonic notches.

Soon after the tragic events of 9/11, Vicki Robin called some friends together to help organize what she was calling Conversation Cafés.[14] She felt that it was essential to create ways of having meaningful conversations in public places—we agreed. Conversation tables were set up in cafés all over town. Anyone and everyone could come and talk about what was on their minds, with no other commitment than to speak your own truth and be respectful of the others at the table. Our starting motto was, "When you put strangers, caffeine, and ideas in the same room, brilliant things can happen."

In thinking about how to make them inclusive and heartfelt, I suggested that we use a simple circle format. We start with a round in which everyone speaks, asking people to hold off before they respond to one another. This makes room for everyone to share what is on their mind, and doesn't leave control of the topic to the first person who speaks. Follow this with another round in which people are invited to respond to each other. This simple process works to allow everyone's voice to come forth. Conversation Cafés have sprung up all over this country and in six others. People are hungry to meet and have meaningful conversation about the issues we all face. Meeting in Circle, listening with our hearts, we discover one another, and find fresh approaches.

To help shed light on seemingly intractable tensions in the Middle East, Tools for Change and Richmond Fisher, a Seattle-based attorney, organized a huge public day of reflection and dialogue. We wanted to have conversations that would be as intimate as what happens in our kitchens, so the facilitators brought their own small tables, complete with tablecloths and flowers. We supplied water, bread, candles, and stones to serve as talking pieces to pass around the circles. Lastly we provided some gummy bears for levity.

The day started and was punctuated with prayers from the different religious traditions, Muslim, Christian, and Jewish. We showed a marvelous video, *The Children of Abraham*, about twenty American Jews traveling through Israel and Palestine listening to peoples' stories.[15] The sum of all of these details set a tone for participants to come from and listen with their hearts. At key moments, we all stopped for shared reflection (using Applied Meditation) to invite people to deepen their sharing.

Conversation about the Middle East is one of the most difficult to have, usually turning polarized and vitriolic within a short time. This day, people were able to hear each other's confusion, fear, rage, and hopelessness without getting hooked or entrenched in their own position. It was for many a transforming moment as they started to be able to think differently about the possibilities for peace. The work of building relationships based in trust is the precursor to any successful political dialog and in a larger sense transformation.

This will require a culture shift in the way we conduct public life. I will never forget an organizing meeting I was in that was addressing the issues of racism. There were many present who had dedicated their lives to justice, and were used to arguing their points and debating. A young African-American man on the panel asked simply, "How many of you have a harmonizing effect when you walk into the room?"

We need to make new ways of meeting together, ways that don't silence us, that honor everyone's humanity. When we set a different stage, we don't get the same old show. There are many different ways to build the set that have been developed in the past twenty-five years, drawing from diverse sources of ancient wisdom, organizational experiences, and the latest in physics, biology, and systems-thinking. There is a plethora of ways to be together that inspire the imagination, that affirm values, and help us share our stories and our visions. Examples include talking in council, a form of sharing that is rooted in many traditional societies, Open Space Technology,[16] the Four Fold Way,[17] and Appreciative Inquiry.

Rational consciousness promotes competitive approaches, whereas spirit creates a field of connectivity. It is vital that we make reflection a publicly shared and collective activity in all our endeavors. Start a gathering of any kind, a meeting, a hearing—whatever it is, begin and end with spirit. It doesn't take long. Ask people to breathe together and remember what is sacred to them. Then invite them to bring to awareness their shared intention. Any group can take a minute to do this, no matter how rushed or diverse. This deepens the shared resonance. Take it further—invite people to imagine their heart and mind connections forming a web that moves from person to person, creating a vibrant fabric that supports their shared work. You can invite people to create a symbol for that intention that will inspire them throughout.

Try story, song, poetry, shared silence, even dance (now *that* is a meeting I'll go to—one that starts with dance!). The challenge is to create fields of energy that foster a spirit of affirmation and welcome—ones that celebrates life, that are authentic, ones in which people listen to one another deeply.

> If individuals and organizations operate from a generative orientation, from possibility rather than resignation, we can create the future into which we are living, as opposed to merely reacting to it when we get there...Create an openness to listen to that implicate order.[18]

Living Into the Changes We Work For

Without vision we recreate the world as it is, we perpetuate the status quo. Vincent Harding, African-American theologian, tells us:

> Above all, where there is no vision, we lose the sense of our great power to transcend history and create a new future for ourselves with others...Therefore, the quest is not a luxury; life itself demands it of us![19]

The Haudenosaunee chiefs think relationally about their decisions and look at the impact seven generations on. Oren Lyons, Faithkeeper of the Turtle Clan, Onondaga Nation, Haudenosaunee, Iroquois Confederacy, spoke to the United Nations in 1992:

> It seems to me that we are living in a time of prophecy, a time of definitions and decisions. We are the generation with the responsibilities and the option to choose the Path of Life for the future of our children, or, the life and path which defies the Laws of Regeneration. Even though you and I are in different boats, you in your boat and we in our canoe, we share the same River of Life—what befalls me, befalls you. And downstream, downstream in this River of Life, our children will pay for our selfishness, for our greed, and for our lack of vision…Given this opportunity, we can raise ourselves. We must join hands with the rest of Creation.[20]

Inspired by the Aboriginal people of the land where she was born, Australian feminist Susan Hawthorn asks us to dream:

> What I hope for is a world full of richness, texture, depth, and meaning. I want diversity with all of its surprises and variety…I want a world in which relationship is important and reciprocity is central to social interaction. I want a world which can survive sustainably for at least 40,000 years.[21]

Let's dream big. The times demand us all to do so. I share this vision not because I expect it to be yours, but because vision ignites the imagination. You may want to read the next section slowly, giving yourself time to imagine what I am suggesting. Take a breath between sentences. Notice what visions arise for you and give them life. There is nothing that has ever been created that wasn't first imagined. Like walking down a path, the further you go, the further you are able to see. We don't have to have the whole picture to start; we are always learning and discovering where to adjust our direction, or when another great element should be added.

A Vision

If we can imagine it, we can create it. What if trust were to society what oil is to machinery? Imagine a world that runs on trust. Imagine a world where we have learned how to be honest with ourselves, and with each other—where the only safe way of being is to be honest. Imagine a world where respect is sacred, where intuition, spirituality, and emotions are all as valued as the intellect. Where our stories weave wonder into the world. Where care becomes the currency of exchange.

Imagine a society that lives in synchrony with the cycles of nature, where human life is sustained on renewable sources of energy as in nature itself, where the earth is cherished, and whatever is taken out of it is returned. Imagine knowing that there would always be a place for you and your family, a place for everyone's family. Imagine being able to take it for granted that there would always be a place for your community, your descendents, for all descendents, for humanity—a place on earth. Imagine how it feels to always belong—belong in a diversified community, for it is the diversity in nature that gives the web of life its strength, beauty, and cohesion. Imagine a time when everyone cherishes diversity in people because they know diversity gives community its beauty, strength, and cohesion. Imagine being able to relax into our connectedness—into a web of mutually supportive relations with each other and with nature.

Imagine a world where what is valued most is not power but nurturance, where the aim has changed from being in control of, to caring and being cared for, where the expression of love is commonplace. The dawn of each day is a blessing, reverence is in the air. We live as though life itself is an act of worship. Imagine a time when generosity is assumed. Creativity and laughter is everywhere.

Imagine a world where responsibilities are of equal importance to rights, where it is understood that enough is good, and that more than enough isn't, where there is a deep understanding of the difference between wants and needs. Imagine a world where greed, opportunism, coercion, and manipulation are all social crimes. Imagine a world where there is collective support in the overcoming of individual limitations, where mistakes aren't hidden but welcomed as opportunities to learn, where there is no reason to withhold information, where honesty is a given.

Imagine a world where power without accountability was history. Imagine a world where bureaucracy, like the dinosaur, is extinct. Imagine a world on a human scale where work has regained its dignity. Imagine a time when work has regained its creativity, where you are part of the decisions that make a difference. Imagine a time when curiosity, inquiry and vulnerability are held sacred.

Imagine a society that reveres patience rather than efficiency. Within patience there is respect, a deep trust—a knowing that in its own time the rosebud will bloom.

Imagine everyone taking pleasure in making their communities beautiful. Imagine the whole of humanity honoring the same sense of responsibility for maintaining the earth. Imagine a world where trust and honesty—not power and deception—are the oil that make society thrive. If we can imagine it, we can create it.

People make history. We can choose respect, trust, and mutual aid. We can choose life. We can choose to heal the earth. We can choose to heal humanity. We can breathe life into this vision.

In relationship, spirit comes alive. May vision-weaving be what we all do with our families, friends, and communities. May we bring vision into the center of public life, discovering what we are *for*.

The Earth and all who live upon her are sacred. Vision and conviction are the fuel and fiber of action. Together we heal present time. May we all live into the changes we want to make. As we embody our visions in the present moment, it makes them manifest. Together we heal future time. Together we heal.

MEDITATIONS

Induction

Many of the meditations in this chapter are very long. Feel free to use only parts of them at a time. They are also rich with questions conducive to collective enquiry.

Focusing on your breathing, breathing calmly, deeply, bring into awareness your physical relaxation symbol...Let your body relax into the earth. Ground yourself...Release any energies you no longer need, as your energy replenishes the earth, the earth replenishes you...Imagine that the earth breathes...Imagine breathing with the earth...Relax into the trust of life's breath.

◆

Bring into awareness your symbol for mental relaxation...Breathe in the sky. Feel the expansiveness of the sky relax your mind...Let the sky open your mind. Sense that your mind is as vast as the sky. In the quiet of your mind you are fully receptive and creative...Feel yourself as spacious inside as the skies...Awareness is vast.

◆

Bring into awareness your symbol for emotional relaxation. Breathe out any "shoulds." Let them drop into the ground by their sheer weight...Feel your heart breathe a sigh of relief...Let go of all the "shoulds"...Offer yourself some loving kindness...Feel as though your heart relaxes into its natural state of loving compassion...of connectedness...Feel yourself relax into the web of life which holds us all...held by life in each breathe you take.

◆

Bring into awareness your symbol for your creative self-restoring center...Feel the universal life force energy that flows through everything, flows through you with each breath you take...Life breathes...Feel yourself part of the natural world...Let yourself be strengthened by an appreciation of interdependence...Acknowledge your gratitude to be part of the wondrous universe...Interbeing.

◆

Take a moment to feel kinship with people...Imagine specific people whom you may not know but you may see them in the routine of your week, people you may imagine have a very different life than your own...Imagine these people...Feel kinship in your shared humanity...As you breathe out, send them some loving kindness.

◆

Here vision is born; here creativity is born...Here we listen to the whispers of spirit...Here we can acknowledge our reverence for life itself...Out of this receptive knowingness we gain the courage to work for a life-affirming world.

With your breath, go deeper and deeper into communion with life itself. Let yourself breathe in the power of the goodness of people, of humanity, of life...As you open to the world inside, the world outside opens...as naturally as breathing in and out. Follow your breath out through the trees, and back into creatures and back to the plants again...Breath weaves life...Interbeing. We are woven together in life. Awesome...

If you like, you can send ribbons of good energy to those in your family and community...to anyone or any being to whom you would like to offer some loving energy...However you imagine this, you can breathe power into the webs of energy that form community.

◆

Finishing what you're doing...

I am going to suggest several affirmations. If you wish to affirm them to yourself, repeat them to yourself after me; feeling their power, evoking their power, attuning yourself to their power...Aligning your energies to the words as you repeat them to yourself...

I believe in life...

I honor the sanctity of the natural world upon which life depends...

I experience myself as part of the whole of life, supported and doing my part to keep the web of life strong...

I live in the spirit of interbeing...

I open to truth...

I cultivate compassion for all people and for all beings...

My personal power is born out of collective life...We gain strength from our connection to the peoples of the world...

I am curious and always glad to discover different perspectives...

Only what is good for everyone is good for me...

I take only my fair share...

I am trustworthy...

I speak and listen from the heart...

I am open and generous...

I honor the dignity of all people...

I am enriched by cultural diversity...

I welcome learning how to be inclusive and transform narrow ways of being; in so doing, horizons broaden...

I observe the impact of all actions on our collective well-being and contribute to re-balancing where needed...

I have integrity. I am honest with myself and others, I am true to principle...

I am courageous, I always put my convictions into practice...

I open to discovering the impact of all actions...

I strive to create a fair, just, and sustainable world in all that I do and say...

As naturally as breathing in and out, I both offer support and receive it…

I learn from the past, I welcome the future…

I trust the future and work to bring about a future in which all life thrives…

Know that in focusing on affirmations, you evoke powers from the depths of beingness itself…powers that manifest both within and around you. In focusing on affirmations, you cause yourself to align your energies with them and you'll discover yourself acting out of these very powers you have evoked. Know that this is so. Expect this to be the case.

If you like, you can invite any spirits from the past or future, nature beings, or friends who you would like to join you in this meditation; do this now…Invite them to join you in your inner work…Let your imaginations sense them…Feel their presence…Greet them…Welcome them…

Circling Together through Time and Space

An induction is not necessary for this, though use it if you like. Use your induction symbols on your own and if you have a symbol for collectivity use that as well. Work with only those paragraphs that are relevant. Leave long silences, especially at the end. Help people stay focused by repeating lines. If there are common areas of inquiry or intention-setting, have everyone imagine the context, then name the specific questions and intentions. Leave ample room between each of your remarks. Refrain from any explanations or asking "why" questions. (The questions should awaken the imagination not beta mind.) Circle members can also chime in and raise a question or intention. Punctuate remarks with long silences to give people the time they need to work with the energies. Feel free to insert relevant passages from other meditations to augment your collective reflection.

After the meditation, go around the Circle and have members share what they experienced. Hold off responding to one another until everyone who wants to has taken a turn. After the round, you may elect to go right back into meditation to reflect on how the different insights and visions weave together. Keep going in and out of meditation and sharing in round format to deepen your collective reflection, insight, and intention as long as you like.

Focus on your breath…Feel breath roll in and out of your body… Breathing…As you inhale, bring to awareness your intention to be here…Breath carries life. Breath weaves life. Let your breath bring you into this moment…Here…As you exhale, let go of distractions…Extend your awareness to include all of us here…Breathing…We share this moment…Feel us all breathing together…Imagine as though when we exhale an energy field begins to come alive and hold us all…Breathe life into our collectivity…Tune to our hearts, they are beating inside each of us.

◆

Feel the presence we create as we share this moment…Sense that our breath and heartbeats move into resonance with each other's…As though there is a field of energy that holds us up…or for you, it may, feel like a web…Energy that embraces us all…it is of us, it is more than us…Feel our Circle Spirit breathing alive here, now…Sense the quality of energy present…Feel resonance…sense the tone…Witness the energy take shape.

◆

We each bring our past here…Imagine that we braid our pasts together to make for a strong circle…a strong web…Each with our particular histories…each with our particular ancestors…Sense the mix that makes for the whole…Imagine that we invite the spirits of the past who we would like to join our Circle…Imagine that we invite them to be with us now…Welcome them…Offer them your imagination to make their presence known…What story do they bring? Imagine…What sensibilities do they offer? Imagine…Commune with them, converse with them…Feel our Circle strengthened by their presence.

◆

All of the past is carried in our Circle, awesome…The molecules that form the substance of our bodies have existed since the very beginning of time…Imagine that as we breathe, as we inhale, we draw on the strengths from all time from time way, way back…Time empowers us here, now. Feel it in our bones…As we breathe, we draw on the great powers that have witnessed all of history…here in the room; in the quiet here…Wisdom… Endurance… Deep…Awesome.

◆

If you like, you can extend your awareness to stretch out into a possible future…Those who live in future time know this moment as history. They can tell you about it…They know the unfoldings…If you like, you can invite a spirit from a future time to join us in our Circle…If you have invited a spirit, or maybe a few, to join us, welcome them now…Know that spirit speaks through imagination…What story has it brought?

◆

There may be spirits in nature or other dimensions who would be happy to join us, who have gifts to offer us…Listen. Open your imagination and listen deeply…Notice the inclinations of your consciousness…Listen…Imagine. Trust your knowing.

◆

Take time to commune with spirits, together spirits weave strong fields of energy. Fields that hold us all up…fields that reveal the emergent realities that carry us into ever greater states of peace, and well-being.

◆

These energies enable us to open and listen to the whispers of spirit, of our collective spirit...brilliant...In the quiet, feel spirit...However you experience this...

Notice if anything is whispering? Listen...Occasionally it shouts...Listen...Is there something that you need to be fully present in the Circle?

Note what the Circle is needing as we breathe with spirit together...Is there anything that would help our Circle bloom into greater being?...Trust your experience.

Tune to each person in the Circle...Share presence with them...Offer them loving kindness, as though you could breathe it out from your heart and offer it...You may want to imagine ribbons of color carrying wonderful energy from your heart.

◆

The room fills with heart-weaving as we all breathe loving kindness.

◆

If there is a particular situation coming up to which you would like to send energy and aim clear intention, do this now.

◆

As you do, listen deeply, the situation may speak to you...or the people...or spirits in the situation may speak to you...Listen...Commune with them; converse with them.

◆

Feel energy weaving, webbing, building strong fields of intention, fields that welcome us when we get there.

Maybe you want to weave strands of love and insight between your hearts and minds...Imagine it. Imagine it in detail.

◆

Set the intention that the energy continues moving between you, especially when it is needed...You might want to invite any spirits to help hold the intention by lending their presence.

◆

Notice what the Circle wants to do or say…

Notice if there is anything that you would like to say or ask of the Circle…

◆

Notice what offering can be made to honor the Circle…

Imagine what offering might be made to honor the spirits…

Imagine how you might carry out what you have discovered in the meditation…What you want to express in Circle…

Thank the spirits…Thank the Circle…

Hope Ripplings

Though you can use this on your own, this meditation is especially designed for groups. Use it in combination with the Circling Together Through Time and Space. *After working with it, do a round of sharing, then meditate again and imagine how everyone's hopeful moments empower everyone else's. Weave your hopes together into great visions that lift everyone into greater power for making change.*

In the end, you may want to read parts of "A Vision" on page 353 in the text. Feel free to embellish on it.

Take a moment, and scan through your experience. Notice what has given you hope. What has inspired you in your past…or touched your heart?…It could be small things—the fresh breeze, a child learning, someone offering kindness, birds singing…It could be great acts of courage…Could be visionary or simple…Scan your experience and notice signs of hope. Small or large, profound or tiny, no matter, find the moments that touched you.

◆

Choose one and recreate the scene...Remember the details...Let the scene touch your heart all over again...Make your heart sing...breathe...open. Feel it make you smile all over again...Sense the quality of energy informing the scene...As though there is an aura surrounding it...It may transform into color, music, sense the good qualities in the air...Now, however you imagine it, breathe this quality in...Feel it inside you...as you breathe, it is as though you have given the energy a boost...Now, imagine that as you exhale, the energy moves out and everyone that it touches is inspired by it too...In their own way they are inspired too. It is infectious...What would happen in the streets?...Follow the breeze—see what it transforms as it travels over the land, through town and city...Imagine it ripples out and touches hearts and minds everywhere...Zero into a few different spots and see the transformation take place...What happens?

◆

Everywhere it touches, people breathe more life into it...and it gains momentum...It is also boosted by the ripples others have started...they join...Great acts happen...Ripples become waves...We are all lifted...Waves of hope, of healing, life-affirming...

These waves turn the tide...Imagine what shifts take place. Zero in on a particular scene, maybe at school, or in the street, or at work...or another place, notice how change takes place...How do people relate to each other differently?...Pretend this is the case...The whole field glows...

Creating Shared Intent for Perilous Times*

When a boat is in dangerous waters, one centered person with strong intention can prevent it from capsizing.— Thich Nhat Hanh

* This meditation was first published in my book, *Meditations on Everything Under the Sun* (New Society Publishers, 2001).

This meditation prepares people to be able to remain centered and unified in the midst of chaotic and potentially violent circumstances.[22] Drawing on people's own sense of the sacred, the meditation weaves their spirits into a web of power so they can hold strong and offer a powerful presence, increasing both their effectiveness and safety. By using symbols, it empowers people to re-access their meditation experience in the midst of stressful circumstances. If people practice this meditation as a group a few times, and participants also occasionally take a moment in the midst of their daily activity to focus on their symbols, it increases the likelihood that they will spontaneously call upon their symbols when confronted with danger.

This meditation is also very useful for opening a meeting or a controversial discussion because it amplifies group cohesion. The first and last few paragraphs make a shortened version that can be completed in less than five minutes—or in less than one minute once people have created symbols. No induction, ending, or count out is needed with this meditation.

Bring your awareness into your body. Notice your body breathing...Feel breath rolling through your body...Feel the rise and fall of your breath...Relaxed and full...

Breath carries life. All that is alive breathes. Appreciate the simple miracle of breath...Breath renews life...As you breathe, feel your breath renew you now...every cell of your body bathed by breath.

Feel your feet...Feel the Earth...Feel yourself supported by the Earth. Feel the stability of the Earth...[*Optional:* grow roots down into the ground...Draw strength from the Earth.]

What you breathe out, the plants breathe in...Breath weaves life together. Breath carries life...Imagine as though the Earth itself is breathing with you...As though the Earth and sky breathe, as though *all that is* is alive...

Remember the sacred.

◆

Life is sacred…Remember the beauty and uniqueness of human beings living in different places on the Earth…All people on the Earth are sacred…Remember the life of the forests…Remember the life of the seas…Feel the power of the forests…the animals…the seas…and deep in the Earth…life everywhere.

◆

Now notice that all of us here are breathing…Remember that we are all here to take a stand for life, for all living beings on the Earth. We are here together; together we are powerful…Breathe the power of life…Imagine that our breathing finds harmonic rhythms…Notice how the quality of energy here is changing as we focus on our common purpose…Bathe in this energy…

Breathing our unity, breathing our common purpose…breathing the power of our shared intention…breathing with the Earth, breathing with each other, breathing the sacred…

Imagine that we weave bands of energy between us…Weaving our power together…attuned to one another…All supported in the web…weaving webs of life…

Now create a symbol or a gesture that represents this energy—whatever feels right to you. [Or bring to mind your symbol/gesture, if you already have one.]…Know that when you call it to mind, you invoke our shared intent. Know that every time you invoke it, its power increases. Tell yourself this now.

◆

As you breathe out, send this power to where it is needed…to work well with one another, to stand with all life…Imagine bathing the situation with this energy.

◆

Tell yourself you'll remember to call upon this energy. Tell yourself this now…Expect it to be true. Envision our success of our shared intent…Expect it to be true.

◆

(*Optional*) Imagine a chaotic situation…Project yourself into it…Call up your symbol. Evoke our shared intention…Feel your feet; feel the Earth…Breathe…Breath creates space…Draw upon the energy around you and imagine channeling it into our shared intention…Feel everyone stand their ground…You might want to imagine roots stretching deep into the Earth, breathing with the Earth, drawing strength from the Earth…weathering the storm.

(*Optional*) Take some time to focus on the issues that we will be addressing in this meeting, and imagine that we remain focused and come up with our best collaborative thinking. [*Name the issues, pausing between each.*]

Begin to move your attention to an outer focus…Bring the power of this shared intention with you…Slowly, coming back to an outer focus of attention…

When you are ready, open your eyes…

Tree Wisdom: Patience, Endurance, Courage

This meditation can easily be adapted to taking an imaginal journey through an actual tree. If you would like to use it this way, skip the first two paragraphs and begin with the one that starts "Imagine the tree…" When you greet it, imagine it as a being with intelligence and share your intention to take an imaginal journey through it. Ask it if this is okay and trust your inclinations; then if it feels right, continue on through the script. Provide long pauses in which to converse with the tree. (Use all of the text through "Appreciate the tree for the gifts it offers.") At the end send it some positive energy and bid it good-bye.

Create a place that seems and feels peaceful. Imagine a tranquil, serene place…Create a place, a deeply peaceful place…Peaceful energy that seems to be primordial. Serenity that transcends space and time as though tranquillity were in this place always...Peaceful energy, that's all around you, breathe it in...Peace...tranquillity...Breathe it into your whole being.

◆

Somewhere nearby, imagine finding a tree, there is a special tree, a tree that is very old.

◆

Imagine the tree...Greet it. Let yourself be in front of this tree, see it from all dimensions, feel it, sense it, imagine the bark, imagine the branches stretching up into the sky, the roots stretching down into the ground...This tree, notice how it fully occupies its place, as though it's merged with this place...It offers life to this place, this place supports its life...As though the tree merges with this place...Commune with the tree...Imagine talking with it if you like.

◆

Imagine that as you breathe you draw into yourself more and more of the sensations of this tree...almost as though you merge with the tree, as the tree merges with the landscape...Let yourself merge with the tree, let your breath enable you to be in communion with the tree...as though your body were the tree and you had roots that stretch deep into the earth and branches that reach up into the sky...Breezes blow through you and the ground is always below you, all around your roots, enabling you to stand...to stand firm, with the wind and all the weather, through all the seasons...Your roots bring up rich nutrients and water from the depths of the earth feeding the whole of your body as you grow up towards the sky...bask in the sun...cleansed by the rain...Life goes on around you. There are the birds, four-legged creatures, and people too.

◆

Tune in to time. This tree has its own way of living in time. Listen, notice how this tree occupies time...Sense the movement of day into night...Sense the different patterns of weather carried by time...rains...winds...the sun...Sense the flow of the seasons.

◆

Feel the endurance you possess. Imagine yourself being this tree, enduring through time, enduring through storms, discover the world as this tree knows it...Basking in the calmness in which this tree lives, growing out of the calm quietness, living fully in each.

◆

Appreciate the tree for the gifts it offers.

◆

Imagine you can bring these ways of being into your life. Imagine this great tree has taught you a different way of being in your life...Imagine the sense of rootedness...rooted in your life...Feel the tree reaching into the sky...feel yourself do this in your life...Feel your way of growing into the sky...Feel calm emanating from the whole of your being...Sense the endurance that resides in your being...Take these qualities into your life.

◆

Imagine taking these qualities and transmute them into patience...Patience, completely present in present time...a well of energy that is strength...present for you always. Patience...primordial patience that enables you to blend with the currents of the moment, carrying you through all times as you move from activity to activity...Move the qualities of how it is to live as a tree into your life, enabling you to be calm, fully present wherever you are. Feel yourself taking your life moment by moment, a step at a time, grounded and open. Standing firm, yet reaching to the sky...Embrace these qualities in your life, and they will enable you to be healthy, basking in the sun, being cleansed by the rain, being enriched by the earth...fully patient...creativity flows through you—just as water flows through the tree enabling it to grow.

◆

Patience gives you a well of strength. While you live in the present, the peaceful present, you are fully receptive to the voices around you and within you. Being fully present, the present moment has expanded, making room for all that is so…You can hear the whispers of the universe…You experience what is so in the moment…Know that this patience creates an openness in which vision is emergent…When you are patient your receptive knowingness is fully present…Wherever you choose to focus your awareness you hear, you witness the subtle messages that tell you what is so and what can be so. You merge with your life as the tree merges with the landscape…Being patient, being peaceful, you can focus your awareness wherever you choose, discovering wisdom in the present moment. As you reside in tranquillity, you hear messages; fully receptive, you come to know what is so…Wherever you direct your awareness, you discover subtlety…

Sensitize yourself to this knowingness, moving forward calmly, knowingly. Living in the present moment, carried by patience. You have strength, wisdom, and vision. Just as the tree endures thousands of storms, know that you have all the endurance you need as you move through life. You stand strong in the storms that may come your way. Imagine this.

◆

As you breathe, experience that patience brings endurance…and endurance brings courage…Courage carries you forward. Courage enables you to act on what you know to be true. Feel this…Courage enables you to put into practice your convictions…just as the tree's roots bring up water, sustenance from the depths of the earth and the tree grows strong and reaches for the sky. As you inhale, imagine drawing up courage from the depths of collective knowingness, draw up courage from the depths of humanity's wisdom…as though you draw it up from the soil…from deep time, for the earth holds all of the past to nourish new life…Imagine this…As you breathe in courage, know that you make it even more powerful when you remember all who stand with you…Remember all who stand with you…Feel your courage grow strong…so powerful it weathers any storm. Make it even stronger, breathe its power, remember all those who stand with you, who have gone before you and who stand behind you…You have lots of people who cheer you on…Feel this…In so doing you grow strong and empowered to reach into the world…expressing your convictions…bring about goodness…Feel courage empower you.

◆

Rooted in courage, give yourself permission to be bold. Rooted in courage, give yourself permission to stick your neck out, to speak up, to act on your know-ingness…Know that you can endure storms…Know the world welcomes your truth and your vision…Imagine filling your whole self with courage to express your full humanity…to stand by your convictions. Imagine yourself expressing what you believe in different contexts in your life, speaking your truth from your heart. Imagine it.

◆

Create a situation in your awareness now where in the past you may have let things slide, knowing that what was happening could have been better, clearer, true to principle…Maybe with someone who operates out of assumptions you disagree with…maybe at a conference or in a public forum or workshop you can speak from the floor. Choose a situation…Create it in your mind's eye…Feeling the scene, now, breathe in courage…Feel it give you the nerve to speak your piece, to go against the tide, to struggle with respect and belief in your convictions…Remember who stands with you. Draw courage from the ground…Imagine expressing what is in your heart…Imagine courage coming right up into your feet, and up your backbone…and let confidence emanate out of you…Express yourself…Give your convictions the eloquence they deserve…Let your convictions come alive…Imagine this now, imagine speaking up.

◆

You may want to create a symbol for all that you are experiencing now…Talk to the symbol, decide how you are going to bring these qualities out into your life, how you are going to act on this knowingness. Honor your convictions…have patience, endurance, and courage. Imagine what you might do to cultivate these energies in your life.

◆

Imagine doing what you've chosen…Notice what will remind you to do so. Feel it all occurring, know that you can dip into the courage of humanity whenever you choose. Know that you are fully capable of always giving life to your convictions. Know that others support you in doing so…We gain strength from one another. Together we have patience, endurance, and courage to heal the world by giving life to our convictions, giving life to our vision.

Exploring Consequence

The questions in this meditation also loan themselves to collective investigation in group settings.

Life regenerates itself; life pulsates through you and around you all the time. Life is the wisest of all teachers, when we listen to the spirit of life we learn…We come to know what is needed to heal our own body, our community, our society, and even the earth itself…Life is intrinsically intelligent. Letting life be your teacher, you can tap into deep knowing. With life flowing through you, listen deeply and discover what is so. Sense the intelligence of the life that percolates through your whole being. Trust nature, trust your own nature. As you open and breathe, the intelligence of life illuminates the truth. Truth is to the spirit what breath is to the body.

◆

Bring into the light of living awareness any concern you may have that you would like to gain clarity about...It could be a project you're involved with, a development in the community, some decision at work, a person who has come into your life, an event taking place in the world...whatever you would like to explore. Choose a particular concern that you would like to gain clarity about.

◆

Like a film, play back scenes that are relevant to your concern, simply play them back and watch them in your mind's eye...Remember them vividly, the whole atmosphere surrounding what is taking place, the quality of energy present...Bring the situation into your awareness now, feel it, sense it, color it in.

◆

Now notice each of the people involved in the situation...Intuitively sense each person...How open and flexible they each are...their intentions...their motivations...what directions people are moving in?...their connections to others...Tune in to one person at a time, sense these things. Notice what values weave through the scene. Notice if some feel more entitled than others, or if anyone feels that others are somehow more important...Witness.

◆

Who does each person trust?...Who are they loyal to?...What are they paying attention to?...Is the natural world present in people's hearts and minds?...One at a time, witness this.

◆

Are people aspiring toward compatible visions?...Are they moving in unison?...What's the quality of exchange between the different people involved?...What kinds of relations are being woven?...How do people feel about one another?...Is everyone equally respected?...Are people inclusive?...What are the possibilities if people think grandly?

◆

Replay the scenes and trust your sense, feel out the situation...Is it flexible in some places and rigid in others?...Is the atmosphere open to change, to learning?...Is respect for life itself present?...Is there reciprocity between people?...What resources are being used?...What is being created?...Notice the ripples out of what is taking place. What happens?...What are the consequences?...Is there damage anywhere?...Where do the benefits land?

◆

Is the quality of the process being attended to?...Are people present for one another?...Are people acting out of the same information?...Is information shared freely...or hoarded anywhere?...How is money related to?...Is power concentrated anywhere?...What's the source of information?...Does it spring from direct experience?...What roles are people playing?...Are there any stereotypes being taken as reality?...Are people open to feedback?

◆

With knowingness, sense the impact of different people's actions...Take a particular action and trace it through time, from the choices that gave it life to what happens along its path...Where does it end up?...What happens along the way?...If you like, explore different actions. Take them one at a time...Witness where they come from and where they're going.

◆

Notice the different perspectives present, see it through other people's eyes...Notice where the support lies for the different points of view...Notice how people align...How does what might take place impact different people?...Different places?...How does it impact the natural world?...What resources are used?...What gifts are offered?...Is there reciprocity in what takes place?…Witness what is the case. Allow all of this to be revealed in your aware-ness…Let the spirit of life be your teacher.

◆

What kind of responses will the situation evoke?…What responses are called for?…Review what you discovered to be discordant with the spirit of life…Does the course of action anywhere need to be adjusted?…Witness if a shift inside yourself would be helpful.

◆

Extend your awareness, notice who can support the changes that might be needed so that the actions that take place harmonize with life?…With the regenerative healing powers of life itself, transform all the energy into an affir-mation of life…Feel it becoming open and flexible, amenable to change. Imagine reciprocal relations being woven…How might things happen differently?

◆

Knowing what is so inside of you and around you, become aware of your allies and sense what can be done so that all that transpires serves life itself…How can whatever constricts the flow of life-giving energy be changed?…How can trans-formation take place?…Imagine being able to work together in unity, respect, and a celebration of life itself…How can you support one another?…What do you need from one another?…Imagine taking joy in one another.

◆

Notice how you can act on all the insights you have discovered…What needs to be communicated to whom?…Choose what you are willing to do and imagine doing it.

◆

Acknowledge life as your teacher…With the intelligence of life you can always see deeply into any situation and intuit consequences…You can come to know what is so…You can join with the forces of the great community of life to pro-tect life itself.

Liberating Ourselves

Now create a place of power, a very special place for you to come and replenish yourself…Create it now, with your imagination, a place where you feel your
personal power; and the power of your culture…It may be a place you've once
been or a place you've often been, or maybe your place of power is solely a creation of your imagination—wherever it is, imagine being there…Create it, feel
it, be there…Experience this place charged with power, power that springs from
the source of life itself…Power that arises out of great feats of endurance and
creativity…Imagine this is the home of spirit…Feel the magnetic core of your
being vibrating with the spirit of this space…

If you like, you can commune with your ancestors here. Welcome ancestors
who would like to accompany you in your inner work…Or there may be other
allies who you would like to invite to join you in this meditation…Welcome
them…You may want to do some kind of ceremony with each other to honor
your connections.

◆

The sounds of these words will carry you deeper and deeper, into the power of
life itself…Feel yourself moving down into the depths of beingness itself…As
you breathe, each exhalation gently releases you into a deeper place…Feel yourself going deeper and deeper into yourself, into your source of knowingness…where you are attuned with the great strengths you have inherited,
powers that are your birthright…Feel them in your breath and bones…Feel
power move through you, feel its presence inside you…It feels good to simply
be present with yourself…to reside in the presence of who you are…Affirm
yourself…Affirm your culture…

Your experience is clear…Your knowingness is always right there, responsive
to whatever is happening right then…fully responsive in the moment, alert to

what is so…Feel your dynamism…your integrity, knowing yourself, defining yourself…knowing you are okay, you are beautiful, fully possessing the space that is yours…Feel that, claim your space, yourself, your integrity.

Remember your allies…Feel your ability to create or reshape reality…Experience the power you have…You can respond however you wish, the choice is yours…Feel that, acknowledge your own knowingness, your own clarity, your own character, acknowledge that your first response is right, for you know what is so for you…You are the only one who knows what is so for you.

◆

Let yourself feel your full intelligence, beauty, power…Give yourself permission to be fully you, to embody your fullest potential…Breathe, fill up your entire self with your power…Love your self…Your body, love your body…Your mind, love your mind…Your emotional and spiritual self, your soul, love your whole self.

◆

Love your expression of life itself…Expressing what it means to be human in your own particular way, trusting your intelligence, claiming your power, claiming your space whatever you do, wherever you go…

Feel yourself moving through the world, fully possessing yourself, claiming your space, interchanging with whomever you see, with integrity, with power from within, power that resides deep inside always…Power offered by allies that accompany you in spirit…Always responding the way you choose, knowing what's right to do to preserve, to express, to assert your humanity, putting forward what is true for you…knowing what's right to do to create the reality you choose, to express your truth…Acknowledge your confidence; you are a powerful being. You determine your choices…

You have fully claimed your personal power…so much so that the energy that emanates from you is so vibrant that it simply wouldn't occur to anyone to tell you what they think "your place" is, what they think you can or can't do, how far you can or can't go…You know you determine your choice for yourself. You define your situation.

◆

If anything comes into your awareness that sabotages your power, that cuts short your choices, that insults your integrity, if anything comes in that keeps you from fully possessing your space, witness the scene…Your knowingness is fully responsive and will tell you what needs to be done to hold your space, to keep your power…Your allies will help…Imagine talking to the characters in the scene…Transform the constricting energy and create an atmosphere of mutual respect…Breathe out constriction, disrespect. Breathe in power from the depth of being and from your allies.

◆

Notice how the very parts of you that others may dismiss are what offer power to you and to everyone in the scene…These parts know how to get through; they're wise, they know…They're survivors…They're needed by everyone now…What you left at the door are ways of being that will shed light and illuminate a path that returns us all to wholeness…They know a different way…how everyone can do things differently…Experience how this is the case.

◆

If any scenes come to awareness in which you have been diminished in some way, rewrite the scenes…If it is in your current life, as you imagine talking to the people, if that still doesn't change the scene, then with agility and knowingness, notice how to maneuver around it…maneuver through it, changing your position…Transform the negativity and redefine the situation maintaining your integrity, your boundaries, your choices…*You* choose it, *you* define it…Offer the situations the wisdom you and your allies have, wisdom that tells us there are ways of being that celebrate us all.

◆

Make room for your power, for your personal power to grow, for you to become even more fully who you are…If you have any anger current or maybe ancient, breathe it out…Let it soak down into the ground. Offer yourself compassion…Healing the bruised child that may reside inside you, softening the scars from all the dehumanizing experiences you never asked for…Be kind to yourself…Quiet your frenzy toward perfection, you are already more than good enough…Love yourself…Transform the energies of the past, re-create your life.

◆

(*Optional*) Replay your past, remember those times when you've been degraded, remember those experiences you never asked for…times you've been dismissed, your feelings disregarded, your humanity ignored…times when assumptions were made and taken as facts, sometimes spoken, sometimes not…times you've been taunted…Remember those times, release them, breathe them out…Transform the energy, let it all soak into the ground, re-create your life, heal yourself, love yourself.

◆

(*Optional*) Fill yourself with gentleness, with kindness, with love for yourself and your people…Remember the times when your abilities were doubted…times your honesty was questioned…times you were distrusted…Remember those times you never asked for…Clear them all out, re-create your life, heal yourself, love yourself.

◆

(*Optional*) If there are any people—in your present or your past—that keep giving you messages to keep you in what they think of as "your place," that keep you down…notice what you're inclined to do…You may want to send them compassion, you may want to simply avoid them, or move them out of your space…Notice what you need to do to re-create the scenes…Some of these messages may be from your own people, your own family, your own community, where you've been told what "your place" was supposed to be...Re-create the scenes so that everybody is respected; everybody defines themselves, and discovers one another, no one molds themselves into imposed roles...Re-create the scenes so everyone has choice...As you re-create the scenes, you heal yourself with the fullness of life itself.

◆

If there are any voices inside you that tell you who you ought to be, what you should and shouldn't do, ground it, let it all soak down into the ground, healed by the earth...Breathe it out.

◆

In doing so you empower yourself, you heal yourself with the fullness of life itself...Now imagine healing yourself with the great powers that come from having weathered hard times, wisdom from history...Breathe in this power...Massage the scars with the affirmation of your life, of your power so clear, so cleansed, that nowhere inside do you see yourself through their eyes. They are the ones who don't understand, they are the ones with the limitations...Heal yourself and feel your horizons expand...Heal yourself and feel yourself become more fully who you are...Stretch the limits, break the limits, and still reach further.

◆

If there were any scenes you couldn't recreate, project a protective shield, like a mirror, a shiny silver mirror...and bounce back all the dehumanizing energy. Bounce back their definitions of who you are and let those who want to keep you down see how hollow their stereotypes really are...Bounce back the energy to anyone who wants to keep you down, bounce it back, bounce back all their projections, all their limited expectations, so they can see what is so and come face to face with themselves, and learn from their own limitations. They can experience their energy for what it is...Bring compassion into the scene.

◆

Know that with your knowingness, with your agility, you can move around these people with ease and maintain your own boundaries, maintain your own integrity. You always have the spirit of your allies with you. Acknowledge your ability to live a life with fullness, to live fully.

◆

Acknowledge all those in your life who have supported you to be who you truly are...Acknowledge the love you share...Feel the connection that you have with others...feel the strength of our differences woven together...creating cohesiveness...It is the diversity in nature that gives the web of life its strength and cohesion...Each of us a different individual...We define our own ourselves...We take it for granted that we each define our own space...collectively, respecting one another...True freedom emerges out of respect for one another...Create a time in your mind's eye where we live in a culture of mutual respect...a time that celebrates cultural diversity...a time where we no longer need our guards, no longer need our shields...a time when you can take yourself for granted and relax into an atmosphere of mutual respect...a time when power springs from within and we celebrate one another.

◆

Breathe in this energy...Let this vision spread a sense of relaxed security through yourself...Breathe it out, imagine it moves through the world and transform all that it touches.

◆

If we can envision it we can create it. Know that this is so. Create a symbol for all that you are experiencing...Tell yourself that you will remember to bring it to awareness whenever you need it and in so doing you call on the power of all your allies and your own great power to stand strong and transform the scene into one in which we are all whole...Imagine it.

Widening Our Horizons by Welcoming Difference

Feel the spirit of humanity flowing through you...Extend your awareness to include the great diversity of peoples and cultures of the world...Just as the earth is magnificent in all its variety...mountains, plains, tropics, deserts—all having a character and beauty of their own, yet each particular place is different...There are no two places upon the earth that are the same...So too, humanity is magnificent in its variety of cultures...each with different language...different traditions...different dress...each with different homes, different rituals, different festivals...diversity in custom as rich as the variety of flowers, diversity as rich as life itself...Life is about expression...Just as all places are *of* the earth, each with soil, and plants and animals and weather, all peoples of the world are *of* humanity...No two persons the same, yet each person and all peoples laugh, dream, and struggle...Everyone celebrates with the food they eat...Everyone appreciates relaxing after hard work...Everyone is warmed by the growing of children...Everyone loves to play...Everyone mourns their dead...Everyone has the spirit of humanity flowing through them.

◆

Take time to appreciate the depth and breadth of humanity...all we have in common with people everywhere...what it means to be human...and yet all the ways that we are different...appreciate the depth and breadth of humanity...Different cultures thrive in different places, there are different cultures that live with one another, some inside one another—cultures are created as ways of being. They are discoveries and expressions of humanity...There are cultures of people with different abilities...There are cultures of people with different sexual identities...There are cultures among people of proclivities, age...cultures as diverse as nature in all of its expressions...Awesome.

◆

Notice your attitude when you bring to mind other cultures. Cultures that are rooted in distant places or have come into being in more familiar places. Witness if you feel that any are somehow deficient, not quite as good as your culture?...Are they exotic, or backward, or not fully understanding what is so?...Take time to wash away the arrogance you've been taught...Imagine the arrogance being transformed into humility and respect...Let yourself be open to what other cultures have to offer...what you can learn from them.

◆

Breathe out the feelings that separate...We make room for our humanity to rise up and flourish in an atmosphere rich in diversity and full of sharing what it means to be human—sharing our passions, sharing our dreams, sharing our struggles...We can make genuine humanizing connections with peoples of other cultures...Imagine it.

◆

Now, like watching a replay of your past, from the very beginning of your life, bring back memories involving people of different cultures than yourself, early memories...beginning to understand or misunderstand who these people were...how they lived, what they did...What you were told...and if the people you knew fit the picture you were told...Reflect on how you felt about it all...Watch your development as you grew older. Give yourself permission to remember, *vividly* remember.

◆

Remember times that were rich with meaningful connection, however momentary...Remember the times you've been in a position of power...And remember the constrained and uncomfortable incidents where the energy simply didn't flow...Remember times at school...in the streets...on the buses...in the stores...in people's homes...at big events...many constrained, uncomfortable incidents...and some that broke the barriers and made genuine connection…and others that may have knocked right up against the unspoken barriers…Replay your life and remember, vividly remember, times leading all the way up to the present…let them parade right through your mind's eye…Re-experience them, how did they feel?

◆

Re-create significant events, remember people's expressions, comments, how they treated one another…Re-create the particular events that somehow stick out. Pay attention to all that ran through your mind in these times.

◆

Now, focus your awareness on the particular situations that stand out…especially re-create the uncomfortable ones…and bring to mind different situations in your life at present in which people different than your self are involved…Notice the atmosphere of each of the different scenes. Notice the quality of interactions.

◆

Now, choose one that has a number of people involved…Remember the details of the scene.

◆

I'm going to ask several questions…Let reflections of these questions shed light on the situation…these questions may uncover beliefs that are in need of transformation.

Witness your responses to each of the people…Look into yourself, notice what beliefs are shaping your responses…Follow them back, where did you get the idea?…Is it current or an attitude you may have picked up that doesn't really fit? Witness.

◆

Are you responding any differently than you would if they were the same as you?…Is there anything you would usually do that you feel you can't in the presence of these individuals?…Can you trust them?…If not, why not?…What do you assume to be so about any of these people?…Follow your assumption back, and notice just where your idea came from.

◆

Now once again bring back into your awareness the depth and breadth of humanity…Remember even though we may feel separated we are each an expression of life, we are all human, distinct, yet within each of us resides the dignity of life itself…We are all human, we each have pains and pleasures, problems and passions.

◆

Remember times when you've made human connections with someone, sometimes maybe in small momentary ways, sometimes maybe in rich, important ways…Remember times where you've made a human connection with people of another culture…times in which you made a connection that enriched your lives…Remember times when you were on equal footing with a person of another culture—each of you respected. Remember the different times that this has happened…If no times come to mind, then imagine what it would be like if you did feel human connection.

◆

Appreciate the generosity of people…Let yourself be enriched by a different cultural experience…When you're in any circumstance with the unfamiliar, learning happens…You come alive…Horizons expand…Open to the learning that comes when you are gifted with the unfamiliar…Let yourself laugh, share, care together…enriched by your differences, comfortable with your differences…Those who are different in some way offer a fresh look at our world…What we thought of as *"normal"* expands…The definition of what's possible expands—the world opens up and comes alive…Horizons widen…Possibilities open up. Open yourself to the wonder of people.

◆

Now extend your awareness through time and envision the future in which this sense of connection that you've had, that you're imagining now, with people of other cultures is commonplace…Just as humanity flows through us all, imagine a time when there is easy, fluid rapport flowing between you and individuals of other cultures, when this is commonplace…Imagine there being strong cultural pride in everyone…Imagine everyone acknowledging the heritage and legacy of different peoples. Envision a time in which there is strong cultural identity and connection, the sharing of human identity across cultures…Feel what this is like.

◆

If you can imagine it, it makes it real, makes it possible…Together we can bring it about…a great humanizing time.

◆

Create a symbol that represents this kind of society, something that embodies this future, a time where cultural differences enrich one another's lives, and all people are experienced as *individuals*—individuals with a heritage…Bring this symbol into your present, into the presence of the world now, a world where sometimes we're scared, sometimes we can't feel connected, we don't know one another, and instead our ignorance fills in the gaps. Now, let the gaps be filled with the quality of your symbol instead.

◆

Let the energy of the symbol spill out into each of the uncomfortable scenes you were focusing on earlier…Ground out the constrained, dehumanizing atmosphere and fill the scene with the energy of your symbol…Let the scenes be filled with laughter, sharing, caring…Let the scenes be filled with respect, trust, and appreciation of everyone's differences. A time when we can openly inquire with each other and learn…A time when we welcome exploring difference.

◆

Now imagine what you could have done differently in these situations...Imagine how an atmosphere of genuine sharing could have been created...Imagine what you'll do next time.

◆

With your symbol in your awareness, let it fill you with confidence to take risks, for it is only in taking risks that you learn...and making mistakes is vastly better than being constrained, always afraid you're going to say something wrong...Let your symbol fill you with knowingness, remembering everyone's humanity...let it give you the courage to take risks, to move out, to move from separation into a sense of connection and respect...the stereotypes crack as you interact in authentic relationship. You learn what is true directly...Stereotypes fall away and real connection touches the heart...Celebrate the life that all of us have, the humanness, the laughter...Let your symbol empower you to do that; let go of the discomfort, and let yourself be filled with courage and openness to gain strength from connection, gain strength from an affirmation of differences. Let the energy heal all the old wounds.

◆

Take time to transform all the dehumanizing, hollow ideas you've been taught, and all the fears and anxieties, let it all soak into the earth...and the earth heals it...Let it all be replaced with a commitment to making a human world, a just world...Feel our humanity rising up and flourishing in an atmosphere rich in diversity, sharing what it means to be human...struggling for a human world together.

◆

Imagine moving through the activities of your life, and whenever you find yourself feeling separate, fearful, guilty, or any other feelings that keep you from moving forward into an affirmation of connection, with your symbol in mind become aware of how you can recognize the separations and move into connection...Keep your symbol in awareness and you'll come to know what is needed...Notice the support you have in your community to help you move into connection; the support there is in other communities to help you move into connection, having the confidence to take risks, to make mistakes, to learn, to connect.

◆

Know that your symbol creates the climate within you to be able to stand up against mistreatment whenever you come across it...Your symbol will enable you to help others move into connection...Imagine it.

◆

Tell yourself you'll remember your symbol whenever you need it...Know that the spirit of humanity flows through all of us...We can create a world that is full of trust, sharing and caring; a world where the integrity of everyone is respected, the integrity of life itself is respected, a world where respect and sharing of differences is commonplace...How good it will feel to feel connected all the time.

Reclaiming the Self for Women

Create a place that supports you. You know well how to support others, how to care for others, how to encourage others, how to nourish others...You know well how to reassure others, how to understand others, how to support others...Bring all these qualities into your place of support, for you deserve to be supported too, you are important...Create a special place in your imagination where you can now *receive* support...You may want to bring in others who believe in you, who care about you, who take you seriously. Invite any others from your past and present who will stand by you...Create your own very special supportive space.

◆

Now you are on the receiving end. Fill up this space with warm, caring, loving energy...As you breathe, breathe in all these nourishing qualities...Fill yourself with care for your own self...You may want to invite spirits who also support you into this place, your place of empowerment...Imagine everyone telling you how *wonderful* you are...Imagine hearing about all the good qualities you have...how smart you are...how strong and resourceful you are...how dynamic and creative you are...how sensitive and interesting you are...Imagine hearing all this and more from those who stand by you...Breathe it all in. Give to yourself as you have given to others...Give yourself permission to take yourself seriously, to believe in yourself...Let yourself be empowered by remembering who you truly are. Fill yourself up with this knowingness, replenish yourself, honor yourself...You deserve it.

◆

It feels good to be cared for...Just as nurtured children grow strong and hardy, feel yourself grow strong and hardy, confident and competent as you receive the nourishment you deserve.

◆

Nurture your personal power and it will grow even stronger; to do this, travel back into the past, take those who stand by you with you, if you wish; you are now going to remember, *vividly* remember, all those times you've been robbed of experiencing the fullness of yourself. Remember, *vividly* remember all those times you had to constrain yourself, restrain yourself..."Don't make waves," "Don't act like that," "Children should be seen and not heard," "Behave yourself," "Stop crying," "Don't get dirty," "You shouldn't talk that way," all those times you were told to curb yourself... Remember them now, re-create them now.

◆

Rewrite the scenes, break the constraints so you get to do what you always wanted to...Imagine being able to push to the limits of your capacities...Discover the fullness of life. Feel yourself growing into the fullness of who you are.

◆

With the fullness of yourself, love who you have become...Let yourself be supported, be encouraged by those who stand by you...Affirm your own character, your own life, breathe life into your creative capacities, give life to your ideas...let your own interests be animated...Take yourself seriously, let yourself be assured, trust yourself to pursue your own creativity, your own interests...Feel yourself as dynamic, capable, competent...You are a creative being. Give yourself permission to pursue what interests you. Imagine doing what you would like to do...With the fullness of yourself, stretch the limits...Break the limits, live up to your potential...Imagine what you might do.

◆

Feel yourself in command of all your capacities, independent, and able...Know that you can do it, let yourself receive support to do it...Believe in yourself, you deserve it...Encourage yourself as you encourage others, receive support for yourself as others have received support from you...Feel yourself empowered to express the fullness of who you are. Imagine how you can be more fully who you are.

◆

Feel strong in yourself, in command of yourself, empowered by who it is that you are...Scan the situations in your life now, relationships, activities and notice if ever you find yourself shrinking from your fullness, shrinking back and making room for another...If ever you say to yourself that what you think or what you feel is not as important...Scan and witness if this is ever the case...whenever you put your concerns aside and care for another...transform all that devalues who you are.

◆

Re-create the situations so everyone cares for one another. Assure yourself that you are just as important and notice what needs to be done to equalize the scenes, so everyone only takes and gives their fair share...Make the relations equal, be loyal to yourself...Others will be fine; give yourself permission to be devoted to yourself, too.

◆

Scan your life and notice when you complain and remember that you can initiate change...Things don't have to stay the same...Notice what needs to change to create balance. Imagine it all occurring...If you find yourself getting stuck, imagine what your allies would say.

◆

Believe in yourself, in who it is that you are, take time to love your body, to reclaim your body...You needn't try to make it what it's not...This is your body, and the beauty of life resides in your body, no matter how tall or how small, how big or how old your body is, the beauty of life, the beauty of you resides in your body...You are a person like none other, like no one who ever has been or ever will be, there is no need to gauge yourself against a model. The integrity of your body deserves respect...Take time to let all the judgments, all the dissatisfactions soak down into the ground and be healed by the earth...Your body is yours, no one else's, there is no place for others' judgments. Ground all of it...Reclaim your body, love your body, possess yourself...Let go of any feelings that tell you you have to fashion yourself...dress yourself...paint yourself to catch the eyes of others...Your body is already fine the way it is...occupy it, reclaim it, honor your body and love yourself.

◆

Reside fully in your power, notice what you need to do to maintain your integrity, to remain in command of yourself as you move through the world...Particularly notice how you can maintain your dignity in any situation...Give yourself permission to keep your integrity and assert your power...Imagine sharing support among others, all of us empowering one another...a strong community of empowered people...Notice what you need to do to maintain your dignity—to protect the dignity of all.

◆

Create a vision of the world in which everyone is cared for...Imagine a world in which everyone is supported in discovering their fullest potential...where there is no such thing as "women's work," as "a man's job"...Instead we all do what needs to be done together...a time when everyone's bodies and everyone's capacities are respected...a time when we live together in mutual care.

◆

Acknowledge the support others have for you...the support you have for yourself...the support you have for others. Go over what needs to be said, what needs to be done to honor who you are.

Becoming Whole: Nourishing Heart for Men

Imagine a very quiet and tranquil place to be...imagine a warm and comfortable place to be. Create your own place of comfort, a place where you can relax and let all the concerns of your life drain away...create your own place of comfort...imagine soothing colors...a gentle breeze...the warmth of the sun...soft music...Create your place of comfort...Be there...Feel this place, this quiet and sensuous place...here you can just be with yourself and relax...Imagine all the details of this scene, relax into the tranquility, security, comfort of this place...Here you can let go and be replenished with the gentle, peaceful energies of this place; let yourself be nourished by this warm and gentle place…Feel the edges inside being soothed…Feel the hard spots softening.

However you imagine all of this, however you experience comforting qualities, be quieted by it all…breathe in the qualities and let them massage you into feeling very quiet inside…breathe in these qualities and let them awaken the gentle and nurturing parts of you, for you are a sensitive being…find the quiet place inside…be receptive to the quiet inside…feel how it resonates with this comforting place you have created. This tranquil and gentle quality that you feel within and around you is very healing, it can make you whole again…Feel the warm, tender, loving qualities beginning to stir inside you, let them fill you, let them heal you…Let them grow inside you.

◆

All those parts of yourself that you may have left behind, you can reclaim them now, make yourself whole again, heal yourself, feel yourself…

As you hear these words move back through your awareness, let these words carry you back into the past, way back into your past, into your childhood…Beginning to remember, *vividly* remember, times in your childhood when you were told, "Don't cry," "Don't show your pain," "Don't be scared," "Don't be soft,"…Remember all those times you were expected to be tough, remember them, re-create them now.

◆

Now with your loving, healing, comforting energies give your childhood self what you really needed…change the demands…let the fears and the hurts be felt and soothed…transform the expectations into sympathetic, tender understanding…soften each of the scenes…reclaim all that you really felt, make yourself whole again…Transform the constrictions and re-create the scenes so you are free to be who you truly are, feeling the fullness of what it is to be human…Change the energy of the scenes, make them fully human.

◆

Now go back to those times where you were afraid but had to pretend to be brave...remember times you were bullied...Rough times, tough times...times you bullied others...hard times, cold times...Remember times you *had* to prove something...Times you had something to prove...remember these times...times with friends, times with foes...fights you had...remember, *vividly* remember, re-create these times in your awareness now.

◆

Now imagine the warmth of the sun, the warmth of your healing self, the kindness of others, let the warmth melt away the hostility, thaw the icy rivalry, let all the antagonisms drain down into the ground...Imagine a gentle rain clearing the air, draining away the pain, the competition, the fear of shame...as the ground softens with the gentle rain, feel the whole scene soften...Imagine everyone letting down their guard...As the rain nourishes the grass and it grows greener, taller, kindness and caring nourishes people and we grow fuller...Fill the scenes, heal the scenes with kindhearted energy...light-hearted energy.

◆

Remember all those times you had to measure up...remember all those times you had to prove yourself...all those times you had to perform to be accepted, to be recognized...remember all those times...bring them back to awareness now...Remember them, *vividly* remember them...re-create them now.

◆

Bring in the warm, tender, kindhearted healing qualities...Reassure your past self that you are already good enough, that you are fine the way you are...Change the atmosphere of the scenes...Ground out all the frenzied striving...create a climate of affirmation of everyone, appreciating differences. Imagine everyone encouraging, supporting, cooperating with one another. You aren't expected to know it all already, instead everyone teaches one another, feeling that it's safe to make mistakes...Drain away the fear of shame...Heal the scenes...Fill the scenes with kindness, encouragement, and respect...

Bring to mind those times when you felt fully alive, empowered from your own sense of self and fully in connection with others. Remember how full your life seemed.

◆

Remember those times when you have been close with other men...Truly close, you may have been working together, playing together or just sharing space in quiet intimacy...It may have been a relative, a friend, or it may have been a complete stranger. What inspired you to get close?...What longing in you did it satisfy to share time with this person?

◆

Remember times when you have been in partnership with a woman, truly equal, mutually empowering, whether it was a relative, a friend, or someone you just met in passing...Remember what inspired the give-and-take, to protect and be protected...to walk together with no expectations. What made it possible? How did your giving feel like receiving?

◆

Feel the quality of energy change within you as you heal the past...Breathe in these qualities...Feel yourself becoming more flexible and caring...As you relax, your feelings flow through you with ease...As you ease up, you become a fuller being...Feel this...As you let go, you become extremely sensitive to those around you, you are enriched by your sensitivity, for it is in sensitivity that you truly discover others. Breathe, feel this.

◆

Now scan your present life, bring to awareness your relationships with your family...your friends...your coworkers...Bring to awareness different things you're involved in...Notice the emotional climate in the different spheres of your life...Look within and find that part of yourself that still feels the need to prove yourself, to perform, to shine out, to dominate...to know it all, to be in control of everything...Find that part that feels alone, like you need to do it or no one else will...What cost are you paying to stay in that place? Find a path of connection. Let go of the isolation, breathe it out...Draw on your connectedness, breathe it in...

Remember the times when you felt connected to others, the qualities of relationship that fostered partnership, bring them to mind. If it was possible then, it is now. Imagine your connectedness deepening in all your relationships.

◆

Imagine taking care of this part of yourself, imagine being compassionate with it, be gentle, be kind...do what you need to do to take care of it, so it too can relax...let go of having to know and loosen up...Let yourself heal so you can be tender and trusting...so you can be sensitive and emotional. As this dominating part of yourself relaxes you can truly join with others, share with others, care with others...be human together...Feel these qualities beginning to spread out into all your relationships now, so these are the qualities that are active. In so doing you can truly connect with meaningful depth.

◆

Imagine being able to express yourself fully, passionately, while remaining within your own space...Express yourself fully while respecting others.

◆

Feel yourself respecting the integrity, the intelligence, the strength of other men and women...Imagine welcoming everyone to express themselves fully...Imagine everyone sharing—discovering who we each truly are...shedding the prescribed roles, free to get to know who we really are...Breathe them out...As we do, we are all healed...We are whole human beings again...Celebrate the kindness, the competence, the strength of other people. Share in equality, imagine it...Imagine the humanizing experience, the creative, humanizing experience of discovering our fullest potential, men being soft and strong, women being soft and strong…All of us supporting one another in discovering our true selves. Imagine the whole society full of creative and receptive people, powerful, yet supportive of each other…

Imagine this time, all the "shoulds" of who one is "supposed" to be, all the shells that imprison us are broken and no one has to perform anymore…No more expectations of who we're "supposed" to be…Feel us joining together…everyone providing room for others to express themselves with passion yet within their own space…Everyone connected, everyone respected…Acknowledge your commitment for creating this time when we can be human beings together, living in a climate of mutual respect and support.

◆

Imagine being open to hearing feedback whenever you fall back into old ways of being…Be gentle with yourself, so you can learn new ways. Be patient with yourself so you can change.

◆

Imagine sharing with and caring for others, creating community…Imagine being able to share with the people in your life, so they too can relax and join with others…With your humanity, with your healing strength, you are all part of healing our culture, creating a time when everyone is safe to express their humanity…A time of sharing, of caring, of trust.

Group Care

Bring to mind the group, the organization you work with. Imagine a place you often meet…Imagine everyone meeting in this place. Re-create the details of the scene, each of the people, what they're wearing, where they're sitting, the atmosphere of the scene.

◆

Feel the spirit that unites you, the convictions that you share…What you all believe in, what you aspire to…the visions that you share…Feel all of this flowing among you. Give yourself a moment to bring to the forefront of awareness the importance of what you are doing…Bring to awareness who you are doing it for…Know that together you make a difference…Feel the spirit that unites you.

◆

Alone you cannot do it; together you can; together you can make a difference; *you need* one another…Feel the spirit of your work…Tune in deeply, experience the heartbeat of your work…the positive core that gives each of you strength.

◆

Acknowledge the qualities that each person brings…Tune in to one person at a time and appreciate the gifts this person brings…Each person in their own particular way is a leader.

◆

Imagine what will foster each person to be able to offer her or his leadership…What might inspire this person to step into their potential even more?

◆

Imagine everyone supporting everyone's greatest potential…Imagine it specifically…Imagine that there are bands of energy weaving between everyone's hearts and minds…weaving a web that lifts your work up.

◆

Joined together you are a powerful force…Building on one another, learning from one another…Feel the dynamism…Experience the vast intelligence of the collective mind you create with each of your qualities joined together.

◆

Imagine that the collectivity is supported and supporting the larger community...Trust the collective mind...Know that together you can come up with the best course of action, together you're extremely resourceful. Let yourself reside in the collective mind of which you are a part...Trust it...As everyone opens to trusting the whole, great power is unleashed...Imagine working in concert, in harmony, dynamic and powerful...Imagine being able to depend on one another, count on each other, rely on your collectivity. Feel how it is to work in unison, all of you joined together in effective work, each person appreciated, each person adding to the whole, everyone building on the others and the whole becoming much greater than the sum of its parts...Great power is unleashed.

◆

Imagine the collective intelligence being so fluid, so cohesive, that it can effectively respond to whatever new situations arise...Feel the agility of the group, responsive and open while staying on course...To do this within your unity, diversity is needed for different strengths are needed at different times. And people have different capabilities...

All the different perspectives dance together, bringing all the angles into clear view; all the complexities, all the subtleties are brought into focus...If you all thought the same you would become dense, brittle, dogmatic—unable to fully grasp the situation, unable to rise to the occasion. Take time to rejoice in your differences. It is out of differences that learning grows, it is out of differences that creativity is evoked. Rejoice in your differences...Concentrating your energies, together you can always come up with the best course of action. Embracing your diversity great creativity is unleashed...Feel the spirit of your collectivity...Trust it...Relax into it.

◆

Feel the circulation of your group, fluid, open...Breath...Feel the spirit of the group breath...Notice if there are any areas in the body of the group that are needing attention...Listen to the group spirit.

◆

Just as you need to care for the health of your body, you need to care for the health of your organization, keep the energy flowing...Notice if some aspect needs attention...Are there areas that need to be revisited?...

Reflect, discover, notice: Where the energy is hot or cold, where it is fluid or dense...How does the energy flow?...Does it stand still anywhere? Is it too concentrated in one place and lacking in another?...What is the quality of exchange between people?...Is there anything that is silenced?

◆

Are each person's talents fully exercised?...Is everyone equally respected?...Everyone affirmed?...Is anyone taking a one-up or one-down position?...Is anyone becoming increasingly isolated?...What would invite everyone to thrive?

Are people there for each other? Is support shared?...Does everyone do the work of caring?...Is there forgiveness and celebration shared?...Is each person reliable?...accountable?...honest and sincere?...What are people's intentions?...Is everyone caring?...principled?...Are people supported in the rest of their lives?...How can the ties to the larger community be strengthened?

◆

Any places that you noticed could be improved, imagine what could be done...What could be said?...Remember the positive core, breathe life into it, and let it breathe life into the places of lack...Imagine this.

◆

Trust the strength of your collectivity, of which you are all a part. Trust the intelligence of your group mind, the agility of your activities...Trust the progress of the work. Is there anything you need to ask for personally?...Imagine expressing your concern...imagine being cared for and supported by the collective resources.

◆

Take time to appreciate each of the people in your group…Imagine everyone expressing their appreciation of each other…Sense the group becoming light-hearted amidst all the important concerns.

◆

Reside in the power you create together…power you can use to affect the world…power you can each use to move through the world more effectively…Honor your shared work…Trust each other…trust life, the flexibility, the resilience, the self-healing power intrinsic to life…Feel the life of your organization always growing, always changing, making a bigger difference in the larger world…learning and meeting the needs of the times. Celebrate it. Trust the future.

Caring Acts Heal the Future

At the end of this meditation, before returning to waking consciousness, you may want to read parts of "A Vision" on page 354 in the text. Feel free to embellish on it.

Become aware of the web of life. Life regenerates itself. Life reproduces itself. Experience the resilience of life itself…All forms of life give life to life of another form. All life belongs to the great web of life…

Focus in on your own life now, the home that gives you shelter, the clothing that gives you warmth, the foods that give you sustenance…Acknowledge the earth for providing for your life…Acknowledge the work of others who produced your shelter, your clothing, your food—all the people involved from gathering, to transporting, to creating, to exchanging, all the people involved in every aspect of providing for your life…the webwork of people producing for each other…the work you do to pay for these things, what your work provides for others. Each act is part of the whole, the whole of society.

◆

Now notice in the constant exchange of energy among people and between people and the earth, notice where there is balance, a give and take that is fair and
equal, where there is as much giving as receiving…Just as your body gets sick,
when it expends more energy than it receives or receives more than it expends,
so too, with society…so too, with the earth…Scan your home life, your work
life, your community life, and notice how balanced the exchanges of energy
are…Notice how every act of everyone relates to the whole, which actions give
it strength and which deplete it.

◆

Notice the repercussions of your own personal life style…Notice how your
actions affect others…Notice how your actions affect the web of life.

◆

As you discover the imbalances, as there are likely to be many in the way our
society is now organized, send them healing energy. Just as you can send energy
to the ailments of your body, so too, you can send healing energy to the ailments
of society, of the earth…The earth cries in some places and so does our society—
give yourself permission to care…From that place of care send healing energy.
Notice what you are inclined to do.

◆

Scan your community now and notice who else cares, who among the people
you know cares?…Imagine awakening the depth of caring we all share…Sense
our caring, awakening all the numb spots…Imagine gaining confidence and
courage out of the connection of mutual care we share…Notice what this caring, healing, shared energy wants you to do…What can you do to make space
for life to regenerate itself, to heal itself?…What can you do to bring the quality of generosity into your life?…Is there anything you are willing to give
up?…How can you revere life?

◆

Let yourself be empowered by the care we share, let yourself be uplifted by the celebration of life...As we care for life, life makes us strong. Imagine that together we care for one another, no one is left out; instead all sharing the caring for each of our lives, for life itself. Together, life makes us strong and resilient...together, we can make each other strong...Freedom means taking responsibility for the future. Feel how our strength, the strength of life itself makes us equal to the challenge...Feel ourselves rising to the occasion, uplifted by life, by one another, to secure the future of life itself...to secure the future of our children...to secure the future of our children's children...to secure the future of the earth. Let yourself move beyond your individual concerns and in so doing you transcend your separateness and join with others in caring, in healing, in securing life itself.

◆

Rooted in the collective strength we share...strength flowing through us like sap through trees, imagine being able to challenge any action you come across that is destructive to life...Imagine being able to transform yourself and inspire others to transform themselves so that all that is done is done in accord with the balance of life...All the imbalances that you discovered earlier imagine what is to be done to regain balance...If you come across cynicism, complaining, powerlessness, envy, greed or any other energies that block the flow, that constrict life in yourself or in others, transform the energy, send it softening, life-giving, healing energy and imagine openness being created...and the openness being filled with generosity and care.

◆

Imagine how it feels to do what is needed...imagine others doing what is needed to regain the balance of life itself. Imagine everyone speaking up and acting on behalf of life itself.

◆

Imagine everyone having the confidence to care for the earth and each other…know that we can do it…We can secure the future of life…Feel everyone returned to the wholeness of life itself. A time when fences and bars have fallen away, a time when generosity and care flows between everyone…everyone returned to the wholeness of life itself.

Count Out

Thank any spirits that have accompanied you through this meditation…

Go over all that you have experienced in this meditation…insights you've gained…any choices you've made. Imagine yourself acting on them in your life…Commitment, conviction and action are the bringers of transformation. Appreciate your own self for the work you have done.

◆

Know that the very fact that you can imagine all these things makes them real—makes them possible. The energy already exists. Remember who in your life you can cultivate these energies with. In relationship spirit comes alive.

Remember all the people everywhere who share care…Imagine a time when all life, all the plants, all the creatures, all the people are held sacred…Reverence is in the air…Care is shared…powerful relations are built which support all of life…Feel yourself supported. Feel yourself supporting the web.

Take a moment and channel loving kindness to anyone or any situation which could use some support at this time.

◆

In a moment I'm going to count from one to five; at the count of five, you'll open your eyes remembering all that you've experienced…feeling refreshed, revitalized, and relaxed...bringing with you the great powers you have tapped...Ready and able to act on them.

ONE—becoming more aware of the room around you...

TWO—coming up slowly now...

THREE—at the count of five, you'll open your eyes feeling relaxed, revitalized, and refreshed, remembering all that you've experienced...

FOUR—coming up now, bringing with you your vision...

FIVE!—eyes open, feeling refreshed, revitalized, and relaxed, remembering all that you've experienced, feeling a sense of well-being. Ready and able to express the visions you have invoked.

Afterword

Recently, when meditating on transforming the feelings of urgency that often plague me so that I could come into a more trusting place, I had a vision: it started out with a group touring the Museum of Natural History in New York City. It became apparent that the world had been at peace, a deep peace for a long time. The huge dinosaur that used to greet you in the rotunda had been replaced by a gigantic armored tank. All the displays of the objects that used to be from the "primitive times" were now displays of the instruments of war.

Then the next part of the vision was outside. The "artifacts" that used to be on display were now back in the hands of the people from whose cultures they had been taken. They were again being used for the purposes that they were made: to hold the world in sacred ways. Our group wanted to know how to live in balance. There was a man from a traditional culture who was helping modern people learn the ancient ways of knowing. There was some clamor in the group to find out what this man had to offer. He turned and said, "What is your hurry? There is eternity."

Notes

Chapter One

1   "Stress is epidemic in the western world. Over two-thirds of office visits to physicians are for stress related illness. Stress is a major contributing factor, either directly or indirectly, to coronary artery disease, cancer, respiratory disorders, accidental injuries, cirrhosis of the liver, and suicide, the six leading causes of death in the United States." See: www.stress free.com/stress.html

2   Silva Mind Control should be credited for being the original inspiration for many of the trainings that spawned the Human Potential Movement, including EST, Mind Dynamics and Life Spring. See http://www. silvamethod.com/ for information about their work.

3   The healing power of mindfulness has been the subject of much study in the last twenty years. See the work of John Kabat-Zinn, which can be found at http://www.umassmed.edu/cfm, especially *Full Catastrophe Living: Using the Wisdom of Your Body and Mind to Face Stress, Pain and Illness* (New York: Delacorte, 1990). See also M. Blacker, "Meditation" in *Holistic Health and Healing*, Mary Anne Bright, ed. (Philadelphia: F.A. Davis, 2002), and *Heal Thy Self: Lessons on Mindfulness in Medicine* (Random House/Bell Tower, 1999).

4   David Bohm, *Wholeness and the Implicate Order* (Routledge & Kegan Paul, 1980).

5   I use the language of alpha, beta, delta, and theta as a metaphoric language to describe consciousness. The last twenty years of body/mind research have

become increasingly sophisticated in mapping the relation of these fre-
quencies to the functioning of the brain. See http://medweb.
bham.ac.uk/neuroscience/jefferys/jjwaves.htm, www.energyscience.co.uk
/notes/rn9706.htm, www.tm.org/news/prsleep2html, www.brainwashed.
com/h3o/dreamachine/bwstates.html

6   Sports scientists have shown that increases of alpha brain waves precede
peak performance. One key difference between novice and elite athletes
is in their brain waves. Just before his best free throws, an elite basket-
ball player will produce a burst of alpha. See http://biocybernaut.com/
tutorial/alpha.html.

Chapter Five

1   Fritjof Capra, *The Turning Point* (New York: Simon & Schuster, 1982). This
book describes, in easily understandable terms, the findings and political
implications of physics, and the limitations of the classic scientific paradigm. Carolyn Merchant's *The Death of Nature* (San Francisco: Harper &
Row, 1980) is a comprehensive book detailing the history of science. See
also *Women and Nature* by Susan Griffin (New York: Harper & Row,
1978), and "Appendix A" of *Dreaming the Dark* by Starhawk (Beacon
Press 1977).

2   Three native American authors show how this world view has had a devastating impact on the earth and her people; especially native people. See
Vine Deloria, *Spirit & Reason: A Vine Deloria Reader* (Fulcrum Books,
2000); and John Mohawk, *Utopian Legacies: A History of Conquest &
Oppression in the Western World* (Clearlight Press, 1999). See also
Haunani-Kay Trask, *From a Native Daughter* (University of Hawaii Press,
1999).

3   Capra, op. cit.

4   Gary Zukav, *The Dancing Wu Li Masters* (New York: William Morrow,
1980).

5   Capra, op. cit.

6   See B. Allan Wallace, *Choosing Reality: A Contemplative View of Physics
and the Mind* (Shambala, 1989) and Amit Goswami, *The Self-Aware
Universe* (Putnam, 1993). See website: www.emergentmind.org for a
comphehensive listing of research in the field.

7   Larry Dossey, M.D., *Reinventing Medicine* (New York: HarperCollins, 1999).

8   Edgar D. Mitchell, *Psychic Exploration* (New York: Putnam, 1974).

9   Princeton University, Princeton Engineering Anomalies Research Group final report of twenty years of research "Consciousness and Anomalous Physical Phenomena," Brenda J. Dunne and Robert G. Jahn, 1995. Dean Radin and Roger Nelson, "Evidence for Consciousness Related Anomalies and Random Physical Systems," *Foundations of Physics* (1989). See also "An Assessment of the Evidence for Psychic Functioning," Professor Jessica Utts, anson.ucdavis.edu/~utts/air2.html (1995)

10   Associated Press, September 12, 2002

11   Benjamin B. Wolman, ed., *Handbook of Parapsychology* (Van Nostrand Reinhold, 1986). For a write up of an experiment that reveals how different expectations on the part of the scientist affects results, see Richard Wiseman and Marilyn Schultz, "Experimenter Effects and Remote Detection of Staring," *Journal of Parapsychology* 61 (1997).

12   See Russell Targ and Jane Katra, *Miracles of Mind: Exploring Non-local Conciousness and Spiritual Healing* (New World, 1999) www.firedocs. com/remoteviewing or www.remoteviewers.com/ index.htm.

13   Jim Schnabel, *Remote Viewers: The Secret History of America's Psychic Spies* (Dell Books, 1997).

14   The arena of parapsychology is vast, the actual demonstrated impacts of mind on the material world are subtle, and the theoretical basis for describing and understanding them is still in its infancy, but a number of studies have revealed the intimate relationship of mind and matter, through PSI, precognition and telekinesis. Those who research these areas even at major institutions are still dismissed by mainstream science. See Dr. Dean Radin, *The Conscious Universe* (Harper Collins, 1997).

15   Arthur Koestler, *The Roots of Coincidence* (New York: Random House, 1972).

16   Joanna Macy, *World As Lover World As Self* (Parallax Press, 1992); see also her *Mutual Causality and Systems Theory* and *Coming Back to Life* for a nuanced and inspiring exploration of co-arising.

17   Arthur Koestler, op. cit.

18   Jerry Mander, Four Arguments for the Elimination of Television (New York: Morrow Quill Paperbacks, 1978).

19   Mander, op. cit.

20   See Susan R. Johnson, M.D., *Strangers in Our Homes: TV and Our Children's Minds* (Zaytuna Institute, 1999) and Keith Bruzell, *The Human Brain and the Influences of Television Viewing* (Wyllaned Institute, 1997).

21   Mihaly Csikszentmihalyi and Robert Kubey, *Scientific American* (February 2002).

22   Federal Communications Commission *Fact Sheet* (July 1,1999). See www.fcc.gov/Bureaus/Mass_Media/Factsheets/factvchip.html.

23   *Media Use in America*, www.mediascope.org; Jean Kilbourne, *Can't Buy My Love: How Advertising Changes The Way We Think And Feel* (Touchstone, 2000). The paperback version of the book is titled *Deadly Persuasion*.

24   FCC, op. cit.

25   Kilbourne, op. cit.

26   Media Arts Center, *Media Literacy and the Young Producers Project* (2002). See www.911media.org/youth/media-literacy.html.

27   Mander, op cit.

28   George Gerbner, Context #38: "Reclaiming Our Cultural Mythology," the Cultural Indicators Research Project (1994).

29   Letty Cottin Pogrebin, *Grow Up Free: Raising Your Child in the 80's* (New York: William Morrow, 1978).

30   FCC, op. cit.

31   Pogrebin, op. cit.

32   Jean Kilbourne, "The Naked Truth: Advertising's Images of Women" speech given at the Woldenberg Art Center (November 13, 1996).

Chapter Six

1   I learned Running Energy at The Berkeley Psychic Institute, which has been training people to reclaim their psychic abilities for the past thirty years (www.berkeleypsychic.com).

2   Larry Dossey, M.D., *Healing Words* (San Francisco: Harper, 1993); *Prayer Is Good Medicine* (San Francisco: Harper, 1996); and *Reinventing Medicine* (San Francisco: Harper, 1999).

Chapter Seven

1 Herbert Benson, M.D., *Timeless Healing: The Power and Biology of Belief*, (Scribner, 1996). See www.mbmi.org. Dr. Benson has made significant contributions to the field of body/mind medicine in his work with what he calls the "relaxation response" and "remembered wellness," a term he uses instead of "the placebo effect."

2 Janice K. Kiecolt-Glase, Ph.D., and Ronald Glase, Ph.D., "Mind and Immunity," *Mind Body Medicine*, ed. Daniel Goleman, Ph.D. and Joel Gurin (Consumer Reports Books, 1993).

3 National Institute for Health Care Management, *Changing Patterns Of Pharmaceutical Innovation* (Washington, DC, May 2002).

4 For example, a major medical school in the Northwest attempted to patent a genetic test in 1999 that was designed to detect sensitivity to a pesticide. This would enable an employer to screen out farm workers who were sensitive to it, and allow them to use a highly toxic chemical with fewer safeguards. See also Troy Duster, *Back Door to Eugenics* (Routledge, 1990).

5 David Baltimore, a Nobel prize–winning biologist, claims: "Instead of guessing about how we differ one from another, we will understand and be able to tailor our life experiences to our inheritance. We will also be able, to some extent, to control that inheritance." In Ralph Brave, "Governing the Genome," *The Nation* (December 21,2001).

6 See Ralph Metzner, "The Split between Spirit and Nature in Western Consciousness," *Noetic Sciences Review* 25, (Spring 1993); also Morris Berman writes eloquently about this in *Reenchanting the World and Coming to our Senses*. (See Chapter Five op. cit.)

7 Ivan Illich, *Medical Nemesis* (New York: Bantam, 1976). The depressing reality is that this is as true in the 21st century as it was twenty five years ago.

8 Dr Barbara Starfield, M.D., M.P.H., of the Johns Hopkins School of Hygiene and Public Health, *The Journal of the American Medical Association (JAMA)* 284, no. 4 (July 26, 2000).

9 Dr. John Wennberg of Dartmouth Medical School, quoted in "More may not mean better in health care, studies find" by Gina Kolata, *The New York Times* (July 21, 2002).

10 Capra, op. cit. (cited in Chapter Five).

11   For a critique of genetic explanation of disease, see Mae-Wan Ho, *Genetic Engineering, Dream Or Nightmare?: The Brave New World of Bad Science and Big Business* (Gateway Books, 1998), and Ruth Hubbard Elijah Wald, *Exploding the Gene Myth: How Genetic Information Is Produced and Manipulated by Scientists, Physicians, Employers, Insurance Companies, Educators, and Law Enforcers* (Beacon Press, 1993).

12   Capra, op. cit. (cited in Chapter Five).

13   Andre Gorz, *Ecology as Politics*, South End Press (1980)

14   Irving Kirsch, Thomas J. Moore, Alan Scoboria and Sarah S. Nicholls," The Emperor's New Drugs: An Analysis of Antidepressant Medication Data Submitted to the U.S. Food and Drug Administration," *Prevention & Treatment*, Volume 5, Article 23, July 15, 2002

15   Gorz, op. cit.

16   Andrew Weil, *SpontaneousHealing* (Ballantine Books, 1996)

17   O. Carl Simonton, M.D., Stephanie Mathews-Simonton, and James L. Creighton, *Getting Well Again* (New York: Bantam, 1978). Over the past fifteen years, their work has continued to deepen and has helped people around the world. See their web site: www.simontoncenter.com. See also the work of Martin Rossman, *Guided Imagery for Self Healing, Revised Edition* (New World Library, 2000).

18   Mander, op. cit.

19   See books by Christiane Northrop, M.D. (www.drnorthrup.com), Herbert Benson, M.D. (www.mbmi.org), Andrew Weil, M.D. (www.drweil.com). The Academy of Guided Imagery offers training to healthcare practitioners on working with imagery and healing. See www.interactive imagery.com for a list of programs and practitioners throughout the U.S. and Canada; see also www.iaii.org for additional listings of healthcare professionals who work with imagery. For books addressing imagery and medicine, see the work of Jeanne Achterberg, Ph.D. (www.thinkingallowed.com), Larry Dossey, M.D., op. cit., Martin Rossman, M.D., op. cit. For books on intuition and medicine, see the works of Caroline Myss (www.myss.com/) and Mona Lisa Schultz, M.D., especially *Awakening Intuition* (Newrenbooks, 2000).

20   Gorz, op. cit.

21   For those of us who are secular, it is important to note that the efficacy of prayer and healing is well documented. Please see the works of Larry Dossey,

M.D. for a compilation, review, and summary of research on the impact of prayer and what he calls the "nonlocal" mind (cited in Chapter Five #28), Larry Dossey, M.D., *Reinventing Medicine* (New York: HarperCollins, 1999). See also his books *Healing Words* (HarperSanFrancisco, 1993), and *Prayer Is Good Medicine* (HarperSanFrancisco, 1996).

22   Herbert Benson, *Beyond the Relaxation Response*, op. cit., and Timeless *Healing* (Simon & Schuster, 1996). See also Larry Dossey, *Be Careful What You Pray For* (HarperSanFrancisco, 1997).

Chapter Eight

1   Jane Roberts, *The Nature of Personal Reality, a Seth Book* (Englewood Cliffs, New Jersey: Prentice-Hall, 1974). All of Jane Roberts' books are good, but this one is required reading for anyone who wants to understand the dynamic relationship between consciousness and reality, experience and beliefs.

Chapter Nine

1   Joanna Macy and Molly Young Brown, *Coming Back to Life: Practices to Reconnect Our Lives, Our World.* (New Society Publishers, 1998) See http://www.joannamacy.net/html/living.html

2   Joanna Macy and Molly Young Brown, op. cit.

3   Rupert Sheldrake is the author of *A New Science of Life: The Hypothesis of Morphic Resonance*, Inner Traditions Intl. Reprint edition (March 1995); *Dogs that Know When Their Owners are Coming Home, and Other Unexplained Powers of Animals* (Random House, 1999). See his website: www.sheldrake.org.

4   James W. Prescott, Ph.D., "The Increasing Psychiatric Disability of Children and Youth in America: Why?" http://webpages.charter.net /jspeyrer/prescott.htm.

5   Donna E. Shalala, www.mentalhealth.org/youthviolence/ surgeongeneral /SG_Site/home.asp.

6   Teen Suicide No. 10 (November 1993), see www.aacap.org/ publications /factsfam/suicide.htm.

7   Patricia Tjaden and Nancy Thoennes, *Nature, and Consequences of Intimate Partner Violence* (National Institute of Justice and the Centers for

Disease Control and Prevention, July 2000) http://ncjrs.org/ txtfiles1/nij/181867.txt.

8 "The National Nursing Home Summary, 1999," U.S. Government Center For Disease Control. See: http://www.cdc.gov/nchs/fastats/nursingh.htm.

9 Dean Ornish, M.D., *Love & Survival: 8 Pathways to Intimacy and Health* (HarperCollins, March 1999).

10 Mab Segrest, *My Mama's Dead Squirrel* (Firebrand Books, 1990)

11 Thich Nhat Hanh, *Anger: Wisdom for Cooling the Flames* (New York: Riverhead Books, 2001). This book, and his many others, are all great offerings toward bringing peace to the heart and to the world. See www.plumvillage.org

Chapter Ten

1 Rainforest Action Network, www.ran.org/info_center/factsheets/ 04a.html

2 Rainforest Action Network, www.ran.org/info_center/factsheets/ 04b.html

3 World Resources Institute, "Worldwide Loss of Soil and a Possible Solution," www.wri.org/wr-98-99/soilloss.html, and Michael Bluejay, "Why be A Vegetarian," http://michaelbluejay.com/veg/why.html.

4 See www.coral.gov and www.coral.org

5 World Summit on Sustainable Development, Johannesburg, South Africa (2002),www.johannesburgsummit.org/html/media_info/pressreleases_fa ctsheets.

6 Rainforest Action Network, www.ran.org/info_center/factsheets/ 04b.html

7 On Biocultural Diversity: Linking Language, Knowledge, and the Environment," ed. Luisa Maffi (Washington, DC: Smithsonian Institute Press, 2001); for more on the relation of biological and cultural literacy, see www.terralingua.org.

8 www.unfpa.org/modules/factsheets/pdfs/linking_health.pdf.

9 Kevin Danaher, *The Global Paradigm Shift in a Time for Choices* by Michael Toms (Gabriola Island, BC: New Society Publishers, 2002).

10 Chellis Glendinning, *Off the Map*, New Society Publishers (Gabriola Island, BC: New Society Publishers, 2002).

11 U.S. Census in 2000, as cited in Gordon Hurd, "Safety Net Sinking," *ColorLines* (Summer 2002). See www.colorlines.com.

12   United for a Fair Economy, Report: "CEOs Who Cook the Books Earn More" www.ufenet.org/press/2002/EE2002_pr.html.

13   Chuck Collins and Felice Yeskel, *Drifting Toward Economic Apartheid in America* (New York: The New Press, 2000).

14   Richard J. Barnet and Ronald E. Muller, *Global Reach* (New York: Simon & Schuster, 1974).

15   John Stockwell, www.thirdworldtraveler.com/Stockwell/JStockwell_ quotations.html.

16   *San Francisco Chronicle* (April 21, 1984). See also Philip Agee, *Inside the Company: CIA Diary* (New York: Doubleday, 1975). He also resigned from the CIA.

17   *Colorlines*, (December, 2001). www.colorlines.com; www.zmag.org/ Crises CurEvts/interventions.htm

18   Thomas Friedman, *The Lexus and the Olive Tree* (New York: Anchor Books, 2000).

19   Gleninning, Chellis, *Off the Map* (New Society Publishers, 2002)

20   War Resisters League, Where Your Income Tax Money Goes, 2003, www.warresisters.org/piechart.htm

21   www.zmag.org/CrisesCurEvts/Interventions.htm and World Watch Institute www.wri.org

22   Eve Goldberg and Linda Evans, *The Prison Industrial Complex and the Global Economy*, (Berkeley: Prison Activist Resource Center, 2001) and www.ojp.usdoj.gov/bjs/prisons.htm

23   www.plumvillage.com

24   U.S. Declaration of Independence, 1776.

25   Vincent Harding, *There Is a River: The Black Struggle for Freedom in America*, (New York: Vintage Books, Random House, 1983).

26   p. cit., and World Watch Institute, www.wri.org.

27   As quoted by Vine Deloria, Jr., *Spirit and Reason* (Fulcrum Publishing, 1999).

28   Felix Greene, *The Enemy* (Random House, 1971).

29   Thich Nhat Hanh, *Interbeing: Fourteen Guidelines for Engaged Buddhism*, Third Edition (Berkley: Parallax Press, 1998).

30   Joanna Macy, www.joannamacy.net.

31   Macy, op. cit.

32   www.ecn.org/communitas/en/en126.html.

33   www.urbanecology.org/gaviotas/ and Alan Weisman, "Gaviotas A Village to Reinvent the World" (1998).

34   www.indymedia.org. See also New Dimensions, which broadcasts inspiring radio programs with a holistic perspective worldwide: www.newdimension.org.

35   Starhawk, *Webs of Power* (Gabriola Island, BC: New Society Publishers, 2002).

36   www.restorativejustice.org.

37   www.avpusa.org/

38   *Yes! Magazine* (Fall 2000), see www.futurenet.org.

39   See the excellent video "Another World is Possible," Moving Images Video Project, www.movingimages.org.

Chapter Eleven

1   Quoted by Christina Baldwin, *Calling the Circle* (Bantam 1998).

2   Harrison Owen, *The Power of Spirit* (Berrett-Koehler, 2000).

3   Among the many circle initiatives see: www.millionthcircle.org, www.fromthefourdirections.org/, www.spiritinaction.net, www.renaissance alliance.org

4   See the work of Christina Baldwin, (cited above) www.peerspirit.com, Jack Zimmerman, *The Council Way* (Bramble Co. 1997) and *Wisdom Circles* by Garfield, Spring, and Cahilll (Hyperion, 1998)

5   Joanna Macy, *Personal Guidelines for the Great Turning*, www.joannamacy.net/html/great.html#personal.

6   See the following websites for more information on Bohemian Grove. www.classic.sacbee.com/news/news/old/local11_19990802.html, www.sonic.net/~kerry/bohemian/bibliography.html, www.sonomacounty freepress.com/bohos/bohoindx.html, www.fair.org/extra/best-of-extra/ bohemian-grove.html, www.counterpunch.org/bohemian.

7   Rupert Sheldrake, *Extended Mind, Power and Prayer: Morphic Resonance and the Collective Unconscious Part III* (Psychological Perspectives, 1997).

8   For more information on the important work of Spirit in Action, see www.spiritinaction.net.

9   This is a powerful and accessible methodology that is solution focused. It's peer-based, works with story and meaning making to surface the best of people's experience and then use it as a basis of planning. See www.appreciativeinquiry.cwru.edu.

10   See Joanna Macy and Molly Brown, *Coming Back to Life: Practices to Reconnect Our Lives, Our World* (New Society Publishers, 1998). This book is full of exercises that are invaluable for Circle work. See www.joannamacy.net.

11   An exercise developed by Claudia Horwitz, *The Spiritual Activist: Practices to Transform Your Life, Your Work, and Your World* (Penguin, 2002). This book is full of resources and innovative approaches for Circle work. See her website: www.stonecircles.org.

12   For a full discussion of building trusting and enduring alliances across social divides, see the two pamphlets I coauthored with Sharon Howell: *Breaking Old Patterns and Weaving New Ties* and *The Subjective Side of Politics*. More information on them is available on our website, www.toolsforchange.org.

13   See www.freedomrising.org/article.php?id=14.

14   See www.conversationcafe.org/. There are Conversation Cafes in many places; if there isn't one in your area, the website has all you need to start one.

15   For information or to order the video, see: www.mideastdiplomacy.org.

16   Harrison Owens, *Open Space Technologies* (Barrett-Koehler, 1998)

17   Angeles Arrien, *The Four-Fold Way: Waking the Paths of the Warrior, Teacher, Healer, and Visionary*, (San Francisco: Harper, 1998).

18   Joseph Jaworski, *Synchronicity: The Inner Path of Leadership* (San Francisco: Berrett-Koehler, 1999).

19   Harding, op. cit.

20   See www.sixnations.org. See also Oren Lyons et al., ed., *Exiled in the Land of the Free: Democracy, Indian Nations, and the U.S. Constitution*, (Clear Light Pub, October 1992).

21   Susan Hawthorne, *Wild Politics* (N. Melbourne: Spinifex Press, 2001).

22   This meditation was written in collaboration with Ruby Phillips to help Seattle demonstrators protest the meeting of the World Trade Organization in 1999.

Acknowledgments

Truth be known, this revision has emerged out of a deep collaboration with my partner in work and in life, William Aal. Bill has brought a depth and breadth of understanding that I could not. Much of new thinking about consciousness and social justice comes out of our conversations. And with his amazing editorial smarts he saved you, the reader, from some of my tangled circular sentences. If I was allowed to break protocol, his name would appear on the cover. Words are inadequate to express my gratitude. Bill, thank you for being the blessing in my life!

There have also been many midwives who have supported the rebirth of *Working Inside Out*. Heart's thanks goes to Susan Nelson who tenaciously researched both the state of the world and mass media; she is a testament to the reality that it is possible to maintain a good sense of humor in the midst of opening to the devastation. Susan also helped think through chapter ten and pitched in with proof reading. Deep appreciation to Autumn Riddle with whom I tossed chapters back and forth through virtual space, piling up versions in our computers, each better than the last. Autumn combed out the rough drafts, occasionally adding key insights rooted in her own years of Applied Meditation and Buddhist meditation practices. I also hold much gratitude for Nina Laboy, who, after reading a section, would always offer encouraging feedback, telling me confidently that most of the work was already done. Though in hindsight there was always more than either one of us thought, without her cheering me on, I am not at all sure the work would have gotten done. Thanks goes to Sharon Howell, with whom I love to collaborate because she always offers new insights. She brought the state of the world and the signs of hope into focus. It makes my heart sing when I think of the participants in my Energy Circles and trainings who shared their struggles and visions, which are an unending source of learning and inspiration for me.

I would also like to express my gratitude to Vivi Curutchet for her perpetual support, to Ruby Phillips for her inspiration as a model of living in a manner that deeply integrates political action and spiritual practice and for our work together, to Linda Stout for her visionary work in bringing spirit into social change work through circles. Thank you all.

The writings of Larry Dossey, M.D., Joanna Macy, and Rupert Sheldrake all accompanied me through the many months of writing and had a deep impact on my thinking. Thank you each for the great contributions your work has made. You might think it hokey, but all the flowers that kept me company and inspired the writing deserve mention. Over the many months, there must have been hundreds that accompanied me. Thanks go to Bill for planting them and the soil for nourishing them.

Additionally, a great big thank you goes to Greg Scott for engineering the sound for the CD. I would also like to appreciate Barbara Moulton for help in the sticky business of contract negotiation. Lastly and most importantly, a great big thanks goes to Sourcebooks for seeking me out and offering to publish this revision of *Working Inside Out*. A special appreciation goes to Deb Werksman at Sourcebooks because she has been a total pleasure to work with.

1st Editon Acknowledgments

The book was born one night six years ago when I was driving home on the Bay Bridge from one of my weekly support groups. I realized that the meditations I led in the group were universally applicable, for I simply led them in response to the concerns of the members each week, the same kinds of concerns that come up for all of us in our day-to-day lives. So I began to get them transcribed and took a pile of transcripts to my mother, Casey Adair, who is an editor by profession, to see what she thought about them. She volunteered to edit this book but said I needed something to tie together all the meditations. That sounded fine to me—the only problem was that I was a teacher, not a writer.

I went to my friend Lynn Johnson, who was a writer, and who about a year earlier, out of frustration, had offered to help me update the handouts I used in my theta workshops. (There was a lag of about three years between what I was teaching and the scripts I gave people to work with.) Lynn was excited about the idea of collaborating on a book. Without Lynn's support, this book would never have become a reality—I am profoundly indebted to him. For the following two years I would go over to his house in the mornings, we would do an energy circle and I'd pace and back and forth dictating the information I taught in the workshops while Lynn typed, occasionally interrupting with a suggestion for improvement. Then Lynn's life took a major turn: he got involved with a business that left him with no time to work with me. There I was, halfway through the book and unable to either type or write; I was forced to become a writer (I have yet to learn to type). I developed a third ear to listen to what I said in my head and then wrote it down.

Above all I want to express appreciation to my mother and editor, Casey, who gave me enormous moral support and was willing to deal with my writing. Her editing was miraculous to me. The original draft of the last half of the book was written in a series of unrelated paragraphs. Imagine a hundred pages of that. The only order to work with was which chapter each bit belonged in. Casey indeed has been a miracle worker! And a dedicated one at that; she has devoted hours upon hours every week for four years.

Thank heaven for the barter system! This book would not have been possible without it. Over the years, participants in my groups and workshops have bartered with me. They offered their skills in lieu of payment for groups, workshops or individual sessions. This book was truly a community effort.

Julia Cato has also played an indispensable role. She has been part of every stage in the development of the book: She transcribed over a hundred meditations which provide the backbone for all the meditations in the book; she wrote large portions of the energy circle chapter; she typed all the rough draft; she helped edit and proofread all the meditations.

I am grateful to Peni Hall who, through the years, kept my workshops in order by being sure the word got out. And thanks to many others who traded with me, helping to transcribe, type and proof over the years. Special appreciation to those who dedicated heaps of time: Gidalia, Judith O'Connor, Kathleen Defendorf, Colette Andrews, Barbara Johnson, and Autumn Riddle. And to others who helped out: John Adair, Peter Adair, Tina Ann, Kathy Bowden, Wendy Cutler, Ginger Gilcrease, Judith Fischer, Virginia Harris, Ann Hershey, Trisha Joel, Hilary Johnson, Diana Lion, Meridian, Nance Massarella, Kirie Pederson, France Montpas, Margaret Smullin, Ellen Trabilcy, Emily Warn, Alison Warner, Batya Weibaum, and Beth Youhn.

Thanks to Maurya Godchaux for doing the research I needed for Chapter Ten. And thanks to Jane Lev, Murray Edelman, Janet Bogardus, Janet Greyson, Marjory Nelson and Roma Guy for taking the time to be interviewed about the impact of energy circles in their lives.

Then there are the folks at Wingbow who agreed to co-publish with me, especially Randy Fingland, who is the antithesis of the ruthless editor stereotype—he spent hours explaining this or that process to me and he was both encouraging and agreeable to all the changes I suggested.

Special credit goes to Sasha Rosen, who spent over a hundred hours coordinating and getting the whole thousand-page manuscript keyed into her word processor and coded for the typesetter. I will always remember her for the time she stayed up all night getting all the dots spaced right in six hundred pages of meditations.

It has been a pleasure working on the production with David Blake, Bob Steiner and Christina Kelly and all the others at Turnaround Typesetting, and an honor to work with the designer, Janet Wood, and the illustrator, Joan Carol, both of whom have superb talent and were enormously patient with me.

My grateful thanks to all those who read the manuscript at various stages of its development and gave me both encouragement and insightful criticisms: Zelda Barnett, Joan Carol, Janet Cole, Vince Dijanich, Hugh Drummond, Linda Farthing, Donnie Goldmacher, Suzie Goldmacher, Paul Kival, Julia Lasage, Tom Mosmiller, Tone Osborne, Freddy Paine, Will Roscoe, Brad Rose, Philip Slater, and Marlene Willis. And to those who both read it and additionally helped me navigate through the publishing world: John Boonstra, David Charlsen, Ruth Gottstein, Roland Dickey, and Sherry Thomas. Special thanks to Roland, who later patiently explained what picas, m-spaces, leading and running heads were.

I have heartfelt appreciation for my comrades, whose support is particularly important to me (having spent years being viewed by political activists as being a little off my rocker), Grace Lee Boggs, Jimmy Boggs, James McFadden, Bill Aal, Rick Whaley, Ellen Smith, and James Jackson, and special thanks to Grace, Jimmy, and Bill, who each spent hours pouring over the manuscript and gave extremely helpful and detailed feedback.

Special thanks to those who organized workshops for me in their home towns. I'm also very grateful to the SPIRIT collective who supported my work in myriad ways. I am appreciative of my housemates and comrades who were willing to relieve me of my responsibilities and do a lit-tle extra for the last six months. Special thanks to my partner, Vince Dijanich, who has shown incredible patience. Thanks to Penny Doran and Sally Davis who provided their homes when I needed to get away to work.

On the spiritual side, I want to express my warm appreciation to everyone in my women's groups who, week after week, year after year, sent energy to the book. I especially want to thank those who have been in it for the long haul: Roma Guy, Virginia Harris, Julia Cato, Peni Hall, and Diane Jones.

There are a few people whose work has had an enormous impact on my internal develop-ment. On the spiritual side, there are José Silva and Jane Roberts. On the political side, Ann Tompkins, who taught me dialectical thinking; David Kubrin, a historian of science who gave me a class analysis of the historical role of rationalism; and most of all, my comrades who, in an atmosphere of mutual respect and dedication, created a context for me to deepen my political understanding by leaps and bounds.

It was a special honor to be entrusted with the experiences of those who came together to talk about the impact sexism and racism had on their lives. These meetings were extremely moving and were a great help in the creation of the meditations. My comrades Rosie Goldsmith, Bill Aal, Melissa Young, and David Marcial were the ones behind the one for white people. Helen Stewart, Virginia Harris, and Lee Woodward immensely deepened my understanding of the impact of racism on people of color. Additional insight for this one was gained from Audre Lorde's essay "Eye to Eye: Black Women, Hatred and Anger" (to be found in *Sister Outsider*, Crossing Press). Tom Mosmiller, Bill Aal and Gil Lopez helped with the one for men. Women in my support groups helped with the women's meditation: Mickie Spencer, Virginia Harris, Roma Guy, Carol Fusco, Tina Ann, Maurya Godchaux and Gail Kimmel. Special thanks to Virginia and Tom, who went over every word of the final drafts with me. And then to finish it off, Colette Andrews, in typing, made a few insightful improvements.

Thank you all—and those whose names somehow slipped through the cracks.

Most of all, thanks to all those who have participated in my workshops and groups over the years. Your support has not only been objective (providing me with a livelihood), but subjective as well, for it has provided me with the opportunity to learn—and feel a part of a community of people. My development came not through my attending any training but by your doing so—thanks for taking me seriously.

Last week when I was driving the other way on the Bay Bridge, I thought of all the support I've received for the book and it quite literally made me cry....Thanks.

Permissions

About the Author

Margo Adair, founder of Tools for Change and codirector of the Tools for Change Institute, has been in the forefront of exploring the connections between consciousness, politics and spirituality. Developer of Applied Meditation, since 1975 she has woven together political, psychological, and spiritual perspectives for personal, interpersonal, and planetary healing. This approach to working with consciousness-integrating intuition, imagination, and mindfulness has been used by therapists and healing practitioners around the world. Her work on trusting one's own awareness, creativity, and intuition has influenced the development of movements for change over the last twenty-five years.

She is coauthor of numerous articles, including two pamphlets: *The Subjective Side of Politics* and *Breaking Old Patterns, Weaving New Ties*. This work reveals that the particularity of what is left out of public life by the demands of assimilation are exactly what is needed to provide the grace and grit to meet the demands of the times and reclaim humane ways of being. She travels extensively, offering workshops, and doing public speaking.

Tools for Change

Tools for Change is a multicultural organization working to promote healing and leadership development, and to create sustainable democratic structures in which everyone can contribute their best. In our work, we call on spirit, heart, history, collectivity, and vision. We offer long-term consultation, large-group meeting design and facilitation, as well as training on power, diversity, and vision-building.

Contact *Tools for Change* to find others in your region to work with:
- Applied Meditation Support Groups: Get together on a regular basis to meditate. We offer information to help start and sustain groups.
- Applied Meditation Training: *Basic*—explore imagination, intuition, and mindfulness; *Advanced*—Hone your practice; *Leadership*—design and lead meditations for individual problem solving and group settings.
- Working Inside Out: a three part workshop. Transformation emerges out of deep listening to the self, to others, and to the planet itself. We work with empowerment tools integrating personal with political and political with spiritual.

Resources Available from *Tools for Change*:
- *The Working Inside Out Applied Meditation Tapes Series*. This includes twenty cassette tapes of almost all the meditations in this book:

1. A. **Relaxing:** *How to Relax in a Matter of Moments*
    B. **Internalizing a Quality:** *How to Cultivate Desired Attributes*
2. A. **Ocean Breath:** *Stress Reduction*
    B. **Affirmations:** *How to Manifest Your Desires*
    Centering for the Day
3. A. **Rehearsing the Future:** *How to Create Positive Experiences*
    B. **Creativity Flowing:** *How to Enhance Your Creativity*
4. A. **Tapping Universal Energy:** *How to be Powerful & Open*
    Stretching the Imagination: *How to Increase Your Imaginative Power*
    B. **Mental Housecleaning:** *How to Clear Out Negative Thoughts*
    Self Protection: *How to Better Protect Yourself*
5. A. **Fear as Challenge:** *How to Make Fear a Friendly Teacher*
    B. **Stretching Your Confidence:** *How to Build It for New Opportunities*
6. A. **Healing with Life's Vitality:** *How to Listen to & Heal Your Body*
    B. **Honoring Your Body:** *How to Create Your Own Healthful Routine*
7. A. **Wise Self:** *Meeting Overwhelming Challenge and/or Life Threatening Illness*
    B. **Respite:** *How to Enlighten the Heart & Relieve Pain*
8. A. **Sexuality:** *Reclaiming the Sanctity of Your Sexuality*
    B. **Enjoyment:** *How to Increase It in Your Life/Bring Forth What Is Needed*

9A. A. **Cultivating Your Best (for Women):** *How to Meet Your Potential Self*

     B. **Exploring Your Life:** *How to Discover and Heal Imbalance*

9B. A. **Cultivating Your Best (for Men):** *How to Meet Your Potential Self*

     B. **Exploring Your Life:** *How to Discover and Heal Imbalance*

10. A. **Liberating Yourself:** *How to Release a Deep Seated Negative Attitude*

     B. **From Trauma to Wisdom:** *How to Turn Defeat into Victory*

11. A. **Habit Control:** *How to Stay on the Path You Choose*

     B. **Getting Unstuck:** *How to Move from Impasse to Insight*

12. A. **Integrity of Life:** *How to Move Beyond Alienation*

     B. **Enriching Connections:** *Turn Competition into Mutual Respect*

13. A. **Choice Patterns:** *How to Cultivate Community*

     B. **Anger Yields Justice:** *How to turn Anger into a Positive Force*

14. A. **Crystal Clear Communication:** *How to Change Conflict into Cooperation*

     B. **Family:** *Healing the Past & Creating a Loving Future*

15. A. **Letting Go:** *How to Move from Holding On Into Openness*

     B. **Trust & Honesty:** *Manifesting Your Highest Values*

16. A. **Caring Acts Heal the Planet:** *Envisioning a Time of Love & Justice*

     B. **Towards a Balanced World:** *How to Distinguish Between Your Wants & Needs*

17. A. **Keeping the Faith:** *Sustaining our Work towards Peace & Justice*

     B. **Self Empowerment:** *Surpassing Culturally Imposed Limitations*

18. A. **Healing the Organization:** *How to Augment Strengths & Remedy Weaknesses*

     B. **Embracing Cultural Diversity:** *Moving From Racism to Respect*

19. A. **What's Going On?:** *How to Discover Who Profits*

     B. **Nourishing Yourself (for men):** *How to Reclaim Your Emotional Life*

20. A. **Patience/Endurance/Courage:** *How to Cultivate Them in Your Life*

     B. **Reclaiming Your Power (for women):** *Giving Yourself What You Deserve*

- Forthcoming audio recordings designed for group use.
- Custom Recorded Meditations for specific individual or group needs.
- *Meditations on Everything Under the Sun*—A cookbook of meditations designed for mixing and matching which cover issues related to personal, family, community and work life.

Additional Publications

- *The Subjective Side of Politics* (co-authored with Sharon Howell), explores how social and historical power relations impact attitudes and assumptions, as well as how we might create just and fair relations;
- *Breaking Old Patterns: Weaving New Ties* (co-authored with Sharon Howell), explores how mainstream culture creates monoculture and provides tools to establish inclusive environments;
- *From Leadership to Empowerment* grapples with transforming our image of the lone leader to leadership that emerges from everyone in different ways. Forthcoming publications on facilitating Circles.

For more information: www.toolsforchange.org

Write: circlework@toolsforchange.org or P.O. Box 14141, San Francisco, CA 94114 or Call: (1-800-998-6657)

Tools for Change Institute (a Nonprofit Corporation)

The Institute is dedicated to inspiring a cultural transformation in which history, heart, spirit, values, and vision are all at the center of public life.

Circles for Change, a national network, is a primary program of the Institute. These Circles are designed to facilitate people discovering and living into their aspirations. They offer a way for people bring the power of spirit into daily life and support one another to develop the clarity, strategies, and courage needed to effectively take action on their values.

The Circles offer a loose structure that people can use to address the issues they care most about. In Circles people come together to develop visions and support one another in achieving them. They are a space of truth-seeking, heart-sharing and vision-making—where people integrate the personal, political, and spiritual aspects of life.

For more information: www.instituteforchange.org

Write: circlework@instituteforforchange.org or 2408 East Valley, Seattle, WA 98112 or Call: (206-329-2201)